Gender, Work, and Economy

Gender, Work, and Economy

Unpacking the Global Economy

Heidi Gottfried

polity

First published in 2013 by Polity Press
Reprinted 2015(twice), 2016

Polity Press
65 Bridge Street
Cambridge CB2 1UR, UK

Polity Press
350 Main Street
Malden, MA 02148, USA

ISBN-13: 978-0-7456-4764-7
ISBN-13: 978-0-7456-4765-4 (pb)

A catalogue record for this book is available from the British Library.

Typeset in 10.5 on 13 pt Swift
by Servis Filmsetting Ltd, Stockport, Cheshire
Printed and bound in the United States of America by RR Donnelley.

For further information on Polity, visit our website: www.politybooks.com

Contents

Figures

Tables

Acknowledgments

Any book is both a solitary pursuit and a collective effort. In this respect, this book represents the cumulative knowledge gained from conversations with colleagues over the years and the expert advice and encouragement from Polity's editorial and production staff. A chance communication from Emma Longstaff launched the book project. Her query regarding the Economy and Society series tweaked my interest in writing a book on gender and the economy. One year into the financial crisis, the book on the global economy seemed even more relevant. Nonetheless, crafting a narrative requires more than a little nudging. I cannot imagine the book coming to fruition without Jonathan Skerrett's encouragement. Throughout the publication process, Jonathan was a one-man rooting section. Authors rely on a good copy-editor whose deft linguistic abilities can turn a tortured sentence into beautiful prose. For this I must thank Leigh Mueller. She always made suggestions for changes without even a hint of a thought bubble inquiring whether I was a native English speaker. Toward the end of the process, Clare Ansell shepherded the book to its publication. Finally, the book benefitted enormously from the detailed comments by two anonymous reviewers and Leslie Salzinger.

Many colleagues influenced my thinking on the issues of relevance to the current era. From its earliest incarnation as a small feminist group meeting at Bochum University, GLOW members have developed a shared body of knowledge on gender, globalization, and work transformation. Though we never realized our original collective fantasy to meet in Bellagio, we discussed and debated our work in the tropical heat of Tokyo, the pastoral retreat of Lowwood, the luxurious landscapes of Monet's Provence, along with many other places in the US and Europe. My ideas have been shaped by conversations with members and others invited to our workshops, including: Joan Acker, Sylvia Walby, Karin Gottschall, Karen Shire, Ilse Lenz, Mari Osawa, Diane Perrons, Ursula Mueller, Judith Lorber, Ann Orloff, Margarita Abe-Estevez, Myra Marx-Ferree, Keiko Aiba, Kazuko Tanaka, Sawako Shirehase, Makiko Nishikawa, Yuko Ogasawara, Jenny Tomlinson,

Susan Durbin, Ursula Holtgrewe, Glenda Roberts, Allison Woodward, Monika Goldmann, Christine Bose, Ulrike Liebert, Sarah Swider, Leah Vosko, and Anne Witz. Frequent visits to Japan gave me a perspective on the importance of gender in explaining the causes and consequences of economic crisis. I want to thank Mariko Adachi, Ruri Ito, and Kaoru Tachi, my hosts at Ochanomizu University, where I spent my sabbatical in 2007.

Convention typically leaves our loved ones' place of honor at the end, even though their imprint is there from the beginning. Early on, Bernhard has taught me to observe the world around me and to open myself to new experiences. The book draws on anecdotes derived from the challenges of motherhood. My choice of the word "challenge" is a way to situate our personal biography in a larger context. However, I apologize to my son if my rapid-fire questioning feels too much like an interrogation, something of an occupational hazard. In the end, I hope that my moral judgment over what to include balances my search for truth with respect for his privacy. Also implicated is my partner of more than three decades. I have lost count of the many versions that he kindly and carefully read. Even though he bloodied the text with his red pen, he offered his criticism in the spirit of comradeship. David Fasenfest kept me on track when my utter frustration threatened to derail the completion of the project. This book is dedicated to them, to their compassion toward others and to their commitment to making the world a better place.

CHAPTER 1

An Introduction to Gender, Work, and Economy: Unpacking the Global Economy

Recently, the near economic cataclysm resulting from the financial meltdown exposed hidden fault-lines in the global economy. Lehman Brothers was not the only casualty on that fateful day of September 15, 2008. Soon after, a suit brought by two female ex-vice presidents against the former head of the derivatives unit of AIG raised the specter that the "'boys club' culture" ignored the impact of risk-taking on women's careers and on working-class communities at large. In this specific case, the boss allegedly admitted his preference for "young (female) workers with 'curb appeal' to those who look like his aunt" (Gallu and Son 2010: 1). Such sentiments, usually left unsaid, express a structural condition valorizing beauty over brains, profits over people's lives and livelihoods. The usual narrative of the financial crisis glosses over the possibility that such corporate leaders' hyper-masculine bravado may have contributed to irrational exuberance born out of their neglect of social responsibility for others. Behind the scenes, their abstract financial investment calculations, and hubris rooted in the expression of hegemonic masculine domination over nature, fostered a culture of undue risk-taking, bringing global capitalism to the precipice. Crises such as this allow a glimpse into both the intricacies of global economic processes and the usually shrouded worlds of work.

Another remnant left in the wake of the crisis has been dubbed "The Great 'He-cession'" (Salem cited in the *New York Times* 2009). Relatively new in this recession, more men than women lost their jobs and experienced long bouts of unemployment. Between 2007 and 2009, the economy shed manufacturing and construction jobs, once the primary engines of muscular economic growth and the underpinning of working-class masculinity and the strong male breadwinner family model. This idea of the he-cession describes a process of economic restructuring already underway. Less clear is what drives the shift from industrial production to service-dominated economies.

These examples cannot be fully understood in the confines of gender-neutral theories of the financial crisis and the he-cession. Though seemingly neutral, definitions of work and economy are themselves gendered. Yet gender is more than juxtaposing men's and women's different work experiences and biographies. What mechanisms systematically and systemically disadvantage women in and at work, and how are differences among women structured depending on class, race and national origin? The rest of the introduction provides a brief for studying gender at work in the global economy.

Why study gender at work in the global economy?

During the closing decades of the twentieth century the work world dramatically changed. In the United States, societal norms gave way to civil rights laws opening up new employment opportunities, and women's paid labor force participation steadily increased. Now, a majority of women with young children work at least part-time or part-year outside of their homes. In addition, young women hold more bachelor's and master's degrees than men, and increase their representation in law, business, and medical schools (Rose and Hartmann 2004). By 1982 women college graduates outnumbered men, and by 2007, women accounted for 57% of college graduates (Skapinker 2010: 11). No longer confined to jobs as domestic servants, sales clerks, secretaries, nurses, and teachers, women gained a foothold in management, earning 43% of all MBAs in 2006, up from only 4% in 1970 (Bertrand et al. 2010: 229). Career paths of women and men have become more similar, yet important differences remain. Despite inroads into male-dominated fields and the high rates of male unemployment during the Great Recession of 2008–9, women still earn less than men and end up re-segregated at lower ends of occupational hierarchies. What seemed like steady progress has stalled and the gender revolution remains unfinished.

It is still the case that women bear disproportionate responsibility for unpaid and, increasingly, for paid labor in the household, which makes it difficult for them to compete equally with men outside the home. Moreover, the current economic system places a burden on American men, who have the longest work week in the advanced industrialized world and consequently the least amount of leisure when employed. In this context, the relative lack of social infrastructure to support working parents in the United States, such as subsidized childcare or paid family leave, requires that families cope on their own either through paying for care and services on the market or by using unpaid labor of family members (usually relying on mothers or other female relatives), especially in times of economic distress.

Meanwhile, government cost-cutting measures deprive individuals and families of the social safety net. State and federal government budget cuts add to the economic tsunami, eliminating 581,000 jobs in its wake. Women lost 81% of the jobs disappearing from the public sector from December 2008 to September 2011 (Institute for Women's Policy Research September 9, 2011). Though men's employment fell by 1.6% at the local level – less than the 4.7% decline for women – men's employment grew by 5.3% at the federal level, likely due to the expansion of homeland security jobs. Increasing unemployment and decreasing prospects for good jobs among men add to the sense of economic uncertainty and insecurity. Precarious jobs and livelihoods are now the economic reality for a growing number of men and women, both in the USA and worldwide. This book considers how economic transformation plays out across social locations, and what effects it has on gender as well as class relations.

Making global connections: unpacking the global economy

Seemingly distant work conditions and processes ripple from one location to another as a result of increasing global interconnections. Financialization of assets, already by the 1970s, generated a crisis of capital accumulation on a global scale. From the 1980s onward, the need to absorb excessive profits fueled speculation and boosted property prices, inflating an already overextended housing bubble (Harvey 2010). Meanwhile, the financial elite parked capital in construction sites of older global cities, or created crystalline cityscapes in actual urban deserts like Dubai and other emergent global cities in India and China. Capital's attempts to overcome the most recent crisis fed the building frenzy, bid up asset values and drove up costs for all residents in the global cities of New York, London, and Tokyo. The built environment, thus, is not merely a façade behind which the real economy must be analyzed. Global urban spaces concretize capital accumulation in both form and function.

Today, old and emergent global cities and countries vie for power in their region, most prominently in Asia, and in the world economy more generally. Once the economic juggernaut in the region, Japan now faces competition from the ascending geographic powers of China and India. These new economic powerhouses' rapid industrialization and urbanization leapfrogged into the 21st-century service economy. Exploring Beijing, Shanghai, Kolkata (formerly Calcutta), and Dubai opens a window into the spatiality of changing economic landscapes, especially migration flows within the region. From the vantage point of these new global cities, migration patterns crisscross rural villages and growing metropolitan areas both within and across Asian countries. For example, female domestic workers and male construction workers, sometimes from the same village, embark on journeys from their homes in south Asia to the wealthy oil-producing nation of Saudi Arabia and to the new shopping mecca of Dubai, and from rural areas in the interior to coastal cities in China. Female care workers from nearby countries such as the Philippines are permitted entry to work on temporary visas in the aging society of Japan (Ito 2005; Parrenas 2011). Women from lower castes support the lifestyles and work of a burgeoning middle class and the elite in cities such as Kolkata. Gender is central to understanding these migration processes and their outcomes in global cities and for the homes left behind.

A unique aspect of this book recasts political economy theory using concepts culled from social geography. Social geography has a ready-made vocabulary to map the spatial dimension of work, and to understand what accounts for the placement and spatial arrangement of concrete work performed by men and women. The social geography frame from a feminist perspective pushes us to think beyond the usual borders and categories common to the sociology of work and traditional political economy, enabling us to unpack the dynamics of the global economy.

Outline of the book

This book integrates gender throughout its study of work and economy to reveal how structural inequalities are produced, why they persist, and how they change. Further, the book advocates using a feminist lens to tells us where to look, and why we must consider work in the intimate spaces of the household, inside the offices looming over old and emergent global cities, and in the factories rusting in the span of old industrial corridors. In so doing, a feminist lens sheds light on the less visible work of care, and how this service work is related to global economic forces and political systems. It provides insight into why the same work, such as childcare or cooking, when performed for pay (market work) or unpaid (non-market work) is treated differently legally, theoretically, and socially. In particular, unpaid labor associated with mothering often goes unnoticed, uncounted, and devalued. Without a feminist lens, we cannot explain transformative processes, which in a lifetime have altered the way we live, how we work, and the cityscapes we inhabit.

What follows unfolds in three main parts devoted to the study of gender, work, and economy. Part I introduces theoretical issues at the heart of work sociology and political economy, interweaving non-feminist and feminist alternatives. Chapter 2 revisits the sociological classics of Marx and Weber in more detail to situate contemporary theories of work and economy. A review outlines their contributions and the gender gaps in both classical and contemporary theories. Then the chapter traces the emergence of three waves of feminism. In the first wave, feminists addressed women's political disenfranchise-ment and economic insecurity, and directed attention to the rela-tively neglected private sphere more likely to be occupied by women. These debates ensuing at the dawn of the twentieth century provided the backdrop for second-wave feminism coming to terms with gender inequality. The remainder of that chapter traces the arc of feminism's second and third waves. Early second-wave accounts introduced and refined the concept of gender (patriarchy) in relationship to class (capitalism). Conceptualizing gender continued as a key concern of later second-wave feminist theory, leading to questions about the sources of male power, how work was gendered, and what constituted the process of gendering work organization. The chapter ends with a short discussion of third-wave feminism to highlight new sensitivities toward complex relationships among women, as well as between men and women, in the division of labor, from the household to the board room. Without third-wave feminist critiques, theorists of work and economy would probably not have trained an eye on the intimate rela-tionship and entanglement between production and reproduction.

Third-wave feminist research on care work and reproductive labor, as detailed in chapter 3, has raised many of the same concerns and conceptual issues that preoccupied first- and early second-wave femi-nist scholarship and politics. Understanding the shift toward service-dominated economies requires our examination of the most intimate moments in people's lives. To know where the family and the house-hold fit into the analysis requires focusing beyond firms, markets, or formal work organizations, and broadening conceptualization of the economy to include both activities and practices in the household and those involving care-giving. An examination of the care sector, by crosscutting the family, paid employment, and the state, points out the necessity for examining the relationships between and within these institutions. Outlining a feminist political economy perspec-tive, the third chapter links care work and domestic labor performed in the household to national and global processes.

The chapters in Part II present case studies and other material on historical and contemporary trends, documenting and explaining forms of segregation, new ways of working, and forms of employment differentiated by gender. With the development of capitalism, cities, and industry, a public sphere dominated by men expanded and restricted the activities performed by women. Chapter 4 examines the root causes of horizontal, vertical, and spatial occupational sex segregation and related pay inequities. The chapter poses several questions, asking how and when industries and occupations change the gender composition of work from male to female (such as the historical example of clerical work), despite other employment categories remaining stubbornly gender-typed (top executives as male-typed and childcare as female-typed)? What is the reason only a small proportion of men enter female-typed occupations, while an increasing number of women seek employment in male-typed professions? It is not enough to acknowledge that some work and occupations are gender-typed. How and under what conditions do jobs become associated with gender-stereotypical images and how does this affect their value? Chapter 5 describes in greater detail the new ways of working, forms of employment, and types of economic activity manifest in the emerging service and knowledge economy. The next chapter investigates the organization, institutionalization, and value of reproductive work and caring labor, as central theoretical and empirical concerns in the commercialization of more aspects of people's lives, including sentiments, love, and affection. Political factors are evaluated to demonstrate that they inform how, and which, services receive support from the state, and the nature of the delivery of services more generally.

Chapter 7 highlights the gender dimensions of political institutions and reviews a range of country-specific policies and regulations in a comparative perspective, integrating usually separate bodies of research on welfare states, employment relations, and policy analysis. Different types of politics, policies, and welfare state regimes have consequences for the reception of women in particular occupations and sectors, and in the paid labor market more generally. Chapter 8 reflects on how new terrains of struggle bring to the surface reasons behind women's under-representation in traditional labor organizations throughout much of the twentieth century, and points to their increasing representation both in some traditional unions and in newer types of worker associations. Greater parity of union membership and the formation of new worker associations raise women's profiles in the workplace, improve women's overall working conditions, and empower women economically and politically.

Part III more extensively explores global connections, initially through a discussion of non-feminist and feminist theories on globalization, by focusing on global labor markets, globalized work, and global cities. Chapter 9 distinguishes between internationalization and globalization, sorts through alternative definitions and accounts of globalization, and highlights what we lose in non-gendered accounts compared with what we gain from feminist theories of globalization. Globalization restructures the location of work and workers in different regions of the world, thereby shaping the contours of power relationships in different places on multiple scales ranging from the city, the nation, to the global. Chapter 10 traces the development of a highly integrated global labor market and the commodity chains interconnecting economic activities across place and space. We cannot understand the value of work and economic outcomes in one part of the world if disconnected from an analysis of the global labor market. Because of their centrality to understanding globalization, chapter 11 surveys the rise of and connections between old and newer global cities. Global cities attract both high-paid professionals in finance and those low-waged workers servicing them. Paradoxically, the global orientation of these cities beyond the nation state requires both local and national government action. Finally, chapter 12 examines new political landscapes encompassing spaces and places for economic governance, and for modes of association at the local and the transnational levels. By cultivating an analysis of new political landscapes in this final chapter, the book captures historical movements occupying the imaginations and spaces in our global economy. The future cannot be known; but having the analytical tools to understand the past and to interrogate the present can improve our chances of arriving at a more just future.

PART I

STUDYING GENDER, WORK, AND ECONOMY

Theory of Work and Economy

So I take phosphates or phosphites – whichever it is, and tonics, and journeys, and air, and exercise, and I am absolutely forbidden to "work" until I am well again. (Gilman 1899)

As evocatively captured by Charlotte Perkins Gilman's lament in her short story *The Yellow Wallpaper*, work has a long, but troubled, history in women's lives and in feminist and non-feminist thought. Although writing around the late 1800s, Gilman anticipates many of the themes taken up by feminists in the late twentieth century. In the above excerpt, the female protagonist's fragile body dooms her to play the part of the "weaker sex" in this Victorian drama. The story comments on the treatment of middle- and upper-class women as prone to infirmity, and thus physically and intellectually unfit for work and political participation in the public sphere. White male critics of enfranchisement invoked gender-stereotypical images of "true" womanhood, arguing that women were too frail and delicate to take on the responsibilities of political activity, a common trope in male political discourse at the time. The virtue of true womanhood was premised on women's and men's perceived different natures. But this ideal depended on the unacknowledged labor of working-class women and women of color, whose bodies suckled elite women's infants and whose physical labor erased the traces of detritus in other women's households. Such assumptions have confined work to, and ultimately defined work against, an implicit masculine standard. More generally, women's life course has been intimately tied to the less visible work of caring labor and reproduction. Looking at work and economy through a feminist lens exposes how restrictions on the type of work available, on where it happens, on its rewards, and even on what counts as work, are related to the gender of who does it (Brush 1999: 162–3).

Recalling the legacy of Marx and Weber highlights the influence of these foundational texts on contemporary theories. In drawing inspiration from the classics, contemporary sociology of work and political economy inherit the vocabulary and preoccupations focusing on non-gendered classes, institutions and work organizations. Further, by elaborating on each approach, this chapter reveals that, like their intellectual predecessors, contemporary theorists do not fully integrate gender and care into analyses of work and economy. The opening section ends by showing that political economy's core categories of worker and citizen, and the institutions of state and economy, are implicitly constructed in terms of a masculine embodiment. Without a systematic analysis of and analytical framework for examining gender relations, traditional political economy cannot account for gender inequality or fully explain global economic change. Three waves of feminism, the focus of the remainder of this chapter, emerged against this backdrop.

Women's political mobilization for suffrage, civil rights, and global citizenship fertilized the growth of three major waves of feminism: the first wave coincided with democratic revolutions of the eighteenth century (Scott 1999: 72) and culminated with women's suffrage at the dawn of the twentieth century; the second wave arose alongside the women's liberation movement of the 1960s; and the third wave, in which we find ourselves at present, was propelled by new transnational women's movements arising in the twilight of the twentieth century. A look back at the first wave finds social reformers who raised the questions of women's economic insecurity and political disenfranchisement. From the earliest writings of Mary Wollstonecraft's *A Vindication of the Rights of Women* in the late eighteenth century, feminists have condemned the theory and practice of separate and unequal treatment of women. These reformers saw that women's inability to fully participate in political and economic activities was connected to their burdens in the family. What united an otherwise divided feminism was the shared recognition of the inter-relationship between reproduction and production, affecting the intensity of both men's and women's market and non-market work.

Feminism encompasses diverse political projects and varied theoretical claims about pervasive, ubiquitous, and persistent gender-based hierarchies at work. As discussed in a later section, second-wave feminism noted the absence of women from social analyses and the social world of sociology. Much of classical sociology had essentially focused on men, male activities and experiences, and the parts of society dominated by men, assuming that the social world was primarily the public world of male activities, from the paid labor force to city life and formal politics. By not sufficiently analyzing the so-called "private sphere" of the social world, early sociology failed to develop an understanding of all parts of that world. Early second-wave feminists brought women and women's work into analyses of the social world and broadened the conception of the social and the economic to include care and emotional labor. Third-wave feminism built on the insights of the second wave, while at the same time acknowledging the limits to structural analyses.

Economic sociology and political economy of work and society

Sociological theory emerged in Europe as a way of explaining modernity and the rise of capitalism. Massive upheavals transforming society after the Industrial Revolution inspired both Marx and Weber to write about the exploitation wrought by, and "spirit" of, capitalism. Both posited that social, political, and economic processes influence one another, but emphasized different relationships between political and economic forces, from which they derived their conceptions of class and power.[1] "The woman's question" also resonated politically at the time. However, since these social theorists primarily were concerned with explaining the emergence of capitalism, its characteristics, forms of development and consequences for the public sphere of social life, they paid little attention to the private sphere more likely to be occupied by women. By considering the antecedents of both conventional political economy and sociology of work, we can see more clearly the gaps in these traditions that have focused on social transformation without the feminist lens.

The Work of Marx and Weber

For Marx, social and political institutions served to reinforce and reproduce a particular set of relations of production. Capitalist production is based on the ownership and control of the means of production by one segment of society. Through that ownership of the means of production, capitalists expropriated profits produced by the labor power (capacities) of workers. The state rationalized and managed this relationship in order to ensure its perpetuation over time, and society's many institutions (religion, education, etc.) legitimate capitalist social relations. This formulation, supported by his more polemical writings, such as *Manifesto of the Community Party* (Marx & Engels [1948] 1978), gave primacy to the economic base of society determining common interests and the differential distribution of power.

Weber ([1922] 1978), on the other hand, focused on institutional rationalization beginning with his analysis of political power and state-making. Weber held that the development of the nation state established basic rules and routines that permitted capitalism to flourish (notably commercial and civil laws and the courts that upheld them). Only then, coupled with the ideological shift to a Protestant ethic, could early entrepreneurial efforts blossom into modern capitalism. Unlike Marx, Weber argued that rationalization and standardization in the economic realm (with the emergence of corporations and bureaucracy) would free up productive forces in the same way the rationalization of power and the rule of law created the modern state. His initial optimism waned as he saw tendencies toward bureaucratization trapping the individual in an "iron cage." Rather than organizing people into classes depending on their relationship to the productive forces in society, as Marx had done, Weber theorized the development of consumption strata, within which individuals in comparable market situations experience similar life chances. For Weber, one's economic interest in the possession of goods, along with one's opportunities for income, determine one's market situation or exchange relations (Weber 2006: 38).

Classical sociology *did* recognize that men exercise power over women, the family, and children. Both Marx and Weber shared a relational view of class rooted in the ownership or lack of ownership of private property (Wright 2000a: 3). In emphasizing class struggles as the central dynamic of capitalism, Marx (and his collaborator Engels, who wrote about the family) neglected asymmetrical gender relations as the foundation of the patriarchal economic system. As Hyman (2006: 51) suggests, "Marx himself noted, in the *Grundrisse* and later in *Capital, Volume 1*, that the exchange value of labor power encompassed both the day-to-day maintenance of the worker (food, shelter, clothing) and the cost of reproducing a new generation of children to become workers in their turn." In fact, Glenn (2010: 208) reminds us that the idea of the relationship between production and reproduction originated in Engels' remark that the "determining factor in history is, in the final instance, the production and reproduction of immediate life." Because Marx's notion of class excluded these activities from productive labor, he subsumed housework and reproductive labor into the larger economic framework of base/superstructure. Weber saw political power and traditional authority involving control by a senior male over other men as well as women, but did not explore how this control contributed to a system of gender inequality. By centering on exchange relations more than on production relations, Weber's class analysis abstracted from the market system, less concerned with identifying the logic of patriarchy. In the end, neither Marx nor Weber addressed the analytically salient and historically specific forms of gender-based domination. The corpus of Marx and Weber laid the foundation of sociological theories of work and economy.

Work Sociology, Economic Sociology, and Political Economy

Work sociology, economic sociology, and political economy span related branches of sociological inquiry into the significance of work and value of labor in society. While the sociology of work studies agency, meanings, and orientations rooted in micro-level interactional and organizational processes, economic sociology and political economy focus on meso- and macro-level institutions and structures. In general, work delimits the set of laboring activities aimed at the production of goods and services. The sphere of "collective production and distribution of resources" defines the economy in a given society (Beamish &Woolsey-Biggart 2006: 233). Overall, a sociological examination of work and economy is central to understanding inequality and the social world (Korczynski et al. 2006: 2).

The sociology of work examines work organization and other social and cultural aspects of production. As a central activity and means for providing economic well-being, work confers social status and power. Work also grounds identity, defining who we are and informing our sense of belonging (Vallas et al. 2009). Who we are, in part, is determined by what we do. Meeting someone for the first time often elicits the question "What do you do?" In posing this simple question, we expect the answer to uncover some deeper essence about the person. Our work becomes a symbol, a repository, a signifier, for who we are. Therefore, work is a social activity. However, what constitutes work is itself debated.

Likewise, many work sociologists analyze paid employment either by zeroing in on status, mobility, and job satisfaction in different occupations or by broadening the view to relate technological innovation to workers' attitudes. A classic in work sociology, *Alienation and Freedom: The Factory Worker and His Industry*, telescopes Blauner's (1964) historical subject of the male worker in different work situations. He looks inside the factory to explain the sequencing of four distinct stages in the development of industrial society (Vallas et al. 2009: 26). Each new work process, starting with craft work, then machine-tending through assembly to automated work, corresponds to workers' attitudes toward freedom and alienation. While his assumption that automated work would free workers from drudgery has been criticized, the paradigmatic use of male-dominated industry to frame his theory falters on other grounds. A more recent example might look at computer technology as an abstract force determining the rise of call-center work and its impacts on people's feelings – a combination of alienation and freedom on both ends of the telephone. Neither historical narrative acknowledges a range of informal paid (market) and unpaid (non-market) labor activities, including emotional labor and care work associated with women, as conceptions of work. Though less apparent today, the fact that much of work sociology applied the concept of gender only to discussions of women's work experiences, and not to those of men, has limited our understanding of work and occupations.

What is gained in terms of rich detail from case studies of work organization and occupations in much of work sociology loses sight of the broader interplay of the structural and institutional archi-tectures of capitalism and patriarchal relations. Most work sociol-ogy pays insufficient attention to political institutions and politics, regardless of their gender sensitivity. When included, studies of work examine policies, such as affirmative action and parental leave, and their effects on the gender division of labor in and outside the house-hold. Why some countries have larger public sectors providing social investments for care, or stronger labor regulations and others rely on market-based care systems remains beyond the frame of work sociol-ogy. Such studies neglect how institutions of welfare regimes are gen-dered in different ways and with different economic consequences cross-nationally.

Economic sociology and political economy connect work to struc-ture in analyzing markets and institutions. Disciplinary conventions and intellectual loyalties divide economic sociology into two main specializations, emphasizing either production relations derived from Marx or political processes and institutions following from Weber. Political economy more specifically names the lineage of theories framing the relationship between political and economic structures and the sets of institutions governing economic and social life. Marxists argue that the state serves the interests of the dominant classes in society. State-organized welfare in the mid twentieth century appears in response to the problems generated by the operation of the capitalist system, including – and especially – the need to reproduce labor power (the capacity to labor). For Marxists, the capitalist state is a set of political institutions, practices, and policies oriented to main-taining the dominance of the capitalist class and to demobilizing the working classes. Democracy is said to be the best political shell for capitalism because democratic procedural principles mask the lack of substantive freedoms caused by the class system. In other words, the state functions to maintain capitalist relations of production. By con-trast, foremost for Weber, political institutions are a form and a force of power in capitalist society. The role of the state shaping social life delineates modernity. In modern society, the state monopolizes legiti-mate authority to raise citizen armies, collect taxes, and intervene in the economy, civil society, and the family (Calhoun 2002: 6). Pitched at a high level of abstraction, Marxist analyses of the capitalist state had ignored the varieties of capitalism. From another vantage point, a Weberian approach differentiates welfare capitalisms reflecting the relative power of capitalist and working classes in society. Political economy and economic sociology draw on insights from both Marx and Weber.

An intervening figure, Karl Polanyi, reflected on epochal change in the world order during the 1950s. Through the marriage of sociology and economics, Polanyi argued that markets are not reducible to purely economic laws of motion, and, rather, that markets are always socially constructed and embedded, although to different degrees across time and place. Polanyi, like Marx, viewed labor in terms of social relations. He posited that labor is "a fictive commodity," by which he means that labor itself is not "produced for sale . . . It is only another name for human activity that goes with life itself" (1944: 72). Through the extension of the social to the economic, economic sociologists consider how densely embedded production activities are fixed in a place, or "different degrees of connection to their production sites" (Collins 2003: 151). Polanyi's influence is most evident in large-scale comparative research on the varieties of capitalism and other meso- and macro-structural approaches. Another great transformation associated with the advent of globalization has led many political economists (Collins 2003; Silver 2003) and economic sociologists to revisit Polanyi's *The Great Transformation* (1944).

Comparative Political Economy: Three Worlds and Varieties of Capitalism

Building on insights of new institutional analyses, comparative political economy formulates variants of national capitalisms. Principally, the observation that social inequality and economic growth vary in systematic ways across countries pushed political economists to establish typologies for comparing capitalisms. Two main theories clustered countries according to the relationship between state and economy. Esping-Andersen (1990) put forth a model for understanding the tripartite division of welfare capitalisms. This theory informs the political dimension of such an approach. Several scholars, steeped in the field of industrial relations, matched countries according to the arrangement of economic governance institutions. The latter theory came to be known as varieties of capitalism (VOC). Both theories seek to define the core principles for organizing variants of capitalism and their social and economic consequences.

The pioneering analysis of "three worlds" captures the consequential variation between different types of welfare capitalisms.

Esping-Andersen identifies the liberal market-based economies in the US, Canada, Australia, and UK, characterized by their modest redistributive welfare policies and minimal social investments; and the social democratic welfare capitalisms in the Scandinavian countries, providing a host of social investments such as childcare, housing, and medical care, funded by higher taxes. The third type, social conservative countries such as Germany, Belgium and France, fall in-between the two polar types. According to the three worlds approach, political principles for organizing social investments and directing economic interventions produce significantly different outcomes. Consistent with expectations, social democratic welfare states reduce income inequality relative to liberal market welfare states.

Emphasizing economic governance more than welfare policy, the varieties of capitalism approach differentiates the logic undergirding the institutional architectures of capitalism.[2] Their neo-Weberian ideal types involve the constellation of complementary production regimes and employment relations systems. Complementary suggests that the institutions operate together to form either a liberal or a non-liberal model of capitalism. Liberal and non-liberal models designate "regimes of economic governance": the former allows for more play of the free market and the latter relies on forms of "hierarchical organizational coordination" to realize non-economic transactions. Germany represents the paradigmatic case of a non-liberal, coordinated market economy with which to contrast liberal Anglo-American capitalism (Streeck 2001: 3–6). Streeck (2001: 6–7) makes an important caveat that liberal economies are neither unregulated nor devoid of institutions. He argues that the dynamism once fueling economic miracles in Japan and in Germany stemmed from coordination among institutions in these non-liberal varieties of capitalism. A second generation, literally students of the original VOC theorists, has pushed the boundaries of their intellectual fathers. Influenced by welfare state theories, this second generation calls for a view that integrates the welfare state into analysis of production systems (Ebbinghaus and Manow 2001b: 304).

Political economy and economic sociology energized theoretical inquiry, showing why political systems and institutional varieties inform our understanding of distributional patterns as a result of work and employment within and across countries. Despite different emphases, liberal market economies exemplify the pivotal type of capitalism with which to compare other models. Both approaches find that greater social inequality corresponds to less regulated liberal market economies. Without a systematic account of the gender dimensions of employment practices, institutions, and regulations, however, varieties of capitalism theories neglect gender relations embedded in the way major institutions are organized, creating blind spots in their political-economic models. Varieties of capitalism theories implicitly refer to work and social regulations designed for a standard male industrial worker and a corresponding form of standard family life. For this reason, the VOC approach is ill equipped to explicate the systematic disadvantage of women in both paid and unpaid work, such as the growth of low-wage services and temporary employment among women. Nor can the theory explain differences among men. By ignoring the importance of gender, like their precursors Marx and Weber, these political economic models miss important factors behind economic growth and distributional outcomes. Non-feminist political economy remains rooted in classical social theories. Returning to these roots in the next section reveals the historical motivation for the emergence of both initial and subsequent waves of feminism.

Social theories, feminist waves

Riding the First Wave: The Woman's Question

First-wave feminism, rising and abating from the late 1800s through the early 1920s, addressed the social ills of the day. Reformers posed "the woman's question" to campaign against sweatshop conditions faced by women workers when large-scale manufacture altered traditional ways of working and disrupted agrarian rhythms of work. One of the few systematic theoretical contributions, *The Origin of the Family, Private Property and the State* by Frederick Engels (1968), offered a compelling historical-materialist conception linking women's oppression to class exploitation.[3] According to Engels, asymmetrical relations between men and women constituted the first class relation. Under capitalism, Engels related male domination to the bourgeois family in which men had an economic interest in controlling individual women's reproductive capacities in order to establish clear paternity lines for the transmission of private property to their male heirs. With rhetorical flourish, Engels (1968: 495) intoned, "The overthrow of mother right was the world historical defeat of the female sex. The man seized the reins in the house also, the woman was degraded, enthralled, the slave to the man's lust, a mere instrument for breeding children." In this critical passage, Engels establishes the basis of women's oppression, but narrowly reduces the woman's question to a class dynamic, and the "female sex" to a class relation.

First-wave Feminism: Home Economics and the Economics of the Home

As a counterpoint to Engels, Charlotte Perkins Gilman published her study of the "economic relation between men and women as a factor in social evolution." In the political ferment at the beginning of the twentieth century, Gilman puts women and economics together in her treatise on "one of the most common and most perplexing problems of human life" (1898: 2).[4] Beginning with the story of Genesis, she evoked the original state of equality between men and women before man succumbed to the tempting pleasures in the bountiful garden of delights:

> Close, close he bound her, that she should leave him never;
> Weak still he kept her, lest she be strong to flee (1)

Her prescient account brought unpaid domestic care work into the economic analysis, implicitly refusing to accept both Marxist and classical assumptions that housework created no economic value. In 1903 Gilman explains the genesis of the downgrading of domestic labor.

> The phrase "domestic work" does not apply to a special kind of work, but to a certain grade of work, a state of development through which all kinds pass. All industries were once "domestic," that is were performed at home and in the interests of the family. All industries have since that remote period risen to higher stages, except one or two which have never left their primal stage. ([1903] 1972: 30–1)

In Gilman's words (217), the drudgery of unpaid domestic labor deprives women of their humanity: "The house-life does not bring out our humanness, for all the distinctive lines of human progress lie outside." Gilman perceptively genders the concept of production and integrates reproductive labor into a broader conception of the economy.

In the antebellum US many prominent Black women abolitionists fought for both racial and gender equality. Best known among them, Sojourner Truth had a profound impact on expanding notions of womanhood. In 1851, Sojourner Truth delivered the speech on "Woman's Rights," when she rhetorically declared, "Ain't I a woman?" Not deterred by either the White men or the White women at the Women's Rights Convention in Akron, Truth used her own life experiences to reveal the "contradictions between the ideological myths of womanhood and the reality of black women's experience" doing hard labor and domestic work (Crenshaw 2011: 32).

> Look at my arm! I have ploughed and planted and gathered into barns, and no man could head me – and ain't I a woman? I could work as much and eat as much as a man when I could get it and bear the lash

as well! And ain't I a woman? I have borne thirteen children, and seen most of 'em sold into slavery, and when I cried out with my mother's grief, none but Jesus heard me – and ain't I a woman? (cited in Flexner 1974: 91)

Crenshaw suggests that Truth's oratory offered a rebuttal to the claim that women were categorically weaker than men. It was in the midst of such emancipation speeches and anti-slavery campaigns that a Black feminist literature emerged to challenge Victorian notions of true womanhood and rigid racial categories (James & Sharpley-Whiting 2000).

Second-Wave Feminism: Gender, Patriarchy, and Discrimination

The adoption of the 19th Amendment[5] ended feminism's first wave. Still, feminist ideas flourished even after the peak of political activity around women's issues.[6] A second wave swept in a more self-conscious feminism. As the women's movement gathered steam during the 1970s, liberal, radical, and socialist feminists debated the root causes of women's oppression. Liberal feminism drew on nineteenth-century political theory in positing that the subordination of women rested on "a set of customary and legal constraints that blocks women's entrance to and success in the so-called public world" (Tong 2009: 2). Like their predecessors in the suffrage movement, liberal feminists argued that unfair discrimination against women derived from the "false belief" that women are less capable than men (Tong 2009: 2). Equal-opportunity laws were seen as the best way to uproot gender inequality in the public sphere. Both radical and Marxist feminists took issue with the central theoretical premise of liberal feminism that female subordination was principally based on customary and legal constraints. On theoretical and political grounds, radical and Marxist feminists dismissed the call for equal opportunities as merely reshuffling hierarchies by giving some women a chance to emulate men without changing the structures of male power and dominance that disadvantaged all women.

The work of Engels served both as an inspiration and as a foil to radical, socialist, and Marxist feminists who applied a historical-materialist method in deconstructing the architecture of capitalism to fashion structural accounts of patriarchal arrangements. Their materialist feminist perspective posited that gender was not simply about a difference between men and women, but a hierarchical division produced by patriarchal domination (Jackson 1998a: 139). Feminists also rediscovered Gilman's ideas about housework and domestic labor, which informed ensuing debates over the concep-tualization of capitalism (Davis 2000) and the relationship between patriarchy and capitalism (Delphy 1977; Hartmann 1979; Walby 1986). This debate over what constituted patriarchy forced feminists to rethink class analysis and to put gender relations and the gender division of labor into the forefront of analyses of work and economy. The attempt to show that capitalism was not indifferent to the gender of individuals in the class structure gave rise to second-wave feminist materialist theories of patriarchy as a system of social relations enabling men to control women's labor. Among materialist feminists, radical feminism gave primacy to the sex/gender system of patriarchy to explain the origins and persistence of male power, dominance, and hierarchy (Tong 2009: 2). Arguing for a view of patriarchal capitalism, Marxist and socialist feminists raised historical questions in their search for the origins of women's oppression in relationship to class exploitation.

Second-Wave Feminism: Capitalism and Materialist Analyses

One of the more faithful Marxist feminist theories gave a nod to Engels, while criticizing his account of women's oppression (Davis 2000: 176). Citing Engels, Angela Davis grounded the structures of women's oppression as "inextricably tethered to capitalism." Though never using the term "patriarchy," Davis went beyond Engels by examining the historical "specificity of the social subjugation of the women who live outside of the privileged class under capitalism" (173). She traced the source of the bourgeois notion that woman was man's eternal servant to the historical consolidation of industrial capitalism severing the new economic sphere of factory production from the old home economy. The resulting cleavage transformed the value of women's work in the home. In the agrarian economy of pre-industrialized North America:

> A woman's work began at sunup and continued by firelight as long as she could hold her eyes open. For two centuries, almost everything that the family used or ate was produced at home under her direction. She spun and dyed the yarn that she wove into cloth and cut and hand-stitched into garments. She grew much of the food her family ate, and preserved enough to last the winter months. She made butter, cheese, bread, candles and soap and knitted her family's stockings. (Davis 1981)

With the rise of the factory system, domestic labor, formerly contributing to the community's survival in pre-capitalist economies, lost its value in the circuits of capital. Housework became an inferior form of work because it did not generate profit, the only value attached to labor in a capitalist economy. Black women were forced to work outside of the home, first to produce a profit for the slave master and later to provide for her own family (Davis 2000: 175). When women entered the wage labor market, and sold their labor power, they did so on different terms from men: capitalists treated women not as "abstract labor power in general but rather as an already socially stigmatized female labor power" (171). Thus, women could be paid less for the work they performed for wages. Within capitalism, women's subordination extends from the domestic sphere to social production.

A new focus on dual systems sought to provide an analytical specificity to patriarchy in relationship to capitalism. The French feminist, Christine Delphy (1977) identified separate spheres, locating the central dynamic of asymmetrical gender relations in a patriarchal domestic mode of production within families, whereby men as a class exploited and benefitted directly from the appropriation of women's labor in the household. Like Gilman, she focused on housework and the household as a key to male domination, and insisted on mainstreaming gender into the concept of production. In collaboration with Leonard, Delphy argued that men and women as groups are distinguished socially because one dominates the other.[7] One came into being in relationship to the other. Just as classes only existed in relationship to each other, there was no bourgeoisie without the proletariat; "[it was] the exploitative relationship that binds men and women together and sets them apart. There would be no 'women' without the opposing category of 'men'" (Jackson 1998a: 135). However, Delphy pays too little attention to women's paid labor outside the home (Jackson 1998b: 17).

Both Sylvia Walby and Heidi Hartmann historicized the connections between patriarchy and capitalism. *Patriarchy at Work* by Sylvia Walby (1986) pushed forward the approach; it wove an intricate theory of patriarchy as relatively autonomous from other structures, with particular reference to a set of patriarchal relations permeating domestic work, paid work, state, male violence, and sexuality in articulation with capitalist relations. Heidi Hartmann (1979) traced women's disadvantage in the capitalist labor market to the late nineteenth century when White male workers and employers settled on a family-wage. A family-wage supposedly compensated male workers for their family's upkeep, supporting the idea of a male breadwinner. Though the working class and capitalists had opposing class interests, the family-wage promoted their common gender interests in maintaining patriarchal gains. The ideology of the family-wage justified the hiring of women in low-wage jobs, which in turn kept women dependent on men for their economic survival, perpetuating a vicious cycle of male and class domination. In both theories, analytically, patriarchy had its own dynamic in relationship to capitalism. Through the general exclusion of women from paid work and the patriarchal relations in the household, reinforced by state policies and violence (Walby) and by the male breadwinner receiving a family-wage (Hartmann), men maintained superiority over women. As suggested by Pollert (1996: 641), this mode of theorizing implied an abstract structuralism, reducing motivations, interests, and strategies for male domination of women either to the abstract needs of capital or to the equally abstract role of patriarchy.[8]

Debates acknowledged the unhappy marriage of Marxism and feminism (Sargent 1981), and expressed ambivalence about the category of patriarchy itself (Beechey 1979, 1987). Although ambivalent, many feminists reserved the concept of patriarchy for specific historical structures, that is, "the patrilocal extended household in which the senior male holds authority" (Acker 1989: 236). While acknowledging the problems riddling the concept of patriarchy, Cockburn defended retaining the concept to define one form of sex–gender system in which fathers exercised customary or juridical rights to and over women. This "father-right" gave way to a more generalized "male-right" through a brotherhood of men under capitalism. Cockburn (1991: 8) sought to analyze the articulations of sets of social relations – that is, the way they were lived and reproduced – and took care to distinguish patriarchy from other possible sex–gender systems. Acker (1989: 239) advocated applying less abstract concepts, such as reproduction, to encompass "all those activities that have to do with caring for human beings." In *Gender Transformations*, Walby (1997) revised her previous formulation to differentiate between private and public patriarchy, with the former rooted in family life and the latter in the labor market.[9] The shift to public patriarchy occurred with the influx of women into the wage labor force in large numbers, segregated into low-paying jobs. Walby addressed the implications of various forms of inequalities and politics for the transformation of gender relations, especially in employment.

The second wave of Western feminist scholarship had coalesced around tripartite divisions of liberal, socialist, and radical political theories, and then splintered into multiple versions expressing the loss of confidence in conceptualizations of patriarchy, sex/gender distinctions, and gender. As Toril Moi (1999: 15) puts the problem: "Gender may be pictured as a barricade thrown up against the insidious pervasiveness of sex." Any broad consensus around a feminist intellectual project centering on overwhelmingly structuralist discussions of gender and sexual divisions of labor, whether in the labor market or in the household, was destabilized in a number of ways and for a number of reasons. The structuralist tone of this research was challenged by developments, particularly within feminist philosophy and post-modernism, which posed serious challenges to early feminist conceptualizations of power and – more significantly – of the very concept of gender.

The postmodern turn and return: conceptual reconsiderations

Until second-wave feminism came of age during the 1960s, there were no adequate theories to explain gender inequality in the labor market. Feminists inherited analytical concepts and theories narrowly conceptualizing sex differences in the division of labor. Within sociology, the leading Parsonian approach posited a dichotomy of differentiated sex roles that implied parallelism, which "constantly collapse[d] into biological differences" (Connell 2002: 35). This binary of sex differences "excluded patterns of differences among women and among men and between alternative masculinities and femininities" (9).[10] Feminists moved away from an analysis of sex differences (individual characteristics and biological essences) to gender relationships. Such a relational perspective called for recognizing diversity of work experiences among women (e.g. in paid domestic work) as well as hierarchies of power among men in such institutions as armies and multinational corporations (Connell 2002: 9).

The central positioning of the category of gender has been questioned. More specifically, intervention by Black and Latina feminists criticized second-wave feminist discussions of the inter-relationship between gender and class for failing to integrate an analysis of race, and rendering Black women and women of color more generally invisible, just as traditional social science had, by and large, rendered all women invisible (Spelman 1988; Collins 1990). Recalling the long but forgotten history of Black women's activism, Black feminists sought to understand the multiple oppressions that Black women face, while emphasizing resistance and the need to interrogate the ways that Black women experienced patriarchy (Guy-Sheftall & Hammonds 2008: 159). Feminists had ignored how their own race functioned to mitigate some aspects of sexism and how it often privileged them over and contributed to the domination of, other women (Crenshaw 2011: 33). Second-wave feminist theories of patriarchy highlighted the history of White women's exclusion from the workplace, all the while ignoring how Black women traditionally worked outside the home in numbers far exceeding the labor participation rate of White women (33). Moreover, "many white women were able to gain entry into previously all white male enclaves not through bringing about a fundamental reordering of male versus female work, but in large part by shifting their 'female' responsibilities to poor and minority (and increasingly racialized immigrant) women" (33). Studies of paid domestic work showed why gender-only analysis distorted the picture of, and complicated, the relationship between women (Rollins 1985; Hill-Collins 1990; Romero 1992).

Conclusion: toward a feminist political economy

Third-wave feminists now acknowledge that women's lives and experiences are shaped not only by gender, but also by class, race, and other distinctions. Most go beyond deconstruction of the category of gender to analyze the interconnections between different dimensions of inequality (Lutz et al. 2011: 9). It was the analysis of Black women's specific socio-economic situation that advanced theories of the "simultaneity and mutual co-constitution of different categories of social differentiation and . . . emphasize[d] the specificity of the experiences shaped by these interactions" (Lutz et al. 2011: 2). The theoretical interventions of women of color led to the call for intersectional analysis "because women of color experience racism in ways not always the same as those experienced by men of color and sexism in ways not always parallel to experiences of white women, [so] anti-racism and feminism are limited, even on their own terms" (Crenshaw 1991: 1252). Neither theories of gender nor theories of race alone adequately addressed how these were "simultaneous and linked" social identities (Browne & Misra 2003: 488) and "structures of domination" (Baca Zinn & Thornton Dill 2009: 91). In their place, feminist analyses grounded women's oppression contextually and allowed for historical contingency, which could avoid the tendency to fix the category of women in an essential difference. Put another way, Browne and Misra (2003: 491) suggested asking questions such as: Do race and gender always intersect? Does intersection necessarily create multiple disadvantages for women of color and multiple privileges for White men? Enduring patterns of gender inequality such as occupational sex segregation, pay inequities, and women's primary responsibility for care might be produced by different mechanisms at different times and in different places.

Revisiting the troubled history of work in non-feminist and feminist thought reminds us of the distance already traveled and the journey ahead in order to craft theories for understanding social inequalities at the intersection of gender, class, race, and nation. Women cannot be simply added to the story – rather the analytical categories themselves must be gendered. If the first wave introduced the woman's question, and the second wave theorized the structure of patriarchy, this third wave integrates structural analysis of patriarchal relations and the process by which gendered meanings and identities are constructed. Throughout the remainder of the book, the chapters direct attention to how jobs and labor activities become gender-typed, and the subsequent consequences over time and place. The book offers a feminist political economic framework for understanding the structures and processes of economic change. The resulting framework integrates an analysis of the whole range of labor activities taking place in old and new locations rather than a narrowly defined economic space.

CHAPTER
3 An Integrative Framework for the Study of Gender, Work, and Economy

THE world of work is undoubtedly changing. Work takes more time and occupies more places, intruding into the spaces of our homes. Home, always a setting of work and part of the economy, now hosts offices for telecommuting throughout the day, the site of cleaning and caring services and the location of other commercial activities. This return of work to the home is certainly notable. However, the everyday work of care and emotional maintenance still fade into the background. As pointed out in the previous chapter, social theories privilege the (masculine) public sphere of power and formal (paid) work and they discount the (feminine) private sphere of emotional and care (usually unpaid) labor (Peterson 2008: 220). The definition of the social and its scope has been limited by the exclusion of large parts of human action and interaction – that is, the social world typically occupied by women. Consistent with third-wave feminism, this chapter fills in the gaps by incorporating those neglected areas associated with the feminine private sphere, such as emotional maintenance, affection, and care, into conceptions of work and economy.

The chapter proposes a new analytical framework for the study of gender, work, and economy. In capitalist societies, gender is a primary way of legitimating differences between men and women and informing the organization of social life. To begin, the chapter elaborates on the basic tenets of feminism, arguing that women suffer discrimination due to their subordinate positions in gender systems of inequality (Delmar 1986: 8). Then, it asks how institutions promote, support, and reduce gender and class inequalities. This ensuing discussion provides a rationale for redefining institutional categories and spheres to include care, reproductive labor, and social reproduction. Without an analysis of gender, we cannot understand how commercialization is encroaching on social life and intimacy, the increasing trends toward financialization and other services, and the variation in distributional outcomes for different groups of men and women.

The spread of work to a home or to a specialized economic zone reveals the impulse of capitalism to colonize space everywhere in pursuit of profits. Social geography offers a guide for surveying the meanings of space and place. Combining the spatial vocabulary of social geography with a new concept of geographies of power, the final section of this chapter explores the changing structures of inequality within intimate spaces of the household, across global cities and within the network of commodity chains transnationally. The framework brings together feminist political economy's attention to gendered institutions with social geography's attention to boundary-making. The result is a new framework better able to explain who does what type of work and why, and under what conditions, to identify the economic consequences and their social meanings.

Feminist political economy: toward an integrative framework

Foremost, a feminist analysis views gender difference as a constitutive "organizing principle in social life, a principle of allocation of duties, rights, rewards and power, including the means of violence" (Acker 2004: 20). Gender signifies a hierarchical division analogous, and related, to class inequality based on material oppression and exploitation (Jackson 1998a: 131). The resulting gender inequality means that men have greater access to, and control over, power, prestige, wealth and well-being – including access to health care, education, and housing – than women (Acker 2011: 2). Systems of gender inequality are rooted in patriarchal relations, constraining women's economic autonomy, denying women's well-being, desires, and needs, and devaluing female-typed traits and work. Other social inequalities *intersect* and mediate gender inequalities: not all men have equal access to sources of power and wealth, and some women are privileged in terms of race and class, but still are disadvantaged in terms of gender. Such a relational perspective recognizes the diversity of work experiences among women, as well as hierarchies of power among men (Connell 2002: 9). Most third-wave feminists also distinguish sexuality, as erotic identities, desires, activities, and practices, from gender. The conflation of gender and sex, according to Jackson, is not an accident; it is the product of a male-dominated, heterosexist culture (Jackson 1998a). In general, the framework proposed here integrates both the structural and the interactional bases of inequality not only between men and women, but among women and among men of different classes and racial ethnic groups.

Third-wave feminists specify gender inequality as being generated both by the social structure disadvantaging women in relationship to men's access to power and material resources, and by a process whereby conceptions and meanings of manhood and womanhood are constructed through social interactions. Structure delimits extensive patterns of social relations, or what Lorber (1999: xix) calls a "lattice-work of institutionalized social relationships, that, by creating and manipulating the categories of gender, organize and signify power at levels above the individual, from cultural meanings to government policies." Gender identities and relations are not simply imposed from the outside by external constraints, such as laws and social norms, but also constructed in a process of doing and acting (Connell 2002: 4). Doing and acting involve everyday social practices and interactions in which norms, idioms, rituals, and rules enforce, enact, and potentially can undo patriarchal gender relations (Glenn 1999: 8). In other words, gender relations and identities are not fixed, but fluid and uncertain, so that asymmetrical gendered power relations are never guaranteed. For this reason, the boundaries of the polarity are policed and sanctioned, symbolically through language and the law, and institutionally through the distribution of and control over resources and power.

The framework offered here combines institutional/structural and organizational/interactional feminist approaches to explain distributional patterns and the processes by which jobs become gender-coded and segregated. Feminist political economy emphasizes how central social institutions, including the economy, the polity, and the family, are gendered to the extent that they privilege men and expressions of hegemonic masculinities on the one hand, and penalize women and emphasize stereotypical characteristics devaluing femininities and alternative masculinities on the other. The idea of hegemonic masculinities draws on forms of rule in class society. Hegemony signifies economic and political power in terms of traits associated with expressions of masculinity. These expressions of masculinity become hegemonic by marginalizing subordinated masculinities and by an emphasized femininity. Control of institutions, through legitimate authority and decision-making capacity, typically rests with men who behave in ways that mobilize hegemonic masculinities (Martin 2001) and that enhance and entrench their own positions of power. Within institutions, hiring practices, organizational barriers, job images, and informal networking constrain women's social mobility by limiting the jobs available. Institutions establish rewards and punishments that make it difficult for women to achieve independence socially, economically, politically, and culturally.

The interconnections between institutions of the labor market, the household, and the state, and gender assumptions built into them, "structure a particular division of labor between men and women and between social classes" (McDowell 2008: 23). However, extant conceptualizations of the economy and the state emphasize labor and work activities primarily in the public sphere. As a result, these concepts already embed assumptions based on gender differences. For the most part, these gender assumptions remain unacknowledged. Therefore, existing institutional categories need to be replaced.

Conceptualizing Care and Reproductive Labor

Conventional political economy theories conceptualize the capitalist economy only in relationship to the production of goods and services that are exchanged for money in the market, and "the distribution of the surplus from that exchange" (Acker 2006: 53). In a sense, the economy appears to function almost alchemically by assuming and deriving value solely at the moment of exchange. This narrow conceptualization wants us to believe that productive work somehow occurs in a vacuum. Such a view cannot fully make sense of valorization processes and distributional patterns because it excludes a range of labor activities and processes vital for making production possible in the first place. Absent, yet vital to understanding how the economy functions, are both unpaid reproductive labor and subsistence production most often performed by women in or around the household. To comprehend the totality of labor necessary to enhance workers' productivity and to sustain the social formation as a whole, we need a broader concept of the economy.

Though care is undeniably important to the health and well-being of individuals, neo-classical and traditional political economy theories either frame it in narrowly individualistic terms, or neglect its effect in organizing institutional priorities. At the core of this viewpoint is the problematic assumption "that the prototypical human being is a self-sufficient rational economic man" (Lynch 2010: 2). This assumption fails to acknowledge the masculine embodiment of a male breadwinner and how he becomes "care-free" (2010). To be care-free means unburdened by and relieved of responsibility to care for others. Waged work in general, and male-typed jobs in particular, assume workers are free from the expectations of outside commitments, such as care work and other reproductive labor. More to the point, as feminist political economists show, "productive work" depends on "reproductive work" (Elson cited in Acker 2004: 25). Reproductive work involves those activities aimed at social provisioning and daily care for human beings, including "caring, feeding, clothing, teaching, and nurturing individuals" (Parrenas 2008: 12).[1] A subset of reproductive work specifically centers on care producing affective relations, nurturance, and healing that enhance workers' capacities to labor and release labor's productive capabilities (labor power). In essence, these activities are necessary to enable workers to be productive in society (12). Even when unpaid, reproductive and care labor can be considered as part of the economy in the sense that they "reduce the wage bill that employers must pay, increasing the surplus that goes to capital" (Acker 2006: 53).

In line with this critique, feminist political economists broaden the definition of the economy to include social reproduction. Social reproduction encompasses those labor activities required for maintaining and enhancing the health, welfare, and capabilities of individuals, families and communities both on a daily basis and inter-generationally (Glenn 2010: 208). Adopting the broader definition extends the concept of the economy beyond the conventionally demarcated confines of firms, markets, and formal work organizations (England et al. 2002). Social reproduction can be organized by the family, the state, or the market. Some reproductive labor can be parceled out to more than one institution and can take place either in the household or in specialized institutions (hospitals, schools, nursing homes). Families may rely on non-kin, including low-paid domestic workers or unremunerated slave or indentured servants, to perform reproductive tasks.

Feminist theoretical interventions go further to explore the relationship between the state and the market, the family, and civil society. Expanding on traditional political economy, the framework not only highlights the division of labor between states and markets, but also includes families into the mix, and details how each contributes to social provisioning of domestic and care-taking labor, and welfare services and goods (Orloff 1993: 313). Such "social provisions affect women's material situations, shape gender relations, structure political conflict and participation, and contribute to formation of specific identities and interests" (303–4). To determine to what extent the state, the market, or the family supports and provides an array of services requires recasting welfare state theories in light of its gendered character.

For advanced capitalist countries, feminist political economists theorize the gendered character of their welfare state regimes and corresponding social policies, as well as women's mobilization directed at challenging power relations. As a political institution, the state influences the balance of private and public involvement in the provision of goods and services, either by socializing costs of reproduction, or by retreating from the provision of care services, or ceding it to family, non-profit organizations, labor market intermediaries, or the market. The welfare state takes over some aspects of social reproduction (health care), either entirely or partially, and subsidizes other aspects, such as childcare, through transfer payments, or means-tested vouchers or services, each depending on the type of welfare state. Further, through policy-making, the state directly and indirectly shapes gender stratification systems (Mandel 2009; Gottschall 2010). The expansion of the welfare state during the 1960s–1970s, and subsequent retrenchment during the 1990s to the present, have had a profound effect on the quality and the quantity of women's employment.[2] Further, through political mobilization feminists can make claims on the state to expand social rights that in turn can enhance women's relative position by reducing gender inequality (Orloff 1993: 304). Specifying the gendered character of welfare states helps explain why patterns of gender and class inequalities differ across places and spaces.

Finally, the full extent of changing patterns of work and employment, increasing commodification of service production, and the current financial crisis cannot be understood in the confines of narrow conceptions of work and economy. Based on the broader definition of work and economy, this new framework can link the often ignored labor "inside" the home with the same commodified activities in the market or provided by the state. Commodification refers to "the transformation of relationships, formerly untainted by commerce, into commercial relationships, relationships of exchange, of buying and selling" (*Encyclopedia of Marxism*). Voracious capitalist appetites for profiting from commodification of everything and every aspect of social life only go so far. Current tendencies toward privatization of social reproduction and commodification of services cannot simply be reduced to the "needs" of capital. Likewise, an economic rationale for seeking the lowest labor costs in a race to the bottom would point to women always replacing men in the production of things and knowledge, based on the ability of capital to pay women lower wages than men. To say that "love is the new gold" points to the distinctive nature of labor extracted from female-typed labor activities associated with feminized traits, such as sentiment, nurturance, and care, as well as its devaluation (Hochschild 2004). Love and care are transferred and transformed along global care chains. As Hochschild's example shows, the changing social organization of care and reproduction are important to understanding the expansion of services and service-dominated economies, both nationally and globally.

Intensification of global competition, developments in communication and other technologies (Floro & Meurs 2009: 6), and changes in the organization of production and reproduction usher in a new era of circulation and integration of people, places, politics, production and reproduction processes, on local, regional, and global scales. With only a few exceptions, feminists as well as traditional political economists have neglected the importance of spatial dimensions in analyses of work and economic transformations. What follows offers a framework that takes account of these cross-border flows and circulations.

Geographies of power: unpacking the global economy

> The need of a constantly expanding market for its products chases the bourgeoisie over the entire surface of the globe. It must nestle everywhere, settle everywhere, establish connections everywhere. (Marx & Engels [1948] 1978)

Theoretical ambition beseeches us to "speak beyond the single case" (Connell 2007: 225). Yet the literature is replete with examples of work and economic structures uncritically place-bound. Work sociology gives short shrift to global connections, regional developments, and country comparisons, while economic sociology tends to reify the nation by differentiating varieties of capitalism and welfare regimes. International and regional relationships tend to be subordinated to national economic institutions in typologies of comparative capitalisms. Interest in the global economy necessarily stretches research beyond the single case. But simply adding more cases underestimates global pressures on national political systems. Instead, theory should investigate the nature of the connections between those cases. Currently, no one theory adequately addresses power dynamics across spaces at different scales. This section introduces a new concept of geographies of power, stitching together Marxist social geography and post-colonial feminism to elaborate on the impulse of capitalism to "nestle everywhere, settle everywhere" over the "entire surface of the globe."

The Marxist geographer David Harvey diagnoses recurrent crises evident in the capital accumulation process in spatial terms. During the 1960s and early 1970s, the US and Europe faced labor scarcities and a relatively well-organized labor movement. To overcome these barriers to increasing profits, employers looked for new sources of cheap and less empowered labor. In the mid-1960s, governments enacted pro-immigration policies opening borders to an increasing supply of low-wage labor. Subsequently, new technologies facilitated reorganization of transportation, communication systems, and flexible specialization whereby capital could coordinate production globally (Harvey 2008: 4). At the same time, flexible specialization of production processes enabled capital to reap lower labor costs by transplanting production to developing countries in specialized socio-spatial economic zones. The result was a global restructuring of both the production process and the labor market. Because of his insufficient attention to gender, Harvey's erudite narrative fails to integrate the work of social reproduction and the feminization of jobs sustaining capital accumulation. Little is said about the contested political and social construction of borderlines to explain uneven economic development, and how gender and racial differences affect and are affected by spatial power arrangements.

Not surprisingly, post-colonial feminists appropriate the spatial language of geography to explain border-crossings, unequal power relations, and cartographies of struggles, usually taking place within and across large regions created by earlier colonial expansion (Mohanty 2006). Post-colonial theory points to the diversity of needs and experiences that complicate the formation of solidarities among women from the Global North and South. However, the vocabulary used to analyze cartographies of struggle is insufficiently grounded in social geography. Drawing on the conceptual tool kit of social geography can aid in the investigation of power relations from above and below territorial borders of the nation state (Robinson 2010).

Place, Space, Territory and Scale

> All old-established national industries have been destroyed or are daily being destroyed. They are dislodged by new industries, whose introduction becomes a life and death question for all civilized nations, by industries that no longer work up indigenous raw material, but raw material drawn from the remotest zones; industries whose products are consumed not only at home, but in every quarter of the globe. (Marx & Engels [1948] 1978)

A starting point for developing a spatially sensitive perspective utilizes social geographer's four main concepts: place, space, territory, and scale (Massey 1994, 2005). The seeming disregard for place in the transplanting of new industries "dislodged" from their national moorings in the drive for profits in fact shows why we must incorporate spatial dynamics to understand what David Harvey calls the enigma of capitalism. Place can be thought of as situational and space as relational. Any place is situated in space; work can take place in the kitchen, on the street corner, on the edge of a city, or in a specialized economic zone. Each of these, however, are located within a particular space bounded by customs, laws, and geography:

spaces which can vary over time. Put another way, place represents the concrete array of people and activities, whereas space delimits its social configuration. In this context, space refers to both a domain over which capital moves and a situation in which capital can mold, all in pursuit of profit maximization (Beynon & Hudson 1993: 182). As analytical constructs, neither place nor space simply demarcates a physical manifestation as such. With the concept of territory, Sassen (2010) deconstructs the master categories of nation and states commonly used in social scientific research. Territory does not presuppose a particular bounded unit such as the nation state, but rather implies and interrogates the constructed nature of political boundaries. A territory can exist within a nation state or exceed its borders. Scale represents the structuring unit of governance, ranging from the local (e.g. city, state, and province), the national, and the regional, to the transnational. Yet territory can transcend any one structuring unit of governance.

Place, space, territory, and scale are core concepts for analyzing meanings and motives fueling the flows and the circulations of capital, labor, and ideas. One contemporary example of the interplay between these concepts involves countries and companies leasing and purchasing land for commercial use in other parts of the world. Investors, both private companies and foreign governments, are leasing large expanses of land in poor African nations. African governments, often the titular owners of the land, displace indigenous farmers who once tilled the fields, sometimes over generations, without a concern for any concept of private ownership (MacFarquhar 2010: A4). To make matters worse, the agricultural output in these new commercial ventures skips local economies, destined instead for profit-generating consumption in wealthier countries. It is often women who work in subsistence farming, as families must fend for themselves and experience hunger, despite bountiful harvests. Here, the agricultural place shifts from subsistence farming to capitalist agriculture in response to changes in the enclosing economic space. In such circumstances, the boundaries of territories no longer coincide with the boundaries of the nation state. As suggested in this example, territories can span national and transnational scales. The leasing of land transforms the geography of political and economic power by transferring ownership from the commons to private property. Now deprived of her access to the spaces of production, the farmer loses control over the products of her labor, which diminishes her ability to secure her family's livelihood, and puts social reproduction in jeopardy. In this scenario, we can visualize the spatial operation of power from a social geography perspective.

Geographies of Power: A Multi-scalar Feminism

An alternative rubric of geographies of power brings these concepts systematically into an integrative feminist framework. Geography of power constructs a conceptual map for a multi-scalar feminist analysis. At the local scale of the household, an intimate geography of power informs gender relations not only between men and women, but among men and among women. In the relationship between mistress and maid, for example, we gain a vantage point from which to view power relations enacted in a single place across different spaces and on multiple scales. Live-in paid domestic workers must navigate and negotiate the symbolic family economy of household spaces. Within the household, some places, such as a dining-room table where the family sit together to share a meal, exclude domestic workers from the zone of family belonging, while other places, such as kitchens, are designated as zones of work. In essence, the social space of the household has been transformed and places within the household take on new meaning as sites of production and reproduction. Domestic staff's living quarters might be spatially segregated from the rest of the household – symbolically demarcated by the downstairs quarters of British domestic servants. On a city-scale, the reconfiguration of the built environment changes intimate geographies of power. A new geography of power emerges as a result of the loss of space for separate domestic living quarters in high-rise apartments crowding people into densely packed cityscapes of old and new global cities. Now, fewer domestic workers live in the domiciles of their employers, creating new topographies of power relations and resistance. Analyzing spatial dimensions can contribute to our understanding of valorization processes – that is, why spaces (such as the domestic sphere) are marked as feminized, and, as a result, are devalued.

Following the lines of spatial thinking, geographies of power draw on a relational comparative perspective in urban studies (Robinson 2010: 8). Analogously, the concept of geographies of power can chart political and ideological borderlines racializing national groupings and calling attention to shifting hegemonies on a regional and transnational scale. Take, for instance, the regional borders of what became known as Asia. "Asia" signified the naming practice by Europeans who sought to racially differentiate the East from the West (Yoda and Harootunian 2006). In this sense, "Asia" demarcated a subordinate political-economic region through an Orientalist gaze that exoticized the other. From its common usage, the category of Asia(n) assumes internal coherence and implies homogeneity, whether referring to a claimed identity or to a region in which people reside (Gottfried 2008b).

The meanings of "Asia(n)" differ when viewed by the people within the constellation of countries composing this so-called region. Contiguous nations bound together in Asia, though sharing a common geographical space, occupy different positions of political, economic, and military power vis-à-vis each other. Within the region, Japan's dominance of its neighboring countries through occupation and military force is but one example of geographies of power at a regional scale. Another instantiation involves both large-scale and intimate geographies of power within the region. When Filipina home health-care workers attend to elderly women in Japan, their position as guest workers on temporary visas is circumscribed by geographies of power between nations. This relationship in the household reflects traces of the colonial past in addition to the economic dominance of Japan in the present. An analysis of geographies of power renders more visible the historical construction of this imaginary Asia(n). To use the term "imaginary" does not mean that Asia did not or does not exist. Rather, it destabilizes the taken-for-granted geographies of economies by unpacking power relations between "colonized" and "colonizers," power relations on different scales. As a result, the geographies of power reveal the social construction of political and economic borderlines.

The concept of geographies of power gestures toward comparative analysis of economic processes at different scales across shifting spaces. This comparative gesture through a feminist lens opens up the research agenda beyond the usual spaces, to investigate emotional labor and care work taking place in the household and the movement of high-wage business services fostering low-wage personal services on the scale of new global cities, such as Dubai, Shanghai, and Kolkata. Selecting cases for comparison, both from within a single region and across regions, decenters the social arrangements that come into view. It keeps the analysis dynamic by considering circulations of people, production, and imaginaries transcending the territorial borders of localities and states. By addressing place, space, territory, and scale, the new framework brings feminism back to large structures, which link power relations at both micro- and macro-levels, and calls attention to resistance ranging from local to global arenas.

Conclusion

Like third-wave feminism, the new framework proposed in this book pays attention to care work in and out of the household. An additional overlay integrates the concept of geographies of power to make more explicit the implicit spatiality in third-wave feminist accounts. In fact, feminism has always been attuned to spatial power arrangements. To say that the separation of housework and industrial production is consequential on gender and class inequalities is to implicitly argue that space matters. To examine transnational chains linking care workers from their homes in developing countries to the homes of their employers in wealthier nations recognizes the importance of spatial connections of power. Unless our framework incorporates a social geography perspective, we cannot fully explain why gender inequality persists, and why patterns of inequality differ across time and place.

Such an alternative points to women's unpaid and low-wage reproductive labor helping to forestall the labor crisis in the early 1960s. With the assault on the male working class in core industries of the Global North, more women entered and remained in the labor force, thereby averting the crisis of reproduction of capitalism. Recurrent crises, beginning with the oil crisis of the 1970s, followed by the Asian financial crisis of the late 1990s, and most recently the Western financial crisis of 2008, externalized and privatized social reproduction costs, intensifying women's paid and unpaid labor, and heaping pressure on families trying to make ends meet, at times by migrating from their home country to find work. Through an examination of gendered work at different scales, the approach in this book links structures of inequality from the household to the global, tying together the economic fate of both men and women in different regions of the world.

The next chapter explores the puzzle of gender segregation from its historical roots to better understand its contemporary divisions. Against this backdrop we can see economic transformations. The historical patterns of sex segregation spatially divided market and non-market work, spatially concentrated men and women in different occupations and industries, and spatially designated men and women in different social locations. Part III of the book takes an in-depth look at these same themes, but in a global context. From this discussion of economic and political globalization, we are better able to conceptualize geographies of power on the global economic grid and to imagine new futures in changing political landscapes on multiple scales.

PART II

POLITICAL ECONOMY OF GENDER, WORK, AND ECONOMY

The Puzzle of Gender Segregation: From Historical Roots to Contemporary Divisions

Tʜᴇ persistence of gender segregation is an enduring puzzle, and represents one of the most intractable issues in the sociology of work and economy. A feminist lens reveals a holistic picture with which to analyze these gendered patterns of work and employment. This chapter explores the origins of gender segregation forms, identifies mechanisms channeling men and women into different types of work, and considers the historical timing of segregation changes and the reasons for them. Two forms of segregation are discussed: horizontal segregation concentrates men in male-typed occupations and women in female-typed occupations along a "manual–non-manual divide," while vertical gender segregation is a form of "hierarchical inequality, specifically men's domination of the highest status occupations within the manual and non-manual sectors of the economy" (Charles 2003: 269). Using the feminist political economic framework discussed in the previous chapter, this chapter highlights third-wave feminist themes of gendered power to uncover the historical roots of gender segregation.

The roots of gender segregation in the labor market run deep. A historical narrative of broad economic and political transformations reveals the factors shaping the contours of gender segregation in the United States. By reviewing the numbers, we can track the steady rise of women's participation in the wage labor force during the 1960s through the 1970s. Push and pull factors, including economic restructuring, legal rulings, and policy reforms, contribute to more women entering and remaining in paid employment, but jobs remain stubbornly male- and female-typed in the midst of these changes. From a feminist political economic perspective, this chapter evaluates both supply-side and demand-side arguments to see which fit the data better to explain the patterns of horizontal and vertical

gender segregation. The chapter concludes by presenting comparative data on cross-national patterns to decipher the puzzle of gender
segregation.

The historical roots of gender segregation in the US

During the Industrial Revolution, the historical transformation of
the family economy put unpaid care labor on a different footing from
wage labor. Moving forward to the nineteenth century brings to the
surface patriarchal structures of work and economy. Occupational
and industrial divides spatially segregated men and women in different spheres of the economy and in different jobs in the fields and the
factories. Critically, political interventions cemented women's disadvantage in the paid labor force and their dependence on men. The
later emergence of a male breadwinner accentuated the separation
of paid and unpaid labor, with the wage-earner shedding responsibility for care labor, thereby devaluing it. By the dawn of the twentieth
century, the contours of gender segregation were firmly in place.

Gender segregation in the eighteenth- and nineteenth-century US

Family structure and gender relations were altered in the aftermath
of the Industrial Revolution, transforming the mode of production once factory employment supplanted the system of household
production. Women's labor, though controlled by others (fathers
and husbands), was visible and valuable in the pre-industrial family
economy (Fraser & Gordon 1994: 322). One of the major disruptions
to the family economy occurred with the ascendance of the factory
system. The rhythms and harsh conditions of factory work extending
10 to 12 hours per day were incompatible with family life and childcare (Vallas et al. 2009: 76). Initially, in Colonial America, the Puritan
ethic emphasized community, and, as a result, mutual support and
hard work informed the conditions of women's labor in the nascent
factory system. Before marriage, young White women were expected
to work under the protective umbrella of paternalistic factory owners.
Upon marriage, women became dependent on their husbands. Wives'
dependence on the father-headed household was codified in the legal
doctrine of coverture (Fraser & Gordon 1994: 319). Marriage deprived
women of citizenship rights, such as the right to own or bestow property, to enter into contracts, or to sue for legal redress (Weitz 2009:
5), in addition to their disenfranchisement. The eighteenth-century
English legal theorist Sir William Blackstone expressed the reason-

ing for the status of women as property: "By marriage, the husband and wife are one person in the law; that is, the very being and legal existence of the woman is suspended during the marriage, or at least is incorporated into that of her husband under whose wing, protection and cover she performs everything" (cited in Weitz 2009: 5). In most states, patriarchal authority limited women's right to own land, which fostered women's dependence on husbands and fathers to insure their own subsistence. Being unable to vote or make a living wage deprived women of the ability to establish economic independence, forcing most women to marry to gain their economic security. Industrialization not only changed the mode of production, but also affected the dominant moral "conceptions of virtue and sin, discipline and leisure, masculinity and femininity" (Vallas et al. 2009: 79).

By the nineteenth century, the rise of large-scale industrial capitalism was accompanied by an emergent laissez-faire ideology stressing the virtues of individualism, achievement, and competition in the economy. At the same time, laissez-faire ideology continued to rest on the opposing principle of women's dependence as prescribed in the idea of the domestic code, which dictated women's place in the home and associated true womanhood with domestic duties (Kessler-Harris 1982). The widespread conviction ascribing women's proper work to within the family as the domestic code helps to explain women's poor economic position confining them to domestic service, laundries, and other extensions of female-typed work found in the household. However, the ascendance of laissez-faire ideology in economic affairs freed non-slave women from their legal dependence on the patriarchal authority of individual fathers. The idea of women's bodies as men's property was challenged by first-wave feminists in the mid-to-late nineteenth century. For example, Mississippi passed the first Married Women's Property Act in 1839. The law gave non-slave married women the right to retain property they owned before marriage and any wages earned outside the home (Weitz 2009: 6). Legal autonomy did not mean economic independence. Regardless of women's self-perceptions and identities, employers used the domestic code to rationalize paying women less by using the justification that women's income supplemented the household budget. Alongside this image of women promoted by the domestic code and supported by protective legislation was the image of a male breadwinner who purportedly earned a family-wage sufficient to provide for the social provisioning of all family members. The upshot was an ideology that emphasized the virtue of women devoted to housework, and saw their incomes as merely supplementary to the family-wage. In this way, the economic position of women workers remained subsumed by the patriarchal authority of the male breadwinner and the family-wage.

The ideology of the family-wage both bolstered White working-men's power over women and children, and facilitated employers' efforts to segment the labor force along gender lines. The combination of the family-wage, on the one hand, and the domestic code, on the other, reinforced women's economic dependence on men. Prior to the institution of the family-wage, women and children were expected to earn enough for their own maintenance. The ideology of a family-wage changed this by supposedly providing men with a wage sufficient to allow women to stay at home to raise children and to maintain the family, rather than having all members of the family working and contributing to social reproduction costs. Even women whose husbands did not earn a family-wage, and who thus were forced to take paid employment to support themselves and their families, were affected by the domestic code and protective legislation prescribing women's roles as mothers and as consumers. Women's labor market status suffered as a result of employers' justification for paying women less based on the assumption that women were secondary workers or merely supplementing the head of household's income.

The majority of women of color could not achieve this ideal of domesticity, since most men of color could not earn a family-wage due to legal and cultural restrictions on where they could work and what type of work they could perform (Glenn 1985). In fact, the ideal of domesticity depended on the unacknowledged but necessary labor of racial ethnic women who performed domestic service in White women's homes (Glenn 1992: 3). Because of legal and cultural restrictions, domestic service was one of the few jobs available to racial ethnic women. As a result, the burden of housework was unevenly borne by women of color and working-class women. Further, employment tracking supported by racial ideologies naturalized the perceived differences between women of color and White women (32). Subsequently, a dual racialized and gender-segregated labor market emerged. The family-wage was unattainable for most men and women of color.

Whether or not the family-wage signified a triumph of the White working class against employers' refusal to pay women commensurate wages to men's remains an open historical question. In one view, the family-wage represented men's reassertion of patriarchal authority once they lost direct control over women's and children's labor (Hartmann 1979). In another view, the family-wage served the interests of the working class as a whole by improving the overall economic well-being of the family (Humphries 1977a, b). While this chapter cannot settle the dispute, the consequences of the family-wage reaffirmed men's association with production and women's with consumption and reproduction. The family-wage supported ideologically a gender division of labor based on the separation of work spheres, freeing men from domestic responsibilities and care while it defined women's work in terms of domesticity. Women's labor market activities suffered as a result of the institution of the family-wage as narrowing the choices and availability of work: women's labor became more closely allied to the household and their waged work notably became seen as peripheral "or even as signaling a moral failure on the part of man judged as an inadequate male breadwinner" (Vallas et al. 2009: 78).

The association of masculinity with the role of sole provider and the cultural ideal in the US of the "self-made man" (Marx-Ferree 1992: 246; also see Marx-Ferree 1990) were made possible by the burgeoning middle class on the one hand and the racialized labor force underwriting social reproduction on the other. Using a feminist lens illuminated gendering of waged work through this ideology of the provider role, which made it difficult for women to achieve equality in both domains. It was not so much the confinement of women in the home, apart from the economy, as it was the historically constructed structural and ideological incompatibilities between the household and the workplace that limited gender equality (Marx-Ferree 1992). This historical narrative traced the roots of segregation to economic structural changes. A more in-depth empirical examination of gender and work underscores the contours of gender segregation over the course of the twentieth century in America.

Contours of gender segregation in twentieth-century America

The contours of gender segregation took shape around the beginning of the twentieth century. Official government statistics estimated that women's labor force participation then averaged 17% of the total (see table 4.1). These statistics probably underestimated women's overall labor activity relative to men's. Official government agencies' definition of labor force participation excluded non-market activities most often performed by women in and around the household. In addition, direct cash transactions (for taking in boarders, doing laundry, and wet-nursing), barter exchanges, and subsistence agriculture eluded official enumeration. These activities were widespread in the interstices of the growing industrial economy. Aggregate statistics also hid variation among women from different racial and ethnic groups. Women's official labor force participation ranged from 10.4% among Chinese-American women, and 16.0% among European-American women, to almost one-third of Japanese-American women (30.1%) and 40.7% of African-American women (Amott & Matthaei 1996: 412).

Table 4.1 Employment status of women 16 years or older (1890–2010)		
Year	Number (000)	% women in the labor force
1890	3,704	17.0
1940	13,783	28.4
1945	19,290	36.1
1965	26,240	35.2
1970	31,543	43.3
1980	45,487	51.5
1990	56,829	57.5
2000	66,303	59.9
2010	71,904	58.6

Sources: figures for 1890–1965 from US Department of Labor Historical Statistics; for 1970–2000 from US Department of Labor, Bureau of Labor Statistics, table 2 "Employment status of the civilian non-institutional population," www.bls.gov/cps/wlf-databook-2010.pdf; for 2010 from Household Data Annual Averages, table 3, "Employment status of the civilian non-institutional population" http://bls.gov/opub/ee/2011/cps/annavg3_2010.pdf.

After the initial feminization of formerly male-typed occupations – such as those of librarians, clerical workers, teachers, and bank tellers – at the dawn of the twentieth century, women made few gains into male-typed jobs until the 1960s.

Popular literature immortalized the plight of the male clerk. Most famously, Charles Dickens' *A Christmas Carol* portrayed a gaunt Bob Cratchit at his desk copying documents into the night. And in the opening lines of Melville's "Bartleby, The Scrivener: A Story of Wall Street," published in 1853, the narrator introduces the scene of the all-male office space. When demand for clerical workers increased in the midst of companies' consolidation and bureaucratization, the job image changed from the lone scrivener depicted in the iconic stories of White male clerks to the lower-paid White female stenographers' pool. The advent of the typewriter facilitated the subdivision of jobs into discrete tasks (filing, answering phones, etc.), cheapening the cost of clerical labor. At the beginning of the twentieth century, White women flooded into clerical work as one of the few alternatives to dirty factory work and the drudgery of domestic service (Bose & Bridges-Whaley 2009: 236), while men abandoned clerical work to enter burgeoning higher-paid professions in finance, law, accounting, and management. Such professions were the business services necessary to the administration of industrial capitalism. Women entered previously male-typed occupations once the job lost status and men opted for better-paying professional positions (236).

In the legal arena, protective legislation in force for much of the twentieth century dictated the restrictions on the type of jobs women could perform, while the absence of equal pay laws permitted dual wage scales. By 1908, the Supreme Court, in *Muller* v. *Oregon*, upheld an Oregon law that restricted women's employment in factories, laundries, and other mechanized establishments to 10 hours per day. This ruling set the legal precedent enshrining the primacy of women's domestic roles and defining all women as potential mothers and housekeepers for the good of the nation. The judicial reasoning likened a woman to a reproductive vessel without the capacity for autonomous action required of full citizenship. The excerpt from the ruling reads:

> physical structure and a proper discharge of her maternal functions – having in view not merely her own health but the well-being of the race – justify legislation to protect her ... the limitations which the statute places upon her contractual powers ... are not imposed solely for her benefit, but also largely for the benefit of all ... The reasons ... rest on the inherent difference between the sexes, and in the different functions in life they perform. (Findlaw.com)

The court paternalistically justified statutory employment limitations by asserting the state's interest in preserving women's maternal functions superseded women's individual right to engage freely in the labor force. In effect, protective legislation gave a legal imprimatur to "public" patriarchal authority, excluding women entirely from some occupations (especially in the manual trades), and supporting the ideology – if not the reality – of a family-wage earned by the male head of household. Protective legislation supported segregation of men and women in different occupations and locked-in a patriarchal gender division of labor.

Throughout the 1920s, fledgeling factory complexes consolidated work and brought more White working-men into a new assembly-line system of mass production. Penned in his *Prison Notebooks* at the time, Antonio Gramsci (1971) excavated the logic of capitalism in his evocation of the cultural and political landscape of American Fordism. He marveled at Fordism as more than a new social organization of work, but also as one relying on both macro-structures of the state and the interpellation of a "new type of man" suited to the new type of work and productive process (286). At a cultural level, American Fordism taught a "puritanical ethic" (303), which subjected workers to rigorous discipline, instilled new habits (298), strengthened a nuclear form of family (300), and regulated sexual "instincts" (295–8). While well aware of the cultural changes shaped in the crucible of Fordism, Gramsci merely hinted at how hegemonic masculinities were being reconstructed at the point of production. The "new type of man" implicitly identified industrial work as a manly pursuit. Indeed, few women worked alongside men on the shop-floor. Closed off from large-scale factory work, women's official labor force participation only inched up slowly in the Fordist era of large-scale manufacturing. Those women counted in the labor force were more likely to find employment in the clerical positions of expanding corporations, in small manufacturers such as food processing plants in the south, or in the still small service sector.

During World War II, "Rosie the Riveter," the name given to the legions of women whom the government rallied to join the workforce, replaced their sons, fathers and husbands soldiering abroad, in manufacturing plants. Despite their experience building airplanes, ships, and other equipment for the war effort, a re-emergent ideology of women's proper place in the home discouraged mothers from staying in the labor force once men returned to civilian life and reentered the factories. Magazines of the day reflected and reinforced this shift: articles that once had published easy-to-make recipes for dinner in 30 minutes, giving mothers shortcuts in their meal preparations so that family responsibilities could be combined with the critical war effort, then instructed women on the proper preparation of three-hour recipes, soon after the war's end. This loss of well-paid manufacturing work sealed many women's fate for the rest of the decade. On the heels of the new decade of the 1950s, ironically featuring the traditional nuclear family in television staple sitcoms such as *Father Knows Best* and *Ozzie and Harriet*, White married women significantly altered their employment biography.

Female Labor Force Participation Trends: Push and Pull Factors

A major economic shift brought an increasing number of women into the wage labor force for longer periods of time by the mid-1960s. Not coincidentally, this structural change precipitated political mobilization and theoretical reflection among second-wave feminists. In the midst of economic and political change, more women, especially mothers entered and remained in the labor force. Only one decade later, half of all women in the US were counted as employed. US women's labor force participation steadily climbed to reach relatively high levels by the first decade of the twenty-first century. Both push and pull factors contributed to women's dramatic influx into the paid labor force during the 1960s and 1970s (Vallas et al. 2009: 207). Economic "push" factors reflected the "cost of staying out of the labor market" (Vallas et al. 2009: 209). More varied factors pulled women into the labor force. Most notably, economic restructuring and educational opportunities encouraged women to seek employment, while political reforms toward equal opportunity and affirmative action, and second-wave feminism, opened up a larger array of options in the labor market.

Economic need and demographic changes pushed more women out

of the household and into the wage labor force during the late 1960s
and 1970s. Already during the 1960s the shift to services eroded the
family-wage as companies shed manufacturing jobs. More married
women entered the labor market due to the decline of male wages.
Married women's earnings became increasingly necessary to ease the
economic burden on families. From midway through the 1960s, when
divorce became more commonplace and acceptable, the rates doubled
from the modest 2.2 per 1,000 persons in 1960 to 5.2 per 1,000 two
decades later. The causal relationship between divorce and maternal
employment, however, is not easily discerned. On the one hand, wage
employment provided women the economic wherewithal to divorce
their partners. On the other hand, divorce compelled many women
to (re)enter the labor force in stalled careers, unable to make up for
lost time. It is not clear whether, and to what extent, divorce pulled
women into employment or women's employment pushed women to
dissolve unsatisfying marriages. Other demographic factors besides
rising divorce rates also encouraged women to participate in the
wage labor force. Declining infant mortality and fertility diminished
women's responsibilities for childcare in the family. In the US, the
average number of children in a family dropped significantly from
the peak of 3.7 in 1957 when the Baby Boom was in full swing to 2.08
children per family in 1960, stabilizing around 1.7 to 1.9 children
throughout the rest of the twentieth century (Hernandez 1996: 243).
Similarly, the mean age at marriage inched upwards from 20.3 years
in 1960, with women delaying marriage until their mid-twenties by
2000.

Political Pull Factors: Judicial Rulings and Legislative Initiatives

Pull factors such as legislation and judicial rulings establishing principles of equal pay, anti-discrimination, and affirmative action broke
down legal barriers to women's economic opportunities. The passage
of Title VII of the US Civil Rights Act of 1964 prohibited employers
from discrimination against women and minorities in hiring and pro-
motions. Two Supreme Court cases in consecutive years erased the last
vestiges of protective legislation. The Supreme Court scrapped legal
reasoning grounded in the protection of women as a special class.
Instead, it applied a new principle of equal opportunity derived from
the "equal protection" clause of the Constitution's 14th Amendment.
In its unanimous decision in *Reed* v. *Reed* (1971), the US Supreme Court
held unconstitutional an Idaho statute giving preference to males in
the appointment of administrators of estates. The court found the
"administrative convenience" explanation of the preference for males
to have no rational basis. The following year the Court took an even

stronger position. An Air Force Lieutenant, Sharron Frontiero, challenged a statute that provided dependent allowances for men in the uniformed services without proof of their actual economic need, but permitted such allowances to women only if they could show that they paid one-half of their husband's living costs.

Eight justices voted in favor of Frontiero's claim, but they split on the reasons for their ruling. On the one side, four justices applied strict scrutiny reasoning:

> There can be no doubt that our Nation has had a long and unfortunate history of gender discrimination. Traditionally, such discrimination was rationalized by an attitude of "romantic paternalism" which, in practical effect, put women not on a pedestal, but in a cage ... Moreover, since gender, like race and national origin, is an immutable characteristic determined solely by the accident of birth, the imposition of special disabilities upon the members of a particular gender because of their gender would seem to violate the basic concept of our system that legal burdens should bear some relationship to individual responsibilities.

On the other side, three justices applied a rational basis test and found the statute unconstitutional on the authority of *Reed* that administrative convenience was not a rational basis for differential treatment.

While judicial rulings and legislation were no doubt important, economic structural change was a major impetus leading to the increase of female labor force participation. As will be discussed more fully in the next chapter, economic change reinforced gender segregation in occupational ghettos. As Oppenheimer (1977) suggests, growth in jobs traditionally relegated to women, mostly service-sector jobs, drove the rising demand for female wage labor. Concomitantly, the decline of good manufacturing jobs depressed men's wages and household income. This economic climate pushed more women into the paid labor force.

Social Change and Segregation

Other social changes during the 1960s–1980s supported women entering, and staying longer in, the labor force. For example, the expansion of educational opportunities gave women more options to pursue careers in professional fields. The women's movement spreading gender egalitarian ideologies and challenging prescribed gender norms gave women the normative space to work outside the home (Vallas et al. 2009; also see Taylor et al. 2009; Charles 2003). From the mid-to-late 1960s, second-wave feminism surged in response to women's labor force participation, boosting it further. Second-wave feminism engendered a community of interest among women around gender equality achieved through economic independence.

Women increased their labor force participation throughout the 1960s and 1970s, but gender and racial segregation continued to define occupational patterns of employment. Economic transformations from "private" to "public" service work exemplified these patterns of gender and racial segregation. Nursing was one of the largest categories of public and semi-public reproductive labor organized along capitalist lines and by the state, rather than defined by the patrimonial mistress/servant model. Capitalist relations of nursing were embedded in a more impersonal, bureaucratic structure governed by more explicit contractual obligations (Glenn 1999: 23), but often supported and subsidized by the welfare state. Yet familial symbolism circumscribed the gender and racial construction of nursing and medical practice. In pre-1940s hospitals, separate spheres delimited the responsibilities and authority of male doctors and female nurses. Doctors took on the mantle of an authoritative father figure, while trained nurses overseeing the care of patients were viewed either as mothers or as dependent children, especially student nurses who were expected to follow orders (24). Most trained nurses were White women, in part because of the exclusion of Black women from nursing schools, most notably in the South (25). A systematic grading of nursing further divided labor through the separation of conception and execution of tasks. Increasing credentialism professionalized the training of nurses, creating tiers among practitioners from the 1930s through the 1940s (28). By the 1970s, additional tiers of nursing aides created jobs primarily employing many racial ethnic women to perform "dirty" tasks in nursing homes, home health-care and convalescent homes (29). From this brief history of the trajectory of nursing, we can see the process by which race, class, and gender structured labor markets. Tracing the historical arc reveals spatial patterning from "private" to "public" service work and its return to the household as a primary site of work, but as permeated by capitalist employment relations.

Throughout the period, African-American women worked, but were restricted to a limited number of jobs. Jim Crow laws in the American South legalized de jure spatial segregation based on race. Even after the repeal of these discriminatory laws, spatial divisions persisted de facto. Still, women's and civil rights' groups mounted legal challenges to blatant discrimination via class action suits. The passage of anti-discrimination laws and legal challenges opened formerly closed male-typed occupations to women, although with mixed consequences for remedying forms of segregation. Looking at a broader canvas of the US economy shows the patterning of horizontal and vertical segregation.

Gender segregation by numbers: manual and non-manual divides

The civilian labor force grew for all groups, most dramatically among Hispanic women and Hispanic men, over the ten years between 2000 and 2010 (see table 4.2). By the end of this period, only a fraction difference separates the percentage of women working during 2010 (see table 4.3). Even though Hispanic women closed the employment gap, they continued to exhibit lower labor force participation rates than other women. Gender differences also narrowed during that decade. Yet men in all racial groups had higher labor force participation rates. It must be noted that Black men's labor force participation fell below the average for other men. Asian men earned the most and Hispanic men the least. Similarly, Asian and White women's median weekly earnings exceeded other women's and those of Black and Hispanic men (see table 4.3).

One way to ascertain the extent of segregation is by constructing the index of dissimilarity measure. An index of dissimilarity, ranging from 0 (complete integration) to 100 (complete segregation), gauges segregation in the overall economy. Occupational segregation declined from 1972, when the index stood at 68 (Hegewisch et al. 2010: 4), to 53 as of 1990. This means that 53% of women (28 million) would need to enter male-dominated occupations to achieve full integration (Reskin & Padivic 1994). The lowest point, at 50 percentage, occurred in 2002, and further progress stalled afterwards. The index lingered

Table 4.2 Civilian labor force, persons 16 and over, by gender and race (2000 and 2010)

Racial group	2000 (000)	2010 (000)	Percent increase
White women	47,689	48,836	2.4
White men	55,040	55,116	0.0
Black women	8,695	9,447	8.6
Black men	7,702	8,415	9.3
Hispanic women	6,767	9,238	36.5
Hispanic men	9,923	13,511	36.2
Asian women	2,908	3,355	15.4
Asian men	3,362	3,893	15.8
Total labor force	142,086	151,816	6.8

Total civilian labor force measures the sum of civilian employment and civilian unemployment (not members of the armed services). For 2000, the total civilian labor force is 142,583,000, and for 2010 it is 153,889, 000, including all other racial categories.
Source: US Department of Labor, Bureau of Labor Statistics, table 5, "Civilian labor force, entrants and leavers, 2000, 2010," www.bls.gov/emp/ep_table_304.htm.

Table 4.3 Median weekly earnings of full-time waged and salaried workers ($), and percentage of population working, by gender and race (2010)

| | GENDER | | | |
| | Women | | Men | |
RACE	Median weekly earnings of full-time waged and salaried workers ($)	Percentage of population working	Median weekly earnings of full-time waged and salaried workers ($)	Percentage of population working
White	684	58.8	850	70.7
Black	592	57.6	633	58.8
Hispanic	508	54.5	560	71.9
Asian	773	57.4	936	71.6

Source: US Department of Labor, Bureau of Labor Statistics, "Population age 16 and over who worked at some time during 2010," www.bls.gov/opub/ted/2012/ted_20120227.htm; US Department of Labor, Annual Averages, 2010, chart 2, "Highlights of women's earnings in 2010," p. 2, www.bls.gov/cps/cpswom2010.pdf (downloaded February 27, 2012).

around 51 most of the period between 1996 and 2009 (Hegewisch et al. 2010: 4). Occupational gender segregation by race and ethnicity saw a similar downward trend. Occupational gender segregation loomed at 55 for Hispanics. Among women the index of dissimilarity was 28 for White women relative to Black women, and 31 for White women as compared to Hispanic women. Men also experienced occupational segregation by race and ethnic background (Hegewisch et al. 2010: 7).

Horizontal and Vertical Segregation by Numbers

By examining specific occupations, a more detailed picture of horizontal and vertical segregation crystallizes. Women entering male-dominated fields accounted for much of the decline in aggregate levels of gender segregation (Vallas et al. 2009: 211). Large strides occurred in occupations such as those of mail carriers (from 6.7% in occupation to 34.9%), lawyers (4.0 to 32.2), and dentists (1.9 to 30.5) from 1972 to 2009 (Hegewisch et al. 2010: 2). Reskin & Roos (2002) found that only three occupations switched from female- to male-dominated. Interestingly, two of these occupations, cooks and food preparation, represented men's entry into the female domain of the kitchen (cited in Vallas et al. 2009: 211). Male cooks outnumbered female cooks nearly 60% to 41%, respectively, in 2009 (United States Department of Labor, "Twenty leading occupations"). The shift to male cooks co-incided with the expansion of restaurants from fast food to fine dining – where top chefs rule the kitchen. Still, the building trades valorizing masculine physical embodiment remained male-dominated, as few women gained traction in these occupations: women were only 5.4%

of machinists (up from 0.5 in 1972), 2.2% of all electricians, and 1.6% of all carpenters in 2009 (Hegewisch et al. 2010: 2). In fact, 39% of men and only 11% of women worked on the manual side of the horizontal divide. On the other side, only 9% of women workers were employed in professional, and 1% in managerial, positions in 1900, rising to 17% of the total in professional specialties and 11% in executive, administrative, and managerial occupations in 1990 (Bose & Bridges-Whaley 2009: 235), reaching 37% of managers and related fields in 2009 (United States Department of Labor 2010: 28). Women accounted for just one-quarter of chief executives and computer programmers, and 14% of engineers and architects, in 2009 (29), while the legal profession, once almost completely segregated, with 0.8% female lawyers in 1900 (Bose & Bridges-Whaley 2009: 235), grew to 32% female more than one century later (United States Department of Labor 2010: 30).

Gender segregation has declined somewhat since the late 1980s. Still, women and minorities have had less access to jobs in authority positions, technical fields, and elite professions than men, a robust finding consistent over time and across countries. Technical fields requiring at least four years of college barely budged: women made up 20.3% of computer programmers in 2009, slightly up from 19.9% in 1972; and civil engineering saw a marked decline after initial gains, reaching a peak of 13.2% in 2005 down to 7.1% in 2009 (Hegewisch et al. 2010: 3). Using an alternative measure of the most common occupations for women and men, we find the persistence of a high degree of gender segregation. In 2010, four of ten women held jobs in female-dominated occupations where at least 75% of the occupation is female (1). Only 4.5% of these same occupations employed men (1). A lopsided occupational structure concentrates women in female-typed jobs, ranging from a high of 96.1% of secretaries, 92.7% of childcare workers, 91.1% of registered nurses and 88.2% of nursing aides, 81.8% of elementary school teachers, and 73.7% of cashiers (table 4.4).

Similarly, women dominated interactive service work and the semi-professions involving emotional labor, nurturance, and care associated with stereotypically feminized qualities. On the other side of the horizontal divide, men occupied manual positions as aircraft mechanics, pipefitters, tool and die makers, electricians, millwrights, carpenters (97–9%), truck drivers (95%), in production assembly (62%), and as construction laborers (84%) (United States Department of Labor 2010: 34–6). These manual jobs emphasize physical prowess and other socially constructed masculine traits. Conversely, fewer men enter female domains in the semi-professions than women in male-typed professions: men represented only 9% of registered nurses, 18% of elementary school teachers, and 26% of cashiers (see table 4.4). Despite

Occupation	Total employed women (000)	Total employed (all) (000)	Percent women	Women's median weekly earnings ($)
Total, 16 years and older	65,638	139,064	47.2	$669
Secretaries and administrative assistants	2,962	3,082	96.1	657
Registered nurses	2,590	2,843	91.1	1,039
Elementary and middle school teachers	2,301	2,813	81.8	931
Cashiers	2,291	3,109	73.7	366
Retail Salespersons	1,705	3,286	51.9	421
Nursing, psychiatric, and home health aides	1,700	1,928	88.2	427
Waiters and waitresses	1,470	2,067	71.1	381
Supervisors/managers: retail sales workers	1.375	3,132	43.9	578
Customer service representatives	1,263	1,896	66.6	586
Maids and housekeeping cleaners	1,252	1,407	89.0	376
Receptionists and information clerks	1,187	1,281	92.7	529
Childcare workers	1,181	1,247	94.7	398
Bookkeeping, accounting, and auditing clerks	1,179	1,297	90.9	628
Supervisors/managers: office and support	1,035	1,507	68.7	726
Managers, all others	1,014	2,898	35.0	1,045
Accountants and auditors	989	1,646	60.1	953
Teacher assistants	893	966	92.4	485
Personal and home care aides	838	973	86.1	405
Office clerks, general	837	994	84.2	597
Cooks	790	1,951	40.5	381

Table 4.4 Leading occupations of employed women (2010)

Source: based on US Department of Labor, Bureau of Labor Statistics, Annual Averages 2010, Women's Bureau, www.dol.gov/wb/factsheets/20lead2010.htm.

some fluctuation, forms of horizontal and vertical segregation continue to channel men and women into different occupations.

Accounting for Gender Segregation: Deciphering the Puzzle

Third-wave feminists have attempted to decipher the causal forces driving the relative stability of the structures of occupational segregation and related pay inequities despite greater female educational attainment, and increasing female participation in the labor market and in politics (Charles 2003; Charles and Bradley 2009). Persistent gender-based hierarchies present third-wave feminists with a vexing puzzle to unravel: men and women not only work in different occupations (horizontal segregation), but also occupy different positions in authority structures (vertical segregation). Enduring occupational segregation and pay inequities are seen as a function of either individual or structural characteristics, and these are related to decisions made by and preferences of either women or employers. Conventional labor market analyses offer a toolkit for examining segmentation, emphasizing either supply-side or demand-side factors.

Supply-side explanations focused on cultural differences in occupational aspirations, choices and preferences of men and women, to explain occupational segregation. Most notably, Catherine Hakim (1995) argued that occupational segregation reflected women's choices. She demarcated three basic types of women, in relation to their commitments and orientations toward family and work: work-centered, home-centered, and the third and largest group made up of "adaptive" women, including women who deliberately chose to combine work and family. Both home-centered and adaptive women's cumulative and collective preferences for less demanding female-typed occupations and/or part-time work contributed to aggregate occupational segregation. This resurgence of preference theory generated controversy and intense debate, especially among feminist scholars in the UK (Bruegel 1996; Ginn & Arber 1996; Blackburn et al. 2002; Crompton 2002). Foremost among the many problems, the three categories reduced women's orientations and experiences to a narrow subset of possibilities and choices (Blackburn et al. 2002: 524). Most critically, the emphasis on individual choice disregarded the social circumstances that constrained it, such as availability and cost of childcare, attractiveness of available work, and relative pay levels (524).

The supply-side argument assumed that women freely gave primacy to family over wage work, and adjusted their investments in skill acquisition and education accordingly, by working shorter hours and choosing fields of study and jobs more compatible with and accommodating of family responsibilities (Bose & Bridges-Whaley 2009: 237). By implication, men chose more time-intensive jobs and fields of study requiring higher skills more consistent with a work biography focused on male-breadwinning. Gender segregation appeared to be a benign outcome of aggregated individual decisions. This account seems intuitively persuasive because it aligns with pervasive gender stereotypes, and seems to conform to the observed experiences of men and women in the workforce. Even though the description correctly points to an association between endowments and economic outcomes, it does not adequately identify the mechanisms that determine the different distribution of knowledge and skills training, or even account for the formation of different preferences. The approach cannot explain why women enter low-skilled female-dominated jobs even when low-skilled male-dominated jobs are available (Bose & Bridges-Whaley 2011: 201). Undermining the supply-side theorist's main assumption, most female-dominated jobs are no easier to combine with family responsibilities than many male-dominated jobs (201). In other words, segregation is not merely a function of preferences for different types of work or an issue in which ascriptive inequality will eventually disappear once labor market outcomes reflect the fit between men's and women's actual achievements and preferences. While the job one occupies is certainly a function of skill sets and educational achievement, the demand-side arguments considered the impact of employers' decision-making on matching people to places in the occupational structure.

On the demand side, feminists argued that employers' discriminatory policies and practices contributed to occupational gender segregation. Their demand-side models attributed segmentation to employers' decisions on hiring, placement, and promotion. According to this perspective, employers engaged in "disparate treatment" by discriminating against equally qualified men and women, and/or used gender-biased selection criteria having "disparate impact" on men and women: the former becoming less salient due to regulatory reforms designed to address explicit gender discrimination, and the latter being more tenacious and difficult to uproot as often implicit in criteria for hiring and promotion (England & Folbre 2003: 11). Structural features of firm-specific internal labor markets produced what Reskin & Padavic (1994: 88) called a "promotion gap." Women more typically worked in dead-end jobs with truncated internal labor markets, in contrast to men who enjoyed longer and broader career paths within and across firms. The lack of mobility chances in these dead-end jobs leads to higher turnover. Where women work is not merely a function of individual characteristics. Instead, job characteristics influence workers' attitudes and ambitions. Demand-side theories emphasized workers' responses to structural features of the labor market (Bose & Bridges-Whaley 2011: 201).

Even as more women entered male work domains, they still ended up in the lower ends of professional occupations in "managerial ghettos" (Stone 1994: 410). Women faced prejudice in commanding the same respect, for example, as "Rambo" litigators (Pierce 1995), and in becoming partners in law firms (Bose & Bridges-Whaley 2009: 235); "Net of qualifications, women managers [w]ere lower in the chain of command, ha[d] limited decision-making power, and tend[ed] to supervise other women" (Stone 1994: 410). Vivid metaphors captured this uneven tempo of mobility by gender, including: sticky floors holding women back at lower levels, glass ceilings keeping women from shattering through to higher levels, escalators accelerating men's ascent to the executive suites (Reskin & Padavic 1994: 88), and "revolving doors" propelling men and women into high-status positions at different speeds and in different directions (Jacobs 1989, cited in Stone 1994: 410).

Accounting for the Gender Wage Gap

The same labor market approaches also applied to analysis of the gender gap in earnings. No one disputed that the pay gap was related to segregation, whatever the causes, although Anker (1988: 14) warned that segregation was only one cause among many for pay differentials. Feminist theories of the gender pay gap followed similar lines of argument. Supply-side arguments proved less persuasive than demand-side arguments.

Human capital theory, a supply-side argument, assumed that pay differences reflected the human capital endowments men and women bring with them to the workplace. Human capital includes those characteristics such as skills and education which make workers more productive (Bose & Bridges-Whaley 2011: 201). Simply put, women earned less on average because they occupied different jobs requiring less-valued qualifications. More specifically, mothers' human capital depreciated over time when they either dropped out of the labor force or reduced their working hours to care for children. Following the same logic as preference theories, women's life choices to prioritize family reinforced the traditional gender division of labor in which men would invest in human capital and be the principal earner or breadwinner.

Empirically, human capital endowments cannot explain the full extent of gender differences in pay. They fail to explain fully, for example, why women with the same or better qualifications earn less than, and have different mobility chances from, men, or how jobs became gender-typed or de-gendered. Why, for example, does an earnings gap persist even among women who have strong labor attachment equal to that of men (Rose & Hartmann 2004)? How skills and qualifications become valued are questions beyond the purview and concern of supply-side theorists. Further, most feminists questioned the assumption that domestic labor contributed zero value to the growth of an individual's human capital (Blackburn et al. 2002: 518). If human capital differentials fully explain earnings, then disparity between men and women should have narrowed even more as a result of women's educational achievements and increasing presence in male-typed jobs. The human capital model failed to explain why men still earned more on average than women in the same occupations when controlling for the same education and experience.

Building on demand-side labor market approaches, feminists highlighted the role of discrimination in contributing to pay inequities by gender. Barbara Bergmann's (1986) crowding thesis argued that women seeking to enter male occupations faced gender discrimination in hiring, leading to an excess of applicants for traditionally female-typed jobs (England & Folbre 2003: 24). The crowding of women into a small number of female-typed jobs lowered wages on average for those jobs. Men also suffered a wage penalty when they worked in those female-typed occupations because employers set lower wages on average in such jobs (25). Yet, men's fate in female-dominated jobs more often yielded positive economic outcomes than was the case for women in male-dominated jobs. A study of male pay scales found that men enjoyed a consistent wage advantage over women irrespective of the gender composition of jobs (Budig 2002: 258), although they earned more on average in male-dominated and gender-integrated work settings (274). While a small wage gap favored men, both men and women earned relatively low wages in female-typed jobs, especially in care work (England et al. 2002). Moreover, men typically experienced faster upward mobility on an escalator than their female counterparts (Budig 2002: 274–5). This crowding thesis did not fully address the mechanisms that contributed to the devaluation of skills and the resulting pay gap, nor how crowding occurred. In general, feminized work tends to be devalued and underpaid regardless of the gender of the job incumbent, but men received higher returns than women in the same jobs (England et al. 2002).

An alternative devaluation thesis located the source of pay inequities in labor market institutions (Steinberg 1990). Devaluation was not simply an artifact of occupational segregation, but also related to gender bias in skill recognition and was a result of male-dominated wage setting institutions. Saliently, the devaluation thesis showed how gender mattered to what counted as skills and qualifications. Then a reassessment of the true value of a job's comparable worth could correct pay levels by comparing male-typed and female-typed jobs to show the relative devaluation of women's work. Breaking down skill into component parts served the purpose of revaluing and recognizing devalued aspects of women's work. Comparable worth campaigns, which flourished in the public sector during the 1980s, gave women workers a political tool for demanding pay equity adjustments (Blum 1991). Despite initial successes, legal challenges (Nelson & Bridges 1999) plus strong employer opposition limited the use of comparable worth as a political mechanism for closing the pay gap.

The above demand-side models showed the strong negative effect of gender (independent of, and in interaction with, other factors) on matching or "queuing" of persons into gender-segregated occupations and on determining income disparities. Demand-side approaches found employers' decisions remained a potent force shaping the gender distribution of employment opportunities. They insisted that discrimination and devaluation of women's work were as important as human capital in explaining the gender wage gap (England 1992). Labor queues developed into gender queues as a result of employers' unexamined gender biases (Reskin & Roos 2002), such as the invisible discriminating assumptions in everyday communication at work (Reskin 2002). Even after gaining entry into male-typed professions, re-segregation channeled women into different specializations that tended to pay less, offer less autonomy, less status, and fewer opportunities for advancement in named partnerships (Bose & Bridges-Whaley 2009: 235). For example, female real estate agents more often sold residential properties, with lower commissions than their male counterparts who marketed commercial real estate, with the potential to yield higher fees and higher overall income. In medicine, women were under-represented in surgical specialties associated with higher salary scales. Similarly, fewer women were employed in the high-paying male-dominated technical fields, and women earn less in the same occupations. For example, male chief executives earn $2,084 per week on average, as compared to female chief executives' $1,553, while male computer and information systems managers receive $1,788 relative to women's $1,411, a difference of 78.9 percent, in 2009 (US Department of Labor 2010: 55).

Gender Differences and Economic Structures

A subset of demand-side arguments attributed the differential outcomes for men and women to economic structural features. This argument further divided labor markets into primary and secondary segments in terms of relative job characteristics. The primary labor market consisted of jobs paying higher wages, offering more promotional opportunities, and according greater job security, which, for manufacturing jobs, were associated with collective bargaining agreements negotiated by unions, whereas secondary labor market jobs paid low wages and offered few, if any, benefits. Those in the secondary labor market often held more than one job to make ends meet, had no job security, and were economically insecure. In other words, the primary labor market was composed of good blue-collar jobs and, more recently, the kind of information processing work performed by stockbrokers and insurance agents, and other "mental" jobs with upward mobility. The secondary labor market worker remained at the low end of the service sector – at the bottom of what we might call "hamburger flippers," but it also included retail clerks, low-end sales workers, janitorial and maid services, and most temporary workers, to name a few (see table 4.5). These dead-end jobs were filled by people

Table 4.5 Labor market structure		
	CORE	PERIPHERY
PRIMARY	Lawyers Skilled trades Insurance agent Investment banker	Same occupations as in core firms, but for small-sized firms
SECONDARY	Clerical workers Laborers	Retail clerks Janitorial workers Maids

who were easily replaced, and led to high turnover because of truncated career ladders for future advancement and salary gains. Jobs in low-waged services have grown over the past few decades and will continue to increase well into the next decade.

Other labor market theorists argued that these labor markets crosscut core or periphery firms in the economy. The core consisted of large-scale companies in oligopolistic/monopolistic markets such as automobiles, steel, utilities, computer hardware, and financial services (investment banks) – companies easily identifiable by name. In the periphery, a large number of small companies competed for market shares. Most personal services took place in one of the numerous small businesses and households on the periphery. Like dual labor markets, core and periphery firms offered different compensation, training and promotional opportunities, and security profiles. Firms in the core bureaucratized and rationalized systems of long and broad internal labor markets, developing extensive job ladders with incremental pay grades and associated benefits. By contrast, competition among small firms in the peripheral sector led to lower wages, minimal and truncated job ladders, weak internal labor markets, and more insecurity as a result of job turnover.

Taken together, "good" jobs were associated with the primary labor market in core firms. These firms offered workers the most advantageous conditions relative to the secondary labor market in the periphery. For example, clerical workers employed by firms such as IBM or GM were apt to face better working conditions than in the periphery. Structurally, female-dominated occupations typically are segregated along the manual and non-manual divide in the secondary labor market and in the periphery.

To summarize, women are far more likely to be paid less than men in any occupation. Male waiters make more. Male nurses make more. Male teachers make more. Women are more likely to hit the "glass ceiling": the barrier that keeps women from progressing to the highest levels of responsibility in their occupation. In the US, White males still predominate in all the highest-paying and highest-prestige jobs, with women and non-Whites predominating in the lower-paid, lower-prestige jobs. Accordingly, the pay gap remains quite large despite women's greater educational parity with men. According to a longitudinal study by Rose and Hartmann (2004), even among men and women who exhibit continuous labor force attachment over the span of a 15-year period, women earned 57 cents for every dollar men earned, a figure still considerably below the often-cited 77 cents, a snapshot of the gender gap in a single year. Even more so, leaving the labor force penalized women's lifetime earning potential. Gender discrepancies in wage trajectories also were a function of women transitioning in and out of the labor-market more than men (Fuller 2008: 177), and the disparity between full-time and part-time wages (Blackburn et al. 2001: 511). Moreover, a pronounced "motherhood wage penalty" underscored the negative impact of children on women's earnings (Budig & England 2001; Fuller 2008: 177–8). The wage gap has been well documented. What has received less attention is the impact of lower initial wages on long-term economic well-being. For the US, lower initial earnings yield lower social security and retirement benefits in old age.

Structural models use large datasets and sophisticated methods in order to capture a panoramic view of persistent barriers and pervasive discrimination in the workplace. These strengths also are, in part, weaknesses. Relying on an inventory of structural factors has forced all phenomena into quantifiable measures. One consequence is that reported gender differences are based on variables that are themselves gendered. The devaluation thesis has gone farthest to uncover the embedded gender biases in the recognition of skill, and to highlight the institutional arrangements and decisions behind lower wages experienced by women: "Despite the centrality of gender . . . [such] accounts explain how gender works rather than why gender is such a major force in the organization of work" (Stone 1994: 416). To understand gendered work and the gendering of work demands a theory and a method attuned to cultural and political processes at the organizational and institutional levels, and one that can explain cross-national variation. Third-wave feminists sought not only to examine structure, as second-wave feminists had done, but also to pursue an analysis that could explain job-allocation processes.

Gendering the organization of work and the gendered work organization

Within the third wave, feminists unpacked the cultural and political processes shaping the expression of male power in the economic sphere. Pioneering the study of gender and organizations, Joan Acker (1990: 140) identified "organizations [as] one arena in which widely disseminated cultural images of gender are invented and reproduced" and where individual gender identities were produced through organizational processes and pressures. By using the verb "gendering," Acker emphasized how gender relations were embedded in the way major institutions were organized. Through an excavation of organizational processes, feminists further analyzed how jobs became gendered – that is, reserved and preserved for either men or women. "To say that an organization is gendered means that advantage and disadvantage, exploitation and control, action and emotion, meaning and identity are patterned through and in terms of a distinction between male and female, masculine and feminine" (Acker 1990: 146). Both "gendering" and "gendered" referred to processes that shaped the distribution of power and the division of labor in and through organizations.

Organizational Processes and Segregation

The feminist lens looked below the surface of jobs to show how skills themselves were socially constructed through gendered idioms and processes. In relationship to skills, feminists asked why some skills and qualifications became socially and culturally valued and typed in terms of gender differences. As a result of their collective power, men defined what counted as qualifications and thereby monopolized productive resources. For example, skilled tradesmen effectively restricted access to apprenticeship through requirements favoring skill sets and experience gained in male-typed jobs. This system disadvantaged women in the skilled trades. Those few women who successfully completed apprenticeship training faced other obstacles on-the-job as male co-workers treated them as less able or even disabled to perform the trade. The link between gender, class, and skill also was evident in female-typed jobs. Feminized jobs welded together femininity and skill "in a construction that relies heavily on class imagery . . . Office 'lady' with its due overtones of gender and class encapsulates this ideal of a white and middle-class femininity" (Pringle 1989: 133).

One of the more influential studies showed how male advantage was sustained in the cultural life of work organizations (Hearn & Parker 1983; Cockburn 1991; Gottfried & Graham 1993; Hearn 1993: 28). In *Brothers*, Cockburn (1983) focused on hegemonic masculinity of the male working class as her subject revolutionizing the study of gender as more than an inquiry about women's lives. Hegemonic masculinity operated not principally by legal coercion or economic compulsion, but by cultural means (Cockburn 1991: 170). Similarly, a study of a Japanese company operating in the US found that job segregation predisposed male and female workers to use gender differences in order to make sense of their positions in class-based hierarchies that valorized hegemonic masculinity as the dominant form of rule in capitalist organizations. In the context of teamwork: "The construction of hegemonic masculinity pushes workers to increase their workload in adopting a 'manly' posture, thereby maintaining capitalist production as a well-oiled machine" (Gottfried & Graham 1993: 625). Working-men controlled machines through the ideology of gender essentialism which naturalized male mechanical prowess.

Segregation and Social Closure

More specifically, organizational processes of social closure and bureaucracy were identified as leading to the relative exclusion of women from positions of authority. In an influential non-feminist view of organizational power, Frank Parkin (1982: 175) revised Weber's conceptualization of social closure as "the process by which social collectivities seek to maximize rewards by restricting access to resources and opportunities to a limited circle of eligibles." He added exclusionary closure as the attempt by one group to secure for itself a privileged position at the expense of some other group through a process of subordination and usurpation (176). The theory of social closure lent itself to feminist conceptualizations of bureaucracy. Interactions between gendered divisions of labor and gendered divisions of authority, when consolidated, produced a formalized structure of gendered bureaucracy (Hearn & Parkin 2001).

Feminists extended social closure to analyze how gendered divisions of labor, both formally structured and informally organized, occurred through processes of inclusion and exclusion, whereby women and men specialized in particular types of work, but not of their own choosing (Hearn & Parkin 2001: 9–10). Walby (1990) further developed the concept by specifying "patriarchal social closure" in order to emphasize the gendered character of exclusionary practices. Spatial distance between male and female workers reinforced social closure, producing forms of horizontal and vertical gendersegregation. It was easier to maintain horizontal and vertical segregation when men cloistered in manual occupations on construction sites and on the shop-floor of many factories only allowed token female representation. Those women in blue-collar occupations often were spatially segregated from men in different jobs and in smaller firms (Bose & Bridges-Whaley 2009: 236). Such spatial segregation diminished the possibility of solidarity across gender divides.

Subsequent scholarship codified this gender paradigm in organizational studies (Cockburn 1991; Hearn & Parkin 2001). A groundswell of new scholarship percolated from Foucault's preoccupation with the micro-politics and technologies of power. The Foucauldian rendering attended to sexual politics (Connell 1987) and discourses of power and sexuality in the workplace (Pringle 1989). With a particular focus on sexuality in organizations, Jeff Hearn (1993) deconstructed organizational cultures in order to "name men as men" (also see Collinson & Hearn 1994). He justified a focus on sexuality in organizations in order to develop a "more accurate conceptualization of patriarchy and public patriarchy" (Hearn 1993). The adjectival use of "patriarchal" combined with other descriptors, such as "patriarchal paternalism" (Calas & Smircich 1989; Collinson & Hearn 1994), summarized the concrete ways in which male power legitimized authority in capitalist organizations. Hearn, in collaboration with Wendy Parkin (2001), further developed an approach relating gender, sexuality and violence intimately involved in social closure. Viewing structural oppressions along with mundane everyday violence, such as disrespect and exclusion, as violations of persons, the authors articulated the case for organizations' central and purposeful role in the existence and propagation of these violations (Keashley & Gottfried 2003: 275). Violence was not an exceptional aspect of authority, but rather one mechanism by which men maintained power in and through organizations. Through their feminist lens, seemingly ordinary expressions of masculinity and everyday violence could be reassessed in terms of gendered power relations in a variety of workplace settings.

Social closure is best illustrated by the glass-ceiling effect, an invisible yet enduring barrier to women's advancement into top levels of the managerial hierarchy, limiting mobility and perpetuating vertical segregation. In 1986 the *Wall Street Journal* first labeled the persistent structural barrier as a glass ceiling (cited in Vallas et al. 2009: 130–1). After a few years, the US Department of Labor established their Glass Ceiling Commission to investigate the phenomenon (130–1). Pioneering women, most notably in Hillary Rodman Clinton's bid for the presidency in 2008, cracked but did not shatter the glass ceiling. This glass ceiling prevents women equally qualified to men from achieving positions at the highest managerial levels, and highly educated women actually lost ground in the ten years from 1996 to 2006, after steadily narrowing the wage gap during the 1980s. The better-educated women actually faced a larger gender pay gap than did the least-educated women (see figure 4.1). More evidence of the glass ceiling can be found in the small number of female CEOs. In 2006, only 10 women ran a Fortune 500 corporation, and only 20 ran one in the top 1,000 (Vallas et al. 2009: 129), that number inching

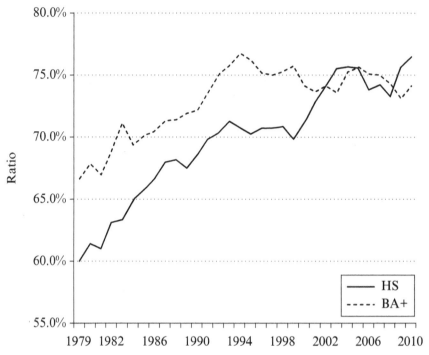

HS = High School; BA+ = Baccalaureate and other higher education.
Source: United States Department of Labor, 2011: table 17, pp. 71–2.

Figure 4.1 Few cracks in the glass ceiling: women's pay as a percent of men's, for high school graduates and college graduates, 25 years and older, 1979–2010 (constant dollars)

upward to 15 CEOs in the Fortune 500 by 2010 (Leonhardt 2010a: B1). In 2010, women held 15.2% of board seats in Fortune 500 companies, a number that barely increases from 2004 to 2009 (Skapinker 2010: 11). Women of color fared much worse with 3.1% of board seats in the Fortune 1000 in 2005. Many women served on several different boards, more likely to fill a token position "reserved" for a woman or person of color. Kanter explained the phenomenon in terms of homophily, the preference for associating with members of one's own group (cited in Vallas et al. 2009: 131–2). The most visible women in politics, Hillary Rodman Clinton and Nancy Pelosi, in fact must tire of hearing about their endless closet-full of pants suits. Such incessant and insistent remarks on their wardrobe implied that they must make an effort to blend into the sea of grey-suited colleagues. It is the unacknowledged embodied differences that make it almost impossible for women to emulate men in male-dominated jobs. Visible markers of gender and race augment this glass-ceiling effect, cementing social closure within work organizations.

Organizational Barriers and Segregation

Several organizational mechanisms promote the glass-ceiling effect and social closure in male-typed occupations. Both formal and informal hiring procedures, unequal access to informal networks for learning about jobs and securing them, gender biases in criteria (height or weight requirements, tone of voice, devotion to the job through face-time and long hours), and implicit stereotypical assumptions that women and men are better suited to perform different types of work (see Charles 2003). Women lack equal access to informal networks due to their outsider status. Such network ties constitute valuable social resources for solidifying relationships and communicative interactions. In turn, communicative interactions provide critical information and expertise as well as social support and friendship, forging close bonds of trust and connections necessary for success in the workplace (Vallas et al. 2009: 132). In addition, power-plays at work involving forms of violence also maintain horizontal and vertical gender segregation. Sexual harassment, bullying, and intimidation discourage women from entering into – and in some cases lead some to exit out of – male-typed jobs, thereby upholding old divides between manual and non-manual work and status hierarchies within non-manual work.

Finally, women are breaking into male-dominated fields, but still face the problem of tokenism, the hiring of one or a few women and minorities, perpetuating group disadvantages. Employers point to the token as evidence of their good intentions and action, implying that the statistical gender gap reflects the lack of qualified applicants rather than discriminatory practices or other barriers. One of the unintended consequences of tokenism is that once a few women are hired, then the urgency for affirmative action no longer applies. The late Harvard legal scholar, Derrick Bell demonstrated the problem of perception, when he threatened to take an unpaid leave of absence until Harvard tenured Black women faculty members – at the time in 1990, of the 60 tenured faculty in the Law School, only 3 were Black, 5 were women, and none were Black women. Some opposed to his campaign implied that such identity politics would lead Harvard to lowering standards, as if no qualified Black female legal scholars could be found. It was his questioning of the implicit norms that struck a chord by revealing the asymmetry in hiring decisions. Few phrased the question why so many White male faculty members populated the Ivy League law schools, and if, indeed, preferential treatment might have produced that outcome.

The gender and organization perspective emphasizes how organizations operate to produce and reproduce gender differences. Through an excavation of organizational practices, the analysis makes visible the active gendering processes and the gendered agents engaged in these processes, and grounds specific forms of male power in relationship to class and other hierarchies in organizations. The discussion of gendered patterns in the US suggests that women suffer long-term consequences due to all forms of segregation. To tease out the factors explaining gender and forms of segregation, it is useful to look at US patterns in comparative perspective. A comparative analysis can show how gendered processes and structures inform varieties of capitalism.

Gender and forms of segregation: a comparative exploration

Both horizontal and vertical segregation are features of different economic systems. Within capitalism, gender segregation exhibits variation across countries. Since segregation is in part a function of educational background and training, it is important to understand the mechanisms influencing "choice" of curricular fields and the factors associated with levels of segregation across fields. Maria Charles (2003) methodically seeks to decipher the puzzle of gender segregation in 10 post-industrial economies, and, with her co-author Bradley (2009), extends the analysis to 44 countries, ranging from the most advanced post-industrial to transitional and developing economies. The importance of this research for understanding gender segregation warrants an in-depth look at their findings. In their large-scale cross-national study, Charles and Bradley (2009: 926) report a high degree of gender segregation in math, science, engineering, and other technical disciplines even in countries with high college enrollments among women.

Gender Segregation across Countries

Probing further, Charles and Bradley find women are under-represented in engineering programs and over-represented in humanities and social sciences across all country types. Engineering programs most consistently exhibit high levels of gender segregation across countries. More mixed results appear in other fields of study: men tend to be over-represented in math and natural sciences; and, conversely, women in health and related curricular fields (2009: 940). Their analysis picks up an intriguingly strong effect of post-industrialism on gender segregation, which they relate to the expansion and feminization of health-care industries and the concomitant proliferation of corresponding degree programs (949). Surprisingly, the study finds more pronounced sex-typing of curricular fields in post-industrial economies than in developing countries. These findings challenge structural functionalist evolutionary theories that expect ascriptive-based inequalities (race and gender) eventually to disappear with the spread of modern achievement values (Charles & Bradley 2009: 924).

To explain this apparent anomaly, the authors argue that cross-national and historical patterns reflect the "enduring cultural force of gender-essentialist ideology (i.e., cultural beliefs in fundamental and innate gender differences), which has proven extremely influential in shaping life experiences, expectations and aspirations, even in the most liberal egalitarian societies. The segregative effect of gender-essentialist beliefs is intensified, moreover, by a strong Western cultural emphasis on individual self-expression and self realization" (Charles & Bradley 2009: 925). But their argument acknowledges that structural features of educational institutions and labor markets may have promoted differences among men's and women's aspirations. Their article "Indulging our gendered selves?" implicates both men and women in self-fulfilling prophesies that predispose them to pursue degrees in sex-typed fields (926, 928). More specifically, the same liberal values of self-expression that give some men and women the "normative space" to transgress gender stereotypes, also leads others to pursue gender-typical choices (929). However, this raises unanswered questions: why do men and women deviate from traditional gender norms, and what factors enable or encourage them to do so?

Like other third-wave feminists, Charles and Bradley move past structural functionalist analysis to account for cross-national differences, and argue against rational-choice theory and neo-institutional varieties of capitalism accounts. These perspectives expect lower levels of segregation where women's economic opportunities are greater. Rational-choice theory posits that women make utility-maximizing calculations in their curricular choices according to occupational opportunities (2009: 933). Perhaps more unexpected, the authors detect a tendency toward greater feminization of humanities and social sciences in countries where women's labor force participation is high overall, and relatively high in the professions more specifically (949). In fact, a higher segregation index in the US than in many transitional economies belies expectations of rational-choice models. Since administrative and financial service jobs are widely distributed across industries (both in traditional manufacturing and burgeoning services), then women's investment in associated credentials could depend on their perceived market opportunities more than on the actual industrial composition of the economy (949–50). Neither rational choice nor the non-gendered varieties of capitalism approach adequately accounts for sex-typing of curricular fields.

Curricular Choices and Segregation Effects

Charles and Bradley offer a plausible account of similarities among countries rather than deciphering all of the interesting comparative puzzles between country types. Solving these puzzles need not get bogged down in detailed national histories that imply ad hoc factors, but rather involve identifying causal mechanisms driving country-specific deviations (Charles & Bradley 2009: 943). Part of the problem derives from the authors' focus on discrediting social evolutionary theories as well as rational choice and neo-institutionalism, and neglect of alternative feminist perspectives better able to explain gendered patterns and processes (Walby 2009a; Gottschall 2010). Curricular "choices" based on gender essentialism no doubt influence occupational segregation and related income disparities. As the authors contend, women may feel more comfortable in caring professions. Along the same lines, women may regard themselves as less status-worthy and competent for leadership positions and without either the requisite, albeit learned, emotional traits for performing in the aggressive legal profession, or the math and science skills for working in engineering. At the high level of data aggregation required to conduct large-scale, multi-country quantitative analysis, the study necessarily loses details about processes and cannot disentangle country-specific patterns and causes. The study cannot easily quantify organizational processes in educational institutions (counseling, classroom practices, few female mentors / role models in male-dominated fields of study), the structure of vocational training and education (Gottschall & Shire 2007) in relationship to the labor market, and the volume and quality of employment among women corresponding to type of welfare state (Gottschall 2010) that contribute to segregation (as suggested by demand-side arguments). The authors readily acknowledge that their observations operate more as baseline similarities than as explanations of significant variability (Charles & Bradley 2009: 928). Nonetheless, their analysis offers insights from which to decipher an enduring puzzle regarding patterns of gender segregation.

Cross-National Patterns of Segregation: Unanswered Questions

A theory emphasizing cultural processes leaves many unanswered questions regarding cross-national patterns of segregation. It is unclear what accounts for the lowest overall levels of segregation by curricular field in Colombia, Bulgaria, and Tunisia, and the highest levels in Finland, Hong Kong, South Africa, and Switzerland (Charles & Bradley 2009: 940–2). These groupings do not fit any of the typologies based on economic development levels, welfare state regimes, or varieties of capitalism. Similar liberal market economies such as Canada exhibit lower overall gender segregation and less male domination in engineering than either the UK or the US. More extreme gendering of health and engineering in the UK is consistent with the high absolute numbers of women in health-related fields, likely due to the large nationalized health service sector. Finally, engineering skews toward men, but health, humanities, and the social sciences reflect a more mixed gender composition, though still female-dominated in the US (940–1). Historical promotion of women in technical fields helps explain lower gender segregation of engineering in the former socialist states (941). Less clear is why women are under-represented in both engineering and math / natural science in social democratic Finland (941–2). It is likely that women's concentration in the public sector contributes to horizontal segregation there. And, what explains weak female representation in engineering and strong absolute female presence in math / natural science in socially conservative Italy (942)?

As the authors note, the extreme segregation of engineering in Switzerland may reflect the historical emergence of this technical field. Citing a case study by Faulkner, Charles and Bradley (2009: 943) positively endorse the explanation that engineering is less hospitable to women when symbolically associated with masculine traits of innate technical prowess and muscularity, and more open to women when associated with formal educational credentials. This historical explanation comports with Charles' in-depth knowledge of the Swiss case. Less horizontal segregation, but more vertical gender segregation in Japan than in the US fits their theoretical claim relating a weak egalitarian ethos with a smaller service sector and a larger and more heterogeneous manufacturing sector in Japan. Overall, patterns of variation do not neatly align with welfare state and varieties of capitalism typologies.

The focus on similarities masks the reasons for differences. It is not clear what fuels post-industrial transition. What we learn, while quite fascinating, is how education, more specifically curricular choices, affect men's and women's positions in fields and specialties with pay differentials. Like supply-and-demand theories, the cultural argument leaves many unanswered questions: why do some countries adopt and adapt egalitarian principles more than others? What accounts for uneven development that keeps some countries economically behind? Since post-industrialism so strongly correlates with horizontal segregation, what accounts for the different size of, and work conditions in, the service and knowledge economy in different countries? What precisely is it about post-industrialism that accentuates gender-segregation? The perspective falters because it lacks a theory of economic transformation and the geographies of power within and between countries in the world economy.

Conclusion

This chapter chronicled the historical antecedents of gender segregation from the Industrial Revolution to the dawn of the twentieth century. Between these two periods, a new mode of capitalist production transformed the family-based economy and small-scale manufacturing. The ensuing upheaval altered patriarchy from its classic rule of the father to patriarchal "dominance of the brotherhood." The formation of segregation should not be viewed merely as the backdrop from which to view the present, since historical patterns, once entrenched, become difficult to uproot. However, it is important to note that history does not predetermine the future. In fact, labor force participation trends do not simply follow a uni-linear direction. Still, the historical narrative situates recent institutional settings in past capitalist developments, which are examined in more detail in the next few chapters on economic transformations.

The puzzle of gender segregation over time and across countries has yet to be deciphered fully. Throughout much of the twentieth century, the contours of segregation remained relatively constant in the overall US economy. More women entered the wage labor force during the 1960s and 1970s than in earlier eras. Both push and pull factors accounted for increasing female labor force participation. Still, women continued to dominate in some occupations and men in others. To make sense of these patterns, theories of segregation emphasized either supply-side human capital endowments or demand-side structural features and employers' discriminatory practices to explain the allocation of men and women across the manual and non-manual divide and within vertical hierarchies. Demand-side arguments identified barriers excluding women from a range of occupations. At the meso-level, organizational processes and practices, such as social closure (through apprenticeships and violence) and the glass-ceiling effect, produced gender-based hierarchies forming horizontal and vertical segregation. Although organizational mechanisms gendering the internal labor market and job ladders in a variety of occupations and industries no doubt affect the variability of gender inequality, the feminist political-economic framework looks to identify the driving forces behind the economic shift toward services more generally.

The comparative exploration adds more explanatory pieces to the puzzle. In comparative perspective, gender segregation appears highest in post-industrial economies. Variation among the most developed capitalist economies vexes those analyses without a framework for explaining transformation toward and organization of services. As suggested in the next two chapters, the reason in part stems from the failure to integrate care and social reproduction into frameworks of work and economic sociology. The following chapter gauges how varieties of service-dominated economies correspond to and shape horizontal and vertical gender segregation.

CHAPTER
5

Serving People: Gender and Services in the New Economy

Tis but thy name that is my enemy;
Thou art thyself, though not a Montague.
What's Montague?
It is nor hand, nor foot,
Nor arm, nor face, nor any other part
Belonging to a man.
O, be some other name!
What's in a name?
That which we call a rose by any other name would smell as sweet.

(*Romeo and Juliet* II, ii, 1–2)

Services encompass a substantial slice of current economic life. A large and growing proportion of workers process information and perform services ranging from "fast food to fast money" (McDowell 1997a: 121). Even more so, the shift toward service production commercializes more and more aspects of daily life. This chapter documents the expansion of and impulse behind the commercialization of services, derived not only from the extension of capitalist relations of production into new social spheres and activities globally, but also from changing structures and meanings of gender relations. By surveying the growth of service work, we can trace how it becomes an increasingly prominent feature of the economy. We must examine the nature of service work, and not just recount the growing percentage of workers employed in that activity, to fully understand the impact of this shift to a service-dominated economy. This chapter suggests that, whether flipping burgers, fixing computers, or serving passengers on an airplane, service work engages workers' bodies and emotions in a kind of performance. For personal services in particular, an employer such as McDonald's requires their workers to project a branded image, present a pleasant demeanor, and follow prewritten scripts aimed at eliciting emotional responses from both the customer and the worker in the pursuit of higher sales. Next, the chapter draws on examples from three different jobs – those of McDonald's workers, flight attendants, and bankers – to show how gender informs the embodied skills and emotional expressions mobilized for use in the service encounter. Services affect both the social worlds of work and the workers themselves by turning everyday interactions into commercial ventures.

To gauge the impact of services not only on the lives and livelihoods of individuals, but also on the economy as a whole, the second half of the chapter presents two sides of service production in the new economy. The nomenclature of "new" economy conjures up a picture of Information and Computer Technology (ICT) in high technology, new media, finance, and knowledge-intensive work. However, as the largest employers in the overall US economy, the chapter focuses on Walmart and McDonald's, offering low-waged jobs to marginalized groups in society. The chapter then examines work in finance and ICT sectors, employing professionals and others in ancillary jobs. Like their predecessors among old industrial firms, these industries standardize work and the product to promote efficiency and extract profits. Service firms such as Walmart and McDonald's rationalize both sides of the service encounter as well as the product in the name of efficiency, while finance and ICT sell customized services in a masculine culture of abstract algorithms, far removed from people's lives. In combination, service-dominated economies reflect new ways of working among a workforce differentiated by employment status.

Taking a cue from Juliet – "That which we call a rose by any other name would smell as sweet" – the analysis in this chapter dispels prevailing images in order to make sense of the gendered meanings behind, as well as the social costs and economic consequences of this burgeoning service production. Gender is significant both in dictating the distribution of jobs – as some women dominate lower-waged personal services and men find work in the higher end of business services – and in shaping the content and context of the job performance. When Juliet utters her fateful words, she foreshadows the tragic power inherent in a family name. Reminiscent of the doomed lovers, disregarding how to label new economic transformations threatens to imperil the scholarly enterprise.

Gender and the growth of service work

In the waning years of the twentieth century, and into the new millennium, service production exceeds, and will continue to outpace, the growth of employment in manufacturing in all advanced capitalist countries. Services account for over two-thirds of total employment

Table 5.1 Percent employment in services (2007)		
REGION	Female	Male
Developed regions	86.4	62.8
Sub-Saharan Africa	25.3	24.8
South Asia	21.5	34.7
Middle East and North Africa	54.7	54.8
East Asia and the Pacific	34.6	35.1
Latin American and the Caribbean	74.7	49.9

Source: ILO 2008 Labor Market database, UNIFEM (2009: figure 4.5, p. 57).

and the majority of women's employment in the US, Europe, and Australia (see table 5.1). In the US, one-third of female and one-quarter of male employment concentrates in sales and service occupations, as of 2007. Further, the ten most prevalent occupations for women cluster in services, including health care (registered nurses; nursing, psychiatric, and home health aides), retail (cashiers, salespersons, first-line managers), office work (secretaries, administrative assistants, receptionists, bookkeepers), and education (see table 4.4). For the US, projected employment growth over the next decade is expected to follow similar trends toward increasing professional and service occupations, with the fastest-growing occupations likely in health-related fields (registered nurses, home health care), computer-related specializations (computer software engineers and applications, computer systems analysis), personal care (housekeepers, childcare, maids), service-related jobs (retail sales, janitors and cleaners), technicians, and office clerks. By 2016, professional and business services, along with health care and social assistance, are likely to expand at more than twice the annual average for all industries, adding 4.2 million and 4.0 million jobs respectively (Bartsch 2009: 3). Clearly, more and more people work in service occupations. Less obvious are the defining characteristics shared by this wide array of seemingly dissimilar occupations and jobs grouped together as services.

At a basic level, service work can be defined by the production process and the product. Service work refers to an activity performed for others and produces an immaterial good. As a labor activity, services can be delivered through either a personal service provided to individual consumers (e.g. health care, personal care) or a business service provided to other enterprises (e.g. data-processing). Vallas et al. (2009: 166) further identify four broad types of services: (1) physical activities (e.g. repairing computers, preparing a meal); (2) intellectual activities (e.g. teaching and training); (3) aesthetic activities (e.g. curating, performing); and (4) recreational activities (e.g. theme park entertaining, hospitality, tourism). A more fundamental aspect of the production process distinguishes services from industrial work. Service work produces an immaterial good – that is, by its very nature, no product as we understand it remains after completion of the work. Though intangible and immaterial, the service leaves behind a trace either as an affect (emotional connection, sensory memory), as a physical presence (art exhibit, tattoo), or as a capability (enhanced knowledge, improved health, social competency). In other words, a service adds value by what it leaves behind. Further, intellectual activities can be transformed into bits and bytes through the encoding of knowledge, and turned into textual form through publications, whereas aesthetic activity can be recorded in another artistic medium through filmmaking or photography. In this way, services alter how the work is performed and the type of labor extracted, in addition to what is produced in the social interface. Its social relational dimension sets apart personal – and to some extent business – services from manufacturing work (Vallas et al. 2009: 166).

Services typically involve a social relationship, an interaction between the service provider and the consumer (client or customer), whether face-to-face or virtually. In other words, services implicate customers in the production process. At McDonald's, for example, when we enact queue etiquette, we habitually play a part in the company's overall efficiency efforts. As customers, by anticipating our order before reaching the register or ushering others to speed-up in line, we help McDonald's maintain an uninterrupted flow of work. Robin Leidner (1993) coins the term "interactive service work" to accentuate this "social relational dimension" of the service encounter. Moreover, as a social activity, a service is "inseparable from the person producing it" (McDowell 1997a: 121; also see Vallas et al. 2009: 166). The social aspect of the interactive service work implicates the self, emotions, and the body (and thereby gender and race) in the construction of job performances and the performer in the service encounter. McDonald's expects its workers to present a happy face at all times regardless of how they feel, even when quelling rowdy customers who get out of control. Similarly, female flight attendants must exude a serene countenance in any situation, calming even the jitteriest flyer, all the while expressing a contained sexiness. Not only is physical labor extracted, but also affective (Clough 2008; Gutierrez-Rodrigues 2010), aesthetic (Witz 1998; Gottfried 2003), nurturance (Lynch 2010), and "emotional, and sexual" labor (Ehrenreich & Hochschild 2003), for profit, in different types of service work. The next section explores in more detail gendering of service work and workers.

Gender in service work

Integrating gender makes visible micro- and meso-level processes whereby jobs become male- and female-typed and differentially valued. Starting at the micro-level, the first section below examines the process of commercialization of feelings and what happens to emotions when they are commodified by capitalist enterprises. Gender segregation and inequality are in part created through organizational processes and practices. For this reason, the next three sections move to an analysis of gendered organizations. Such analyses conceptualize gender as embedded and embodied in work styles and organizations.

Emotional Labor, Gendered Selves

"Now girls, I want you to go out there and really *smile*. Your smile is your biggest *asset*. I want you to go out there and use it. Smile. *Really* smile. Really *lay it on*" (emphasis in the original, Hochschild 2003: 4). A veteran pilot admonishes the flight attendant trainees to use their smile because it is their biggest asset. In this short excerpt reiterating "the value of a personal smile," Hochschild highlights the transformation of feelings and sentiments into a serviceable commodity. With the publication of her pioneering study *The Managed Heart* (1983), feminist sociologists inherited a concept that addresses the absent (repressed) expressive rationality at the heart of commodity relations. Hochschild's concept of emotional labor and emotion work launched a plethora of workplace studies (Leidner 1993; Pierce 1995; Steinberg & Figart 1999). One of the most far-reaching insights recognizes the significance of emotional labor in interactive service work (Leidner 1993). This stream of feminism flows from Goffman's dramaturgical approach, viewing the presentation of self in everyday life as a kind of social performance concerned with the creation and management of impressions. In different ways and in different proportions, analyses of emotional labor situate the everyday rules of face-to-face interaction in larger organizations and structures of meaning to uncover the construction of gender-based hierarchies in service jobs.

Introducing the concept of emotional labor calls attention to the management of impressions in ways consistent with occupations, and to employers' roles in directing not only employees' physical movements but their emotional ones as well (Erikson & Wharton 1997: 189–90). Female-typed occupations, most notably those of secretaries, nurses, and flight attendants, require workers to manage their own emotions (emotion work) and the feelings of others (emotional labor)

(Sotirin & Gottfried 1999). The study of emotional labor interrogates the frozen smile on flight attendants' faces in relationship to male passengers, the jockeying of door-to-door salesmen with their female customers, and the sexualized banter between waitresses and male short-order cooks.

In *The Managed Heart*, Hochschild sets out to explain the "filigreed patterns of feelings and their management" in the form of emotional labor (2003: 11). Her theory of emotional labor eclectically weaves together elements of Goffman and Marx. The analysis draws on Goffman to better understand the small and seemingly trivial "rules of face-to-face interaction" so important to the display of feelings (10). Out of these micro-interactions, she formulates the concept of emotional labor defined as "the management of feelings to create a publicly observable facial and bodily display" in the service encounter (7). Though Goffman's influence is apparent in the way she appropriates Marx, as seen in the language that "when emotional labor is put into the public marketplace, it behaves like a commodity" (14), Hochschild recognizes that Goffman's perspective alone cannot explain why and how companies harness emotional labor to maximize profits. For this she turns to Marx. By analogy to Marx, emotional labor is comparable to physical labor in manufacturing: both are sold for a wage and have an exchange value. Emotion work refers to those same emotional tasks performed "in the private context where they have a use-value" (7). As with the example of the laborer, the company lays claim to the service worker's physical motions, but also manages her emotional actions and extracts emotional labor for profit (7–8). In other words, emotional labor produces exchange value for capital. The service worker, like her counterpart in the factory, decides how much emotional labor to give (work effort) and how much to withhold (8). Unlike her counterpart, she produces a sentiment rather than an object. Nonetheless, the job of flight attendant involves the transmutation of feelings into a serviceable commodity. As a result, the service worker becomes estranged from aspects of her self.

To make her case, Hochschild deconstructs a gesture, the ubiquitous smile on flight attendants' faces. The seemingly simple gesture of a smile represents acting to transform feelings as a sense into a commodity. As one flight attendant observed, this smile appears "on them" rather than "of them" (2003: 8). The job requires her to coordinate her own and others' feelings. This paradigmatic smile is socially engineered and organized by the company. Training regimens and manuals invoke detailed bodily gestures that will evoke the desired feelings and sentiments in the service encounter. Hochschild's strategic choice to study flight attendants is based on several features of the job. First, flight attendants are more vulnerable to social engineering by the company. Second, the job employs both men and women, thereby allowing Hochschild to compare men and women doing the same work in a female-typed job. Third, the emotional labor performed by flight attendants is illustrative of the handling of other people's feelings, and their own, that is a feature of many service jobs (13–14).

The outward frozen smile required of flight attendants serving passengers and empathy expected of nurses on duty are unacknowledged and undervalued emotional labor and embodied skills in feminized service performances. Whether or not employers intervene to reshape workers' moods, demeanor, appearance, and attitudes, Leidner (1993) convincingly argues that interactive service workers and their customers must negotiate an interaction in which elements of manipulation, ritual, and genuine social exchange are subtly mixed. Workers manage customers through "ethnomethodological competence," the capacity to make use of unspoken norms of behavior to control interactions (Stinchcombe 1990, cited in Leidner 1993: 7). This competency draws on emotional resources such as the use or "withholding of personal charm and effort and vengeful retaliation against troublemakers" (Leidner 1993: 41). Leidner (201) also identifies the gendered associations between the many skills used to establish and maintain rapport, including drawing people out, bolstering their egos, displaying interest in their interests, and carefully monitoring one's own behavior so as not to offend – the so-called "womanly arts." More specifically, interactive services engage the provider in a performance utilizing what has been called "soft skills" that "pertain to personality, attitude, behavior rather than formal and technical knowledge" and "in part derive from how people present themselves" (Vallas et al. 2009: 167; also see Leidner 1999), in terms of their demeanor, appearance, and style of speech. These skills imply social learning, interpretive capacities, and interpersonal abilities by which male and female actors enact gender in and at work.

Emotional Labor: Masculinity and Femininity in Service Work

Subsequent research identifies a spectrum of emotions that corresponds to sex-typing and gender-coding of jobs as either feminized or masculinized. Male-typed occupations of police officers (Vallas et al. 2009: 168–9), lawyers (Pierce 1995) and managers (Martin and Wajcman 2003) evoke emotional displays ranging from aggressiveness to dispassion. Doctors, although they must care about their patients, assume a posture of dispassionate distance, which accords with the (male) emotionally distant (father) figure of the rational professional. This act of masking emotions renders such emotional labor invisible even as it marks professional authority in hegemonic masculinized terms. Emotional labor silently attaches not only to many female-typed jobs, but also to many male-typed jobs. In *Gender Trials* (1995) and subsequent research, Pierce casts the work of "Rambo litigators" as a dramatic "performance and presentation of an emotional self tapping into cultural conceptions of masculinity with class inflections" (1999: 356–8). Gender- and class-based appropriate codes of conduct, including tone of voice, cadence, body language, and dress codes are strategic choices, not simply individually selected, but also institutionally constrained. The structure of the profession, including formal and informal professional norms, affects a "style of self-presentation to create a desired impression" (365). Organizations sanction gender-appropriate performances of emotional labor, and determine their value.

The example of managing highlights the changing impact of emotional labor on gendering work in another elite profession. In their study of managerial careers, Martin and Wajcman (2003) investigate the understudied repertoire of positive emotions, such as passion and enthusiasm, which is emerging as more critical to managerial performance as a result of the erosion of mechanisms for securing loyalty from the organization in the context of flexibilizing firms. Women have been at a disadvantage in managerial career tracks as long as gender displays coded as emotionality remained out of place in the rational world of work. As positive emotions gain importance to managerial performance, such symbolic resources either could become the basis of social closure fortifying the glass ceiling or could break down existing barriers to women's mobility in the firm. This analysis theorizes the complicated ways in which gender is constructed and embedded in management systems, norms, practices and technologies. There is more to gender equality than allowing women access to organizational positions once monopolized by men.

The privileging of certain emotions over others contributes to gender-coding of jobs and gender identities. Emotional traits associated with hegemonic masculinity, such as dispassion, aggression, and ruthlessness, are valued in elite professions and authority positions. Interestingly, fathering (though not often used in this active verb form) takes on similar attributes of rational authority. Or, stated differently, authority is rooted in the notion of an abstract, disembodied patriarchal norm. As a result, women appear out of place when performing work contradicting gender-stereotypical expectations.

In a more general sense, the "doctrine of feelings" indexes anger as rational and appropriate for male workers, but as a sign of weakness or an instance of excessive emotionality in supposedly emotionally prone women (Hochschild 2003: 173). The same emotion is treated and interpreted differently when expressed by a woman or a man. On the presidential campaign trail in 2008, the media response to tears shed by Joe Biden and Hillary Rodham Clinton provides insight into the doctrine of feelings. Joe Biden's tear humanized him in media representations, whereas Hillary Rodham Clinton could not escape the chorus spinning her tearful interview to raise doubts about her ability to serve as commander in chief. This double standard rests on gender associations of authority and power at work. The doctrine of feelings dictates different emotional requirements in jobs associated with women's work. Emotional displays associated with feminized stereotypical traits such as nurturance, empathy, and care tend to be devalued. However, men in female-typed jobs experience different expectations and rewards from women doing the same work. Male flight attendants in Hochschild's study could wield emotional skills such as taking charge and disciplining unruly passengers from the repertoire of emotional tasks associated with men's specialization. Similarly, a male nurse can shift from exhibiting nurturance to exercising rational authority without suffering the consequence of seeming abrupt and not being "nice." As Hochschild (171–2) suggests, women's feelings are accorded less respect and given less weight than men's because of gender hierarchies. Unacknowledged emotional labor receives unequal compensation and respect depending on who performs the work, all of which reinforces gender inequalities.

As a broad process then, emotionality and rationality are constructed as if they are opposing principles of organization in public and private spheres, and thus deemed appropriate in different types of work associated with essentialist gender-coding. Hochschild challenges the classic Weberian proposition that the process of organizational rationalization banishes emotions from modern bureaucracies. On the contrary, she finds that employers rationalize sentiments for use in the service encounter. In so doing, some types of interactive services alienate workers from their feelings, which Hochschild (2003) equates with the dispossession of workers from the fruits of their physical labor in the transition from feudalism to capitalism at the heart of Marx's *Capital*. Unlike in manufacturing, where employers' control over the pace of work and standardization of the product is more amenable to technological intervention, it is the person and persona that must be managed in service production. Employers must develop other mechanisms that harness emotions to control the service encounter. Most notably, scripted performances and training minimize workers' discretion in an attempt to standardize and control the interactive service and server (Leidner 1993). Organizations assign different values to emotional labor associated with the type of service work.

All the above studies make visible the cultural valuation associated with emotionality in the job performance. Emotional labor has been differentially rewarded, often depending on the gender expectations of the occupation. The performance of feminized emotional labor and emotion work by women contributes to the reproduction of gender-typing of occupations and the division of labor along gender lines that helps to sustain horizontal and vertical segregation. The focus on emotions hints at embodied forms of labor, but does not distinguish between different types of labor activities. New feminist scholarship has paved the way for an appreciation of gendered embodiment in work styles and organizations.

Embodied Labor, Gendered Bodies

Body matters have a tenuous link to class and gender domination both in Marx and in some feminist theories. While Marx wrote passionately about the brutality of the capitalist machine destroying workers' bodies, he failed to incorporate this compelling portrait into his analysis of alienation. The laborer in question implicitly has a gendered body. For different reasons, and many years later, second-wave feminists "side-lined body matters and fore-grounded gender matters . . . in an effort to retrieve woman from the realm of biology" (Witz 1997: 2). As a result, feminists paid little attention to how gendered bodies and embodied labor were used and misused at work. For example, nursing assistants suffer high rates of back injuries in caring for their patients, and carpel tunnel syndrome afflicts many keyboard users. This neglect by second-wave feminists was especially notable given the centrality of bodywork and work on the body to the performance of feminized labor. Women's work often involves the care of others' bodies as well as the management of their own body. Reproductive work most centrally deals with women's bodies on both sides of the service interaction. A new attention to body matters developed out of post-structuralism and the deconstruction of the concepts of sex and gender.

Third-wave feminist theory, under the influence of post-structuralism, mobilized the body to break up the "unholy alliance" between the concepts of sex and gender. Judith Butler moved feminist analysis beyond a notion of a sexed body as a substance upon which gender could work. More generally, analyses noted that the social construction of bodies was a political process, involving and "reflecting different groups' competing interests and differential access to power" (Weitz 2009), enforced normatively, by law and through means of violence. Some feminists emphasized how "gendered body practices, exaggerate and minimize differences and similarities among people" (Lorber & Martin 2011: 284). The key to their analysis is encapsulated in the following statement: "In short, by judging, rewarding, and punishing people of different body sizes, shapes, weights, and musculature, members of a social group persuade and coerce each other to construct socially acceptable (and similar looking) bodies" (284). Subsequently, research on the body provided a fresh look at the social construction of femininity and masculinity, a new exploration of the relations between sex and gender (see Aiba 2004), and a new focus on embodiment.

Launching a new approach, Joan Acker's (1990) influential body of work on the body at work in bureaucratic organizations draws attention to the process of gendering, embodied labor, and embodiment to explain the fault-lines of labor market segmentation (Witz et al. 1996; Halford et al. 1997; Tyler & Abbott 1998; Gottfried 2003). The process of gendering (see chapter 4) is difficult to discern because organizational logic seems on its surface to be gender-neutral (Acker 1990: 142). In theory, bureaucracy supposedly strips personal characteristics from the job unit. In its place appears a job description abstracted from the worker. This disembodied worker does not exist in reality. Jobs in fact assume a gendered (male) worker whose life centers on work without "outside" responsibilities. There is no place in the gender-neutral organization to recognize "bodied" processes such as human reproduction and the "free" expression of emotions (152). A feminist lens alternatively reveals the implicit masculine standard by which employees were assumed to be free of attachments and care responsibilities. By focusing on bodied processes and practices, Acker exposes how systems of gender, race, and class hierarchies come into play within and through organizations.

Building on this perspective, Halford et al. (1997) propose a paradigm of "gender and organizations" that sees gender as both embedded and embodied. Embodiment referred to modes of being in bodies (Morgan 1998: 655): "gender rests not only on the surface of the body, in performance and doing, but becomes embodied – becomes deeply part of who we are physically [corporeal capabilities], psychologically [and socially]" (495). Taking this approach one step further, Witz links embodiment and gendered work to an analysis of new forms of labor market segmentation around "aesthetic labor," particularly but not exclusively in service industries where employees are increasingly being called upon to develop particular forms of embodied skills in the service encounter. According to Witz (1998), "aesthetic labor described the mobilization of embodied capacities and competencies possessed by organizational participants. This definition foregrounds the sensible components of social interaction." Women must achieve and maintain a particular "state of embodiment" (Tyler & Abbott 1998: 434), expressed through modes of speech, accent, and style that conform to a set of gender attributes that embody socially sanctioned but variable characteristics of masculinity and femininity (McDowell 1997b: 31). For example, temporary help agencies not only dispatch flexible employees to job placements, but they also select, produce, and manage gendered bodies to fit people into organizational cultures. In order to sell labor power as a commodity, temporary agencies select and seek to manage the body. The treatment of body management in terms of aesthetic labor is particularly resonant in characterizing the Japanese work world where stylized uniforms, along with linguistic and gestural forms, mark workers' place in the social order. These practices burden, exclude, and constrain female embodiment from the conception of full-time careers, and represent a good example of aesthetic labor in which cultural idioms shape bodies for temp(t)ing work (Gottfried 2003). In a more general sense, organizations police and demand "constant vigilance regarding gender self-presentation at work" (Wajcman 1998: 10).

Using the conception of embodiment, some feminist political economists explore the ways that organizations shape bodies at work and configure work around gendered bodies. A meso-level analysis complements such micro-level analysis of social interactions. Witz specifically calls for a shift to the meso-level as a means of "confronting the possibility that modes of embodiment are not only mobilized by individuals but also are produced by organizations" (Witz 1998: 9). Bureaucratic organizations validate and permit forms of male embodiment and invalidate or render impermissible forms of female embodiment (5). For women, the discursive construction of the reproductive body assumes particular importance in disqualifying them from authority positions and is continually evoked as the kernel of embodied difference (Halford et al. 1997: 213; Witz 1998: 6). The sexualized body qualifies women for certain front-stage (waitresses and receptionists) and subordinate organizational functions (Witz 1998: 7; also see Adkins & Lury 1999). These dual processes of qualifying and disqualifying particular aspects of female embodiment shape the development of sexualized cultures in which organizational gendering takes place.

Organizational practices are tied to embodied characteristics of gender, class, age and race, to notions of appropriate behavior and style (Halford & Savage 1997: 116), and to the processes of knowledge creation. For example, the corporeal capabilities called upon in manufacturing work are often defined in terms of masculine physical labor (heavy lifting) and valued more in terms of compensation than tasks performed by women processing information in feminized clerical work. In a study of merchant bankers in London, Linda McDowell (1997a, b) reveals that the construction of a dominant version of hegemonic masculinity revolves around a variant of an embodied, manly, heterosexualized, class-based masculinity that disempowers a range of "Others," not only women but men from different class, ethnic and educational backgrounds. Women as a group are constructed as the "Other" in the everyday social practices enacting roles and referencing images derived from normative familial or sexualized hierarchies. The "social construction of the female body as nature, not culture, for pleasure, not work, may continue to mark women as different from, and inferior to, an embodied but still ideally masculinized worker," according to McDowell (1997b: 140). The relationship between a female body and lack of power is part of the reason why women are forced to act as if they are men to achieve success. However, women who attempt to behave like men are often "distressed to find not acceptance but distrust from their male peers" (154). Women, according to McDowell, therefore seem to be in an impossible situation. On the other side of the gender divide, some working-class men cannot find jobs as a consequence of gender-specific work preferences by employers in many of the feminized personal services: "growing numbers of men are disqualified from even low-wage, low-status jobs in the service sector by their inappropriate (stereotypical) gender attributes . . . the characteristics of docility, deference and a neat embodied performance that are valued by employers of labor at the bottom end of the service sector are mostly closely mapped onto the socially constructed attributes of femininity" (McDowell 2008: 21). Workers . . . "are disciplined to produce an embodied performance that conforms to idealized notions of the appropriate 'server'" (McDowell 1997b: 121).

Feminized Services: Emotional Labor and Embodied Skills

Feminist political economy highlights the gendered aspects of service production. Services not only produce immaterial goods, but also shape gender at work in organizations. Gender attributes are not merely imported into the workplace, but rather are recreated, sanctioned, and mobilized in the processes and practices of capitalist organizations. More specifically, service employers utilize gendered characteristics in the selection and evaluation of work and workers, and call upon emotional labor and embodied skills in the service encounter. Embodied skills and embodiment are built into job requirements, but with different values depending on who does the work (Peterson 2008: 214). On the one hand, feminized forms of embodiment often involve unrecognized and thus undervalued emotional and aesthetic labor. On the other, hegemonic masculinity privileges the expression of power in dispassionate and other "care-free" emotional displays that appear as natural and rational. In other words, the rational professional is seemingly unemotional and disem-bodied. As the examples indicate, meso-organizational processes and micro-social practices shape gender inequality at work. To ascertain the significance of service production, we must situate these organi-zational practices in the economy as a whole. The next section names the distinctive features of service production in increasingly service-dominated economies.

What's in a name? Services and the "new" economy

Service production spans a range of labor activities, involving mass production and consumption on the one hand, and customiza-tion and the intensive use of knowledge in the production process, on the other hand. Macro-structural approaches tend to focus on only one segment or one subsector of the service economy. For example, McDonaldization (Ritzer 1996) and the Walmart phenom-enon (Macionis 2010) are theories about the extension of Taylorism to new areas of service production, distribution, and consumption. Taylorism – or, more precisely, neo-Taylorism applies the principles of time-management to the subdivision of conception from execution in the labor process in service production. Through rationalization of service provision and the service provider employers cheapen labor costs by making labor more interchangeable. Conversely, theories of financialization and the spread of ICTs emphasize the growing significance of abstract instrumentalities (e.g. knowledge and infor-mation) over concrete production (Castells 2000). Finance capital, the epicenter of the most recent crisis, is emblematic of a fundamental shift from the manufacturing of tangible products to the production of immaterial goods. Finance capital and new media circulate infor-mation electronically through highly complex algorithms removed from the communities that they affect. Cross-cutting these latter approaches, organizational innovations such as the emergence of call centers and networked processes feature new spatially dispersed practices and staffing arrangements enabled by ICTs on a global scale. Each of these types of services incorporates gender in differ-ent front-line and back-room activities and has different effects on patterns of inequality. A more detailed discussion of the impact of McDonaldization and the Walmart phenomenon on structures of class and gender relations follows.

Two Sides of the Same Coin: McDonaldization and the Walmart Phenomenon

McDonaldization and the Walmart phenomenon are discussed as two sides of the same coin, transforming production, distribution, and consumption through standardization of services and service providers. On one side, McDonald's attempts to standardize and homogenize the services provided as well as service providers; and on the other side, Walmart logistically ties together far-flung low-wage manufacturers by trucking low-priced goods for sale in their mega-stores. Low-priced goods supplied by low-cost producers combine with low wages of Walmart employees. These ubiquitous retail outlets have surpassed GM as the largest employers in the US. Today, Walmart employs over 2 million people in stores worldwide, almost triple the number at GM's peak of over half a million employees. In contrast to the 1960s, when the largest employers assembled cars, fabricated steel, manufactured appliances, and installed telephones, services define the core mission of 2010's leading employers, dispatching temporary workers (Kelly), producing computers (IBM), delivering packages (UPS), and dispensing fast food (McDonald's; Yum, which owns Taco Bell, KFC, and Pizza Hut) (Duhigg & Bradsher 2012). McDonaldization and the Walmart phenomenon epitomize one side of the shift from industrial to service production.

The McDonaldization of society dictates that jobs are created for efficiency, predictability, uniformity, and automation (Ritzer 1996). These characteristics standardize the product and the process of production, which limits the creativity of humans who work in the job. The process of McDonaldization goes one step further. The service provider, along with the product, must be standardized in order to control costs of production and to ensure uniformity of the product. McDonald's serves a unitary product in thousands of small outlets sandwiched among brand-named franchises along Miracle Miles off exit ramps, seemingly on every corner in large and small communities. Starbucks follows a similar business model at the upper tier of consumption. Any Starbucks sells the same menu of expensive Italianate coffee drinks. The formulas, the Italian-inspired terminology, and the décor look much the same from place to place. As a coffee junkie, I have found my caffeine fix tucked away in the Forbidden City compound in Beijing or in otherwise nondescript office buildings in business districts around Tokyo. Minor cultural adjustments gesture to the local setting – for example, silver thermoses dispense sugary syrup alongside milk canisters in Tokyo Starbucks. Otherwise, I can order, in English, Arabica beans or Americano at a Starbucks below street-level in the warrens of Tokyo train stations – a post-modern

Metropolis. These large companies, through the dispersion of uniform outlets, sell convenience and a way of life – one needs only to drive-through to get a Big Mac or a venti cappuccino seemingly everywhere in the world.

The Walmart phenomenon frames a production strategy in which a low-wage workforce produces goods, often in off-shore factories, and sells low-cost items at stores located in rural areas or on the edge of cities. When a Walmart opens in a small rural area, local businesses can't compete and so they close their doors. While small businesses suffer due to "big-box" stores like Walmart, the general population gets better deals and more competitive pricing. However, one way these kinds of stores can keep prices down is to keep wages low and provide no or minimal benefits. In some cases, Walmart employees cannot even afford to shop at Walmart. In *Nickel and Dimed*, Barbara Ehrenreich (2008) documents the problems faced by low-wage women working in big-box stores. Women may not earn enough to stay afloat above the poverty level.

A class action suit addresses the issue of alleged sex discrimination at Walmart.[1] One of the named plaintiffs, Christine Kwapnoski, is a 46-year-old single mother of two children, earning $60,000 after 25-year tenure at Walmart. She asserts that Walmart promoted men faster and paid them more than women. Her claim goes to the heart of gender discrimination when she states that "She never heard a supervisor tell a man, as she says one told her, to 'doll up' or 'blow the cobwebs off' her make-up" (Sherman 2011). Statistics back up her claim. However, the numbers available only date back to 2001, the year when the suit was filed. According to documents accompanying the filing of the suit, women earned an average salary of $13,000, about $1,100 less than the average for a man. At that time, "women held 14 percent of store manager positions compared with more than 80 percent of lower-ranking supervisory jobs that are paid by the hour." Once the suit was filed, Walmart changed some policies, for example by posting all job vacancies electronically. Kwapnoski acknowledges that Walmart elevated more women into management positions in response to the threat of the class action suit, but she also contends that promotions among women slowed down thereafter and now, once again, favor men over women (Sherman 2011).

In both McDonald's and Walmart, the proliferation of low-wage jobs creates a class of workers whose part-time work schedules fluctuate and whose full-time income often isn't sufficient to support a family. Those workers eligible for health benefits receive insurance packages offering limited coverage. At McDonald's, their mini-med plan requires workers to pay an annual out-of-pocket fee of $730 for benefits of up to $2,000. For over double that premium, workers can pay about $1,660 to receive up to $10,000 of coverage. Almost 30,000 workers subscribe to these mini-med plans offered by McDonald's – less than 10%, in a company with 385,000 employees in 2009 (my calculation, based on Hoovers 2010). While company executives extol the benefit of their health-care plan, the monetary caps deny workers access to many medical procedures and treatments costing more than $2,000 (such as MRIs, many cancer therapies). McDonald's workers who earn less than $20,000 (below the poverty level for a family of three) cannot afford to pay even the lower premiums (Leonhardt 2010b).[2]

No less profound than Fordism symbolically encapsulating new business practices of the industrial era, McDonald's and Walmart are two faces of the new economy. These companies do not overtly sexualize their demands on workers' self-presentation. For the most part, workers don uniforms not particularly designed to accentuate their sexuality. Filling of jobs still can be considered a bodied practice. The people selected to dispense coffee or scan items or stock shelves or greet customers look the same, from one store to another, whether in Paris, France or in Paris, Texas. Part of the standardization process is the erasure of gender and class markers and traces of place, while hiring practices and job expectations draw on gender and class idioms for creating a low-wage work force.

More specifically, hiring preferences reproduce gender and class inequality by diminishing the ability of their workforce to earn a living wage. McDonald's and Walmart drive down wages in their retail outlets and among suppliers in a race to the bottom. The cost of production is sensitive to the price of labor. From the perspective of the company, the search for a low-wage workforce is just good business practice. The rules of the game appear as abstract and disembodied. In reality, the ability to pay low wages assumes that the worker does not live on their own wages. These eponymous retail giants hire women, youth, and retirees for full- and part-time employment so they can provide minimal benefits. This staffing decision is underwritten by the organization of social reproduction, both privately and publicly provided. It assumes that these groups are dependents of others, drawing upon other sources of support through husbands, parents, Medicaid, social security, and Medicare to secure their livelihoods. Paying low wages in turn reinforces economic dependence of the worker who must rely on support from a husband's wages or on the public sector to make ends meet.

Price to Pay? Financialization and Knowledge

Likewise, finance capital (financialization) and/or the increasing use of information and computer technologies (ICT) have changed the production process (Castells 2000). The almost magical quality of financial operations beyond the comprehension of most people mystifies financialization as an abstract and disembodied process. A closer examination finds that financialization contributes to the transnational growth of service production in a new economic geography of global cities – much as Fordist mass production and consumption once transformed the built environment of regional economies during the 1940s and 1950s. Large-scale factories once clustered in what have become rust-belt cities scarred by deindustralization. In much the same way, finance and other business services are attracted to specific places, whether by historical accident or by existing institutional infrastructures. Social geographers tell the story of Silicon Valley as the incubator for new media design in California (Benner 2002), and its predecessor along Route 9 linking medical technology and microchips credited with the Boston recovery, or the accumulation of financial services on Wall Street and in other global cities (Sassen 2001). Highly educated, well-paid professionals in finance and other business services perform knowledge work in global outposts. As will be discussed in more detail in chapter 11 on global cities, finance capital attracts and spawns an array of low-wage personal services as well as business services (intellectual and aesthetic activities) to these areas, to sustain the life and lifestyles of the global elite.

A postmortem of the financial crisis in 2008 lays bare the anatomy of the new economy. This financial crisis swept across the economies of industrialized nations of Europe and Asia like a man-made tsunami, leaving economic destruction in its wake. Though not central in most news stories, the less visible gender-based causes and consequences of the crisis are only now being written about by feminist scholars (Young 2008; Walby 2009b). The priorities and practices of Wall Street are oriented toward financial capital and global profit maximization at the expense of the "real" economy of Main Street. Theories about the gendering of "financial architectures" (Elson 2002, 2010) and governance bodies reveal that gender has both causal effects and consequences. For example, few women have become partners at investment banks. Goldman Sachs, one of the central actors in the financial crisis, ended 2010 with only 13% of women among its partners, slightly more than double their numbers in 2000, but still low relative to their increasing presence in large financial firms on Wall Street (Craig & Dash 2010: A3). More specifically, men in decision-making capacities, whether deemed as rogue traders or financial alchemists, traffic in securities and other instruments, taking risks seemingly without concern for the havoc that might ensue for homeowners and communities. In fact, risk assessment usually does not assign a value to social costs of financial transactions. Social considerations are outside the parameters of abstract profit calculations. These calculations are gendered to the extent that they disregard responsibility for the care of others.

Preliminary evidence also indicates gender-differential consequences of the financial crisis. Unemployment and precarious employment have risen and wages have declined as a result of the crisis. Women experience higher rates of unemployment on average, but gender differences in unemployment rates are lowest in the developed countries and highest in Latin America, the Caribbean, the Middle East, and North Africa (Walby 2009b: 9). The extent of informalization among women workers in the Global South renders employment more vulnerable to catastrophic economic shocks, and thus results in their higher relative and absolute rates of unemployment.

Despite the impression that Information and Computer Technologies (ICT) dominate the industrial landscape, ICT industries account for a small percentage (less than 5%) of total male and female employment in new economy sectors in the United States and the other major economies of Germany, Japan, and the UK (see figure 5.1a). Within the ICT sector, men and women work in different occupations as well as exhibit different levels of employment (Shire 2007). In the emblematic film *The Social Network*, although heightened for dramatic effect, tireless young male programmers sit in front of their computer terminals at all hours to give birth to the social networking site Facebook. Employment statistics bear out the image of men operating computers or writing code. In the US, three-quarters of computer programmers are men whose entrance into the occupation dramatically increased over the decade of the 1990s. Overall, gender disparities worsened in the first decade of the twenty-first century: women's representation in computer science and math declined from 30% in 2000 to 27% in 2009 (Holmes 2011). Female computer programmers lost ground during the 1990s, saw an uptick in employment in 2008, yet earned less on average than men in the same occupation. For example, male computer and information system managers' median annual earnings of $95,400 compares with women's $82,540, in 2008 (Leon-Guerrero 2011: 106). Female computer software engineers ($77,070) and computer programmers ($68,920) rank among the more highly paid occupations for women, but they receive $20,000 to $30,000 less than their male counterparts (106). ICT jobs available to women typically reside at the lower end of occupational hierarchies, and are marked by routinization and low wages. Most prominently, data-entry keyboard operators are overwhelmingly female (81%), and

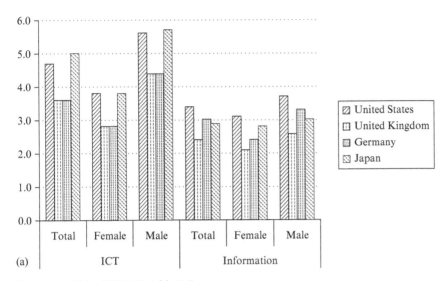

Data source: Shire (2007: 66, table 2.4).

Figure 5.1a Percent of total, male, and female employment in ICT and information, for the United States, United Kingdom, Germany, and Japan (2002)

the occupation grew at a faster rate than more highly paid computing jobs.

Taken together, in the US, knowledge-intensive industries account for 40% of total employment and over half of women's overall employment. The vast majority of women within knowledge-intensive services are employed in female-typed health fields and social work. Interestingly, the education sector only makes up 5.3% of women's total knowledge-intensive employment in the US (Shire 2007). Seen in comparative perspective, the low percentage of women in the education sector seems unexpected. However, against the backdrop of the larger market-oriented service economy, women's employment spreads out in other business and personal services in the US.[3] Women have made inroads into knowledge-intensive industries (see figure 5.1b). The technical fields of engineering and computer sciences remain male-dominated while health, education and social work continue to be female-dominated – a finding consistent with Charles' comparative study of segregation discussed in chapter 4.

From McDonald's to Goldman Sachs: What's in a Name?

The review of theories and empirical evidence suggests that the new economy elevates the human/machine interface (digital divide), the importance of access to knowledge, and the influence of networked relationships between firms, flows, and finances. Capitalism

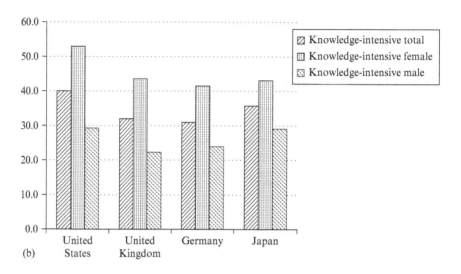

Data source: Shire (2007: 66, table 2.4).

Figure 5.1b Percent of total, male, and female employment in knowledge-intensive industries, for the United States, United Kingdom, Germany, and Japan (2002)

intensifies networked interactions of the productive forces, radiating out from the Global North to the Global South in a new international division of labor. Along the network, knowledge creation and distribution spreads unevenly across populations and regions. But scholars emphasize different driving forces behind post-industrial developments still in flux. Some focus on the ascendance of business services in financial circuits of capital, and others on the prominence of personal and social services reorganizing work and the economy. In either case, what to call the new economy eludes precise specification in part because of this dual nature of post-industrial service production.

At one end of the economy, McDonaldization and the Walmart phenomenon rationalize the labor process and standardize the service provided and the product served. Flipping burgers or restocking shelves exemplify neo-Taylorist deskilling of labor. Neo-Taylorism not only means boring jobs, but also means companies can offer low wages and minimal fringe benefits. At the other end, finance and knowledge-intensive work deskill some activities and reskill others so that the labor force and compensation varies depending on the status of the position. Gender inequality results from structural disadvantages based on the jobs available to women, who end up stalled in secondary labor market jobs and under-represented in higher-paying professions. In aggregate, a typical woman earned about $14,792 a year, compared to a typical man, who earned $21,104 in 2010 (Tavernise 2011: A10).

This chapter uses "new" in a more generic way to describe current economic trends toward increasing knowledge-intensive work and service production, and how these jobs and occupations are gendered. The ICT sector and finance, thought to be the leading-edge of the new economy, employ a small percentage of the workforce in post-industrial countries. Knowledge-intensive services by far span more occupations and industries. Health and social work and education are the largest industrial subsectors with a high concentration of women's employment. Within knowledge-intensive services, gender determines who has access to specific jobs – men monopolize authority positions and technical specialties, and women end up in lower-paying female-dominated subsectors and tend to earn less than men in higher-paying professions. More subtly, women process information, but are less likely to participate in the transformation from tacit to embrained knowledge. Less visible, but no less critical, is the work of those serving and caring for professionals. The new economy is also associated with a proliferation of sales and other services that are routinized and pay low wages. An expanding service-dominated economy boosts women's labor force participation, but also splits their distribution in two, at both low and high ends of occupational hierarchies. No one questions the numerical growth of service production or the fact that women dominate on the lower occupational rungs. What accounts for the concentration of women in these jobs cannot be discerned from the functional needs of capital based on their ability to pay women low wages. Linkages between gender and class inform the trajectory of capitalist development and associated inequalities.

Conclusion: in the service of service

Revisiting "What's in a name?" brings us back to the question posed at the beginning of this chapter. Names for the new economy derive from a narrow focus on one subsector of services, either at the low end, such as McDonald's and Walmart, or at the high end, such as financialization and ICT. None of these conceptions fully captures the novel aspects of the service economy. The failure to identify what's in a name in part stems from the tendency to reduce gender to an outcome of otherwise abstract economic and political processes rooted in capitalism. It does not escape these theories' notice that women are the preferred workers in low-wage personal services, and men in high-wage business services. Without a feminist lens, the theories at best consider one aspect of the new economy. Hiring women is only half of the story. Gender and feminized work are central to understanding the transition to a service-dominated economy.

The "new" service-dominated economy reflects the shift from traditional "in-services," often confined in the home, to the widespread production of immaterial goods. From the nineteenth century, the master and servant exemplified the British case of "in-service" that demarcated the spaces and places of class, and symbolically represented class hierarchy in the architectural quarters of upstairs and downstairs. At that time, only the elite class could afford to buy the labor power of others for their personal services. While services are a necessary part of any economy, the next change involved the expansion, and substitution, of many tasks once performed without pay in the home. Fast-food and convenience stores created new commercial spaces for production, augmenting household labor and the busy work schedules of dual-earner families. Consuming these services no longer solely marked an upper-class position. One of the consequences was the double-duty or second shift, an experience among women, albeit differentiated by race and class. Working-class women, many of whom found employment in low-wage personal services, couldn't afford to displace their own labor by a myriad of paid services. On the other side of the class divide, women in the upper class could off-load their domestic labor through purchasing a variety of old and new services, most exotically through the use of in-house personal concierges.

What makes the new economy post-Fordist is commodified service insinuating itself into the fabric of everyday life. Some services apply the Fordist logic of rationalized production. In the new service economy, old forms of "in-service" continue, but are transformed into a class relation. Unlike in previous eras, service work in the new economy crosses and creates a new class structure: investment bankers and lawyers in elite jobs, with childcare workers and taxi drivers in lower-paid occupations serving these elites. More fundamentally, the new economy signifies production of services in the service of other services and service providers. Services produce something ephemeral, leaving a trace, an immaterial good. By involving workers' bodies and extracting emotional labor, interactive service work extends commodification into the most intimate aspects of who we are, what we do, and how we feel and relate to one another. This extension of commodification to feelings and bodily practices and displays takes the process of alienation farther than imagined by Marx. It is the commodification of everyday experiences, affective relations, and sentiments that set apart service from previous modes of production. The commodity form intrudes on everyday interactions and intimacy, and increasingly inhabits and colonizes the life-world. Service-dominated economies exhibit new fault lines of inequality, not only based on gender, but also on race, caste, immigration status.

The new post-industrial service-dominated economies, as Esping-Andersen hypothesizes, will probably produce an increasingly polarized class structure (cited in McDowell et al. 2005: 443). More diversified employment relationships, from formal to informal, full-time and part-time, characterize the range of service occupations. Part-time work is concentrated in female-typed and racialized jobs, including sales, cleaning, and canteens, whereas other feminized jobs, such as clerical and secretarial work, are more likely to remain full-time (2005). Those working in low-wage services may be unable to afford their subsistence: too poor to pay for health care and nutritious food and not poor enough to qualify for means-tested benefits – limited in the US – and for decreasing entitlements in other welfare states. Equal opportunities, parental leave, and expanding civil rights sit uneasily with these economic changes – a topic taken up in a later chapter. Overall, the reproductive bargain in service-dominated economies devolves responsibility for support of a family-wage and the standard employment relationship to individual workers. A more stratified class structure results from such differentiated employment conditions, outcomes, and expectations.

Only when we examine care and reproductive labor can we begin to get a holistic picture of the new service economy. Reproductive labor, whether fully or partially remunerated, both underwrites and fuels further the expansion of the service economy. Because this labor is less visible in theories and in practice, reproductive labor has not been given adequate analytical attention. The organization of and institutional support for reproductive labor varies across time and space, which helps to explain the varieties of capitalism. Though implicated in them, social reproduction stands outside of capitalist enterprises' calculations. In the new economy, less responsibility for care and social reproduction among corporations fuels the growth of more services provided either by the market or by the state, or defaulting to the responsibility of family members, usually women. To fully understand the changing content and context of service production and the economic consequences, we need to examine the social organization and delivery of care and reproductive labor from a feminist political economic perspective. As the next chapter will show, paid care and reproductive labor are at the cutting-edge of service production: increasingly important for the economy as a whole, and consequential for gender relations more specifically.

CHAPTER
6

Caring for People: Gender and Social Reproduction in Service Economies

A woman tucking a child in bed or sweeping a kitchen floor is such a normal state of affairs that the activities seem to require no explanation. When viewed through a feminist lens, this common-place scene begs the questions how and why care and reproductive labor stubbornly persist as a female-centered and devalued activity? The social and monetary value of care has been attributed to its close association with devalued women's work (Perrons 2007), and the unrecognized and thus unremunerated tacit knowledge and emotional labor in this type of service (Nishikawa & Tanaka 2007). Devaluation of care work may stem from the cultural construction of motherhood (England et al. 2002: 457), which is based on an ideology of domesticity "underpinned by a set of gendered moral obligations," as well as an economic rationale that deems the activity outside the realm of the money economy (McDowell et al. 2005: 448). If mother-hood is viewed as a putative labor of love, then compensation for care would seem to "make the sacred profane" (England et al. 2002: 457). Commonsense understandings expect care to be given freely, rewarded in terms of its intrinsic use-value rather than compensated either in the "profane" medium of money or with an abstract right of citizenship. Seemingly then, the logic of care (like emotionality) appears to function according to organizational and ethical princi-ples in opposition to the market and exchange-value, and thus seems to operate outside the circuits of capital. Such assumptions are preva-lent in conventional economic theories.

This chapter revisits third-wave feminist political economic theories to interrogate these troubling definitions of care and reproductive labor. In their place, the chapter refines the definition of reproductive labor and care work, shows that these activities produce and extract a specifically gendered type of labor, and indicates that the organiza-tion of care and social reproduction informs the social construction of gender identities for both men and women. To understand economic transformation and the growth of the service economy, this chapter more specifically assesses the value of housework in capitalist society, and the significance of moving care and social reproduction out of the home and into the market economy, and how their gendered context carries over from previous devalued, unpaid housework. An in-depth examination of childcare and cleaning highlights two paradigmatic examples of low-wage feminized and racialized services. Today, the household increasingly is the scene of paid childcare and cleaning. Looking at domestic services in Kolkata provides a close-up view of the intermingling of love and exploitation, care and money, and the sacred and the profane.

Analysis of the social organization of care and reproductive labor in this chapter adds a key piece with which to decipher the enduring puzzle of gender segregation of the labor market and transformations of work and the economy on both a local scale and a global scale. Women in and from the Global South leave their own homes, traveling short or long distances in pursuit of jobs often involving the performance of reproductive labor for other women. Kolkata is the site for a case study of domestic servitude in a country "grappling with modernity." Undergoing rapid transition, combining elements of its feudal past, rudimentary industrial production, and high-tech services, India gives us a chance to witness economic shifts currently in progress. Caught in this conjunction of economic systems, domestic servitude exhibits both old and new relations of paid domestic work.

Troubling definitions of care and reproductive labor

Traditional economic theories represent care in terms of human capital models, which has an impact on women's income in two different ways. In the first instance, paid careworkers' low compensation reflects the "true" market value of care work. In another sense, time out of the labor force to care for children depreciates the value of education and other productive assets. The more time out of the labor force, the less valuable are other skills when women re-enter the labor market. Both viewpoints assume that women specialize in care labor, paid and unpaid, either because of their preferences (often not explained) or because of rational economic calculations in the family. Power inequity is absent from these accounts.

On a broader canvas, traditional political economic models typically value care labor in the market by deriving it from the logic of capitalism. Women shoulder the burden of paid care because employers can pay them low wages, on average. If an economic rationality alone determines hiring practices, then we would expect women to replace men in all instances, such as in automobile assembly or steel mills. One historical precedent illustrates the way that gender and race determine who performs care labor. In California until 1880 and in Hawaii until 1920, Asian men, initially Chinese and later Japanese, filled the majority of domestic service jobs due to the scarcity of female immigrants from Asia – in large part due to legal restrictions. Once Japanese women's immigration reached sufficiently high levels, then they "inherited the mantel of service" (Glenn 1992: 9), so much so that, just prior to World War II, nearly half of all Japanese women in the San Francisco Bay area and in Honolulu, including both native-born and immigrants, were employed either as servants or as laundresses (9). In other regions of the US, White female immigrants served as housekeepers and sometimes as supervisors of domestic staff, while racial ethnic women performed dirty tasks such as scrubbing floors and doing laundry (10). Consistent with other economic theories, traditional political economy overlooks the mechanisms by which care work is devalued and allocated to women.

Feminist political economists argue that care and reproductive labor produce something novel, and generate affective relations, forms of life, and well-being (Hardt 2008), different from material objects forged in the crucible of the Fordist era. Care and reproductive labor are performed with or without pay via market or non-market relationships, using routinized or non-routinized methods (Lynch 2010: 11–12), through intimate face-to-face interaction in which the provider enhances the recipient's human capabilities (e.g. "physical, emotional and cognitive skills; and proclivities of empathy and self-discipline": England et al. 2002: 455).[1] The activity can take place in a variety of institutional settings, both public and private. Not only do feminist political economists redefine care and reproductive labor as enhancing capabilities of others and as deploying the skills of emotional competence and bodily capacities, but also they explain the devaluation of these activities in the context of the larger economy. More specifically, devaluation of care is rooted in the social construction of housework as women's duty rather than as a form of productive labor. Because providing care is so closely associated with familial relationships, housework retains the cast of patrimonial and pre-capitalist relations from the context of the family.

Unpaid reproductive labor within the household: meaning and value of housework

The social construction of housework as a distinctive form of labor emerges as a consequence of industrialization (as discussed in chapter

4). It presupposes the institutional separation of paid work and unpaid domestic work. Today, hauling water, cultivation of food for subsistence, processing of raw materials, and piece-work in manufacturing (e.g. of garments, matches) all comprise housework in developing countries. But more commonly in developed economies, housework entails the unpaid labor of preparing meals, cleaning, and childcare in and around the household. Despite the variation in the tasks performed, the same unchanging label of "housework" marks a spatial sphere of quintessentially gendered labor, referring to "a set of culturally and historically specific tasks [physical and emotional] that convey social meanings about masculinity and femininity," evoking power relationships (Marx-Ferree 1992: 247). Both motherhood and fatherhood involve a labor of love underpinned by a set of gendered moral obligations that are not reducible to purely economic trade-offs. While the overall amount of time spent on housework may or may not change, the intensity on each task may shift over time and place. This is why the intensity of motherhood does not necessarily decline as a result of the introduction of labor-saving devices like washing machines and dish-washers. How one performs motherly duties is shaped by cultural meanings of femininity in relationship to masculinity, as well as by the political-economic context. For this reason, feminist political economists investigate the intra-household allocation of care and reproductive labor not only in terms of the amount of time spent on housework, determined by an economic calculation of opportunity costs, but also as a set of gendered obligations associated with the cultural and social expectations of motherhood and fatherhood.

An examination of intra-household time allocated to care and reproductive labor reveals that the amount of time devoted to housework by men and women varies with levels of economic development and with different institutionalized systems of care. The United Nations Development Program Human Development Report estimates gender-based time allocation on housework across the Global North and South (Floro & Meurs 2009: 27). Generally, women spend less time on cooking and cleaning and childcare in developed countries than women in the developing world. In Mexico, for example, many women are too poor to ease their workload by paying for services. More generally, higher fertility rates among women in developing countries translate into more time spent on childcare. Nowhere are these activities taken over by men or shared equally between male and female partners.

Men's relative time spent on unpaid housework remains minimal – men's time spent on childcare ranges from 4 minutes per day in South Africa to 24 minutes in the US (see table 6.1). Such estimates may not accurately reflect the "true" amount of time spent: men may exaggerate their input while women may not account for all of their care and reproductive labor. Studies based on diaries of time spent find a gender bias in self-reporting on housework. Diaries register perceptions of time elapsed that may seem longer or shorter, depending on the person's sense of their duty to perform the work tasks. Due to its routine nature and relative invisibility, women may take for granted the time it takes to plan and coordinate activities as well as their everyday emotional work, and thereby underestimate their overall contribution. Conversely, men overestimate their efforts, more conscious of the choice to participate in a discrete set of tasks. Though the reported time spent may not exactly measure actual effort, studies indicate gender differences in the type of housework performed by men and women. Commonly, men avoid day-to-day labor such as cooking and cleaning. By contrast, men's relative share of time dedicated to childcare exceeds their relative share of time spent on other daily activities. Some countries exhibit lower gender disparities in the allocation of housework. For example, in social democratic Norway, men help out with childcare more than their male counterparts in other countries. Still, Norwegian men contribute only half as much time to this task as their female partners. Unpaid housework continues to be female-centered, regardless of women's employment status.

The time women spend growing food for subsistence, gathering fuel and water, doing childcare, caring for the sick and elderly, and carrying out domestic chores (not included in GNP) co-determines time spent in paid, market work (Floro & Meurs 2009: 25). Women's participation in the wage labor force and access to decent work often hinges on their double burden of, and responsibility for, combining unpaid reproductive labor and paid employment (2005). Inversely, demands for increasing housework put limits on the time for labor outside the home. More specifically, the presence of children and the systems of childcare are important factors associated with the intensity of women's labor force participation. A comparative perspective teases out the ability of women to manage the second shift and juggle responsibility for unpaid housework and employment. Women work a second shift when they return from their first shift of paid work to unpaid tasks waiting for them at home. Hochschild coined the idea of the second shift in order to capture the double burdens and the never-ending demands on women's time and sense of responsibility. The division of housework and its meanings are constructed in the larger context of a reproductive bargain, which in turn is based on economic development and welfare systems.

Table 6.1 Time spent on household tasks, by gender and country (various years)						
	Cooking and cleaning Time spent (hrs.: mins.)			Childcare Time spent (hrs.: mins.)		
Country	Women	Men	Ratio M/F	Women	Men	Ratio M/F
Norway (2000–1)	2:14	0:52	0.24	0:34	0:17	0.50
France (1989–99)	3:04	0:48	0.16	0:28	0:09	0.32
Germany (2001–2)	2:32	0:52	0.22	0:26	0:10	0.38
Korea (2004)	2:36	0:20	0.09	0:55	0:15	0.27
US (2005)	1:54	0:36	0.23	0:48	0:24	0.50
Mexico (2002)	4:43	0:39	0.06	1:01	0:21	0:21
South Africa (2000)	3:06	1:00	0.33	0:39	0:04	0.10

Source: United Nations Development Programme (2007: table 32).

Children, Childcare, and Maternal Employment

The transition to motherhood is one of the most consequential life-course stages for many women. Both the age and number of children affect the intensity of women's labor force participation. Not surprisingly, the presence of young children negatively correlates with maternal employment because it intensifies the amount of necessary reproductive labor, care, emotion work, and emotional labor. Furthermore, moral judgments of what it means to be a good mother are largely based on childrearing practices and dedication to childcare. However, the impact of young children on women's labor force participation is mediated by fertility, institutionalized systems of care, social norms, and gender-type of occupation.

An interesting paradox emerges with regard to birth rates and women's labor force participation (De Laat & Sevilla-Sanz 2011: 88). We know that women's labor force participation varies with the presence and number of children in their household. Not surprisingly, women are more likely to work outside the home when no or few children reside at home. In general, considering national labor force participation, we find that the greater the number of children in a household, the lower the labor force participation of any given woman. Yet nationally, a low birth rate (i.e., number of women having a child) does not correspond to high overall labor force participation among women.[2] So logically, why doesn't low fertility translate into higher labor force participation for a country? Unraveling the logical puzzle can offer clues to how the reproductive bargain within a country, structures options and actions related to the gender division of labor in the household, and its consequences for women's labor force participation in the wage labor market. The contrasting cases

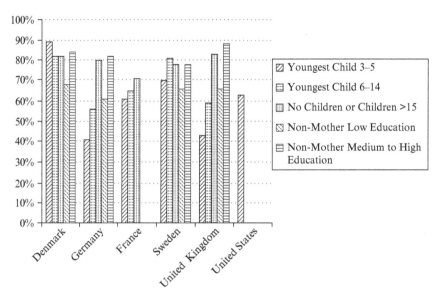

Data source: De Henau et al. (2010: 74) based on their own calculations of wave 8 of
the European Community Household Panel (1994–2001), except for US. For US, *source*:
Women's Bureau, US Department of Labor, Employment Status for Women and Men
in 2007. This figure reflects a wider sample of the female working population (age 16
or over). Interestingly, for the US, 60% of women with young children (under 3) were
in the labor force in March 2006; an increase of nine percentage points (from 51%) on
March 1986.

Figure 6.1 Employment rates of women 25–44, living with partners, FTE employment
(2001)

of Japan, on the one hand, and Sweden, on the other, can clarify what
appears like a statistical disjuncture. Japan is a country where low
birth rates do not correspond to low overall female labor force participation. Consistent with our expectations, however, Japanese women
with few children tend to participate in wage labor at higher rates
than their counterparts with larger families. Conversely, Sweden,
combining the highest female labor force participation with steady
fertility rates, represents a country providing support for the care
of children, thereby enabling women with two or more children to
sustain employment. As demographers suggest, fertility decisions
are sensitive to economic and political factors and contexts. A clearer
picture of this relationship emerges by exploring the impact of young
children on maternal employment.

Using a measure of full-time equivalent employment rates, figure
6.1 demonstrates the negative impact of young children on mothers'
ability to maintain their same employment status in different countries (De Henau et al. 2010).[3] Compatibility of motherhood and career
depends on availability of childcare. Although childcare coverage

does not indicate causality – that is, whether the low rate reflects the lack of adequate supply or low demand – it does suggest that insufficient infrastructure of care services is associated with lower women's labor force participation. For children under three years old, childcare coverage ranges from 54% in the US, to 34% in the UK, 13% in Japan and 10% in Germany. Coverage increases for older children, prior to starting kindergarten: 78% in Germany, 70% in the US, 60% in the UK, and remains relatively low at 34% in Japan. Though not shown here, childcare coverage in the southern European countries of Italy and Spain resembles that in Germany and Japan. Correspondingly, women's labor force participation remains low: 20 points less than in the Nordic countries; dual-earner families are still a minority in Spain (31%) and Italy (42%) (Garcia-Mainar et al. 2011: 144).

The hours of childcare services must mesh with work schedules. In Sweden and Denmark, nearly all childcare facilities stay open 11.5 hours per day to accommodate full-time working schedules. Danish mothers' full-time equivalent employment remains at the high rate of 89%. France, with its cradle-to-crèche childcare and fairly long childcare opening hours, resembles the social democratic countries more than social conservative Germany. Though women are responsible for two-thirds of childcare in both France and Germany, state-subsidized reproductive services support French women's full-time employment, mediating the negligible time men spend on childcare in the home. Faced with insufficient childcare services and little help from fathers, Italian, Japanese, and German mothers are more likely than French mothers to drop out of the labor force when their children are young. Evidence from Germany shows employment rates precipitously declining to 41% for mothers with young children, as compared to 80% for childless women. German families, especially in male breadwinner households, exhibit high levels of gender inequality in the intra-household allocation of time; childcare is a mother's duty with little help from fathers (Garcia-Mainar et al. 2011: 131). Parents, usually mothers, amass midday to pickup their toddlers from small, informal, as well as large institutional, childcare – a common scene played out in neighborhoods all over Germany. Most childcare facilities open only half a day, and half as long as those in Sweden, forcing many women with young children to find informal arrangements if they want or need to work full-time in Germany.

My partner and I, as visiting scholars at Hamburg University, experienced firsthand the difficulties of coordinating half-day informal childcare arrangements for our toddler in Germany. Word-of-mouth networks enabled us to literally translate our colleagues' local knowledge into a slot in a Hamburg neighborhood *Kindergruppe*, a small group of children aged three to six years old supervised by two childcare teachers. The relatively affluent group of parents could afford to pay a reasonable salary to the teachers, both of whom had degrees in child development. Our flexible work schedules facilitated what could have been a nearly impossible negotiation of transporting our son from childcare to home at midday. We could stroll our way to the *Kindergruppe* in the neighborhood just a few blocks away from where we lived. Like many working mothers in Germany, we relied on a variety of arrangements, from a *Tagesmütter* (childcare worker, or – translated literally – "Day Mother," contracted directly to take care of the child at one's own home) to employment of many US study-abroad students who worked sequential shifts during the afternoon and evening hours. Friends and colleagues who also had flexible work schedules as professors or as freelance journalists were better able to coordinate their childcare needs around their employment demands, although not always seamlessly (Henninger & Gottschall 2007).

For welfare states in continental Europe, North America, and Japan, higher birth rates and higher relative female labor force participation co-exist in countries where the household division of labor is more equitable (De Laat & Sevilla-Sanz 2011). In the US, men spend 13.8 hours per week on housework, and a higher proportion of women participate in the labor market. At the other end of the spectrum, Scandinavian countries report the highest female labor force participation rates and the most egalitarian division of housework. For example, Danish fathers dedicate over twice as much time to caring for children (19.38 hours per week) as men in southern Europe (7.45 and 7.97 hours per week for Spain and Italy respectively) (Garcia-Mainar et al. 2011: 119). In Mediterranean countries, mothers who devote around five times as many hours as men to housework have low labor force participation in comparison with other European countries (142).

To make sense of this variation, we can see how systems of child-care structure choices for individual women and their partners when allocating time to paid and unpaid labor. The transition to mother-hood is not uniformly negative for all women within a country and among women across countries. While still female-centered, caring work doesn't have the same deleterious impact in all countries. An infrastructure of childcare supports more continuous maternal employment. An uneven employment biography punctuated by periodic gaps is in part induced by the lack of available, affordable, and good-quality childcare. Care is not only a gender issue, but also a class-based issue in terms of access to good-quality and affordable care and the choice of type of care (in-home, state-based, or subsidized services). Inadequate and expensive market-based care may exacerbate class inequalities among women (McDowell et al. 2005). Care responsibility often defaults to the unpaid labor of women in the absence of available care services.

Employment, Marital Status, and Motherhood

In most countries, education mediates the negative effect of children on maternal employment status. Women with higher qualifications tend to return quickly after childbirth and to work full-time. Conversely, women with lower qualifications are more likely to return in part-time employment (note the high rates of part-time employment among women in the UK). Single mothers with limited education are least likely to combine paid work with motherhood (McDowell et al. 2005: 448).[4] As will be discussed later, the pattern differs in Japan whereby educated women's labor force participation barely budges after childbirth. All things being equal, education does not uniformly translate into higher maternal employment in all occupations.

Data on occupational distribution suggest that some occupations are more or less compatible with marriage and motherhood. Wives are half as likely as husbands to work in elite occupations of executive management, or as doctors and lawyers, whereas single men hold only a small edge over single women. Another study finds that long, unpredictable, and inflexible hours in elite occupations, especially in finance and corporate management, do not mesh well with the rhythms of everyday life and the calendar of children's school and after-school activities (Bertrand et al. 2010: 230). Put another way, elite occupations are configured around a form and a norm of masculine embodiment based on non-responsibility for care and social provisioning. For this reason, women without children are more likely to follow men's career paths (Leonhardt 2010a: B6). At the highest levels of the executive and judicial branches of the US government, many of the most prominent women remain childless, including: Supreme Court Justices Elena Kagan and Sonja Sotomayor, and Cabinet Officers Janet Napolitano and Condoleessa Rice (B6); or wait to pursue political office once their children are grown, such as Hillary Rodman Clinton who was elected to the US Senate, ran for President, and subsequently was appointed to the Cabinet position of Secretary of State, all after her daughter Chelsea left home. Organizational features and processes influence how hospitable an occupation is to mothers working full-time.

Still, mothers experience better chances of employment in some elite professions than in others. A longitudinal study of highly qualified professionals' labor force participation found that female MBAs had a more difficult time combining work and family life than female physicians, Ph.D.s, and lawyers: the employment rate 15 years after graduation is the highest for mothers who are MDs at 95%, then

Ph.D.s and JDs at 90%, and MBAs at 85%. Even greater disparities exist for mothers who remain in the labor force: maternal employment is the lowest for MBAs (50%), then Ph.D.s and JDs (55%), and the highest for MDs (65%). A similar pattern of labor force attachment appears when looking more generally at the number of hours worked among mothers: just 30% of mothers with MBAs work full-time, as compared to 38% of Ph.D.s and 43% of MDs (Bertrand et al. 2010: 253). A recent study tracking MBA graduates from the University of Chicago Business School finds men and women initially earn similar income and work the same number of hours. Ten years after graduation careers diverge, with men earning about 60% more than women. Much of the difference is the penalty women experience as mothers when they take time off or work part-time (228). In fact, the highest-paying professions in finance and corporate management demand more than a full-time commitment, incompatible with parenting and care responsibilities. This suggests that the incompatibility of motherhood and employment in elite occupations is more than opportunity costs for women. If these were solely the reason, then women should be able to substitute paid services in order to reconcile their work schedules. Time allocation and job flexibility do have an impact on maternal employment, but so do the cultural expectations of the occupation. As more women work full-time, they increase their demand for paid personal services, creating new class and racial divisions among women and between women and men.

Accounting for the value of marketized care

The day-to-day activities of cleaning and caring for people are necessary services in a variety of settings, from the household to the corporation. Firms always retained a few "in-house" workers designated to carry out a certain amount of cleaning and other "housework" functions. Now, a larger share of these services, and even new types of activities, are becoming commodified and entering the market. Care work, reproductive labor, and other personal services increasingly are commodified in market-based relationships.

Paid Domestic Services: Childcare and Cleaning

The gender and racial composition of paid care work can be seen in microcosm by examining the state of Massachusetts (Albelda et al. 2010). An overview of the service economy reveals nearly one-quarter of all workers employed in care work, as compared to 11% in information services, as of 2007 (7–8). Women comprise three-quarters of all care workers and only 41% in all other industries. Immigrants, who make up 18% of the state's workforce, account for nearly 40% of all nursing, psychiatric, and home health aides, 31% of personal and home care aides, and 23% of childcare workers. Black and Hispanic women are over-represented in care work (8). This profile of a single state illustrates the significance of care work to women of color's overall employment in the new service economy.

Looking at the national US economy, official estimates put the number of childcare workers at 1.3 million in 2008. The US Occupational Outlook Handbook differentiates childcare workers based on where they work: either in private households, in their own homes, or at childcare centers (United States Bureau of Labour Statistics 2010b: 1). Of those who hold childcare jobs, 19% care for children in either a daycare center or private household (4). Childcare employment is expected to increase 11%, in line with the average projected increase for all occupations, by 2018. Building cleaners, maids, and housekeepers fill approximately 3.7 million jobs, made up of about 2.3 million janitors and cleaners, and about 1.4 million maids and housekeepers in 2010.[5] The vast majority of maids and housekeepers work either in private households (30%) or in hotels, motels and other private establishments (29%). Growth (4% for janitors and cleaners and 6% for maids and housekeepers) is projected to fall below the average for all occupations over the next decade. A more in-depth look at childcare and cleaning reveals the racial and gender division of reproductive labor. Women comprise more than 95% of childcare workers (Macionis 2010: 95); and, as in Massachusetts, Hispanics (20.0%) and African-Americans (17.4%) are over-represented in childcare nationally (Macionis 2010: 301), with 28.2% and 18.4%, respectively, in cleaning services.

Compensation in childcare and cleaning services is low, regardless of an individual's educational attainment; childcare is among the ten lowest-paid occupations. Yet, nearly 50% of childcare workers earned qualifications beyond a high school diploma (Hegewisch et al. 2010: 8), and almost half of those had some college education (Hegewisch et al. 2010: A18). Despite relatively high educational attainment, the Occupational Outlook Handbook reports that the lowest-paid 10% of childcare workers earned $7.04 an hour in 2009. In addition, most childcare workers receive minimal or no fringe benefits (United States Bureau of Labour Statistics 2010b: 5). Female childcare workers' median earnings of $364 per week remunerate a full-time schedule. A single mother with two children, even if she works full-time year-round as a childcare worker, earns an income just above the official poverty line at $18,310 (Hegewisch et al. 2010: 11). As in other occupations, male childcare workers earn more than women on average.

Still, men in childcare receive lower wages than they could earn in male-typed jobs in manufacturing and construction. Low relative wages "cannot be explained by low unmeasured human capital or a disinclination to bargain for high pay among care workers, because these individual characteristics would presumably affect their pay in all jobs" (England et al. 2002: 468). Instead, gender biases undervaluing care and reproductive labor help to account for unexplained differences. Similarly, the lowest-paid 10% of cleaners eke out wages of $7.41, though median hourly wages hover at $10.31 as of May 2008. Local government pays cleaners the most ($12.82), and private residences the least ($9.31) (4). When compared, childcare workers earn less on average than cleaners.

At the same time, informalization is a common factor for many workers in these low-waged services. Labor relationships range from informal direct hires to third-party subcontracting, often involving migrant workers from Central America, Mexico, and Asia. One-third of childcare workers were classified as independent contractors in 2008 (United States Bureau of Labour Statistics 2010b: 4). Nearly 14% of cleaners are classified as self-employed, and around 33% of janitors work for companies contracting out services (United States Bureau of Labour Statistics 2010a: 4). Contracting companies are expected to expand their share of the delivery of cleaning services in response to increasing demand from private households and hotels, according to government reports (3). Such informalized employment status deprives workers of benefits and social protections.

Commodification of household tasks also has spawned new occupations, such as concierge services for men and women in the middle and upper classes (Sherman 2010). What makes concierge services a commercial possibility also complicates its viability. In trying to create a market for household and care-related services, concierges confront "difficulties of commodifying gendered labor associated with the home and family" (36). Concierge services in the home embody a feminized service more likely to involve highly educated women and some men whose class position is more closely aligned with their customers. Like unpaid care work, concierge services retain the flavor of intimacy and informality of pampered personal services.

Impelling the shift from unpaid to paid care work is a variety of economic and social forces. Social choice and economic need compel more women to seek waged employment. Women working both increases demand for new services, and in turn brings more women into care and other service occupations. In this context, dual-earner couples and working single parents may turn to alternative sources of, and substitutes for, labor to perform and deliver care and cleaning services. Moreover, households increasingly make use of purchased goods and other services (e.g. restaurant meals, house-cleaning, laundry services, and daycare centers), thereby reducing unpaid labor in the household (Floro & Meurs 2009: 26). As capitalism shifts toward more market-based service production, it makes available inexpensive goods from big-box stores like Walmart and fast-food meals from McDonalds (as discussed in the previous chapter), which further encourages the growth of these services to replace unpaid production in the household. These factors, along with the retreat of the state from support of social reproduction, contribute to increasing commodification of caring labor. Interestingly, the household remains a site for these activities even after the transformation of social relationships. For this reason, the next section analyzes reproductive and care labor not only as a set of occupations, but also as a system of social relationships.

Paid Domestic Services: Back to the Household

"At a bus stop between a middle-class residential district and a squatter settlement, a group of domestic workers, clutching plastic bags, stand apart from the urban women returning home from work and shopping" (Ozyegin 2001: 126). This seemingly mundane scene of waiting for a bus evokes the intersecting everyday worlds of middle-class and poor women. The scene is emblematic of the intimacy shared by women in the domestic sphere, even as they occupy unequal power relationships. Paid domestic service workers operate both separately from, and as a part of, the same spaces as the women who employ them. It is the intimate life world of social interaction, in a space ideologically designated as outside the circuits of capital, that complicates both legal regulation over employer-and-worker relationships in paid domestic service, and their sociological conceptualizations. The blurring of public and private forms of power is exemplified by women who meet in the patrimonial relationship of "mistress" and "maid." Bakker and Gill (2003: 40) use this example to illustrate the hybridity of the social space of the household, which they characterize as follows: "For the 'Mistress' it is a private realm, but for the 'Maid' it is a semipublic workplace." Paid domestic service in the household becomes a microcosm of, and a way to see, old and new fault lines of inequality where gender, class, race/caste, and citizenship intersect.

Domestic service, after waning through much of the mid twentieth century, thrives again in the Global North as well as persisting in the Global South.[6] These trends belie expectations of conventional social theories. Most prominently, modernization theory predicts the gradual disappearance of this patrimonial relationship of master and servant with the diffusion of modern values of meritocracy upending ascriptive characteristics matching people to jobs in post-industrial countries. But the lineage of domestic service is not simply a vestige of either the feudal past or colonialism, but rather reflects both "continuity and change" (Qayum & Ray 2003: 522). To understand what drives expansion and shapes employment conditions of paid domestic labor, Qayum and Ray summarize two inter-related feminist strands. The first emphasizes globalization and immigration processes propelling women to join old migratory routes and embark on new ones. Women leave their poor countries of origin in a "reproduction migration" from the Global South to urban destinations either in home countries or in wealthier nations, mostly of the North (Hondagneu-Sotelo 2001; Parrenas 2001; Gutierrez-Rodrigues 2010). A related strand considers dual-career couples' increasing demand for paid domestic service as more women seek to remain in the labor force after childbirth. In the US, families resort to private solutions because of inadequate public subsidies to supply and support care services. Both strands take as their departure points the re-emergence of paid domestic service and the repercussions on social inequalities worldwide.

Two exemplary studies analyze the structures of inequality in paid domestic service. One of the most compelling early contributions draws on Marxist labor process, feminism, and critical theories of race. M. Romero's (1992) *Maid in the USA* conceptualizes paid domestic service as an employment relationship structured by intersecting systems of capitalism, racism, and sexism. Contemporary capitalism imposes a class template of proletarianized labor relations in domestic service, but with a difference based on this gender-coded and racialized service. In addition to physical labor, employers attempt to extract emotional labor, both given "freely" and sometimes withheld by domestic workers. Low wages reflect the super-exploitation of racial-ethnic women relegated to domestic service. G. Ozyegin positions the Turkish domestic workers that she studied in culturally and economically constituted structural relationships of inequality (2001: 126–7). In *Untidy Gender*, Ozyegin describes domestic workers as actively engaged in the messy work of negotiating control over their pace of work, discretion, autonomy, and supervision in their employer's household. She argues that inequality is shaped contextually and relationally through "negotiations between employer and worker in the daily interaction within the domestic service encounter" (130). By emphasizing symbolic negotiations as well as material inequalities, Ozyegin restores workers' agency in recreating and contesting class relations in routines of everyday interactions.

A new approach defines domestic servitude as an institution, forging a middle-range theory in-between a macro-economic structural theory and a micro-interactional perspective. Culture of domestic servitude refers to the idioms, symbols, rituals, and practices that enact "the form of dependency and submission in relation to paid domestic work" (Qayum & Ray 2003: 548). As a social institution, domestic servitude structures hierarchies of social relationships rooted in the larger political economy. A case study looks at this institution in Kolkata. India, like other emergent economic power-houses among the BRICs (Brazil, Russia, India and China), projects a fledgeling and burgeoning middle class that adopts a lifestyle built on former colonial and feudal ties and emergent capitalist systems of domestic servitude.

Through in-depth interviews with 38 first- and second-generation employers both from middle and upper classes and from lower castes, S. Qayum and R. Ray (2003: 548) trace the "unbroken" social and cultural legacies of domestic servitude in India. Excavating shards pieced together from richly detailed oral histories, the authors uncover a "constitutive continuity of the institution": a turning point in which the confluence of political partition, creating the sovereign nations of India, Pakistan, and Bangladesh, with rural economic crisis dispossessing peasants from ownership and use of cultivable land, sent as many as 220 million migrants on a path away from their homes in the countryside to the city. Even before the independence struggle successfully dismantled British colonial rule in 1947, migrants from the hinterland soon outnumbered native-born residents of receiving cities like Kolkata (525). These internal migratory waves supplied an ever-expanding pool of labor that could be paid meager wages, both in domestic service and in other labor-intensive industries. Caste as well as class and gender dictated appropriate tasks and jobs in the household: men and women from the lowest castes were relegated to the dirty or "impure tasks" of cleaning bathrooms and washing dishes while male cooks hailed from the upper Brahmin caste (526).

Three premises underscore contradictory cultures of domestic servitude, sitting uneasily between pre-independence India's feudal past and current capitalism: first, servants are the hallmark of a well-run household among the elite; second, "servants are 'part of the family' and bound to it by ties of affection, loyalty, and dependence"; and third, servants express their own "distinctive lifestyles, desires and habits." Contemporary practices and discourses undercut and challenge each of these premises. Contrary to the first premise, the feudal master and servant paradigm fits uneasily with the contemporary capitalist ethos viewing employment relationships in terms of "free" wage labor. As Marx and Weber argued, capitalism unfetters the forces of production and frees labor from the shackles of feudalism. As a result, capitalism loosens the previous culture of servitude's patrimonial hold on servants' loyalty and deference. Despite traditional and rhetorical deference and reference to family belonging, the modern notion of privacy leaves little space either ideologically or physically for servants to be part of the nuclear family and to live in small apartments without separate servants' quarters, undercutting the second premise. At the same time, the rapid urbanization that is changing Kolkata's built environment no longer accommodates large single-family compounds that once housed wealthy landowners and their live-in servants. As more servants reside in densely populated shanty-towns, the exposure to "a political culture where democratizing discourses circulate in both state and civil society" provides an alternative means of identification and organization (Qayum & Ray 2003: 527), thereby undermining the third premise. Those very conditions that anchor the institutional moorings of domestic servitude also are responsible for its possible undoing. This historical narrative reveals the changing "relations of paid domestic work intimately tied to the self-conscious evolution of [a] modern Indian elite" (527). It casts light on the spatial aspects of class, caste, and gender re-formation through the lens of domestic servitude in one of the world's fastest-growing cities – Kolkata's population, teeming at 15.6 million, ranks eighth among the largest mega-cities in the world. The case study depicts a city on the verge of global ascendance in which emergent classes are grappling with economic transformation. Importantly, labor relations in the domestic sphere take on a different cast.

Recent scholarship raises the question of whether the structural conditions of paid domestic service centered in the household diverge from the rationalized industrial workplace. From the institutional perspective, we can draw both parallels in, and distinctions between, cultures of domestic servitude at different historical moments and in relationship to other institutional settings. On the one hand, in the industrial workplace, "worker and employer rarely meet in person, where job requirements are well defined and where compliance with job requirements is achieved through a technical division of tasks and through disciplinary practices" (Ozyegin 2001: 129; also see Qayum & Ray 2003). On the other hand, domestic labor relations do not neatly conform to the specificity of either "the factory or the field" (Ray 2008). Its location, in the household rather than in a specialized institution as with care taking place in hospitals and clinics, significantly shapes cultures of domestic servitude. A female employer is interjected in the domestic employment relationship, recreating the "mistress" and "maid" duality in the "semi-public workplace" of the household. In other words, "Domestic service confuses [and fuses] and complicates the conceptual divide between family and work, custom and contract, affection and duty, the home and the world" (Qayum & Ray 2003: 521).

The complexity of labor relations in the institution of domestic servitude derives from this in-between status of patriarchal, feudal, and capitalist relations. Labor relations are mediated through a diversity of informal and formal employment arrangements and institutions, neither fully feudal nor fully capitalist. For example, maid services in the US may consist of a single individual or a network of cleaners whose employment status categorizes them either as dependent employees or as pseudo-independent contractors. Other hybrid enterprises operate with a manager directly dispatching teams of sub-contracted house-cleaners to jobs. By contrast, cultures of domestic servitude retain elements of feudalism and colonialism in a country grappling with rapid economic transformation. Histories of slavery and immigration in the US, and the caste system and the colonial past in India, produce different racialized class and gender hierarchies. In India, most domestic servants are Indians whose class and caste differentiate them from their employers. A more thorough discussion of globalization and immigration of domestic service follows in later chapters on global linkages.

Conclusion: caring in and out of the household

This chapter frames care labor performed in the household – both paid and unpaid – and in the market, as part of the economy. Unpaid housework remains a burden unequally shared. Shouldering the bulk of unpaid housework in turn influences the intensity of women's labor force participation. Because women continue to bear primary responsibility for childcare, the presence of young children and the number of children often lowers their intensity of labor force participation, but the impact is not the same everywhere. Support of childcare, either from fathers doing more of the work or from public financing of affordable and extended childcare hours, mitigate the negative effect of children on women's labor force participation. Though education tends to boost mothers' labor force participation, some occupations are less compatible with motherhood than others.

A general trend toward reorganization of social reproduction and re-division of reproductive and care labor, both unpaid and, increasingly, paid, fuels the transnational growth and feminization of services and the transformation of employment relationships in the new economy. The service economy increases the number of well-paid professional jobs in finance and ICT, which in turn fuels the demand for and the intensification of care and reproductive services – in service to service workers, as discussed in the previous chapter. In particular, the substitution of paid personal services relieves some women of responsibility for unpaid household tasks by transferring the burden onto other women who perform such feminized (also racialized) labor for low wages in insecure employment relationships. To keep wages low, many women in-service are drawn from migrant labor pools. Through market-based services, more paid work takes place in the home and extends the working day both in time and in space. Home is different from other workplaces, filtering relationships through the template of the family. It is not so much that family life once stood as a bulwark against the heartless world of capitalism, but rather that now all aspects of social life are subject to the logic of profit maximization. The expansion of services increases commodification of everything, everyone, and everyday life. No aspects of people's lives, bodies, and selves are free from the tug of capitalist production. Commodification of care, "commercialization of intimacy" (Hochschild 2005: 79), and outsourcing of household tasks interjects more aspects of everyday life and social relationships, such as care, love, and intimacy as well as food preparation and cleaning, into the market, swept up into the circuits of capital. One of the most dynamic aspects of the new economy in some ways is the least novel. The transformation of housework in part contributes to the growth of the new service economy. Housework increasingly is externalized either by locating this work outside the household or by bringing in other women to perform these tasks usually for low wages.

As distinct from other service work, care and reproductive services can be organized and provided directly by the family, by the market, and/or by the state. The extent to which care and reproductive labor are embedded in non-market activities in the home or supported by the state or by the market has consequences for gender inequality. Through support of childcare services, the welfare state provides a bridge for reconciling maternal responsibilities and employment. How the welfare system intervenes affects whether or not care work and social reproduction remain in the purview of private households or shift to the market or to the state. The role of the state both as a provider of services and welfare, and as an employer of service workers, bears on the cost of reproduction and the valuation of reproductive labor. Welfare state support for childcare mitigates the negative effect of children on women's labor force participation. However, the ethos of care as a collective good is under assault. What will be the new division of responsibility for care when welfare states retreat from and decrease involvement in social reproduction in the face of fiscal crises and the neo-liberal agenda for smaller government? Who will pay for, and perform, these services? Chapter 7 considers how state-based policies and politics shape the distribution and conditions of employment by gender.

State and Economy: Gender, Policy, and Work

Political economy is an approach to studying political and economic forces in relation to other institutions in society. Previous chapters focused on economic structures and work organization to document and explain gender inequalities in the labor market, and alluded to the importance of political forces influencing employment and distributional patterns. This chapter uses a feminist lens to reveal how gender informs and structures political institutions and policy priorities, influencing the size of the gender pay gap, the degree of women's economic autonomy, their risk of poverty, and patterns of gender segregation in the labor market. Sorting through conceptual differences and gendering comparative perspectives on the welfare state and varieties of capitalism, chapter 7 clarifies how the political factors shaping patterns of gender inequality vary, and what accounts for this variation.

Beyond identifying institutional variation, the chapter compares policy initiatives that are more or less women-friendly. Latter parts of this chapter look at policy formation through a feminist lens. Because of the centrality of gender relations, the gendered body, and the gendered character of social reproduction in comparative feminist theories, the policy examples discussed in this chapter come out of the realm of care and sexual relations in the workplace, most notably the development of parental leave and sexual harassment law.

Gendering comparative perspectives on welfare states and policy analyses

"The state" refers to political institutions through which those in power rule. As a set of institutions, the capitalist state maintains social cohesion of the polity (Eisenstein 1984), facilitates capital accumulation, coordinates economic governance, and regulates individual and collective norms. To that end, capitalist regulations govern behavior normatively, based on cultural traditions, and formally, through state-based statutory rights and social protections. Those expounding state and economy theories characterize political institutions and political actors as having more (Skocpol 1980) or less (relative) autonomy (Jessop 2001) in relationship to the market. Inspired by Weber, the first approach suggests that state actors may pursue their own interest in expanding their organizational power, thereby exercising autonomy even if their actions conflict with entrenched societal groups. Drawing on Marxism, others point to the role of the capitalist state in reflecting the systemic needs of capitalism, demobilizing the working class and facilitating capital accumulation, constraining political actors and their actions. Nevertheless, debates over the degree of state autonomy in capitalist society tend to neglect how the state reinforces structures of male dominance and hegemonic masculinity as well as extends rights and benefits to subordinate groups in society. Using a feminist lens makes visible "the rules, laws, and institutional arrangements of social groups that organize and maintain the differences between women and men" (Scott cited in Marx-Ferree et al. 1999: xxii).

The welfare state more specifically represents a set of political institutions and social policies mediating conflicts arising out of "deeply entrenched societal inequalities ... [and] often express[ing] political commitment to fairness and social solidarity" (Acker 2011: 2). Welfare states can affect the quality of men's and women's lives and livelihoods as well as shape gender relations, identities, and political participation (Orloff 1993: 303–4). Feminists ask "how gender is constructed in welfare state policies and how these policies are a force in (re)ordering gender relations through an examination of a wide range of contexts" (Sainsbury 1999: 4). Another key feminist insight brings the family into the constellation of what are considered meaningful institutions relative to state and economy. The family is presented in today's ideology as if it is private and thus unrelated to public functions of the state. Zillah Eisenstein (1984) suggests that whether a woman chooses to bear a child is supposedly her "private" affair. Yet whether the law gives her options to do otherwise is not understood as a reflection of indirect patriarchal control by the state. *Not* providing paid maternity or parental leave or not building day-care centers puts the burden of childcare coordination on the shoulders of individual women, which has employment consequences. More expansively, feminists argue that full and equal participation in the polity and economy presupposes that women control their own bodies and "bodily capacities," including sexuality and reproduction (Orloff 1993: 307). Finally, within this political economy tradition, feminists argue that the welfare state operates not simply in opposition to or augmentation of markets, but also delivers care and reproductive services and shapes public and private forms of power. Though clearly consequential, the state is part of an ensemble of institutions, along with the family, civil society, and economy, that impact on the distribution and conditions of employment by gender.

A critical review of comparative non-feminist and feminist scholarship reveals how the role of the state and policy formation shapes systematic patterns of gender and class inequalities. These theoretical frameworks array countries along different axes, emphasizing power relations within and across labor markets, households, civil society, and the economy (see table 7.1). As mentioned in chapter 2, traditional political economy defines types of welfare capitalisms or varieties of capitalism. These "three worlds of welfare capitalism" – liberal, conservative, and social democratic welfare state regimes – are based on the political principles for determining the extent of state intervention in the economy. Under liberal capitalism, economic institutions are less constrained by regulation than under non-liberal varieties of capitalism. Neither of these two non-feminist theoretical frameworks incorporates gender systematically into their typologies. Feminists, while sharing common concerns, express different understandings of state and economy relationships by conceptualizing gender contracts, gender regimes, or state feminisms. Gender contracts distinguish between strong, modified, and weak models, based on the extent to which institutions are organized around a male breadwinner norm. Next, gender regime differentiates private from public forms of social relations, depending on the system of gender relations in the labor market, civil society, the household, the state, for the society at large. Finally, state feminism delineates strong to weak forms, measured by whether or not policy formation and government agencies are women-friendly. The next section elaborates on the defining features of each framework.

Comparative Institutional Perspectives: From Three Worlds to Gender Models

Non-feminist theorists recently have integrated feminist insights into their welfare state models (Korpi 2000; Esping-Andersen 1999). One of the most influential approaches, the three worlds of welfare capitalism initiated by Esping-Andersen, differentiates between social democratic, liberal market and conservative welfare capitalisms on the basis of distributive principles governing the relationship between state and economy. Social democratic countries provide universalistic benefits in accordance with social citizenship and an equality ethos, liberal market countries means-test many entitlements and emphasize an individual's work ethic, while social conservative

Table 7.1 Theoretical frameworks: gender, state, and economy in comparative perspective					
FRAMEWORKS	US	UK	Germany	Sweden	Japan
Welfare state regime[a]	Liberal	Liberal	Conservative	Social democratic	Hybrid
Varieties of capitalism[b]	Liberal	Liberal	Non-liberal	Non-liberal	Non-liberal
Gender contract[c]	Weak male breadwinner	Modified male breadwinner	Modified male breadwinner	Weak male breadwinner	Modified male breadwinner
Gender regime[d]	Public	Public	Public/ domestic	Public	Public/ domestic
State feminism[e]	Weak	Moderate	Moderate	Moderate	Weak

a. Esping-Andersen (1990, 1999, 2009).
b. Crouch & Streeck (1997); Streeck (2001).
c. Lewis (2001); Gottfried & O'Reilly (2002).
d. Walby (2004, 2009a).
e. Mazur (2001); Stetson & Mazur (1995).

countries link social insurance to employee and employer contributions and rights based on class and status (Daly 2011: 91). An innovative aspect of Esping-Andersen's original model differentiates welfare capitalisms along axes of commodification and de-commodification. De-commodification occurs when services are provided as a right, not merely as a function of employment status, and it enables livelihoods to be sustained outside of the market economy. This principle is most developed in social democratic countries (Esping-Andersen 1990: 21-2). The practical design of social security and de-commodification are not the only elements that define significant differences between welfare capitalisms. The theory takes into account the state's role in relationship to other institutions (Daly 2011: 95).

Revisiting his three-worlds' model of welfare capitalism, Gosta Esping-Andersen's (1999) analysis of the post-industrial state borrows the feminist concept of defamilialization to denote provision of services outside the family by either state or market. In his recent venture, Esping-Andersen (2009) incorporates a life-course perspective to explain what he refers to as "the incomplete revolution in gender relations." Though women are more equal to men, new class inequalities polarize women who have different levels of educational and skill qualifications. But he misses other key aspects of feminist theorizing about sexuality, violence and the body. Moreover, an impoverished concept of gender leads him to underestimate the contradictory effects of de-commodification. Though Esping-Andersen acknowledges the progressive impact of labor force participation on women's autonomy (commodification of women's labor power), he reserves the category of gender for analysis of the family and class for analysis of the economy (Walby 2009a: 145). As a result, his welfare state typology overlooks the gender character of capitalist institutions. Various approaches to theorizing varieties of capitalism or welfare state regimes are unsuccessful because they neglect structures of gender relations and political mobilization and their impact on the division of labor and the quality of employment. Significant differences between types of political and economic systems cannot be fully explained without reference to class and gender power relations.

One alternative feminist comparative approach constructs a typology that clarifies the factors and the forces affecting the boundaries of public and private responsibility for social reproduction. J. Lewis' (1992, 2001) concept of the male breadwinner model highlights policymakers' assumptions about family forms, and the ways in which this contributes to the social organization of care. Subsequently, the introduction of the concept of gender contract elaborates on "the historical forms of the tacit gender bargain as embodied in laws and institutions regulating mutual obligations, rights, and relations between women within and between the area of production and reproduction" (Gottfried & O'Reilly 2004: 30). This framework revises welfare state approaches to compare institutionally embedded male breadwinner models ranging from strong to weak. A strong male breadwinner model "channels men and women in different spheres" (von Wahl 2005: 82) and creates incentives for married women and mothers either to work in non-standard employment or to drop-out of the labor force as a means of reconciling work and family life. In strong male breadwinner models, women's access to benefits has been derived from and mediated by their relationships to men (Orloff 1993). Typifying a modified male breadwinner model, the social conservative welfare system of Germany and the hybrid system of Japan provide insufficient public resources to build social care infrastructures, rely on women's unpaid reproductive labor in the household (Gottfried & O'Reilly 2004: 50–1), and create strong internal labor markets for men in core industries. Generally, current policies supporting women's labor force participation and reconciliation of work and family life have modified, eroded, and weakened the male breadwinner model. Still the legacy of the male breadwinner model continues to inform policy formation, albeit to different extents across countries.

The language of contract initially had intuitive appeal, but its legalistic connotations caused problems when applied to gender relations writ large. Contracts set out terms and conditions enforced by legal imprimaturs. More broadly, the notion of social contract in the post-World War II era came to define a negotiated social "compact" of expanded workers' rights, extended restrictions on the freedom of contract, recognized collective rights and obligations of labor unions to represent workers' interests, and established welfare state protections against market risks. As a doctrine, the social contract inscribed distributive principles under-girding political consent as a necessary scaffolding to support the design of institutional architectures that ensure social cohesion (Zunz et al. 2002: 1). Social contracts have varied in accordance with dominant political principles operating across different types of welfare states and varieties of capitalism. On the one hand, access to the market was the primary means of "democratization of wealth" advocated by liberal US policy-makers. On the other, "institutionalized social protection" was pursued by most European states (Zunz et al. 2002: 2). Uncomfortable with the notion of contract, some feminists find other concepts to delimit the institutional and normative framework.

For this reason, Ruth Pearson's (2007) innovative concept of the reproductive bargain immediately resonated as an institutional term closely allied with the concept of gender contract. A reproductive bargain composes an ensemble of institutions, ideologies, and identities around social provisioning and care for human beings (Gottfried 2009a, 2011). A bargain constitutes a hegemonic framework within which actors negotiate rules and rule-making. "Bargain" implies a set of normative rules and institutions regulating interactions, self-conceptions, and social relations. This notion of "bargain" not only implies a bounded agreement (structure) proscribing and prescribing conduct (habitus), but also injects a dynamic notion of boundaries being made (agency). As a social process, agents interpret rules and influence rule-making that can call into question and alter the boundaries of any bargain. However, agents negotiate from different structural positions of power with different resources (material, symbolic, and associational). The arena of bargaining can range from the factory floor to the kitchen table. Most formally, collective bargaining between legally recognized representatives of labor and capital establishes industrial jurisprudence and determines benefit packages for those covered by the agreement. Out of this comes the division of responsibility for care and reproductive labor in the household. It is the latter that has been the implicit part of the strong male breadwinner reproductive bargain.

Variation of reproductive bargains corresponds to the ensemble of institutions involved in social provisioning, and the institutional locus of reproduction in either private (household) or public spheres (state or market-based). Welfare systems supporting the family as the preferred site of social reproduction create a host of mechanisms, including the "lack of nursery schools, short school days or lack of home services for the elderly, economic incentives like the marriage subsidy, care allowances and the 'family wages'" (Montanari 2003:

25), that limits women's ability to remain employed full-time. In liberal market economies, the state intervenes principally by enabling market-based solutions for the provision of care and reproductive services. The intervention of the market weakens the male breadwinner model while at the same time reinforcing class differences between families. As a result, low-waged labor of women, often among women of color and recent immigrants, increasingly substitutes for the formerly unpaid labor of women in their households. Whether or not, and how much, reproductive labor is remunerated and its organization influences women's autonomy and financial independence (gender equality) and contributes to the health, economic well-being, and livelihood security of families (class inequalities) and communities (Osawa 2007). The framework of a reproductive bargain identifies normative rules governing types of work available to different groups of women and men (see table 7.2 and table 7.3).

An increasing number of non-governmental organizations populating civil society provide care and other personal services in the space between state, family, and economy, and thereby alter the reproductive bargain. Non-profit non-governmental organizations fill a niche for the delivery of services in what some call a "third" sector. These organizations, in contrast to market providers, often operate according to need of the clients rather than the profit motives of the organization. Indeed, many of these non-governmental organizations

Table 7.2 Reproductive bargains in comparative perspective

| Institutional locus of reproduction | Private sphere: family | Reproductive bargains | | |
| | | Public sphere | | |
		Civil society	Market	State
Informal employment relations	Paid (direct or through third-party labor market intermediary) and unpaid (family members)	Paid and unpaid (volunteer)	Paid, unregulated	Third-party subcontracting, temporary, and part-time
Formal employment relations	Paid (direct or through third-party labor market intermediary)	Paid (direct or subsidized by state)	Paid, regulated	Civil servants, dependent employees
Mode of regulation	Normative	Inter-subjective	Thin	Thick
Coordination	(Laissez-faire) Social conservative	–	(Liberal) Neo-liberal	(Non-liberal) Social democratic
Service provision	Family-centric	NGOs and commercial orgs.	Transfer payments	Service-provided
Male breadwinner	Strong	Weak	Modified	Weak
Interest intermediation	Individual/network organizations	Network organizations	Low-density Service unions	High-density Public-sector unions

Table 7.3 Locus of reproduction cross-nationally

Reproductive work	US	UK	Germany	France	Sweden	Japan
Locus reproduction work[a]	Market-oriented	Market-oriented	Family-centered	State-centered	State-centered	Family-centered
Care economy	Market-based	Mixed	Family	State-based	State-based	Family
Health	Market-based	State	Mixed	State	State	Mixed
Childcare	Market / transfer payment	Market / transfer payment	Family allowances	State	State	Family allowances
Gender regimes	Public	Public	Public/domestic	Public	Public	Domestic
Gendered welfare state	Dual-earner	Modified male breadwinner	Strong male breadwinner	Dual-earner / female care-giver	Dual-earner	Strong male breadwinner
State as employer (size of public sector)	Small	Medium	Medium	Medium	Large	Small

[a] Montanari (2003) identifies institutions responsible for reproduction work as in the family, the market, or the state. These categories are not mutually exclusive, but rather indicate the primary locus for carrying out, managing, and bearing costs of reproduction work.

are embedded in the communities in which they serve. Civil society organizations can alter the distributive principles for the delivery of care and reproductive services. Currently, however, non-governmental organizations at best augment rather than displace other institutions as the primary site for the provision of care services.

Finally, feminists contrast countries with different gender regimes (Connell 1995, 2002; Ostner & Lewis 1995; Fagan & O'Reilly 1998; Walby 2009a) or inequality regimes (Acker 2011). They share in common the usage of the term "regime" to characterize governing principles (logic) that structure systems of social, political, and economic relationships. At an abstract level, gender regimes refer to "a system of gender relations in the market and household economies, the polity, and in civil society, that includes inter-personal violence and sexuality" (Walby 2004: 55). Modernization of the gender regime entails women's increasing participation in public spheres and expanding civil, social, and reproductive rights (Walby 2009a). Walby (2011) conceptualizes the relationship between the structure of patriarchal relations (varieties of gender regimes from private to public) and the structures of capitalist relations (varieties of class regimes from neo-liberal to social-democratic), to show that they don't necessarily map onto one another. She constructs empirical indicators to distinguish analytically between class-led and gender-led employment protections and welfare provisions. With respect to class and the economy, she uses a measure of the extent of employment regulation (strictness of employment protection) and of public provision of services; and in relation to gender and the economy, she looks at regulation for equality in employment (strength of equality regulation) and state provision of childcare. Consistent with her theoretical proposition, she finds that there is no statistically significant correlation between countries that have strict employment protection legislation and strong equality legislation. Based on her statistical indicators, she shows that class-led forms of organization (unions) and mobilization are linked to higher levels of employment protection and state welfare provision. Likewise, gender-led forms of organization, realized by women's representation in unions and in parliament, are linked to stronger equality legislation and childcare expenditures. Analytically, patterns of complex inequalities reflect the separate, but intersecting, trajectories of the class regime and the gender regime.

Building on earlier organizational analysis, Acker (2011) moves to a societal level in her recent conceptualization of inequality regimes. For the broad economy, inequality regimes encompass relationships within and across social categories of gender, race, and class. Acker emphasizes processes of inequality formation within a political economic framework. It is a deeply historical perspective concerned with the "ongoing intersections between [mutually constitutive] gender, race, and class processes." Analytically, inequality can exist without poverty. For this reason, Acker (2) distinguishes the two concepts, defining poverty as an economic threshold "below the level necessary for health and participation in the society." In most societies, poverty afflicts those occupying positions at the lowest levels of inequality. Three primary mechanisms produce inequalities: (1) wage-setting and the creation and distribution of jobs; (2) gender and race segregation of occupations and jobs as a result of economic processes; and (3) political processes maintaining power over the creation and distribution of resources, including wages (3). The process of wage-setting generally is controlled by owners of capital and those with organizational power. While capitalists seek to maximize profits through minimizing allocation of the surplus, workers influence wage-setting and resulting wage inequality by means of their organizational muscle, exercised primarily by means of unions. Typically, organizations set actual wages whether by bureaucratic fiat, by individual negotiations, or by union rules. A host of decisions regarding who to hire, where to locate production, who is best suited for particular types of jobs all constitute inequality-generating processes (5–6).

One of the more innovative aspects of her argument regards visibility of inequalities and political mobilization. Inequality regimes can change when class, gender and/or race disparities become more visible, leading those in subordinate positions to take action against the systems of inequality – the Occupy Movement and their slogan, "We are the 99%," is a way of talking about visible class inequality. A single transformative act of self-immolation by the Tunisian street vendor Mohamed Bouazizi called attention to the country's harsh economic conditions and extreme disparities of wealth, sparking the cascade of protests culminating in the Arab Spring of 2011. Inequality regimes persist through processes of control, both direct and indirect, and compliance, sometimes motivated by fear, despair or by feelings that no viable alternatives exist. Control may function economically, in the sense that workers fear losing their job if they protest, especially in the face of tight labor markets and high unemployment, despite legal prohibitions against discrimination or unfair treatment. Finally, political processes create, maintain, and can change inequality regimes. Both welfare states and labor unions can reduce inequalities produced by capitalist economies. Countries with strong labor unions, usually affiliated with political parties, leverage the welfare state for greater social protections nationally and for collective rights at the workplace. Women's movements similarly respond to and address visible gender inequalities. This meso-analysis allows Acker to theorize the historical processes by which complex inequalities systematically and systemically develop and change.

This extensive review of the literature distinguishes between theories in order to make sense of the variation in patterns of gender inequality across welfare capitalisms. We gain an appreciation of the salient institutional settings that structure gender and class relations from this inventory of theories. Some theories emphasize structure and others process, either at the macro-level or the meso-level, and view gender and class as either mutually constitutive or analytically independent. In each case, comparative feminist research integrates the family and civil society in relationship to the economy and the state. By gendering institutional characteristics, feminist analyses highlight the persistence and change of both public and private forms of power in the context of political interventions and political systems.

Feminist Policy Analysis

Turning to analyses of policy processes and structures internal to the state, feminist policy formation research overlaps with state feminism approaches. Feminist policy analysis attempts to explain the extent to which contemporary welfare states pursue feminist/ women-friendly policies (Kahn & Meehan 1992; Stetson & Mazur 1995; Mazur 2001, 2002). State feminism focuses on those "activities of government structures that are formally charged with furthering women's status and rights" and "institutionalization of feminist interests" (Stetson & Mazur 1995: 5, 10). Accordingly, the emergence of women's policy machineries inside the state helps to account for the effectiveness of feminist policies in improving women's social status. "Women's policy machinery" refers to government agencies established by statute, administrative directive, or political resolution, and devoted to women's policy issues (Stetson & Mazur 1995: 5). Feminist comparative policy theorists credit the role of femocrats[1] and feminist organizations with bringing feminist issues to bear on political institutions at multiple levels of polities (Mazur 2001).

Extending this approach further, Mazur (2002) uses the secondary literature to elaborate eight subsectors of feminist policy to explore whether, how and why governments pursue feminist-oriented actions, and measures their impact on gender inequality. Three of the eight subsectors – equal employment, reconciliation of work and family life, and sexuality and violence policies – are particularly relevant to the study of gender, work, and economy. For example, public policy and regulations can protect male privileges through framing of fathers' rights in family laws (inheritance) and mandatory motherhood through tax codes (incentives for women to work part-time) and protective legislation (as discussed in chapter 4). The absence of provisions recognizing and criminalizing the legal concept of marital rape, and unavailability of contraceptives can put women at risk of unwanted pregnancy and limit their reproductive rights. Each of these initiatives deprives women of control over their bodily capacities and their ability to participate fully in the labor market. Further, labor and gender regulations can either positively or negatively affect labor force participation and fairness in the workplace by:

1) easing or constraining (re)entry into, and the exit from, the labor market;

2) increasing or lowering penalties for interrupting labor force participation, through childcare policies, parental leave policies, and reproductive choice;

3) boosting or undermining employment quality through the expansiveness or the narrow remit of labor standards, such as minimum wages and working-time policies, and equal treatment of standard and non-standard employment;

4) enabling or restricting action against violence through effective sexual harassment laws; and

5) expanding or limiting career opportunities through affirmative action and equal employment policies.

State policies are critical to defining possibilities, but also the nature of enforcement will help determine labor market outcomes for both men and women.

Feminist policy analysis also considers the framing of social policies in order to reveal the social construction of gender, race, and class in welfare reform. US welfare state policies emerged during the 1930s, a period of capitalism's economic collapse, to prevent citizens falling into poverty as a result of circumstances beyond their individual control. An array of labor policies under the rubric of Franklin Delano Roosevelt's "New Deal" addressed dislocation due to injury (workman's compensation), channeled government assistance to workers (unemployment insurance), legally recognized collective bargaining, promulgated industrial jurisprudence (rights at work, though not rights to work), and established labor standards framed around the male working class (male breadwinner). This implicit male standard excluded many women and racial-ethnic workers in fields exempted from legislative coverage, such as agriculture, domestic service, and nursing. Extending rights based on a full-time, full-year threshold similarly limited social protections initially accruing to White men, regionally concentrated in the industrial corridors of the Northeast and Midwest (McCall 2001: 178–9). Labor regulations continued to be framed around the male standard employment relationship even after reforms of welfare policy shifted rhetorically from economic security to economic opportunity. However, during Lyndon Johnson's administration, a series of "Great Society" policy initiatives, most notably the Civil Rights Law and Equal Opportunity Act, aimed at providing access to occupations previously closed off to people of color and women (178–9). How gender has been inscribed in subjects of legislation affects the distribution of employment protections, risks, and opportunities. For example, regulations framed with regard to money privilege the commodity form of labor over all other forms of non-waged work. This has left some aspects of workers' lives, especially those related to women's work and work biographies – such as unpaid care and emotional labor – outside formal regulatory frames. By explicating the gender subjects implicit and explicit in grammars of regulation, feminist policy research critiques current work arrangements and denaturalizes gendered norms implicit in the language of labor regulations and welfare policies.

Feminist scholarship has made important strides, improving our understanding of the forces behind gender (in)equality by either advancing gender-sensitive perspectives on policymaking processes and comparative welfare state developments or offering rich case studies and theoretical contributions to analyses of work organizational transformations. Comparative feminist approaches assess different public stances toward gender and workplace policy, and how policy is intricately embedded in social, economic, and historical forces that vary by nation or regime. Welfare state theory typifies national cases through excavation of regime logics. In contrast to welfare state theory, feminist policy formation and state feminist approaches treat the state as internally differentiated structures and processes. Neither approach expects coherence or unity across policy areas. On the one hand, state feminists avoid welfare state theories' generalizing about national policy styles. On the other hand, theories of feminist policy formation sometimes lapse into descriptions of isolated policy areas. These theories are not mutually exclusive. Alternative feminist approaches point to different aspects of policies and institutional arrangements that are consequential for explaining gender stratification patterns across countries. Gendering institutional analysis enables feminists to explain variation of inequality across countries. A review of empirical studies shows that gender assumptions built into institutional architectures differentiate patterns of gender stratification that vary across types of welfare states.

Comparative theories of the welfare state and gender inequality

Adopting the three worlds of welfare capitalism approach through a feminist lens, Mandel (2009: 712) uses a range of indicators of gender inequality to make her persuasive argument that the "nature of gender stratification varies across countries in accordance with different modes of welfare state intervention and divergent ideological approaches to gender stratification." She constructs a set of variables measuring employment patterns and outcomes, including: women's overall labor force participation; employment among mothers with pre-schoolers; household forms (percent of male breadwinner households); and wage-related data broken down by gender (gender composition of quintiles 1 and 5, and gender wage gap). Importantly, the analysis also includes the degree of poverty among single mothers either in or out of paid work.

Consistent with the three worlds approach, social democratic countries support a predominance of dual-earner households. An expansive welfare state through its family-friendly policies has enabled mothers to continue working after childbirth and during child-rearing years. However, the same forces supporting high rates of women's labor force participation in Scandinavian countries contribute to extreme horizontal gender segregation (see chapter 4). Much of the growth of women's employment concentrates in health care, education, and public administration in social democratic countries. By contrast, liberal market economies exhibit relatively high rates of female labor force participation and provide women with the highest access to managerial positions. Likewise, dual-earner households outnumber the percentage of male breadwinner families, yet there are a large percentage of poor single mothers in liberal market economies (see table 7.4). Socially conservative welfare states support the modified male breadwinner family even though maternal employment has increased over the past decade. In the cluster of conservative welfare states, the presence of young children depresses female employment levels.[2] For example, in social conservative Germany, mothers are more likely to drop out of the labor force than their counterparts in the US and the UK.

Despite nearly equally high employment rates among women and mothers in the US and Sweden, the gender wage gap and poverty more generally looms larger in liberal market economies than in social democratic welfare states. More specifically, poverty rates vary significantly across welfare state types. The risk of poverty is highest for single mothers in liberal welfare states, with the United States at the higher end and social democratic welfare states at the

Table 7.4 Means of gender inequality factors by welfare regime clusters (percent)

Gender characteristic	Social democratic[a]	Conservative[b] Italy and Spain		Liberal[c]
All women's labor force participation rate[d]	80	56	41	71
Labor force participation rate among mothers of pre-schoolers	78	50	42	63
Percent dual-earner households[e]	85	48	28	68
Percent male breadwinner households[f]	9	39	58	21
Percent working mothers work after birth and during child-rearing period	75	52	46	56
Access to managerial positions[g]	37	47	43	73
Occupational segregation[h]	61	54	51	53
Women's representation in quintile 1[i]	27	25	25	27
Women's representation in quintile 5	11	16	19	13
Gender wage gap[j]	16	11	7	20
Educational wage gap among women[k]	29	38	40	58
Poverty rate among single mothers[l]	6	26	23	49

a. Social democratic countries include Denmark, Finland, Norway, and Sweden. Definition of all the indicators and sources for this table can be found in Mandel (2009: 714–15).
b. Conservative countries include Italy, Spain, Austria, Netherlands, Belgium, France, and Germany. Data for Italy and Spain are listed separately.
c. Liberal countries include Canada, the USA, the United Kingdom, and Australia.
d. Labor force participation rate (LFPR) for women aged 25–60.
e. Married or cohabiting couples, both with earnings.
f. Married or cohabiting couples, only men with earnings.
g. Net odds of female being employed in managerial positions.
h. Index of dissimilarity (drawn from Anker 1998: table 9.1). An index of dissimilarity, ranging from 0 (complete integration) to 100 (complete segregation), gauges segregation in the overall economy.
i. This and the next row refer to working women in the top and bottom quintiles of their country's earnings distribution (based on hourly earnings quintiles).
j. 100 * [1– (average female hourly wage / average male hourly wage)].
k. 100 * [1– (average annual earnings of low educated / average annual earnings of high educated)], based on Luxembourg Income Survey standardized education levels, with up to compulsory education or initial vocation education equals low education, and university or college education or specialized vocational education equals high education.
l. Poverty is a relative measure based on disposable income in a country. Those in poverty earn disposable income less than 50% of the average equivalent disposable income in their country (Mandel 2009: 714–15).

Source: Mandel (2009: 700, table 1)

lower end. Still, single mothers *not* in the labor force experience high rates of poverty everywhere. Conversely, paid work depresses poverty for single mothers in all countries. Even though working boosts single mothers' earnings, it does not guarantee an escape from poverty. Social democratic countries are most successful in shielding single mothers from sinking too far into poverty. By contrast, single mothers fare much worse in liberal market economies where one-third of single working mothers earn incomes below the poverty level.

Similarly, single mothers do not fare well economically in conservative welfare states. Interestingly, a high percentage of single mothers work full-time in Japan. This apparent paradox stems from the particular way in which the male breadwinner family bias primarily channels benefits to wives rather than to mothers in Japan (see Ezawa & Fujiwara 2003). For different reasons, workfare denies sufficient benefits to support single mothers, who are compelled to work often in low-wage jobs in order to make ends meet in the liberal market US welfare state. Economic independence and livelihood security is out of reach for most single mothers, though welfare state policies can mitigate the severity of poverty or leave individuals to fare for themselves. Thus, household structures and family forms (single-female, male breadwinner and dual-earner) affect mother's risk of poverty in the context of the welfare state.

However, countries do not neatly align with Esping-Andersen's tripartite demarcation of welfare states. For example, Australia deviates from the liberal market welfare state cluster and exhibits characteristics more similar to continental European countries' patterns of gender inequality. This variation stems mainly from the relatively low level of maternal employment, but also the relatively low gender wage gap and access to highly paid jobs. Another significant difference from other liberal market welfare states is women's high rate of part-time employment at 44.6% overall, which spikes to 63.1% among mothers with two or more children in Australia (see Campbell et al. 2009). But, consistent with other liberal market welfare states, single mothers suffer high rates of poverty in Australia. Mandel attributes the divergence of Australia from other liberal welfare states to institutional features of the welfare state and its employment relations systems. The low level of female labor force participation among mothers is linked to the historical commitment to a strong male breadwinner model in which women tend to claim their social rights on the basis of care-giving (Mandel 2009: 707), while the comparatively low wage differentials among women and between men and women are linked to the system of centralized wage-setting in Australia. Like other liberal market welfare states, Australia's less generous support to single mothers puts them at a relatively high risk of living in poverty (707).

The US and the UK, as liberal market regimes, also differ from each other significantly when employment status is taken into account. The part-time workforce is composed of younger and older, male and female workers, using the arrangement during education and before and after retirement, in the US. By contrast, women are more likely to work part-time when they have dependent children in the UK. Mothers in the US tend to work full-time whereas the reverse holds true for mothers in the UK and Australia. In the UK, 74% of childless women, as compared to 64.5% of mothers, are employed full-time. More strikingly, only 10% of women work full-time if they have a child under the age of five in the UK (Daguerre 2005: 14).

The relatively high labor force participation among mothers in France and Belgium, with their well-developed social investment in infrastructure and availability of childcare, diverges from that in other continental European countries and appears closer to Scandinavia. Two countries in the conservative welfare cluster also differ. German mothers are slightly more likely to work full-time than their Japanese counterparts. Still, nearly half of married women with children work part-time, for less than 20 hours per week, in Germany (Daguerre 2005: 14).[3] By contrast, Italy and Spain rank lowest in terms of maternal labor force participation rates. In these latter two countries, the strong male breadwinner model depresses labor force participation and leads to higher levels of economic dependence (Mandel 2008: 707–8).

The tripartite division of welfare capitalism designates the logic of economic governance based on political principles between clusters of countries. Most consistent with the typology, social democratic countries support higher labor force participation among women in general, and mothers in particular. Based on the narrow wage gap and high female labor force participation irrespective of marital status, women workers fare relatively well in Scandinavian countries. However, women's economic fate varies within and across types of welfare states. Anomalous cases within each cluster suggest that the "three worlds of welfare" capitalism framework needs more than a little tweaking. For the Australian case, the lower wage differential between men and women derives from the historical development of employment relations. No explanation is given for why a larger number of mothers work full-time in the US than in the UK. Mandel fails to fully explain the reason for the variation within clusters of welfare states, in part because she does not systematically integrate employment relations systems and social reproduction into her formal model. Thus, it is necessary to go beyond the tripartite division of welfare state typology primarily constructed with class in mind.

To identify the factors behind unexpected differences and anomalies, feminist political economy considers the gender character of political institutions and suggests that the organization of social reproduction affects employment patterns and gender stratification. Most of the literature on the welfare state and policy development neglects the role of the state as an employer. Yet the extent and nature of state intervention affects female labor force participation and their working conditions through direct and third-party employment opportunities. Public-sector employment is particularly consequential for women as a result of their over-representation in state-supported paid reproductive work. Gendering political institutions and policy analyses requires an examination of the structure and function of the state vis-à-vis other institutions. In this way, we can see how the service economy has grown and explain the institutional location and valuation of different services. More specifically, treating the state as an employer broadens the analysis of gender and work in the service economy.

The State as Employer

The state not only is a political institution affecting economic governance and well-being through policy and regulations, but also is an economic sector significantly structuring job opportunities and employment quality for men and women. Women have been chief beneficiaries of welfare state expansion, both as clients of state services and as employees delivering those services, and, in this period of neo-liberal state shrinking, the primary victims of job loss. As an employer, the state directly influences the size, composition, and conditions of employment among women and men in this sector. At the pinnacle of the state bureaucracy, elite political positions can be more open or closed to female participation. The extent to which women are integrated into the state bureaucracy affects and reflects broader gender power relationships in society. An exemplary study of the state as employer adds a critical piece of the puzzle for understanding why extreme horizontal segregation combines with lower economic disparities between men and women in some countries and not in others (Gottschall 2010). K. Gottschall contrasts four welfare state types: Germany (social conservative), Sweden (social democratic), the UK (liberal market), and France (hybrid between social conservative and social democratic). Including the fourth type of welfare state to the three worlds reveals that distributional patterns by gender deviate from those linked to categorizations of welfare states and varieties of capitalism (also see Kroos & Gottschall 2010). Typically paired with Germany in the social conservative category of welfare states, when the state sector is taken into account, then France resembles the social democratic regime of Sweden. Similarly, the UK's large public health sector sets it apart from the usual market provision of services in other liberal economies such as the US.

The expansion of the welfare state and the extent of publicly provided social services concentrate ever larger amounts of women's employment within the public sector. Welfare states employ a huge swath of the overall labor force – more than 19 million (13%) in the

Table 7.5 Public-sector employment and female labor market participation (2006)[a]			
Country	Total (000)	% of labor force	% Women
United States (liberal)	19,734	13.0	45.0
United Kingdom (liberal)	5,850	20.2	65.2
Germany (social conservative)	5,721	14.6	50.4
France (hybrid)	6,718	29.0	59.4
Sweden (social democratic)	1,270	34.4	73.0

[a] Following Gottschall (2010: table 2, slide 5/6), public sector employment defines all work for the government, including education and health, and state-owned enterprises for those 15 to 64 years old.

Data sources: Gottschall (2010) for European countries; US Department of Labor (2010); US Census Bureau (2010), author's own calculation from Local, State, and Federal figures for 2010.

US and over 5 million in Germany (15%) and the UK (20%), nearly 30% in France, and more than one-third in Sweden (see table 7.5). Sweden leads other countries with more than 50% of women's overall employment in the public sector. Moreover, women's relative share of total public sector employment ranges from 45% in the US, to a little more than half in Germany, two-thirds in the UK, and three-quarters in Sweden. Social democratic countries' commitment to universal health, education, and childcare services has enlarged the state sector by socializing some aspects of reproduction. One of the unintended consequences, despite family-friendly policies such as generous parental leave and paternity benefits, is that a high degree of horizontal sex segregation exists in social democratic Sweden (Charles 2003; Estévez-Abe 2005). The index of dissimilarity for sectoral segregation puts this gender bias in stark relief. Based on data from 2007, this index reaches 42.7%, reflecting the high concentration of women in Sweden's public sector (Gottschall 2010: 3). The smaller public sector in the US leaves the majority of reproductive services, including health and childcare, to the private sector. However, women, and particularly women of color, benefited from the expansion of employment opportunities in the US public sector.

Despite rhetorical exaggeration of the bloated federal government for political effect, the reality of public-sector employment has fluctuated since the end of the World War II in the US. In 1946, 2.4 million people were employed by the federal government, increasing to 2.9 million in the late 1960s on the heels of "Great Society" programs. The number stabilized around 2.8 million during the Nixon and Carter administrations, reaching its peak of 3.1 million under Reagan. Then federal employment decreased to around 2.9 by the time Clinton left office. While public-sector employment declined in the first few years of George W. Bush's administration, the federal government subsequently added more employees. Much of the employment growth in the public sector occurred at the local level, mushrooming from 2.7 million in 1946 to 14.2 million (US Census Bureau 2010). In fact, the vast majority of public employment takes place in local municipalities (60%), with the state level accounting for 25%, and only 4% at the federal level. Women outnumber men at the state (52%) and local (61%) levels, predominantly as teachers, according to 2011 estimates (Institute for Women's Policy Research [IWPR] 2011). The federal government tilts more toward men's employment (57%) as concentrated in postal service jobs, management, and security (IWPR 2011). Overall, the US has a small welfare state supporting fewer public-sector jobs than other developed countries.

Disaggregating employment by state function and redistributive principles shows a smaller percentage of women employed in the social conservative welfare state sectors of France and Germany than in both social democratic Sweden and liberal market UK (Gottschall 2010). Publicly provided health care comprises a core function of European welfare states. However, the state's role in financing and providing health-care services varies from country to country in unexpected ways. The British National Health Service (NHS) inflates employment levels in the public sector of this otherwise liberal market economy. By contrast, Germany's public sector covers a smaller percentage of the overall labor force, in part due to the mixed public and private organization of health-care delivery. German doctors may own their medical practices and may act as private employers (2), diverging from the fully government-run model in the UK. In Germany, doctors, mainly men, receive reimbursements for their expenses out of pooled health insurance contributions from employers and workers. This mixed system contrasts with the largely private-based insurance and medical practice in the US. The more expansive socialized health-care systems in both the UK and Sweden support the higher share of female labor force participation. By contrast, the larger, more extensive male-dominated state bureaucracy, along with French state-owned enterprises, tips the balance toward men's higher relative share of public-sector employment in both Germany and France (3).

Public versus Private Sectors

A comparison between public and private sectors' employment also highlights vertical sex segregation in authority structures. The state as employer offers more women professional positions managing the bureaucracy in the government. Not surprisingly, Swedish women fare particularly well in obtaining senior civil service (44% of the total) and public-sector management positions, as of 2009. The German state is less hospitable to women at higher levels of government: women held only 13% of senior civil service positions in 2009 (Gottschall 2010: slide 8). In France, women comprise 15% of senior public-sector management positions. France looks different from Germany, a country typically paired together with it as another social conservative welfare state. A more egalitarian civil service combines with a more male-dominated pinnacle of the state bureaucracy to characterize one difference between France and Germany (slide 8). This seeming paradox in France arises out of Republican rhetoric endorsing the pervasive role of the state in society, on the one hand, and the still heavily male-dominated composition of elite universities which channel students into upper levels of the state bureaucracy, on the other. Another side of Republicanism recalls the French Revolution, when men defined themselves as equal to each other, and different – by virtue of their bodies and sexual reproduction – from women, and used this politically created difference to reserve citizenship rights only to men and to restrict women's bodies for motherhood (Scott 1996). While, clearly, French women enjoy citizenship rights today, state-sponsored pronatalist ideologies linger in the service of French Republicanism.

A detailed picture of lagging female representation in positions of political power comes into view using a different set of indicators (see table 7.6). High-level positions in the government and in the Congress remain largely a boys' club in the US (14.3% women), more closely aligning with France (17.6%) than the three other liberal market economies. Conversely, a relatively high percentage of women have won elections to represent constituents in the Bundestag (parliament) and hold government positions in Germany (46.2%). The election of women to political office, however, as we will see later in this chapter, does not necessarily translate into feminist-oriented policy projects. Yet their relative share in the bureaucracy and in elected positions advances policies impacting on gender inequality, as suggested by Walby (2009a) and state feminist theorists (Stetson & Mazur 1995).

An examination of the private sector tells a different gender and class story, and puts it into comparative perspective. Leadership in private business favors women in France, Germany, and the UK more than in Sweden. Based on 2008 data from the four countries in the study, France ranks highest with a 40% female share of business leaders[4] while Sweden stands at the other end with 26%, Germany has 30.8%, and the UK has 33.4% (Gottschall 2010: slide 8). The private business world accommodates women more than the public sector in France (slide 8). Still, women are twice as likely to become members of the highest decision-making bodies of large companies in Sweden (27%, as compared to only 10% in France). Interestingly, management

Table 7.6 Women in political office, by welfare state clusters (2005)					
Welfare regime	Country	Women in government at ministerial and Cabinet level (% of 2005 total)	Legislators, senior officials, and managers (% female 1999–2005)	Professionals and technical workers (% female)	% seats filled in Lower or single House
Social democratic	Sweden	52	30	51	47
	Norway	44	30	50	38
	Finland	47	30	55	42
Liberal market	Australia	20	37	56	25
	Canada	23	36	56	21
	United Kingdom	29	34	47	20
	United States	14	42	56	16
Social conservative	France	18	37	47	19
	Belgium	21	32	49	35
	Germany	46	37	50	32
	Austria	35	27	49	32
	Netherlands	36	26	50	37
	Switzerland	14	8	22	30
	Italy[a]	8	32	46	17
	Spain	50	32	48	36
	Greece	6	26	49	16
	Portugal	17	34	50	21
Hybrid	Japan	13	10	46	9
Other	South Korea	6	8	39	13
	India	3	N/A	N/A	8
	China	6	17	52	20
	Costa Rica	25	25	40	39
	Chile	17	25	52	15
	Philippines	25	58	61	20
	Mexico	9	29	42	23
	UAE	6	8	25	23

[a] The shaded area indicates those Southern European countries sometimes clustered together as family-centered social conservative welfare states.

Source: Social Watch Gender Equity Index, 2007, figures rounded, www.socialwatch.org (downloaded, April 28, 2012)

hierarchies are more open to women in liberal market economies than in social conservative welfare states (see O'Connor et al. 1999; Orloff 2009). To explain why the figures in France and Sweden seem counterintuitive requires an understanding of state formation. Both countries qualify as statist welfare capitalisms, but operate according to different political principles for targeting economic intervention. The French state, with its strong President, chooses national champions and nationalizes industries run by men, and its male-dominated bureaucracy leaves little room for qualified women. Sweden's more expansive state sector absorbs women's employment with more opportunities for advancement. Clearly, the glass-ceiling effect is apparent across different types of welfare capitalisms, but this uneven pattern of women's integration into the labor market across public and private sectors does not align with either welfare-state types or varieties of capitalism.

Focusing on the state as employer enables Gottschall to disentangle gender from class inequalities in more state-centered versus more market-based service economies. A subgroup of highly qualified women benefits in the more open labor markets of liberal market economies. Women might profit from better chances of climbing the job-ladder in professional positions, lessening vertical sex segregation, but at the same time risk ending up as low-waged earners in the less-regulated, market-based service sector, accentuating horizontal sex segregation and class differences. In countries with a large public sector socializing reproduction, female workers gain economically from a more compressed wage structure. The public-sector wage structure tends to be more redistributive (Gottschall 2010: 6), in part because of stronger union presence than in the private sector, as will be discussed in the next chapter.

Different working-time schedules also lead to cross-national variation of the gender pay gap (Gottschall 2010). More full-time or longer part-time work for French and Swedish public-sector workers narrows the gender pay gap, while shorter part-time and mixed work schedules for women in the UK and Germany create larger earnings disparities (see Gottschall & Kroos 2007 for a detailed examination of Germany in relationship to France). Subcontracting and informalized employment relationships, whether in the public or private sector, are associated with negative economic consequences. Although the complex history of the French Revolution cannot be chronicled here, both the more egalitarian civil service and the high levels of full-time employment among women are rooted in the formation of the Republic, with a strong state struggling for its independence from the Church. The French state developed an infrastructure for social reproduction in order to encourage women to work outside the household and produce future citizens of the nation. At the same time, strong pro-natalist policies dovetailed with the state's attempt to consolidate its power over the Church. Socializing reproduction was a political means by which the French state could "liberate" society from the stronghold of the Church at the time.

This section focused on the state as employer structuring employment opportunities, labor market institutions, and economic outcomes. The state is a "model" employer associated with more compressed wage levels, but not uniformly for all women. Gottschall's study reveals why gendering institutional analysis of the state helps to explicate similarities and differences in women's integration in the paid labor force across countries. Comparative feminist perspectives must consider in more detail how state intervention affects the organization of social care, and the extent to which the state, through policy formation, promotes either familialism or women's employment, especially among mothers.

Social care policy in comparative perspective

A way to calibrate state support of maternal employment gauges the relative extent of "defamilialization" (Orloff 1993). Defamilializing policies make possible relatively high maternal employment levels and generate female employment by increasing demands for child-care services, ranging from publicly provided and subsidized care (service-intensive) in Nordic countries and France to more market-based care services and tax incentives (transfer-intensive) in the US and Canada. More specifically, policies that provide childcare for young children, and maternity and parental leave, allow mothers to maintain employment continuity (Gornick et al. 1998). In response to increasing female labor force participation, especially among mothers with young children, and changing norms about work and family, all industrialized countries have moved from some sort of maternity leave to either parental or family leave policy. Further, the focus on leave policy provides a lens to clarify how such policies both reflect social norms and/or perpetuate historical gender imbalances. A comparison between advanced capitalist countries' policies on parental and maternity leave underscores the tension between dual wage-earner and female care-giver reproductive bargains.

Balancing Work and Family: Parental Leave Policies

Parental leave and maternity leave programs play an important role in allowing women to take up employment on more equitable terms by guaranteeing income security when they must attend to care-giving. Haas (2004) compares 15 EU countries in terms of key policy features, including the length of leave, payment, flexibility, and incentives for fathers to share in childcare.[5] Maternal employment is higher in France, Belgium, and the Nordic countries due to an array of policies providing childcare, parental leave, leave compensation (income replacement levels), and job protections during leave (De Henau et al. 2010: 47). In countries where leave provisions are generous but other employment supports are not well developed, then maternity leave may reinforce the traditional division of labor and women's non-employment. Germany and Italy are two such cases. The most traditional countries, including Greece, Portugal, and Spain, offer the least generous parental leave without remuneration and with minimal protection of individual-based entitlement, associated with lower maternal employment. The liberal market economies of the UK and US both provide unpaid parental leave, but the UK differs in offering paid maternity leave, though income replacement remains relatively miserly. Neo-liberal ideology that limits government intervention, except in cases where the family fails, gives women few options in the US and the UK: women either exit from the labor force or reduce their hours in waged labor in the UK and remain in (often low-waged) work in the US.

A more detailed picture of the forces supporting or constraining maternal employment emerges from in-depth case studies. At one end of the spectrum is Sweden, retaining and strengthening universal, egalitarian principles despite neo-liberal pressures to privatize care services. Privatization of childcare has not abrogated public responsibilities – rather, private childcare is "publicly regulated and financed" in Sweden. The Swedish state, despite devolution of responsibility from the national to the municipal level, has spurred growth of high-quality childcare services (Bergqvist & Nyberg 2001). To ensure quality and more universal access, Sweden moved pre-school responsibilities from the Ministry of Health and Social Affairs to the Ministry of Education and Science in 1996 (2001). Even when the Swedish Social Democratic Party lost the election in 1976, their longevity in power created a "widespread political consensus" on the role of the state in family policies (Bolzonaro 2010: 595).

A major shift in policy debates among EU nations, as discussed by Haas, recognizes the need for incentives to encourage fathers' participation in caring labor. Sweden comes closest to an egalitarian society, supporting dual-wage earners, in that policies effectively provide male employees incentives to share in the care of young children. In Sweden the non-transferable entitlement for fathers has not only significantly increased men's use of the benefit, but also positively affected their time at work. The persistence of sex-based occupational segregation indicates trouble in Swedish feminist paradise because of the deeply entrenched gendered power relations resistant to policy innovation from above.

Many countries with social conservative welfare states provide care privately with little development of public services for the care of young children or general support to families with children (Gottfried & O'Reilly 2002; De Henau et al. 2010: 47). These familialistic welfare states, such as Japan, Taiwan, Germany, and Italy, produce inadequate social infrastructures for daycare and elderly care (Miyamoto 2009). The result has been more, yet inadequate, childcare facilities provided during hours unable to accommodate full-time work schedules for working parents. Social conservative Germany is a case in point. Germany "more readily gives direct financial assistance to those taking on the tasks of child or elder care in the family, rather then investing in an expansion of public social services" (Bird & Gottschall 2004). The public educational and dual vocational training systems that are unique to Germany also are important background conditions: the former because of the short hours and lack of aftercare programs, and the latter because of the gender bias in training toward men in manufacturing and devaluation of traditional women's work in service occupations. Constructing motherhood cohorts based on the birth of the first child, Gottschall and Bird measure the impact of the four important policy reforms ("mother allowance," maternity leave, family leave, and parental leave) on women's work choices and chances in Germany. The progression from mother allowance to family leave has had the effect of shoring up the male breadwinner, female-carer model, despite the diversification of family forms. On the positive side, family leave also contributes to increasing female labor force participation. Essentially, leave regulations have standardized a "baby break" among women. Further, Gottschall and Bird's analysis indicates a strong path-dependency to the development of regulation and, perhaps more critically, shows how changes in workplace policy can directly impact – for good or ill – leave-taking on the part of female and male employees.

Finally, an assessment of policies to balance work and family in Japan provides a case study in which entrenched social values clearly run counter to the application and use of leave and flexible working policies (Roberts 2004). A variety of dynamics are converging in Japan that portend changes in the work/life balance, particularly for women. Educated, younger women are putting off marriage, and the government is becoming increasingly concerned about declining birth rates, giving rise to various legislative initiatives to create "gender-equal" workplaces. Despite these trends, the societal value placed on corporate men supported by stay-at-home wives renders real change slow and marginal at best.

Wage-Earner and Care-Giver Models in the United States and Canada

A comparison of maternity and parental leave in the United States and Canada reveals differences between these contiguous liberal market welfare states, and indicates why the US has lagged behind other industrialized nations, both in the late timing of policy enactment and in the lack of remuneration, despite more recent attempts to shift financial resources from unemployment compensation to pay for family leave (Wisensale 2004). In the US, leave policies have developed incrementally in fits and starts over a long period. As far back as 1942 the US Women's Bureau recommended the establishment of maternity leave, but the initiative fell on deaf ears. In 1961 President John F. Kennedy established the President's Commission on the Status of Women and appointed Eleanor Roosevelt as chairwoman. The report issued by the Commission in 1963 documented substantial discrimination against women in the workplace and made specific recommendations for improvement, including fair hiring practices, paid maternity leave, and affordable childcare (www.factmonster. com). Consistent with the history of other labor standards, incremental policy innovations began with the framing of maternity leave in the language of anti-discrimination rather than as either an entitlement or a social right.

The Pregnancy Discrimination Act (PDA) of 1978 represented the first law prohibiting discrimination against pregnant women, reversing a 1976 Supreme Court case ruling that denial of benefits to pregnant women was *not* sex discrimination. The passage of the PDA mandated that employers who offered health insurance for temporary disability include coverage for pregnancy, childbirth, and other related medical conditions. Unable to expand employment rights to encompass maternity leave, the PDA instead equated pregnancy to a temporary disability, requiring that employers "treat a pregnant woman who can't perform her job due to a medical condition related to her pregnancy the same way [they treat] all temporarily disabled employees" (Rosenberg 2012). By treating pregnancy as a disability, the law excluded men and some women from the benefit. The framing of the law ensured that only women could receive the benefit and reduced motherhood to a bodily (dis)function. The law not only proscribed the benefit, but also extended it only to those women working for companies already providing health insurance to its employees.

Then, in 1987, the US Supreme Court case *Cal Fed* v. *Guerra* brought to light inconsistent provisions between, and the minimal coverage of, state and federal laws. A woman employed as a receptionist at California Federal Savings & Loan Association (Cal Fed) took a pregnancy disability leave in 1982, but, when she notified her employer that she was able to return to work, she was informed that her job had been filled and that there were no similar positions available.[6] At issue was the conflict between many state laws requiring that pregnant employees be treated in a special manner (sex differences) and the federal mandate that they be treated the same (gender-neutral) as other workers. When the US Supreme Court upheld California's maternity law providing for special benefits to pregnant women workers, liberal feminists argued for a gender-neutral policy, while radical feminists supported special treatment acknowledging gender differences. Both attacked the framing of pregnancy as a disability.

During Clinton's administration, both at the beginning and at the end of his term-of-office, a national leave policy took shape. After much debate and several failed efforts in Congress, Clinton's first piece of legislation signed into law established the Family and Medical Leave Act (FMLA) of 1993 (US Department of Labor 2010). The FMLA finally created a national standard, entitling employees in companies with 50 or more staff to take 12 weeks of unpaid leave to care for newborn children or sick relatives, or to deal with their own health problems.[7] Before leaving office, President Clinton issued an executive order allowing states to use unemployment compensation money for working parents to take time off to care for a newborn or an adopted child. Only the Massachusetts legislature approved the use of unemployment money for family leave, but the Republican Governor Mitt Romney vetoed the measure (Marquis 2002: A22). Two years later in 2002, President George W. Bush repealed Clinton's executive order, setting back this experiment in compensation for family leave (Marquis 2002). While a step forward, the FMLA does not offer income replacement for parents to care for children and dependent adults (Wisensale 2004). One small step taken by the California State legislature provided paid leave, yet the lack of remuneration elsewhere prevents many men and women from taking leave and burdens men and women with fewer resources to cushion time-off for the purpose of care-giving. The US federal system allows for significant variation among states in the quality and content of family leave regulations (Foote 2000: 158).

The US generally relies on the market to supply care, and the tax code as an indirect mechanism for support of care. In contrast to state-supported services in Sweden, tinkering with the tax code characterizes the US' indirect and transfer-intensive approach to care. Tax instruments, such as deductions, exemptions, and credits are the chief mechanisms through which families can save money to pay for dependent care. But tax deductions and credits tend to benefit the affluent rather than the middle class (Folbre 2001: 189). The poorest, owing no income tax, can apply for the Earned Income Tax Credit (EITC). However, the EITC phases out for those whose earned income passes the poverty-line (189). Some employers provide pre-tax flexible spending accounts for the purpose of paying for childcare. Otherwise, the only other support comes from income transfers to help the poorest women in need of childcare. None of these mechanisms directly supports building new childcare centers or provides direct childcare services. Further, the shift from federal funding to federal block grants after welfare reform in 1996 gave states the purview for public spending on childcare. As a result, spending varies from state to state and over time depending on economic conditions (189).

Childcare left principally to market forces often operates in a non-regulated environment and in mostly for-profit venues. For-profit childcare tends to yield a continuum of care services in accord with consumers' ability to pay leading, in many cases, to low-quality care for those with few financial resources and to low wages for childcare workers, and to high-quality, expensive care for those who can afford to pay additional costs (Folbre 2001). Minimal public subsidies for childcare and reliance on means-tested vouchers and tax deductions put the burden on individual women and families to buy private services or supply the services themselves. Unpaid family and parental leave similarly requires individuals to bear the financial burden of taking time-off. A market for services has created low-wage jobs for working-class women and freed professional women from many domestic chores and care tasks. In the US, labor regulations initially exempted domestic workers from legal mandates and later imposed thresholds effectively depriving many of benefits and rights.

Canada also belongs to the liberal cluster of welfare states, yet differs from the United States in significant ways. Trzcinski (2004) provides a historical assessment of Canadian workplace policies specifically focusing on a variety of leave programs – maternity, parental, and sickness – and highlights comparison with US approaches. In addition to providing a window on the Canadian policy approach to balancing breadwinning and care-giving, this study also specifically addresses the balance in cost between public and private wage replacement programs, and allays concerns that governmental wage replacement programs will be used to the exclusion of private programs with large attendant societal costs. Market responses are not sufficient to meet needs and/or demands for leave. Thus, even the more generous leave policies in Canada do not fully address the needs of female workers to create an optimal work and family balance.

Maternity, parental leave, and childcare policies affect the extent of support for balancing work and family life. It is clear that market solutions have prevailed over social benefits in the US to a greater extent than in most of the other nations examined. The research from Canada and European countries indicates more comprehensive and less market-driven care-giving policies. Most countries' policies implicitly exempt fathers from care or provide only minimal incentives for fathers to take leave. Income replacement certainly supports mothers in taking time off, but does not necessarily change the gender division of labor. In fact, mothers' labor force participation is high in both Scandinavian countries and the US, with radically different approaches to parental leave and social care. Poorly educated women's labor market position responds strongly to public policies, since they depend on access to maternity leave with high income replacement and affordable and accessible childcare (De Henau et al. 2010: 65). Parental leave, then, is most effective in support of maternal employment if buttressed by the availability of publicly supported childcare, especially among the poorest women (59).

A new emphasis on social care and the need for male and female workers to balance family and work-life is evident in the proliferation of policies on childcare, elder care, and leave schemes. As the comparisons highlight, the relative roles of the state, the market, the family, and civil society networks (Daly & Standing 2001: 3) shift the boundaries between public and private responsibility over time, and vary across countries. Welfare states have pursued policies for care but few have "promoted the capacity of men and women to engage in and share it" (10). Even where care has shifted to some extent to institutions other than the family, policies often do not attend to either the quality of care or the quality of care work (in terms of wages and benefits). Care work, especially in the private sector, often pays low wages and is undervalued. The quality of care work is associated with the quality of care services.

With the ascendance of neo-liberalism more generally, we can observe the shift of sites for the collective provision (Perrons 2007: 188) and the social organization of reproduction across and by families, markets, states, and civil societies (Orloff 2008). Neo-liberalism pushes states to relinquish responsibility for social reproduction, privatizing risks. As a result, women and households bear "increasing shares of the cost of reproduction of labor" (Pearson 2007). This shift intensifies the search for low-wage alternatives to perform reproductive labor, with female migrants picking up the slack in some cases. More intensely, liberal market economies' move toward workfare forces women to take up low-waged jobs, reducing workers' abilities to secure their own livelihood and that of their dependents (McDowell et al. 2005: 444).

Defamilializing policies positively affect female employment levels by enabling partners to better balance work and family life. A comparison between advanced capitalist countries' policies on parental and maternity leave underscores the tension between dual wage-earner and female care-giver reproductive bargains. Ironically, low-income women performing private care work are not able to secure care for their own children, intensifying unpaid work by relatives or other mothers at the bottom of the class structure and undermining efforts to get past female care-giving. The advent of defamilializing policies has left a positive imprint on female labor force participation. Clearly, more women have entered the paid labor force. Such policies do not necessarily address power relations either in the household or in the workplace. To examine the balance of power within the workplace, the next section discusses the example of sexual harassment and standards of gender equity.

Regulating sexual relations in the workplace and standards of equity

Equal opportunity and anti-discrimination policies were "a watershed in the history of welfare state egalitarianism" (Esping-Andersen 1999: 43). After the initial wave of civil rights legislation in the late 1960s US, legal interpretations extended standards of equity in the workplace. One legal area most directly targets sexual harassment as a form of discrimination against women. Sexual harassment policy addresses a uniquely problematic aspect of gender relations in the workplace because it operates at the intersection of public and private or social and workplace norms. Further, it is embedded in the most problematic of gendered relationships – sex. Studies show that success, implementation, and enforcement of sexual harassment policies have varied widely cross-nationally due to differences in legal systems and legal strategies. A comparison of sexual harassment policy in the US and Germany assesses a workplace policy that deals explicitly with the context of gender inequality and gendered power relations at work.

Sexual Harassment Policy in Germany and the US

The advent of sexual harassment policy came earlier in the US than in Germany, and through different legal channels. Sexual harassment and enforcement practices are embedded, respectively, in German labor law in the form of workers' protection regulations and civil rights law in the US (Zippel 2004). German labor law defines sexual harassment as "mobbing," recasting the issue in gender-neutral terms, emphasizing fairness and respect for all workers, and favoring workgroup or organizational cultural solutions to harassment. Because the approach in the US is legally and individually based, the policy focuses on individual behaviors, formal reporting, and often adversarial investigations, and ultimately punitive solutions. Further, in the US, the dynamics of implementation have emphasized individuals' legal redress, individual reporting, and lawsuits, which have affirmed employers' responsibilities to prevent sexual harassment by institutionalizing policies and educational programs. By contrast, because of the absence of strong anti-discrimination laws in Germany, the implementation of policies against sexual harassment depends on the political will of unions, employers, and emerging state equality offices for women – offices that are often stronger in the public sector (see Gottfried & O'Reilly 2002). Federal systems of government in both Germany and the US hamper implementation of sexual harassment laws enacted at the national level and must be implemented at the state level. Lenz (2004) notes the more progressive development of equal opportunity law in the federal state of Nordrhein Westfalen, with a long history of progressive politics. With their federal systems, both countries impede implementation because of tensions between state and national regulatory action. An examination of the origins of sexual harassment law can reveal the political sources and social forces contributing to policy variation across countries.

Different political opportunity structures have shaped whether sexual harassment law came mainly through changes in case law (US) or by the passage of new laws (Germany). The approaches to sexual harassment mirror the different ways that women's movements have pursued their agendas in the two countries (Young 1999). US women's groups have relied on the court for extending rights, whereas German women's groups have worked through organized political actors (political parties and unions) to affect social change. Thus, the courts have been an important mechanism for social action in the US, absent other political vehicles that exist in Germany and other European countries. The priorities and agenda of women's movements are influenced by political opportunity structures in different countries.

Legal systems also can significantly affect the implementation of policies relevant to the workplace. For example, large settlements, either through individual or class action suits are rare in Germany. The legal arena exerts less pressure on German employers to take action on issues such as sexual harassment and discrimination. Class action suits and settlements have been more successful in the US than in more collectively oriented countries like France or Germany (Mazur 1995). Such class action suits aggregate individual interests as a mechanism to foster substantive legal changes for the group. There is reason to believe that class actions will be less viable and harder to assemble in the future due to the ruling against the large size of the class claiming redress for wage discrimination at Walmart. Taking their cue from the US-style legal strategy, women's legal advocates bring suits against companies in Japan. Yet these widely publicized trials in Japan serve a symbolic function to shame companies and the state into addressing sexual harassment, more than an attempt to win large monetary rewards (Hirakawa 1998). Legal battles that can take ten years may end up with an apology as the final resolution in Japan.

A brief digression on certification of class actions in the US reveals the difficulty of pursuing legal strategies to address intersecting inequalities through the courts. Certification of a legal "class" for redress against discrimination is fraught by the court's power to define categorical boundaries. The courts certify a "class" on the basis of imputed shared interests among those in a social category. Drawing categorical boundaries has limited the remedial scope and the possibility of claims based on multiple disadvantages. In one case, the court refused to recognize the possibility of compound discrimination against Black women and analyzed their claims using the employment of White women as the historical base (Crenshaw 2000: 215). In another, the court arrived at a different conclusion. *Hughs Helicopter* v. *Moore* precluded Black women from using statistics to reflect disparate impact of the overall gender disparity in supervisory and upper labor jobs because Moore had not claimed discrimination as a woman, but "only" as a Black woman. The underlying assumption in the certification of Moore as the "class" was that she could not represent all women. Finally, another case ruled against Black women representing an entire class of blacks due to presumed conflicts in cases where sex additionally disadvantaged Black women (215–16). The court's refusal to allow the multiple disadvantages of Black women to represent others who may be singularly disadvantaged, such as White women or Black men forecloses the possibility of a "bottom-up" approach that would combine all those discriminated against to challenge the entire employment system (213). "As a result, Black women – the class of employees which, because of its intersectionality, is best able to challenge all forms of discrimination – are essentially isolated and often required to fend for themselves" (213).

The courts have been the chief mechanism for enforcing equal opportunities regulations and other civil rights provisions in the US.[8] An important turning point occurred in the middle of the twentieth century, when civil rights advocates discovered that litigation could become an effective tool for broad social change.[9] The landmark filing of *Brown* v. *Board of Education* in 1954 culminated in passage of the Civil Rights Act ten years later. The Civil Rights Act paved the way for further litigation by inviting plaintiffs to sue as a means of opening up the workplace to women and minorities (Eviatar 2002: 23). The more common recourse to legal remedies in the US than in Europe has been attributed to "the decentralized American system [which] forces Americans to take their problems to court," as compared to

Britain's and Germany's "centralized systems with powerful regulatory agencies to provide safeguards and with generous social welfare
benefits to cushion life's blows" (Burke cited in Eviatar 2002: 21).

The US stands out from other welfare states in the reliance on the
courts and on litigation based on interpretations of civil rights laws.
Within the purview of civil rights laws generally, and in sexual harassment cases particularly, gender and race are recognized categories for
redressing discrimination at work in the US. Multiple disadvantages,
however, are difficult to adjudicate in the current system. Germany
provides stronger labor protections for the group, but subsumes
gender policies under the rubric of workers' collective rights. As
a result, anti-discrimination law tends to be relatively weak in
Germany. By distinguishing the gender context of the legal systems in
Germany and the US, we see the significance of political opportunity
structures selecting and limiting the course of anti-discrimination
action.

Gender policy, politics and political institutions: comparative conclusions

The studies referenced in this chapter provide in-depth descriptions
of welfare state systems in particular countries over time, and help to
assess the relative weight of global, national, and sub-national forces
in explaining the presence or absence of particular policies, and
details their consequences for gender inequality. When read side-by-
side, the case studies here point to both convergence and divergence
with regard to policy sets across country clusters. Clearly there is a
general tendency toward path-dependency, indicating the resilience
of the nation state and national social values in shaping the policy
process. The attention to historically specific contexts helps gauge
why some policies are more resistant or open to negotiation, compromise, and change.

Revisiting the "three worlds of welfare" capitalism brings us back
to the importance of fine-tuning assessments of alternative typologies. Admittedly, the demarcation of liberal, conservative, and social
democratic is robust for indicating the broad contours of employment patterns as a function of economic and political relationships.
Most consistent with the three world perspective and various feminist alternatives is an array of countries along a continuum. At one
end is the US, paradigmatic of liberal (and neo-liberal) capitalism,
basing the provision of health care and childcare principally on the
market, and creating the sharpest class inequalities for access to these
services. At the other end, social democratic welfare states are more

family-friendly and supportive of the balancing of waged work and family responsibilities. However, data presented in this chapter do not correspond to a one-to-one mapping of welfare state types and gender stratification in the labor market. Feminist political economy revises class-based varieties of welfare capitalism to correct for their neglect of gender power relations, and goes beyond the narrow focus on the job in work sociology. Feminist-informed typologies gendering institutional analyses more readily produce an understanding of the dynamic relationship between the state, family, civil society, and economy which leads to meaningful differences that explain gender and class inequalities across countries.

Feminist political economy systematically incorporates the organization of social reproduction normally left out of welfare state models, shedding light on public and private forms of power within and across different institutional arenas. More specifically, the type of welfare state and its reproductive bargain shapes gender relations either by socializing costs of reproduction or by ceding the delivery of care and social services to the family, non-profit organizations, or the marketplace. In this way, the state's role varies from minimal support of care to delivering care primarily through services directly, via third-party arrangements (public subsidies), or through transfer payments (taxes and welfare benefits). The extent of state support for care bears on both the quality and quantity of services, and on the quality of employment. If left either to the family or to the market, care and reproductive labor receive no or little remuneration. A comparison between advanced capitalist countries' policies on parental and maternity leave underscores the tension between dual wage-earner and female care-giver reproductive bargains. The welfare state consists of more than a set of policy prescriptions and income transfers – it also plays a significant role as an employer in the new economy. More compressed wage differentials and more generous benefits characterize employment in the state sector relative to private-sector services, thereby improving gender-based disparities and inequalities.

Theories of state feminism take us inside the policymaking process to get a closer look at the political machinery transforming feminist ideas into women-friendly policies. Through defamilializing policies, the state positively affects female employment levels by enabling partners to better balance work and family life. The countries enacting strong defamilializing policies do not always fit the expected patterns. Low female representation among political office-holders and weak state feminism can co-exist with strong state-centered social infrastructure for care, as in France. In addition, comparative policy analysis of seemingly gender-neutral workplace policies, such as the minimum wage and tax policies, would be well served by "mainstreaming" gender into the analysis of alternative policy options and attendant policy outcomes. Such policies often affect women more than men because of gender-based hierarchies and the concentration of women in low-waged jobs. These types of policies, while not explicitly tied to gender, have differential effects on male and female workers and, without a consideration of such effects, policy research will be missing important potential externalities, opportunity costs, and inequities in impact and outcome. While there may be heuristic value in differentiating between policy types, the analysis of gender policy should be drawn broadly and not ghettoized. For example, the political backlash against policies like affirmative action, particularly in the US, has significant potential effects on gender as well as racial balance in the workplace. Along the same lines, there are a number of other feminist-inspired issues, such as domestic violence and reproductive rights (abortion, access to contraceptives, family planning, and side-effects of contraceptives) that have significant impacts on women and their ability to work. Violence such as sexual harassment disrupts bodily security, which disables women from full participation economically and politically. Sexual harassment laws can change the balance of power within the workplace. However, the effectiveness of this and other policy initiatives depends on the legal systems and reproductive bargains in place, and on political pressures from organized interest groups.

Reference to the reproductive bargain and gender regime points to the role political representation plays in negotiating and possibly renegotiating gender arrangements. Women's political participation and mobilization, either through autonomous movements or within larger organizations (such as unions) and political parties, affect the type, locus, and effectiveness of policy. Employment relations systems both reflect and determine the likelihood of different groups of workers belonging to a union, which in turn has gender and class effects depending on the institutional forms and regulatory norms established in a country. Turning to the history of labor organizing in the next chapter, we can determine why some countries have enacted policies extending workers' rights, as well as women's rights as workers, and others have not.

More broadly, this chapter focused on the state as both a political institution and an economic sector. Understanding the winds and whims of politics is notoriously difficult – like accurately reading tea leaves. However, the feminist political economic framework introduces gender regimes, reproductive bargains, and inequality regimes to conceptualize intersecting power relations in varieties of capitalism. The role of the state in perpetuating patriarchal gender relations escapes notice in class-based typologies. Feminists not only insist on bringing the family into the constellation of institutions, but also argue that analysis of work and economy must integrate both public and private forms of gender power relationship within and between state, family, civil society, and economy. So-called "private" forms of power, when viewed through a feminist lens, magnify the importance of bodies, violence, and sexuality as central to male dominance and the expression of hegemonic masculinity. It may seem far-fetched to blame the state for these more intimate interactions and orientations, or to situate them in the economy at all. How, if, and when the state intervenes severely constrain the deployment of labor power in the economy. In this sense, the state helps to pick winners and losers in the casino of capitalism.

Both this and the next chapter focus on institutions at the national level, and thus might leave the impression that other scales, such as the local, the regional, and the global, are less important. The analysis of welfare states in this chapter necessarily limits the investigation to the most advanced capitalist countries. Part III moves from the national to the global to pick up the new storyline concerning globalization of migration and transnational care chains traversing, and creating, new global spaces of production and reproduction. In the final section of the book, the chapters underscore that nation states are not political containers of economic processes, and that policy formation, political institutions, and political mobilization increasingly cross national borders. From the perspective of geographies of power, the book ends with an account of globalization transforming economic conditions in the household, in global cities, and in regional political assemblages.

CHAPTER 8

Terrains of Struggle: Gender, Work, and Labor Organizing

As the US economy slipped into recession on the cusp of the new millennium, the iconic symbols of Fordism faltered on the edge of bankruptcy – General Motors, Chrysler, and Ford, the titans of the automobile industry hemorrhaged cash and shuttered more factories, adding to the ruins of Detroit and its environs. Old industrial unions, most prominently the United Automobile Workers Union (UAW), saw their membership shrink, putting their future, and the labor movement's, at risk. In the wake of this massive restructuring, many working-class jobs providing a living wage disappeared. Invoking the UAW recalls the institutional legacy of a central actor in establishing the post-war employment relations system in the US. The institutional rules governing employment relations and the organizational forms of unions set the historical backdrop against which women have joined unions and increased their gender representation throughout the twentieth century and into the twenty-first. Gender representation means more than increasing female composition of union membership, and leadership of labor organizations. It also informs how gender becomes the basis for forging solidarities and identities, strategies, goals, and associational forms, with their potential to advance claims for gender justice.

This chapter begins with a discussion of the underlying logics of collective action in a capitalist society. Two logics of collective action describe power differences between labor and capital, and workers' rationale for organizing unions to promote their collective economic interests and to gain associational power. Why women have been under-represented in unions for most of the twentieth century requires a feminist lens for analyzing terrains of struggle. The chapter examines institutionalized employment relations systems in comparative perspective and finds a common pattern of industrial unions primarily organizing male workers centered in large-scale manufacturing, from sprawling automobile assembly plants to belching-smoke-stacked steel-making complexes. Through an in-depth comparison of the US and Japan, the chapter details how unions' policies and practices shaped possibilities for women's self-organization, either within the larger framework of trade unions or in separate women's and feminist organizations. The feminist political economic perspective, adopted here, shows that looking beyond the usual industrial cases reveals patterns of female union membership and new forms of labor organizing among woman across different welfare states as well as in global cities.

Two logics of collective action

In a general sense, the class structure creates reasons for workers to organize and join unions (Wright 2000b). Unions are "an organizational structure of social relations among workers consciously directed toward the realization of immediate economic interests" (Wright 1978: 101). Yet unions have more consistently aggregated the interests of working-class men in mines, mills, and manufacturing than those of women in offices and services. While women have made in-roads, closing the gender gap in union membership in most capitalist countries, men and women still largely inhabit different worlds of trade unions because of occupational segregation and economic segmentation. Gender intersects with class in ways that complicate collective action, and mediates whether and how women participate in traditional labor organizations and movements (Gottfried 1992: 99). An examination of two logics of collective action identifies workers' economic interest in organizing and forming unions. Given this interest, we must ask what barriers have limited labor organizing and what conditions enhance or diminish workers' capacities to pursue their collective interests through union organizations?

Class and Logics of Collective Action

By virtue of workers' subordinate positions in the social structure they must engage in collective action in order to change the class system of inequality. Such structural asymmetry between capital and labor corresponds to two logics of collective action, a theoretical proposition specifying how structural power organizes capital's advantages in relationship to workers at a disadvantage in the class structure (Offe & Wiesenthal 1980). Power derives from position in the social structure: controlling access to economic resources privileges forms of capital, including physical plant, financial and cultural assets, and knowledge. Each side of the class divide pursues different logics of collective

action derived from their social location. On the one side, the capitalist class are only partially dependent on the supply of labor; they can
introduce labor-saving devices and release themselves partially from
this dependence. Corporations' decision-making power to hire and
fire individual workers complements their structural power in society.
For example, a corporation's implicit or explicit threat of downsizing
and plant-closure can devastate a community relying on jobs for its
residents and revenue streams to fill local government coffers. Under
these conditions, workers may make concessions to save their jobs. On
the other side, workers cannot release themselves from their dependency on capitalists' willingness to employ them. Since workers cannot
merge like capital, they must associate to partly compensate for the
structural power advantage of capital. In the absence of associational
efforts on the part of workers, via unions or other organizational
vehicles, individual workers have little bargaining power to change
working conditions and address more deep-seated social inequalities.
Labor must engage in dialogic exchanges in order to forge a collective
identity to realize associational power.

Gender and New Forms of Associational Power

The transformation to a more service-oriented and knowledge-intensive economy alters the primary terrains of production, creates the
possibility of establishing new bases of identity and solidarity, and
prompts workers to develop new organizational strategies for representing the varied interests of an increasingly diverse labor force.
Going on strike, the main weapon in the union's arsenal, disrupts
the flow of traditional capitalist production. The shift to service-dominated economies and commodification of care changes employment
relationships, and affects opportunity structures for mobilization in
particular places and around the nexus of working life, well-being,
and care issues. In particular, the possibility of disrupting consumption lends service workers their "associational power" and creates
employers' vulnerability (Otis 2012: 162). Service workers can inflict
damage by tarnishing an employer's brand or reputation, by using
rhetorical and other discursive strategies besides resorting to strikes,
or by withholding labor power – all tools honed in the crucible of
industrial capitalism. A labor organization may draw distinctions
to reveal gaping disparities between consumers and producers of
services, whether at a luxury hotel (Otis 2012), at an elite university
(Nussbaum 2007), or in a household (Ehrenreich 2010). Ruining a
reputation through collective pressure and shaming practices may
be more effective than withholding labor through the traditional
channel of going on strike[1] – a last-resort strategy, especially among

low-waged workers who are easily replaceable. What makes union organizing different in this economic environment relates to the distinctive gender-based quality of the labor extracted in the service encounter. Unions, primarily representing women workers, can draw on the ethos of care to highlight the way that working conditions affect the quality of the care delivered in a variety of feminized services. Workers may enlist their patients, clients, and constituents in the push for better services as they confront employers. Organizational strategies are gendered not only because they largely involve women who work in these sectors of the economy, but also because a caring ethos is deployed as a rhetorical resource for realizing associational power.

Conflict and discontent are part of the social system supplying the logic of collective action. Before workers can act, however, the group must consciously recognize the need and possibility for change and have the capacity to mobilize. Capacity depends on structuring opportunities and resources available for mobilization. Structuring opportunities can range from the socio-spatial congregation of workers on the assembly-line in factories to the meeting of childcare workers in city parks and laundromats. Yet the most aggrieved or poorest workers may not be among the most active in a labor movement because they lack associational and other resources for collective action. Dispersed in individual homes or concentrated in small workplaces, low-waged service workers are the most in need of unions and the least likely to belong to them. Workers' capacities to engage in collective action both determine and reflect institutional histories of employment relations and models of unionization.

Employment relations and industrial unions in comparative perspective

While the institutional histories of collective action cannot be chronicled in-depth here (see Gottfried 2000), a comparison of employment relations systems can uncover reasons for the under-representation of women in the rank-and-file, as well as among the leadership, of traditional unions. It is now fashionable for scholars and academic programs to abandon the nomenclature of "industrial relations" in favor of the alternative terminology of "employment relations," because the former too narrowly reflects the old Fordist economy based on mass production and the latter more broadly delimits the full range of occupations and industries in the new economy. In the same spirit, I use "employment relations" to designate the institutional relationships between labor and capital in national contexts. What Beverly

Silver (2005) calls the "organizational residue" of unions, born in the big bang of capitalist consolidation and subsequent institution-alization of employment relations, bound trade unions to industries located in the modern nation state as the principal arena for collective bargaining and for the establishment of labor regulations. Through a comparative perspective, we can identify how different employment relations systems initially disadvantaged women in industrial unions, and anticipate services as new terrains for organizing.

Gender Representation in the First Unions

Labor organizing flourished in the latter years of the nineteenth century and into the twentieth. Marx presciently observed the advent of large-scale manufacture's reliance on a "socialized" labor process predicated on "co-operation" (1976: 1024), creating conditions for the associated producers to take over production. Marx states that: "Under capitalism labor should not be seen as labor only but as the combined or collective labor of all those whose labor is indispensa-ble to produce the final product" (1019). Initially, unions organized workers in a trade rather than in an industry. Industrial unionism grew up in response to, and enabled by, the new mode of mass pro-duction. The origins of industrial unions date to the 1930s when the rise of Fordist mass production dominated the economic landscape. Though Gramsci did not differentiate gender from class analysis, his essay on "American Fordism" proclaimed the birth of hegemony in the factory (Gramsci 1971: 285) that taught a "puritanical ethic" (303), which subjected workers to rigorous discipline, instilled new habits (298), strengthened a nuclear form of family (300), and regulated sexual "instincts" (295–8).[2] Fordism was a new mode of production that interconnected legions of male workers along an assembly-line for mass production of branded products. As a new organizational form at the time, workers established industrial unions, often after pitched battles with security on the companies' payroll or with the local police force. Fordism both enabled unions to flourish and provided police to break strikes. In the golden age of Fordism, the state took on a new role in employment relations by legally rec-ognizing workers' right to join unions and to engage in collective bargaining.

Successive waves of collective bargaining and the formalization of bargaining relationships institutionalized a reproductive bargain (Gottfried 2000). To varying degrees, this reproductive bargain was based on the male breadwinner norm and its implicit masculine embodiment of non-responsibility for human reproduction. But the male breadwinner ideology was a largely unacknowledged legacy of many traditional trade unions, as "working class men in the factories forged solidarity around laboring ... as the key constituent of masculine identity and common interests seemed clear" (McDowell 2008: 21). Craft and industrial unions came to represent a community of interest among unmarked male workers in similar trades or industries. Even the mandatory issues of collective bargaining were narrowly focused on wages and working conditions. Women joined unions, though typically in different sectors because of segregation and economic segmentation. As a result, their membership and influence lagged behind men's for much of the twentieth century.

A similar history played out in most advanced capitalist countries. However, those countries manifest different types of employment relations systems. They range from tightly coordinated and institutionalized bargaining between representatives of labor and employers (corporatism) at the meso-level of industrial branches in Germany and at the micro-level of enterprises in Japan, to more decentralized forms of bargaining in the United States and in the United Kingdom (see table 8.1). Such institutional features and arrangements of employment relations systems reflect different organizing strategies and opportunity structures that influence the openness to organizing women. As Suzuki (2004) suggests, "the extent to which labor unions are embedded in employment relations institutions forms the background for organizing strategies of labor unions" and informs different receptions to the organization of women workers. Unions embedded in employment relations institutions tend to be more "conservative and *not* strongly committed to organizing beyond unions' 'traditional' membership base (i.e., male blue collar workers)" (emphasis added). Indeed, corporatism institutionalized bargaining relationships between organized male workers and capital, often to the exclusion of women's participation. Even though Germany exhibits high union density compared to Japan, embeddedness of unions in employment relations institutions produces low relative union membership among women in both of these two coordinated capitalist economies. By contrast, "unions try to increase their membership by mobilizing rank-and-file members and activists, when their leaders perceive labor unions as a part of social movements rather than as actors in institutionalized socio-economic systems" (5–6). The gender composition of unions is more equal in liberal market economies, though overall union density tends to be low. Unions everywhere adopting this mobilization model, or dialogic communicative practices, have been more successful recruiting women and representing women-friendly issues. Gender representation, consequently, varies in and is shaped by different institutionalized employment systems in particular historical conjunctures.

Table 8.1 National comparisons of labor market regulations and class-based employment regimes

	US	UK	Germany	Japan
Production regime[a] Production system[b]	Uncoordinated Low skill, numerically flexible	Uncoordinated	Industry- coordinated Diversely qualified	Group-coordinated Flexible specialization
Unfair dismissal				
Standard jobs	Weak	Moderate	Strong	Strong
Non-standard jobs	Weak	Moderate	Moderate	Moderate to weak
Institutionalization of industrial relations				
Extent of interaction	Decentralized	Medium	Dual-level	Decentralized
Wage-setting	Firm/pattern	N/A	Industry/plant	Enterprise,
Power of labor	Low/weak	Moderate	High to moderate	coordinate
Intensity of labor/ capital	Bi-lateralism	Tri-partitism	Meso-corporatism	Low/weak Micro-corporatism
Union density				
% of all workers	13.4[d]	29.1[f]	32.2[k]	20.7[n]
% of male workers	15.0	29.0[g]	31.0[l]	23.2[o]
% of female workers	11.6	28.0[h]	17.7	12.4
Full-time	14.7	32.0[i]	N/A	N/A
Part-time	6.8	20.0	N/A	2.7[p]
% female share[c]	44.0[e]	50.0[j]	31.0[m]	17.0[q]
Training system	General education	General education	Vocational[r]	Firm-based, in-house

a. Huber & Stephens (2000: 113).
b. Ebbinghaus and Manow's summary of varieties of capitalism features in their table 1.1 (2001a: 1–24).
c. Walby (2007: 28).
d. 2001, members in union, News, US Bureau of Labor Statistics, www.bls.gov/news.release/union2.t01.htm (downloaded February 2, 2008).
e. Calculated from data in *Monthly Labor Review* 2004 (cited Walby 2007: 49).
f. 2001 numbers (Brook 2002: 343).
g. This is down from 42% in 1991 (Brook 2002: 343).
h. This is down from 32% in 1991 (Brook 2002: 343).
i. Brook (2002: 346).
j. From Hicks & Palmer 2004 (cited in Walby 2007: 49).
k. Japan Institute of Labor, Trade Union Density Rate (2003), www.jil.go.jp/estatis/eshuyo/200301/e0702.htm (downloaded March 3, 2004).
l. For West Germany only; union membership for East Germany declined from 39.7% in 1992 to 18.5% in 2000; East German women saw their union membership drop precipitously from 43.5% in 1992 to 16.1% in 2000 (Schnabel & Wagner 2003: 213).
m. European Industrial Relations Observatory On-line 2004, data for 2003 (cited in Walby 2007: 49).
n. Basic Survey on Labour Unions, Statistics and Information Department, Ministry of Health, Labour and Welfare, March 2002.
o. These 2006 statistics are based on a presentation given by the Director of the Gender Equality Office of RENGO in March 2007.
p. The 2001 estimate for unionization rate of short-term workers, defined as working less than 35 hours (Japan Institute of Labor 2002: table 2).
q. 1997 data from Broadbent 2005 (cited in Walby 2007: 49).
r. Long-tenure, low turnover for dual training; school based vocational training with less well described career paths and higher turnover in some low paid feminized occupations (Krüger, 1999).

Gender Representation in Unions: From the 1960s to the 1980s

The 1960s marked the most propitious era for narrowing the gender gap as a result of new unions mobilizing workers in the burgeoning public sector. Public-sector unions now account for the lion's share of women's overall union membership in all welfare states. More specifically, the welfare state as an employer has been more inclined to recognize trade unions as bargaining partners, and more hospitable to hiring women workers (as discussed in chapter 7). Getting union recognition often involves taking members' concerns to the street to rally favorable public opinion. More than in the private sector, workers seeking to form unions leverage political symbols for their cause. Reception to these demands among women depends on the nature of the union's partisan politics, of the existing body politic, and of the government in power. Although not always, conservative local or national administrations are less receptive than left-leaning parties to unions' collective bargaining demands and even challenge their right to negotiate on a variety of issues, as evident in Wisconsin during the 2011 budget battles in that state. Nonetheless, unionization increased in the public sector overall and among women during the period of welfare state expansion.

The same forces contributing to the expansion of the welfare state make the public sector more open to union recognition. Throughout the 1960s and 1970s, welfare state expansion absorbed much of the rise in women's labor force participation and accounted for most of their subsequent unionization. Most dramatically, Swedish women's unionization surged by 90% from 1970 to 1980, due to the significant growth of women's employment (87%) in public sector jobs encompassing health, education and social services (Curtin 1999: 13). Similarly, through their participation in public-sector unions, women nearly achieved parity with men's overall union membership in the UK and in Canada, but later than in Sweden (Walby 2007: 27). While low by international standards, women exhibit higher public-sector union membership than private-sector unionism both in Japan and in the US, where overall union density remains relatively low in comparison to other welfare states (see table 8.1). More specifically, US public-sector union membership rose during the 1960s and 1970s, peaking in the early 1980s, as the decade ended with close to two-fifths of all government workers belonging to unions (Cobble 2007). Size of the public sector is one predictor of women's union membership, and accounts for some of its variation cross-nationally.

Women's employment opportunities and their overall union membership are affected by the type of the welfare state and its level of socialized reproduction. Socialized reproduction reflects the negotiated bargain regarding the role of the state vis-à-vis the economy and the family. The socialized health-care system accounts for higher trade union density in the UK than either the market-based system in the US or the mixed private and public system in Germany (Gottschall 2010) – even though trade union coverage reaches relatively high levels among men in Germany and lower levels in the US (Walby 2007: 28). In the UK, women constitute half of all trade union members largely because of their high representation in public-sector unions, most prominently in health care; nurses are government employees of the National Health Service (Walby 2007: 28). When negotiating with the government, unions can leverage public sentiments regarding state responsibility for providing necessary services and collective goods to citizens. Appeal to the caring ethos becomes a discursive resource used for the purpose of union recognition and collective bargaining among women workers.

Additionally, a union's policies and politics toward gender inclusiveness impact levels of union membership and leadership among women. In this respect, the labor movement has an uneven history of developing policies for promoting women's leadership. The historical legacies of unions' egalitarian commitment toward solidaristic politics must be taken into account to explain variation across countries. Unions' militancy and co-determination with the state kept non-standard employment at a relatively low level for French women in the public sector (Kroos & Gottschall 2012). Labor confederations with explicit policies for increasing women's leadership, either through reserved seats or quotas, have higher rates of female representation in top positions. For example, a comparative study conducted by Jennifer Curtin (1999) found that, as of 1993, women accounted for 30% of top positions in Italy, with its quota system, and 31% in the UK, with its system of reserved seats. Despite their high union density, Swedish women trade unionists fared less well than their counterparts in Italy and the UK. Without a specific strategy for increasing women's leadership either in the LO (the blue-collar federation) or in the TCO (the white-collar federation), Swedish women's leadership grew modestly to 13% and 20% in each federation, respectively (Curtin 1999: 13). By contrast, few women have attained top leadership positions in the larger labor confederations in the US (9% in the American Federation of Labor and Congress of Industrial Organizations [AFL-CIO]) or in Japan. At the time, neither of the largest union federations pursued active policies of inclusion. It wasn't until 2005, with the formation of Change to Win, the 5.5-million-member rival to the AFL-CIO, that Anna Burger became the first woman to head a union federation in the US (Hananel 2010).[3] More generally, as Curtin's study suggests, affirmative action policies implemented by unions boost women's leadership in unions.

Initially, unions formed by male workers in the trades and industry negotiated expanded rights for male industrial citizens. Gender representation varied within the union movement more generally, as well as across countries. In most countries, women gained a presence in unions, particularly in the public sector during the period of welfare state expansion, yet remain under-represented in traditional unions. Employment relations systems create different opportunity structures for gender representation. Behind the increasing representation of women is the reality of segregation of men and women in "two worlds" of trade unions (Milkman 2007).

Gender representation: two worlds of trade unions

Most notably, women and men largely belong to different unions, occupying, as Ruth Milkman (2007) aptly calls them, "Two worlds of trade unions." Two worlds of trade unions is a way to describe gender segregation in unions. A typical male union member is a blue-collar worker in the private sector, whereas a female union member typically is a white-collar or professional worker in the public sector. Union membership among men and women is a function of occupational segregation, economic segmentation, and employment relations systems. A comparison between the US and Japan provides a more detailed understanding of nationally based economic and political factors giving rise to differences of gender representation in unions. The US as a liberal market welfare state and Japan as a hybrid welfare system, and both with decentralized employment relations systems, share similar legal challenges, and structural barriers to unionization more generally.

Gender Representation and Trade Unions in the US: "Two Worlds of Trade Unions"

The increasing presence of women in unions reflects the changing economic structure and political climate as well as personal preferences favorable toward unions. In the US, narrowing of the gender gap brings a larger share of women into the rank-and-file of unions. Gender equity in part is a statistical artifact of declining union membership among men. During the 1980s and 1990s (and even earlier), US unions experienced waning membership and loss of political and bargaining power as large manufacturing companies restructured by closing plants, relocating off-shore, and down-sizing workforces (Suzuki 2004). In 1983, 25% of men, as compared to 15% of women, belonged to a union. Men's 10-percentage-point advantage

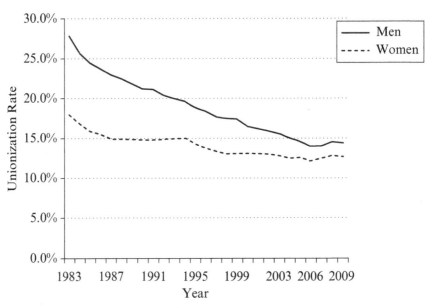

Source: United States Department of Labor (2010: 91).

Figure 8.1 The declining gender gap in unionization rates, United States (1983–2009)

dissipated over the next two decades, as their union membership fell by 50% while women's union membership dropped by 30% (Milkman 2007). As of 2009, approximately 14.7% of men and 12.7% of women belonged to unions. Given these trends, women's increased union membership must be seen against this background of men's diminishing membership (see figure 8.1). Even though union membership among women and men is statistically near parity, the labor movement remains segregated in two worlds of trade unions. In the US, female union membership is concentrated in three industry groups: education, health care and public administration, accounting for 70.9% of women's union membership and 39.2% of the female wage and salary workforce (2007). Milkman fills in the historical factors and sociological reasons why the two worlds of trade unions emerged.

Perhaps the single most cited factor shaping distinct gender regimes of individual unions is the gender composition of membership, which is highly variable because of persistent occupational and industrial sex segregation (Milkman 2007). Moreover, the gender composition of a union significantly affects the likelihood of women occupying leadership positions. Some unions with relatively high levels of female membership, such as the Communication Workers of America, the United Food and Commercial Workers, and unions in the textile and garment industries established in the 1910s, have low levels of female leadership due to a paternalistic, top-down male organizing style (2007). Women's leadership, like their membership, reaches higher levels in public-sector unions, among the few unions that experienced growth over the past few decades (Cobble 2007). So, partly as a result of this union growth, there are more leadership positions opening up in the public sector.

A short history documents the changing gender representation in US trade unions. Union membership is not simply a function of either individual preferences or ideological orientations toward the merit of unions. Milkman (2007: 76) makes the important point that

> unevenness of unionization is an artifact of the US employment rela-
> tions system, which since 1935 has not been based on individual deci-
> sions about union affiliation, but instead on a winner-take-all electoral
> process that leads to unionization (or not) of entire workplaces. Given
> limited organizing, in most cases the main determinant of whether a
> given individual is a union member is where she or he happened to be
> employed and whether the workplace became (and remained) union-
> ized at some previous time.

Further, white-collar unionism remains low in the US because labor law denies basic collective bargaining rights to employees categorized as managerial and supervisory, regardless of whether or not they exercise actual discretion over decision-making. Women, who are more likely than men to occupy such positions at the lower rungs of management and supervisory ladders, are legally ineligible for union membership even though they could benefit from union representation (Cobble 2007). In the hands of corporations, such restrictions on legal recognition of unions can lead to reclassification of workers out of possible bargaining units. This indeed occurred in the mid-1970s when the former telecommunications monopoly, ATT, promoted female operators to first-line management positions – after a consent decree directed the company to address statistical discrimination following a class action suit. Classifying some female telephone operators in management stripped them of their right to remain members of the Communication Workers of America. Precautionary measures in the event of a strike more easily slotted these former telephone operators into their former jobs. Telephone operators among the first-line management profited from their promotion, receiving higher pay, but also benefitted from the union's presence. Though no longer members, managers' compensation packages tended to rise, with increases advanced through collective bargaining agreements. So, unequal gender representation partly is the result of a legal framework that defines eligibility criteria based on occupation and employment status.

Another challenge derives from the US legal framework channeling workers' rights on a two-track system: union organizing and collective bargaining are covered under New Deal labor legislation and anti-discrimination falls under Civil Rights law (Crain 2007). Although not always at odds, unions on the one side and women's and civil rights movements on the other have split loyalties, with the former more narrowly defining workplace issues through (male) industrial citizenship and the latter advocating for a broader conception of civil rights (e.g. affirmative action) in and beyond the workplace. From the mid-1950s onward, industrial citizenship expanded rights principally at the bargaining table (Burawoy 1985), while women's and civil rights organizations accomplished gains in the legal arena through legislative action and litigation.

Legal impediments aside, new unions originating in the late 1960s and 1970s, at a time when women became a more substantial part of the waged workforce and when notions of gender equality were more widely accepted, tend to be more women-friendly (Milkman 2007). Despite an often troubled history of recognizing gay rights and an uneven record on dealing with sexual politics, there has been greater receptiveness to women and sexual minorities by public-sector unions, which came into being during the ferment of the 1960s and 1970s social movements (Hunt & Boris 2007), coinciding with the second major expansion of the welfare state, the first being in Franklin Delano Roosevelt's time. More specifically, workers' organizations that are consciously committed to nurturing women's leadership and to internal democracy, such as 9to5 (Nussbaum 2007), the Harvard Union of Clerical and Technical Workers (Firestein 2007; Savage 2007), and Yale's clerical union (Gilpin 1988) register greater success organizing women in unions than do traditional unions (Milkman 2007). Clerical unions at Harvard and Yale mixed creative strategies to mobilize collective action, including one-to-one personal contacts to empower women and engaged in less hierarchical and bureaucratic organizing styles. In We Can't Eat Prestige, John Hoerr narrates the lively strategies leading to unionization of the largely female clerical workforce at Harvard University. Both the Harvard and Yale campaigns exposed the disparity between the elite status of the university and the gender and race inequities within it. Feminist activists and feminist principles influenced and informed unions' political commitments aimed at gender equity and gender equality.

The two worlds of trade unions reflect both the internal policies regarding democracy and the segregation of men's and women's work and employment in different spheres of public and private sectors in the US. Public-sector unionization, along with men's declining unionization, accounts for most of the increase in women's relative share of union membership in the US. The public sector was one of the few bright spots for union growth during the last few decades of the twentieth century. Because of the relatively small public sector and larger privatized service provision rooted in principles of the liberal market, union density remains low overall and among women in the US.

Gender Representation and Trade Unions in Japan: Different Worlds of Trade Unions

Different worlds of trade unions appear even more starkly in Japan. Gender differences in union membership partly reflect horizontal gender segregation, whereby women are concentrated in service occupations and in smaller manufacturing firms with low union rates and without a history of strong union presence. Unionization rates correlate with size of company, varying from a high of 54.2% for 1,000 or more employees to 16.8% for 100–999, and a low of 1.3% for those in firms with less than 99 employees, in 2002 (Araki 2002: 164). The corresponding numbers in 2006 ranged from 47.7% of workers in the largest firms to 15.0% among workers in middle-sized firms, and 1.2% among those in small firms. As the 2006 figures suggest, downsizing by large enterprises had the impact of reducing union density even further (Japan Institute for Labor Policy and Training 2010: 71). Women's low union membership is rooted in the structure of the labor market and the employment relations system. The coordinated intermediation between labor and employers in large Japanese corporations resulted in the negotiation of a reproductive bargain tying benefits to employment status at the enterprise level, and generating strict employment regulations over unfair dismissal that protected male workers. Corporate-centered welfare and industrial regulation left a patchwork of residual policies over work conditions at the national level (Gottfried 2009). What had been strength as long as the economy was expanding in the 1960s and 1970s turned into weakness for workers and their unions, tied to the fate of particular firms, when the Japanese economy entered the lost decade of the 1990s. Unions' membership declined overall and the two worlds of trade unions continued to characterize the Japanese employment relations system and organized labor.

Japan's employment relations system of enterprise-level bargaining with its strong institutional embeddedness "either have weak commitment to organizing activities or prefer organizing strategies based on a partnership model [with management]" (Suzuki 2004: 22). Unions' embeddedness at the firm level limits the scope and scale of negotiations over workplace issues. Japanese enterprise-based unions have projected and represented gender interests of the male breadwinner and a work pattern based on a male norm of non-responsibility for reproductive labor and care work. These organizational priorities and practices centering on core male workers undermined the traditional labor movement's capacity to counteract declining union membership when the economy slowed down in the 1980s and later hit the skids during the recessionary 1990s.

Japanese union membership saw a downward slide throughout the 1980s and 1990s period of workforce restructuring that included a "hiring freeze, 'voluntary retirement', and replacement of regular workers with non-regular workers" (Suzuki 2004: 10). From the 1980s to the early 2000s, union membership dropped steeply for both men and women: from 33.6% to 23.2% among men, and from 26.3% to 12.4% among women, widening the gender gap in union membership.[4] Union density declined to 18.5% overall by 2009 (Fujimura 2012: 6), down from 20.7% in 2001 (see table 8.1). To stem hemorrhaging of union membership in 1989, most enterprise-based industrial unions unified under the umbrella of a new national labor federation, the Japanese Trade Union Federation (RENGO); communist-leaning unions coalesced around a smaller radical union federation. In addition to the national center based in Tokyo, the national federation set up 47 local RENGOs in each of Japan's prefectures.[5] This institutional reorganization did little to either organize new members, especially among women, or limit the loss of membership.

Declining union membership and the lack of new organizing among women is not surprising given that few women have attained top leadership positions in unions, a key to organizing success. By 2005, there were no female presidents of RENGO-affiliated unions, and only six affiliates have one woman in the top three positions (figures provided by RENGO). Still, women's integration in top leadership positions grew to 22.2% in the national office of RENGO, although affiliate unions averaged only 7.2% of leadership positions. Recently, RENGO and some affiliate unions, especially in the service sector (public-sector unions and retail unions), have articulated successive action plans both to promote gender equality and to recruit more women, especially in part-time jobs. These action plans are rhetorical documents, expressing an interest in increasing women's membership without transforming exclusionary practices of and hierarchies in unions.

The Japanese employment relations system presents unique challenges for organizing women workers. A male-dominated state bureaucracy produces few job opportunities for women in a relatively small public sector. Horizontal segregation means men and women work in different firms and sectors. Moreover, traditional enterprise-based unions have generally excluded women, immigrants, and part-time and temporary workers from union's rank-and-file, or have been ineffective in addressing their concerns. From the 1990s through 2009, much of the growth of women's employment has been concentrated in part-time and temporary jobs, those areas least touched by enterprise unions (Gottfried 2009a). Yet few traditional unions have successfully extended union membership to part-time and temporary workers – the union membership among short-term workers grew modestly from 2.7% in 2001 to 5.6% by 2009 (Hashimoto 2012: 26). This is in part due to the fact that few unions affiliated with RENGO "explicitly advocated an organizing model stressing social justice, mobilization and alliance with social movement organizations" (Suzuki 2004: 4). For this reason, campaigns, though directed at women, have not significantly boosted women's union membership. Traditional unions' failure to make strategies and structures more women-friendly is partly to blame for the lack of organizing success.

Gender Representation in Trade Unions: Comparing the US and Japan

Even though unions suffered a decline in overall membership in both the US and Japan, the gender gap in union membership widened in Japan but narrowed in the US. Union density among women is slightly higher in Japan than in the US: 12.4% as compared to 11.6%, respectively. Conversely, the low female share of union membership – around 17% in Japan – compares to the higher 44% in the US. So, even though union density is higher among women in Japan than in the US, the gender composition of unions remains more starkly male-dominated in Japan. Notably, US women's union membership still lags behind men's, despite the gender gap closing over the course of the 1990s and into the first decade of the twenty-first century. An in-depth comparison of the US and Japan contrasts different employment relations systems influencing gender representation and composition of unions.

Institutionalization of employment relations establishes a framework for the extent of interaction between bargaining partners, the level of wage-setting, and the intensity of labor and capital relationships (see table 8.1). Overall, union membership dipped below already low levels in the US and Japan, where decentralized employment relations weakened the labor movement's national power at the ballot box and in the economy as a whole. With wage-setting at the firm in both countries, and some pattern agreements in the US manufacturing sector and the Shunto in Japan, collective bargaining limited benefits to union insiders as industrial citizens rather than translated into strong employment protections as statutory rights. Looking more closely, micro-corporatism supported the group-coordinated production regime in Japan. In the US, bi-lateralism lowered the intensity of labor and capitalist relationships, leaving workers more vulnerable to employers' reaching an impasse, emboldening employers to step up anti-union campaigns, and making it easier for workers to decertify extant unions at companies (Clawson & Clawson 1999).

Each employment relations system, built on different reproductive bargains, created different constraints and opportunities for women's repertoires of collective action and their likelihood of belonging to a union. Japanese unions' commitment to protecting the industrial citizenship of their mostly male membership limited benefits to insiders under the umbrella of collective bargaining at the enterprise. Firmly embedded in the enterprise, Japanese traditional unions sought to preserve a reproductive bargain that reinforced a strong male breadwinner family model. Japanese women who worked in smaller industrial settings and in different enterprises remained largely outside of the traditional labor movement. High levels of part-time employment among women further dampened their overall and relative share of union membership in Japan. Despite high hurdles for certifying unions, depressing union organization overall, the individualism of the US employment system paradoxically makes unions more open to those women who secure employment in the same establishments. Mostly, gender representation reflects both the decline in men's membership and the rise of women's membership in health care and the public sector in the US.

Despite these challenges, new organizations have turned these disadvantages into a means of appealing to workers. In Japan, the dramatic increase in non-standard employment has threatened traditional union membership, leading unions to search for strategies to counteract decline (Suzuki 2010). However, limited success thus far raises the question of whether bureaucratic organizing models, modes, and ideologies are ill suited to bringing non-traditional workers into traditional unions.

Repertoires of collective action: new organizing strategies and organization forms

As more women are drawn into waged labor globally, new forms of work and working change terrains of struggle, and, as a result, foster the emergence of new sources of associational power, and vulnerabilities at different scales. In moments of broad social, economic, and/or political change, disarticulation of former economic arrangements and social structures cultivates a fertile terrain for new cycles of organizing activity and the emergence of new organizational forms.

Thus, it is not surprising today to detect a similar impulse toward the development of community-based campaigns, community-based net-works, and "cross-constituency organizing" (Briskin 2008) as means of aggregating interests across occupational, skill, and other divisions. Workers and their advocates have fashioned new hybrid associational forms and community organizing models in response to the changing gender and racial composition of the workforce and ways of working. Many of these new labor organizations represent associational hybrids, combining features of non-governmental organizations with workplace organizations, and operate in civil society spaces rather than exclusively or primarily at the worksite.[6] The multiplication and diversification of these groups enrich associational life, interject new voices, issues, and solutions, and contribute to democratization of the labor movement. Innovative oppositional politics and practices counter older repertoires of collective action among workers and point to new organizations, acknowledging differences and mobiliz-ing around mobile and multiple communities, collective identities, and new sites of production and reproduction.

From networks to workers' centers, new labor organizations address a multiplicity of issues and identities rather than either a narrowly based workplace interest or a singular identity formed at a fixed workplace or space. In the US, new organizing strategies and organizational forms include professional associations that engage in union-like practices, most notably collective bargaining (Cobble 2007: 7). The National Education Association, the largest professional employee association with 2.7 million members, turned to collective bargaining during the 1960s in order to compete more effectively with its rival, the American Federation of Teachers, the union organ-izing teachers since the beginning of the twentieth century (Cobble 2007).

Another new hybrid form, community unions, cross workplace borders, but take their impulse from community organizations rooted in a geographic space. Community unions counter the more traditional styles of union organization. The community organizing model, more than the industrial union model, serves "no wage" workers involved in workfare (Tait 2007), care workers dispersed in private homes (Boris & Klein 2007; Fine 2007), and other workers in precarious jobs (Vosko 2007). Likewise, the role of the state, not only through the formulation and the enforcement of policy, but also through provision of services and funding, complicates the industrial model of unionization predicated on a dyadic relationship between the collective worker and the employer. Further, the nature of many care-giving jobs and the associated labor process require "the making of workers and defining of employer" (Boris & Klein 2007: 178), due to the absence of a central or even well-defined workplace. As one of the newest types of hybrid organizations in the United States, workers' centers are situated between the community and the workplace.

Workers' Centers: Representing Gender, Class, and Citizenship

Workers' centers promote workers' interests rooted in a combination of employment and citizenship status and gender relations, providing an array of resources and political advocacy to those immigrant workers relegated to low-waged precarious jobs with minimal access to traditional unions (Fine 2007). There are 137 workers' centers, operating in over 100 US cities that serve as advocates for immigrant workers' rights and as an interface between immigrant communities and various institutions (government, unions, and employers) (Fine 2007). Their hybrid form derives not only from cross-cutting advocacy for workers and immigrants and often women's rights, but also from their organizational strategies and practices, often filtered through a feminist lens. As community-based and community-oriented, these centers take a page from feminist social movements and community organizing methods. This section draws on Janice Fine's comprehensive study of workers' centers in general, and The Workplace Project more specifically, to get a more detailed picture of these new hybrid organizations that merge race, gender, and citizenship status with labor organizing, and address key elements and conditions of new service jobs.

Workers' centers mobilize participants from all regions of the world, but largely from Mexico, Central America, and South America, although about 15% of workers come from the Caribbean and East Asia, and another 8% from African nations. The concentration of workers from Latin America reflects the larger number of immigrants from that region, which in turn stems from the history of immigration and proximity of their country of origin. Some workers' centers exclusively focus on women in female-dominated jobs, such as Asian Immigrant Women's Advocates in San Francisco, the Garment Workers Center in Los Angeles, and Domestic Workers United in New York City. Others establish women's committees within the worker center to address the specific needs of women, as in The Workplace Project on Long Island, or women of color in the Carolina Alliance for Fair Employment (Fine 2007: 216).

As one of the longest-standing worker centers, established on Long Island in 1992, The Workplace Project advocates for Central and South American immigrants who migrated to New York in large numbers during the 1980s. The Workplace Project seeks to represent women's and workers' rights simultaneously. A women's committee called

Fuerza Laboral Feminina (FLF) was set up early on to give women an autonomous space where they could discuss their own issues and build a sense of community. The community-building strategy begins with outreach designed around the everyday rhythms of women's lives. In the suburbs of New York City, FLF organizers look for domestic workers in laundromats, supermarkets, and churches – the spaces women frequent on their days off. In initial encounters, organizers approach potential participants by administering a survey that has multiple purposes, including: compiling useful data on workers' lives, eliciting conversations, establishing rapport, and ending with an invitation to attend a four-week course at the worker center. The course not only teaches Basic English skills, but also encourages socializing among women who are usually isolated at work. Such group processes enable women workers to articulate their personal stories, from which issues of common concern emerge, laying the groundwork for collective action in the future.

Labor feminism often is an explicit organizing principle of these groups and informs the language used to frame issues and identities as well as modes of organizing. From women's own words, the FLF tailored campaign language around notions of respect and dignity, and dropped the term "trabajadoras domesticas" (domestic workers) in favor of "mujeres que trabajan en casa" (women who work in the home). This latter phrase's subtle linguistic shift signifies the importance of labor feminism to setting the political agenda and to determining strategies and practices sensitive to the group.

A common theme in women's stories points to the fact that employment placement agencies have routinely ignored and violated state and federal laws. The FLF developed an innovative community-based campaign based on these stories. The triangular relationship between the employment placement agency, the client family, and the domestic worker had complicated organizing up to that point (Fine 2007: 226). To optimize their impact beyond a single employer, the FLF's first campaign targeted employment agencies that charged exorbitant fees to women who sought placement as housekeepers. Agencies sometimes charged double or triple the legally allowed fee of 10% of the first month's wage, demanded the fee upfront even though the law allowed a ten-week installment plan, and knowingly placed workers in jobs paying $2.00, well below the official minimum wage of $5.15 in 1999. This employment agency practice occurred in the context of high poverty rates among an alarming number of long-term and more recent immigrants living in New York City: "More than a fifth of New Yorkers who were long term U.S. residents ... in 1999 ... and more than a quarter of recent immigrants were living below the poverty threshold" (Adler 2010).[7] Moreover, non-citizenship deprived these

migrant workers of eligibility for many statutory entitlements and
legal protections. Because neither federal and state anti-discrimination law nor the Family or Medical Leave Act applies to workplaces
with a single employee, domestic workers are particularly vulnerable
to employers firing them without notice or with unfair cause (e.g.
pregnancy) (Fine 2007: 217). Women's stories about their employment
conditions form the basis of the FLF's non-traditional campaign.

Ambitious and innovative strategies grew out of the earlier campaigns. In 1997, FLF, in cooperation with The Workplace Project,
embarked on a campaign for a Domestic Workers' Bill of Rights
that put forth a set of guidelines for good practice in New York City.
Agencies signing would appear on a "Good Agency" list, distributed
to area churches and synagogues and through the media, while those
not on the list ran the risk of a consumer boycott of their services. The
campaign mobilized allies, most prominently religious leaders who
had moral authority in the community and the families who employed
domestic workers. While five out of six agencies ultimately agreed to
sign the Bill of Rights, workers won a pyrrhic victory, since there was
no effective way of monitoring and enforcing the agreement. To gain
more control over their collective working conditions, 12 of the women
workers formed a housecleaning co-operative called UNITY. All of the
UNITY members found work because of the ties already established
in the community and through additional outreach efforts. Women
working in the co-op earned $20/hour (in 1999), and plowed back 10%
of their wages to maintain operating expenses. Several years later in
2004, the co-op had grown to 81 members (Fine 2007: 220). However,
collectives such as this co-op probably will have limited impact on
altering labor market dynamics because of their modest scale (226).

New repertoires of collective action are creative responses to economic transformation. Workers' centers are among the new hybrid
forms of organization crossing workplace borders and merging interests across class, gender, and citizenship status. Unlike traditional
unions, workers' centers mobilize associational power beyond the
workplace, often rooted in imagined, but geographically bounded,
communities. In particular, workers' precarious employment and
citizenship status preclude the usual on-site organizing style of traditional trade unions. These new workers' organizations leverage
associational power to access local political, social, and religious
institutions to improve working conditions among male and female
workers. To overcome difficulties of organizing workers in services,
particularly domestic and care work scattered over many households,
workers' centers innovate new strategies that enlist the larger community in their efforts. These new strategies to some extent draw
on the power of women's stories to make compelling appeals to the

broader community and to political actors. In this way, workers' centers turn women's spatial and social disadvantages into possibilities for collective action. New forms of worker organization increasingly populate terrains of resistance.

Networks within unions and unions as networks

New labor organizations, such as networks, mobilize individuals to join in association with other workers who share similar work conditions, employment statuses, or diasporic identities.[8] Networks link together workers, either proximately at the same workplace or across borders in different locales. These networks engender associational power, characterizing the accumulated resources gained from alliances forged across different types of borders, including different workplaces in a bounded geographic space and among workers in similar occupations or companies along supply chains trans-nationally. Networks make possible, and even necessitate, cross-border alliances between workers, who are similarly situated in their social locations, but who do not necessarily share the same places of work. Thus, while spatial dislocation of work and workers, temporal discontinuities of work schedules, and contractual variation in employment relations create difficulties for organizing workers, doing so contributes to imagined communities forging new organizational forms that cross borders to empower workers, especially those in precarious employment.

Networks Within/Alongside Unions in the US

Networks involve micro-political processes aggregating interests across occupational, skill, and other divisions, developing strategies beyond a single organizational logic, and relying on and mobilizing information for communicative interaction (Lenz 2004). Three types of networks organize either *within* unions, *alongside* unions, or *as* unions. Each represents a new modular organizational form aggregating interests across borders of different types.

Networks within unions are among the newest types of labor organizations. Two service unions, primarily organizing public-sector workers, the Service Employees International Union (SEIU) and the American Federation of State, County and Municipal Employees (AFSCME), sought to "reenergize" existing organizations by adopting a new set of strategies for mobilizing members and increasing membership involvement in union activities. These unions developed new recruitment programs, such as Workers Organizing Workers and

Justice for Janitors, which employ peer-to-peer networking and the rhetoric of democracy and equality to recruit new constituencies, including women, minorities, and workers in occupations that traditionally have not been unionized (such as home health care workers, janitors, graduate students, and part-time workers). Such reform efforts have resulted in some success: US unions that adopted peer-to-peer recruiting strategies scored some of the largest organizing victories during the 1990s. In addition, the AFL-CIO and Change to Win, along with their member unions, have shown greater openness to working with support and advocacy groups that developed within and around traditional unions to give greater voice to women and minorities (Clawson 2003).[9] However, while America's "new unions" adopt more democratic, peer-to-peer strategies for bringing new members into the organization, in many cases, their fundamental organizational structure remains unchanged.

Networks also developed alongside traditional unions, as in the examples of the Coalition for Labor Union Women (CLUW) and the National Association of Office Workers (NAOW). CLUW is a network of affiliated individuals who belong to traditional unions. Dedicated to internal union democracy, the organization encourages women to become shop stewards and to seek other leadership positions,[10] but CLUW lacks monetary resources to fund large-scale organizing campaigns that might increase awareness of unions among unorganized women workers. The 9-to-5, National Association of Office Workers, the precursor to the SEIU local 925, organized women in a female-dominated occupation associated with low levels of unionization. Karen Nussbaum, one of the founding members, gives a first-person account (2007) that traces the rise and stagnation of 9-to-5 to economic and political conditions. She attributes the origin in 1973 and growth of the organization to economic restructuring and to the influence of civil rights and women's rights movements during the 1970s. Restructuring not only squeezed household incomes, leading more women to seek to join the paid labor force, but also created demand for women workers in the burgeoning office economy. New career prospects for many White middle-class women channeled discontent over dead-end jobs into individual mobility paths. Local 925 networks with 9-to-5, National Association of Office Workers to provide women with a safe organizational home for pursuing better working conditions.

Networks-as-Unions in Japan

The embedded institutions of worker representation and collective bargaining at the enterprise in Japan set the stage for the emergence of networks-as-unions. Japanese reform efforts largely have been premised on the idea of creating a new, more democratic structure that serves the needs of marginalized workers. These new network-based worker associations include women-only unions (Broadbent 2005), community unions, part-time workers' unions, temporary workers' unions (Gottfried 2003), and even a managers' union (Dean & Guevara 2001). The origins of community unions date back to the mid-1950s, a time when the model of enterprise unions had only recently gained a foothold in large, mostly industrial, firms (*keiretsu*). At this time, community unions as networks set their sights on organizing small and medium-sized firms that were less likely to already be unionized.

Though initially successful, community unions lost momentum. However, they left a "legacy" spiriting the resurgence of the "second wave" of community unions from the 1980s onward (Suzuki 2010). A survey conducted by Akira Suzuki in 2010, estimates 30,000 to 100,000 members belong to community unions out of a total of 10 million union members overall. Most of these community unions average a membership of 292 with 1.3 full-time staff members. Despite their small size, these networks-as-unions are more successful than traditional unions in organizing categories of workers largely excluded from enterprise unions. In fact, women make up 36.4% of members, compared to 29.1% in traditional unions; and similarly, workers in non-standard employment account for 44.2%, compared to only 7.0% in traditional unions.

A second-wave network-as-union brought together women workers to form the Women's Union Tokyo (WUT). Founded in 1995, WUT seeks to advocate for both women's and workers' rights by building an anti-bureaucratic structure. To mitigate the tendency toward bureaucratization, WUT relies on active participation and empowerment of its more than 250 members. Adopting a community-based organizational model, the WUT recruits women from a variety of companies and occupations, rather than workers from a single firm, industry, or occupation, located in the Tokyo metropolitan area. Most members are clerical workers (59%), but among their members they count professionals (22%), service workers and store clerks (12%), and blue-collar workers (3%). Individuals generally approach the union when they encounter on-the-job problems, usually gender-related issues (e.g. pay inequity, sexual harassment). WUT does not exclusively serve associated members, and also will respond to calls from non-members. This organizing strategy utilizes a unique provision under Japanese labor law that permits "collective" bargaining for individual workers. The network-as-union enables the organization to aggregate members' interest across borders of class, occupation, and industry.

Networks in the US and Japan: A Comparative Perspective

A comparison of organizing strategies adopted by network unions in the US and Japan reveals both similarities and differences, due to historical legacies of gendered employment relations institutions and ideologies. American reformers focus on adopting more democratic and inclusive strategies within existing institutional structures, while Japanese reformers focus on building new institutions based on more democratic organizational forms. This is because reform movements act on legal terrains not of their own making. US labor law constrains collective labor representation to circumscribed group interests, whereas individual bargaining became a defining feature of community-based unions in Japan. Although the two reform movements differ in significant ways, both recognize the benefits of and embrace peer-to-peer networks in building grassroots movements. Peer-to-peer networks are flat (non-hierarchical) and democratic, structured along person-to-person ties across organizations, and based on demographic (such as gender, ethnicity) rather than enterprise affinity. Both draw inspiration from second-wave feminism in their attempts to put into practice anti-bureaucratic organizations.

Networks have several advantages that facilitate reform movements' goals, and disadvantages that thwart the growth potential and limit organizational capacities. Networks develop strategies beyond a single organizational logic, relying on and mobilizing horizontal information and communication. Yet a network has inherent vulnerabilities that derive from its innovative form. Networks must aggregate resources and spread risk across a membership stretching beyond a single organizational site. This extended membership requires that the network expend valuable resources to renew and nurture attachments among current members, as well as provide for organizing new members. Each associational form has different advantages and disadvantages.

On the one hand, networks within existing unions can benefit from drawing on a larger pool of resources, but may be constrained by the larger organizational mission. In addition, bureaucratic governance in large-scale unions competes with the democratic organizational logic of collective action, undermining the ability of networks to reform traditional unions' organizational structure. Such tension does not necessarily consign networks within unions to an inevitable iron-cage of oligarchy. Although the jury is out, these networks might succeed in the long run.[11]

A complementary form of networks developed alongside unions. Networks alongside unions, like their counterparts within unions, bring the interests of network members to the traditional union.

Such networks gain semi-autonomy by maintaining independent organizations. But, similar to networks within unions, networks alongside unions are still largely dependent on traditional unions for their membership and/or for financial resources. After initial growth of networks alongside unions, the failure to expand further suggests impediments that may stem from their inability to pursue goals inconsistent, or in conflict, with the larger organization's priorities.

On the other hand, networks-as-unions gain from their flexibility in responding to grassroots needs, but may not have sufficient resources to support organizational goals. The effectiveness of networks-as-unions stems from being organically grown and locally embedded. Their strength derived from acting locally on the grassroots, however, can become a weakness as these organizations increasingly function on multiple levels. Networks-as-unions must remain rooted in local communities or lose contact with constituents, but their effectiveness and power increasingly depend on reaching out to other groups and extending beyond regional geographic bounds. Fully autonomous network as unions risk losing membership because they are not anchored in a common workplace.

More generally, networks-as-unions and networking among unions can foster cross-cultural dialogue and build the labor movement from the bottom up. My experience as co-principal organizer, with Anne Zacharias-Walsh, for a Center for Global Partnership (CGP) project sheds light on strategies and practices in a series of workshops bringing together several network unions from Japan with their counterparts from the US. The process of developing the CGP proposal began with conversations to ensure that the project, and ultimately the workshops, were relevant to the group's goals. At the first workshop, held in September 2004 at Wayne State University, representatives of working women's organizations from the United States and Japan provided written and oral presentations on their organizations and activities, and shared information on current working conditions for women in each country. The reports focused on each organization's structure, strategies, current projects, long-term goals, and major problems faced and problem-solving efforts to date. Coupled with historical and theoretical perspectives provided by American and Japanese scholars, the organizational reports gave the participants a concrete basis for specific strategy and materials-development discussions in the subsequent workshops. The immediacy of information-sharing provides the intellectual space for corrections and illuminations. At the first workshop, participants struggled over the meaning of "collective bargaining." The professional translators correctly and dutifully selected the correct English words, but were not equipped to elaborate on the legal background of the concept.

Invited scholars explained that "collective" bargaining permits advocacy of individual workers in Japan, as compared to representation of group interests in the US. The exchange enriched scholars' knowledge and enlightened the groups by opening new ways of understanding, and approaching, problems faced.

Our first workshop intensified networking among Japanese-based non-governmental organizations. Following the workshop, participating Japanese women's organizations scheduled regional and national meetings in preparation for the second and third cross-national workshops. The Women's Union Tokyo coordinated an open satellite meeting to report on the first workshop to non-governmental organizations in other areas, distributed translated versions of the workshop papers, and identified shared criteria and goals for a new leadership skills development program in Japan. Similar meetings took place in the Fukuoka, Hokkaido, and Osaka regions. Representatives from these satellite meetings convened for a two-day seminar in Tokyo, and later synthesized the information gathered from each region.

Information technologies pushed the frontiers of these networks by intensifying interactions at the local level and sustaining connections over electronic media. For example, the Internet and teleconferencing offered personalized communication alternatives, enabled organizations to establish networks of social capital of varying quality, facilitated collective action efforts by more rapidly disseminating knowledge and creating shared meanings, and permitted NGOs to collectively locate, motivate, and coordinate individuals who in the past were extremely difficult and costly to organize effectively. Following the first workshop, the Japanese participants, with support from the researchers, established an online discussion forum to enable geographically dispersed women's groups to continue working together between meetings and after the workshop series had concluded. It is important to note that online communication would not have been as effective without first establishing face-to-face contact at the workshop. The personal relationships established at the workshop will spur, and already have spurred, dialogue within Japan and between Japanese and US participants. This type of research engagement will only become more important with the expansion of NGOs in civil society.

Finally, networks-as-unions can forge ties across place and space, moving from the local to the regional and even transnational scale. Cultivation of ties networks horizontal relationships. The movement toward transnational networking provides opportunities to enlarge perspectives on issues that can enhance the local agenda, and can foster cross-cultural understanding of the goals, strategies, experiences, and social and political context of organizations with similar goals across countries. Such an understanding enables local network organizations to evaluate other countries' practices for local relevance and provides a basis for creating new strategies and thinking about how existing strategies could be modified to better fit local circumstances.

Networks and other hybrid worker organizations are gendered forms and use gendered strategies, though not exclusively. Many of these organizations represent gender interests in part because women constitute their core membership. Exclusion from or lack of power in traditional unions has inspired women to form alternative worker organizations. Gender representation goes beyond composition of a network's membership. Networks forge associational power around issues of particular concern, such as sexual harassment in the workplace and responsibility for care, in their own households and often in their jobs – to working women. As a form of organization, networks build on feminist non-hierarchal, democratic principles for empowering women vis-à-vis male unionists and employers. Through networks, feminist labor activists seek to maintain spatial and political semi-autonomy through loose ties among networks alongside formal unions or stronger ties among networks in unions. The feminist lens used by networks enables its members to connect separate spatial domains of their work and to make explicit and revalue gendered types of labor activity (emotional, aesthetic, care). These new forms of organization promote gender representation in the labor movement.

Conclusions: gender representation in traditional and new labor organizations

Women remained under-represented in official unions throughout most of the twentieth century – though women did not fare well in traditional trade unions born in the mines and the factories, they did form one of the first labor associations in the early northeastern US mill towns. In recounting this history, we cannot forget that unions formed and organized in the context of already-existing class and gender structural divides. As organizations representing the interests of their membership, then, it is not surprising that unions promoted and protected their predominantly male members. As a result, the institutionalized system of employment relations and internal governance of unions tended to reflect the male-dominated gender regime within unions, the unacknowledged masculine embodiment of its male membership, and the negotiation of a reproductive bargain based on the male breadwinner's non-responsibility for care work. While negotiation for the social wage at the bargaining table

or through national legislation was a high priority, few industrial
unions addressed non-market issues such as parental leave and childcare, and the inequality of circumstances for mothers and fathers
entering the labor market. The terms of the institutionalized system
of employment relations created different impediments to collective
action along class and gender lines. Gender representation in trade
unions did not significantly change until the public sector expanded
with the major wave of welfare state reforms beginning in the mid-
1960s. Women's union membership increased primarily in the public
sector, and the density of unionization is highest in those countries
with extensive socialized reproduction. For this reason, gender representation is more equal in some countries than in others. But women
and men still largely belonged to two worlds of trade unions, even in
countries like Sweden where union membership has reached gender
parity. The feminist lens used in this chapter provides insight into
union decline and its possible revitalization.

Women and men forge associational power under different conditions and from different social locations on new terrains of resistance.
New organizing strategies and forms of organization promote gender
interests among workers. The rise of hybrid organizations, most
notably networks, provides those formerly excluded from traditional
unions with a vehicle and a voice for realizing gender equality in the
workplace. New repertoires of collective action in general, and the rise
of network organizations in particular, reflect new economic realities
in which work, especially non-standard employment and services,
does not take place in a single location or for a single employer in a
bi-lateral employment relationship over workers' life courses. Under
these conditions, the logic of collective action has changed. Labor
organizing has become more mobile, both in form and in content.
New voices and organizations coalesce around the intersection of
labor and gender issues, production and social reproduction, at multiple sites and on multiple scales. Forms of networks vary depending on
the history of institutionalized economic and reproductive bargains
in a country. As a form rooted in the history of immigration in the US,
workers' centers organize around workers' and women's rights among
migrants whose precarious work leaves them outside of traditional
union settings and often without legal protections. The effectiveness
of these new associational forms in realizing broad social change
remains to be seen, given the obstacles that networks and workers'
centers face. Though the second wave of community unions may ultimately abate, organizational memories can spirit a new wave in the
future. Globalization, through economic restructuring and increasing
mobilities of labor and capital, is shaping new terrains of struggle and
possibilities for new subjects and sites of collective action.

PART III

GENDER, WORK, AND ECONOMY IN A GLOBAL CONTEXT

Thinking Globally, Global Thinking: Theories of Internationalization and Globalization

Previous chapters alluded to the importance of global processes and structures for understanding economic transformations. Though it is intuitively apparent that we live in a global world, analytically it is still necessary to distinguish globalization from earlier phases of internationalization in order to delineate the precise nature of globalization and decipher what makes this current phase of capitalist development new. Before turning to an examination of economic transformations, this chapter reviews where thinking globally and global thinking fit with regard to theories of internationalization and globalization of work and production. Internationalization and globalization theories situate economic transformations on local, regional, and global scales. Globalization is said to intensify interconnections between people, political institutions, politics, and production processes transnationally, while internationalization more simply refers to capitalism's expansion from one part of the world to another. In either case, gender has not been central in non-feminist theories of either internationalization or globalization.

Feminists critical of gender-blind globalization narratives (Sassen 1996; Bergeron 2001; Freeman 2001) recast globalization theories in light of labor market restructuring and its impact on gender and other power relations (Browne & Misra 2003). A feminist critique is necessary in order to understand economic transition and the consequences of that transition. To understand the distance traveled since the early 1970s, a review of feminist scholarship begins with an introduction to and criticism of the "women and development" approach. Initial forays put women into development paradigms, raising concerns about women's status in relation to international economic forces. Each feminist wave provided layers of depth to explain economic processes of development and characterized gender relations unfolding in these processes. The limits of early second-wave accounts can be traced to their narrow frame, firmly anchored to the logic of international development within an internationalization formulation. Women and development research thus can be seen as a reaction to the way that development projects incorporated men into mines and factories, and largely ignored and devalued women's role in subsistence agriculture and in other "housework." Their project, both theoretically and practically, sought to elevate and make visible women's role in development, raising awareness that women's work – much as it had been during the emergence of capitalism – was central to social reproduction and supplemented the wages of men. Capitalism takes specific forms depending on the way gender relations, bodies, and practices are incorporated into production and reproduction.

By contrast, the process and consequences of globalization represent a qualitative shift in the way of thinking about the international system of capitalist production, invite new questions as a result of the destabilization of the old gender order, and discuss the fuller integration of women into circuits of capital. Feminist political economy traces the arc of a new narrative featuring the flows within and across the Global North and South. A new geography of power results from increasing mobility across places and spaces on a global scale

New geographies of power? Internationalization versus globalization

Out of the ashes of World War II destruction emerged a geo-political map of international relations, an East/West divide with North/South implications: the former along political lines, the latter reflecting the stage of economic development. In its aftermath, countries rebuilt physical infrastructures and reconstructed political and economic institutions in the context of US hegemony. Social scientific research followed in the footsteps of the new world order. In particular, research conducted by US-based scholars in area studies programs often took the form of in-depth analyses of single cases carved out of a political geography from the international system of nation states and imagined regional clusters, defined against the politically relevant backdrop of West and East (East Asia, Western Europe, and Far East). Modernization theory, emergent during the 1950s when the West clearly dominated the rest, exhorted so-called "backward" countries to modernize by adopting the values of "successful" economies, as the means by which countries could reach higher levels of economic – and social – development. The evolutionary arc of modernization theory defined set stages of development, not coincidentally following a path prescribed by Western liberal ideology. At the time, both modernization theorists and their opponents still saw the world in terms of the inter-national system, whether through "linked" development in modernization theory or through dependent and distorted development in critical theories.

By the late 1960s and into the 1970s, reaction against evolutionary structural-functionalist approaches in the social sciences re-energized comparative and transnational research. The commanding approach of Barrington Moore (1966) inspired a rich sociological tradition comparing European cases, including the monumental studies of nation-building by Charles Tilly (1975), and of states and revolution by Theda Skocpol (1979). On an even broader canvas, world systems associated with the work of Immanual Wallerstein (1976), and dependency approaches characterized by André Gunder Frank's (1978) development of underdevelopment, grouped country cases into larger units for transnational comparisons. For example, world systems theory formulated macro-economic structures forming core, semi-periphery, and periphery regions of the world economy. Though these theories emphasized different relationships between the historical process of state formation and emerging economic forces, they shared a common intellectual agenda analyzing big structures within the historical trajectory of capitalism. However, none fully integrated gender into their accounts of these large-scale economic and political developments, either as a factor in its formation or as a consequence of social and economic development.

More recently, theorists have taken up the concept of globalization to define the changing integration and inter-relationships of these clusters and production processes. Beginning in the late 1970s, new patterns of globalization became evident in the formation of horizontally integrated transnational corporations spreading and intensifying the international division of labor, and internationalizing money and financial capital; the development of supra-national political institutions (such as the European Union); proliferating international agreements (North American Free Trade Agreement, or NAFTA); and the formation of transnational organizations (ranging from the World Trade Organization to other non-governmental organizations). By the end of the 1980s, these changes significantly altered geographies of power. Throughout the 1990s, researchers tried to make sense of the new economic realities of this shift from internationalization to globalization.

Scholars debated the meanings of globalization and the viability of sovereign nation states as units of analysis (Katzenstein 1999), raised fundamental questions concerning the content and context of implied integration (Hirst & Thompson 1999), and pointed to transnational actors and inter-societal relationships influencing political and economic boundaries and cultural identities (Amin 1997; Woodiwiss 1999; Jameson 2000). Despite disagreement on the precise nature of globalization, scholars increasingly recognized that real qualitative shifts (as well as quantitative changes) had altered political economic institutions on a global scale. While globalization may not have rendered the nation state obsolete, greater interconnectedness and wider networks deepen relationships between firms and among people. Globalization theories trace the movement and intensity of interactions of people, processes and production traversing nations in the Global North and South.

Those who see recent economic transformations as qualitatively different from those found in the post-World War II period embrace the language of globalization to identify the novelty of current structural changes. While agreeing that globalization represents something new, theorists emphasize different aspects of economic, political, and social processes in their definitions of globalization. The definitions that appear below offer alternative, but closely aligned, political economic approaches.

1) Ash Amin (1997: 124) defines globalization as a macro-structural social "process of linkage and interdependence between territories and of 'in-here out-there' connectivities." As a social geographer, Amin explores the spatial scales of globalization. Further, for Amin globalization processes affect a growing number of chains of economic, social, cultural, and political activity that are worldwide in scope, and an intensification of levels of interaction and interconnectedness between states and societies (129). In this sense, the internationalization of the economic order and political interdependence can no longer be contained by politics of metropolitan nation states.

2) For Michael Aglietta (1998: 65), "globalization [is seen] as a multiplicity of distinct but interconnected processes. Occurring at different speeds, in different sequences and in different places with varying degrees of intensity, these processes are far from coherent." Aglietta neither assumes a uni-linear nor a totalizing process of change. Rather, it becomes imperative to analyze processes on different scales and in different places, rather than generalizing from a single tendency or trend.

3) Ilse Lenz (2004) suggests that globalization represents a qualitatively new stage in a long, on-going process of unequal internationalization promoted by Western modernization and colonialism that is connected to, rather than a rupture or

break with, modernity. She identifies three new qualities of globalization: ecological interdependence, producing new risks and chances; communicative interaction through new and old media and personal mobility (e.g. migration, tourism, scientific exchanges and conferences); and the formation of international institutions and organizations (e.g. the European Union, NGOs).

4) Joan Acker (2004: 18) discusses the contested nature of globalization as a process and as a concept. She cites those who suggest that globalization is a euphemism for Americanization, "serving an ideological function in mystifying the current configuration of capitalist expansion." Despite her doubts about using this politically charged concept, she defines globalization in terms of the "increasing pace and penetrations of movements of capital, production, and people across boundaries of many kinds and on a global basis." Rather then view globalization simply in terms of increasing interactions and connections over space, she considers both political and economic developments, including the growth and consolidation of transnational corporations, along with new forms of decentralization and subcontracting. Globalization is associated with "free-marketization" reducing state and contractual controls and extending the potential reach of "commodification."

Several common elements appear in these definitions regarding the nature and effects of globalization in relationship to, and distinct from, internationalization. Each emphasizes process over a static configuration or an end-state; processes are seen as interdependent and linked, contradictory, complex, and multifaceted; and processes are uneven in effects across time and space. Points of disagreement remain, however, raising a fundamental question about whether or not globalization represents a new or an on-going process – capitalism has been international almost from its inception. Is globalization qualitatively different from internationalization? Is globalization about domination of the South by the North? Is globalization synonymous with Americanization? Is globalization place-bound even as the processes result in changing territoriality and inter- and transnational relationships? Can the inter-national (connections between) be differentiated from the global (inter-relationships)? Key to the debates is the unsettled question of whether and how globalization differs from internationalization. Do globalization theories provide a new political cartography for understanding patterns of social inequalities? To what extent, and how, does a feminist lens illuminate processes of globalization? How does integrating gender make visible the

Table 9.1 Differentiating internationalization and globalization

Relationships	Internationalization	Globalization
Economic relationships	Simple extension of economic activities across national boundaries	Functional integration has occurred among geographically dispersed activities
Political relationships	Nation states are primary agents of change and sites of struggle	Extra-national forces constrain and condition (but do not completely determine) strategies of nation states and national political struggles
Cultural relationships	Primary interchanges are between and around nation states	Complex re-articulation of cultural forms and channels at a range of scales

Source: I am grateful to Amy Bromsen who created this table based on material taken from Dicken et al. (1997).

causes and consequences of economic transformation generally, and the transition to service-dominated economies more specifically?

Globalization after internationalization: a new cartography of production and reproduction

Any definition must consider whether or not globalization represents a new phase of economic, political, cultural, and social transformation in the late twentieth century. Capitalist development always has been associated with expansion across the globe. However, it is possible to differentiate the current phase from earlier colonialist and imperialist expansion. Table 9.1 contrasts globalization and internationalization in terms of economic, political, and cultural relationships. Internationalization involves the simple extension of economic activities across national boundaries. By contrast, globalization is associated with functional integration across geographically dispersed economic activities. In other words, globalization involves increasing frequency and intensity of interactions on multiple scales. Nation states are the primary agents of political change and sites of struggle in the period of internationalization. Extra-national forces constrain and condition, but do not completely determine, strategies of nation states and national political struggles as a result of globalization. Finally, primary cultural exchanges principally take place between and around nation states in an earlier epoch, while globalization furthers the complex re-articulation of cultural forms, and cultural channels extend to a range of scales (Dicken et al. 1997).

Scholars, however, disagree on the nature and impact of globalization on work and workers. Bergeron (2001) characterizes the debate

Issues/ dichotomies	Global imperative	National management
Table 9.2 Approaches to globalization		
Focus	Economic forces of transnational capital flows and global markets; convergence into homogeneous world economic and cultural system	Cultural conditions of globalization (emergence of global village, coca-colonization); increased heterogeneity of economic and cultural forms
Penetration of global forces	Capitalism has created a truly global economic, social, and cultural system	Logic of global capital reserves social power to nation states
Politics / nature of capitalism	Unfettered free market capitalism is seen as only alternative; coupled with neo-liberal politics	Retention of some power in nation state permits maintenance (or reinstatement) of some forms of social safety net; shelters citizens from worst ravages of globalization
Resistance	Global resistance is necessary to counter global capitalism; however, globalization has created the conditions under which this is possible	Nation states retain sufficient power to be centers of resistance to global capitalism

Source: I am grateful to Amy Bronsen who created this table based on material from Bergeron 2001.

in terms of its emphasis on either a "global imperative" perspective or a "national management" perspective. Table 9.2 compares these two perspectives along several dimensions: focus, penetration of global forces, politics and the nature of capitalism, and resistance. The "global imperative" perspective focuses on economic forces of transnational capital flows and global markets. Capitalism has created a global economic, social, and cultural system. Transnational resistance is necessary to counter the excesses and negative consequences, such as poverty and uneven development of global capitalism, and globalization creates the conditions under which this resistance is possible. The "national management" perspective argues that the logic of global capitalism reserves social power to nation states, in that they retain sufficient power to be centers of resistance to global capitalism. Neither the expectation of convergence into a homogeneous world economic and cultural system, nor the emergence of a global village with an increased heterogeneity of economic and cultural forms, adequately captures the nature of globalization and the relationship between the global and the international. Bergeron criticizes both perspectives for their construction of the global or the national as monolithic or unified subjects. The assumption of an all-powerful capitalism that privileges the macro-level leaves little space for theorizing "contradictory potentials" (2001: 998) that arise out of globalizing production and labor markets and the contestation of globalization from below. Consequently, neither approach can recover the concrete work practices of men and women in particular places such as global cities.

Social geography interjects global cities to differentiate globalization from internationalization (Sassen 2001). The introduction of global cities allows for the decomposition of the nation state, previously as a unitary concept, into a variety of sub-national components moving beyond the "duality national/global" (Sassen 2004: 377). Rather than posit a dichotomy between the national and the global, Sassen's notion of global cities suggests that globalization creates a new socio-spatial dynamic transnationally. In this view, the nation state is no longer considered a primary container of polity and economy. Global cities weaken national sovereignty as work processes and workers become untethered from the nation state and decoupled from a bounded territoriality. Importantly, the social geography perspective cracks open the nation state to analyze new political assemblages and the globalization of production and reproduction in particular places across spaces and at different scales.

Distinguishing globalization and internationalization, the concepts of "global commodity chains" (Gereffi & Korzeniewicz 1994) and "global value chains" (Gereffi et al. 2005) emphasize integration and connectivity of firms and workers on a global scale. A global value chain "describes the full range of activities that firms and workers do to bring a product from its concept to its end use and beyond" (www.globalvaluechains.org/concepts.html, downloaded April 30, 2012). A value chain encompasses economic activities that can produce either goods or services, while a commodity chain characterizes the "structure and dynamics of global industries" (ibid.), linking low to high ends of value-added production across countries of the Global North and South. The metaphor of chain describes the full array of economic activities at different stages from production to consumption, "decreasingly confined to a particular geographic space and its local and established practices" (Rosenau 1977: 360). Though originally applied to manufacturing and to unmarked male workers, the conceptual armature lends itself to the discussion of other types of global value chains. Feminists have appropriated the concept to theorize the development of transnational care chains (discussed in chapter 10).

Globalization signals an epochal change "akin to the 19th century and 20th century development of a national capitalist labor market" (Standing 2007: 41–2), but ushering in a new international division of labor and globally integrated labor market (44). So, while internationalization of production may not be new, the current phenomenon of globalization can be defined as "complex and multifaceted processes of worldwide economic, social, cultural and political expansion and integration which have enabled capital, production, finance, trade, ideas, images, people and organizations to flow transnationally cross the boundaries of regions, nation-states and cultures" (Chow 2003: 444). In this way, globalization differs from internationalization in the intensity and frequency of interactions. Globalization accentuates old fault lines of gender, race, and class inequalities, and creates new ones in strategic sites and places over changing spatial boundaries and time scales. These general accounts of globalization are a good starting point from which to analyze economic transformations.

We turn to feminist critiques of gender-blind theories to demonstrate what we gain from integrating gender into analyses of globalization. Feminists criticize gender-blind theories of globalization as "narratives of eviction" for expelling women's concrete work practices in the portrayal of abstract, disembodied global capital (Sassen 1996); as "rape scripts" for counterposing "a dominant, invasive, penetrating global capital to subordinate or disunified nation-states" (Gibson-Graham, cited in Bergeron 2001); as "erasures of gender" (Freeman 2001: 1008) when characterizing the economic dimensions of globalization at the macro-level and leaving gender to describe intimate relations in the family; and as "neo-liberal rhetorics" justifying privatization and non-responsibility for care for human reproduction and the environment (Acker 2004). Such feminist interventions challenge non-feminist globalization theories for missing the importance of family dynamics, intra-household relationships, and non-market activities, in addition to not applying gender to other spheres of activity. According to feminist political economists, non-feminist theories tend to assume that narrowly defined economic interests, predominantly or solely, drive human activity (Fernandez-Kelly & Wolf 2001: 1244). It is necessary, but not sufficient, to note the absence of gender in non-feminist accounts. Feminist criticisms show how this absence constrains our understanding of global forms and meanings of work transformations (Freeman 2001: 1010).

Feminist critiques: beyond "women and development"

Feminist critiques progress from women and development to gendering globalization theories. By tracing the lineage of current feminist literature on globalization to an older generation of "women and development" research, this review shows both the continuities and distance traveled from the previous terrain of debate (Beneria 2001; Floro & Meurs 2009). New feminist scholarship on globalization owes a debt to these important, albeit limited, studies of women at work in Latin America, Africa, and Asia, while acknowledging the need to go beyond the category of women to analyze specific forms and cultural expressions of gendered power in relationship to class and other hierarchies (Fernandez Kelly & Wolf 2001). The origins of feminist scholarship on globalization, work, and economy can be found in the framework of "women and development." This field of study came on the heels of post-colonial struggles and arose out of the heyday of second-wave feminism when scholars began questioning the exclusion of women in development theories and projects. One of the founders of the approach, Ester Boserup (1975), called for the integration of women in development to address the ways in which countries undergoing industrialization had marginalized women's work and privileged waged employment among men (Beneria 2001: 45, 47).

In the first phase of women and development research, feminist economists noted that the shift to implantation of cash crops and waged labor relied on women's unacknowledged labor in household production and subsistence farming (Sassen 1996: 11). At that time, feminists launched a research agenda and development projects showing how economic changes had disadvantaged women as a group. Economic transformation and US development aid reinforced a division of labor depriving women of an independent means of existence. Women lost ground in the process by which more land was converted into capitalist agriculture alongside intensive extractive industries employing male labor. However, as Ruth Pearson (2007: 4) suggests, the women and development model's "focus on women as a perpetually disadvantaged group in terms of patriarchal structures and gender discrimination" isolated the analysis of women from that of men, and treated women as an undifferentiated group thus "seldom acknowledg[ing] differences between women in terms of age, life cycle, religion, ethnicity, class, (dis)ability, sexuality, morbidity, etc." As a result, the perspective had "no room to interrogate men and masculinity " (4). The research agenda under the rubric of "women and development" ultimately proved limited.

As more women were drawn into the global assembly-line, the next phase of feminist research turned to the internationalization of manufacturing and the feminization of the working class. Feminist analyses of the internationalization of manufacturing theorized the strategic "nexus between dismantling high-paid labor in major industries in the north and formation of an off-shore proletariat" (Sassen 1996: 14). Global production off-shoring manufacturing jobs brought a disproportionate number of women into paid work in the industrial economy. This scholarship, more than the first phase, uncovered the gender dynamic that could explain why women predominated in some labor-intensive industries, most notably in garment and electronics assembly, regardless of a country's development level (Sassen 1996: 14). What needed to be explained in this second phase was not so much that women were left out of waged work, but how, why, and where they were integrated into industrial production. Thus, the second phase of feminist scholarship can be seen as a reaction both to the limitations of the women and development framework and to changing economic realities. In part, women's work on the global assembly-line prompted the transition in second-wave feminist thought. Even further, this phase of research moved away from a focus on women to an analysis of gender and class structuration, in order to understand the rationale for companies hiring women in low-waged, labor-intensive industries. Though an advance over women and development, second phase accounts failed to go sufficiently far beyond the development paradigm and internationalization to be able to fully analyze global transformation of economic activities (15).

Gender and globalization theories

The current generation of third-wave feminist scholarship moves from "development to globalization" in gendering political economy analysis and "putting gender at the center of considerations of globalization" (Basu et al. 2001: 944). In this generation, feminist theories frame and assess the conditions of globalization around the world, examining the different roles women play in the global economy, and consider the extent to which patriarchal arrangements and masculinities and femininities change as a result of greater economic integration of women into circuits of capital. Much of feminist scholarship on globalization seeks to go beyond either top-down or bottom-up approaches. On the one hand, "globalization from above" typically focuses on capitalist structures and capital accumulation processes. On the other hand, "globalization from below" celebrates either non-governmental organizations or coalitions resisting capitalist domination (Basu et al. 2001: 944), or conducts micro-analyses focused on women's work in global production and consumption only at the local level (Freeman 2001: 1007). According to Freeman, some feminist accounts have failed to consider the larger patterns and structures shaping women's experiences (1013). Yet globalization is neither a "process imposed solely from above by powerful states or multinational corporations" nor simply a response from social movements at the local level (944–5). This recent scholarship complicates and problematizes the simple dichotomies representing the "colossus power of exploitative corporations against the exploited victims" (Fernandez-Kelly & Wolf 2001: 1247), and allows for a new appreciation of changing work conditions on multiple time and space scales (Sassen 2001). In other words, the current generation of feminist

theories seeks to "avoid macro-generalizations as well as romanticiza-
tion of micro-level as an alternative" (Basu et al. 2001: 944).

Still, much of this new generation of research prefers concrete
analyses to abstract, disembodied theories (Freeman 2001; Salzinger
2004). Examining the concrete instances where globalization touches
down to the local, such feminist scholarship documents unequal
and uneven globalizing processes and effects on women's and men's
work patterns and their social consequences (Fernandez-Kelly & Wolf
2001). More specifically, this feminist scholarship acknowledges the
need to analyze specific forms and cultural expressions of gendered
power in relationship to class and other hierarchies (1244; Gottfried
2008b), and to uncover power relationships among women, which
often remain hidden or are left unexposed (Mohanty 2006: 224), in
order to understand how different groups of women and men fare
in increasingly globally integrated labor markets (Gottfried 2009b).
And some go even further to question how gender – femininities and
masculinities – constitutes and is constituted by globalization. We
need not only to know that "gender shapes labor markets but how
it does so" (Salzinger 2002: 2). Gender and gendering (de-gendering
and re-gendering) are seen as historically and culturally variable
categories and processes. Such theorizing thematizes the complex
articulations of gender and class in specific contexts, and explores
relationships between macro/micro, global/local, public/private and
production/consumption, economy/family, abstract/intimate, pairs
coded implicitly as masculine and feminine (Basu et al. 2001: 943).
Working toward a more dynamic and concrete perspective, feminist
theories of globalization highlight the impact of restructuring on the
complexity of relationships between, and the interconnectedness of,
social inequalities within and across countries.

One of the major advances in feminist theory of globalization,
gender, and work emerges under the microscope of Joan Acker (2004),
whose keen analysis magnifies how gender is both embodied and
embedded in the logic and (re)structuring of globalizing capitalism.
This extends the case she made in her earlier pioneering research
on how gender relations are embedded in the organization of major
capitalist institutions. For the study of globalization, Acker (2004:23)
posits that the gendered construction (and cultural coding) of capitalist production – separated from, and built around the assumption of
non-responsibility for, human reproduction – has resulted in subordination of women in both domains. The gender-coded separation
of production and reproduction became the underlying principle
for not only the conceptual organization of work, but also the physical, spatial, and temporal relationships between unpaid work in the
home and paid work, "bodily movements through time and space, the

general organization of daily life, and the ways that groups and individuals constructed meaning and identities" (Acker 2006: 92).

Through this analysis of globalization, Acker chronicles the historical legacy of a masculine form of dominance associated with production in the money economy that was exported to and embedded in colonialist installation of large-scale institutions. She borrows R. W. Connell's notion of "globalizing masculinities" to distinguish colonial from contemporary expressions of hegemonic masculinities. During the colonial period, hegemonic masculinities were shaped in the act of conquests and empire-building by direct and explicit engagement in violence against colonized people. Ego-centric individualism was a core constitutive element of hegemonic masculinity, whereby the colonizer believed in and imposed their superiority over others. By the late twentieth century, large-scale institutions promoted images and emotions that projected economic and political power in terms of new articulations of hegemonic masculinity. In the current era of globalization, "transnational business masculinity" is still rooted in egocentrism, but also is an expression of conditional loyalties and a declining sense of (paternalistic) responsibilities for others. Violence occurs, not necessarily openly as in the colonial period, but rather institutionally in what appear as rational business practices and outcomes, such as the violence of leaving people without a means of survival. So, the logic of hegemonic masculinity in part drives globalization processes and practices.

From a different perspective, Carla Freeman (2001) begins with a local case study of market intermediaries known as "higglers" in their Caribbean context, to show how globalization operates at local levels and is configured in particular places, for particular groups of people, and to particular ends (1009). She seeks to recover and make tangible the corporeal presence and embodiment practices of real people's "flesh and blood" activities through higglers' practices, reimagining the relationship of local and global (1010). Higglers, both historically in their role as buyers and sellers of agricultural produce and goods transported from rural areas to public spaces of markets both at home and in neighboring islands (1019), and contemporarily in their position as "suitcase traders" or "informal commercial importers," traverse space and destabilize the dichotomies of mother and worker, provider and consumer, local and global (1020). The local is neither a simple effect of the global nor an isolated site for studying individual actions. Gender is at the center of her analysis of how global labor markets operate.

Global restructuring does not merely relocate work and workers, but also reorganizes the types of people employed and the work that is performed. Leslie Salzinger (2004) documents the making of gendered workers in Mexico's global factories on the border with the US. In these Maquila factories, women assemble electronics and garments for companies with household names. She finds that gendered structures of meaning, "transnationally operative and locally applied," reproduce the gendered structure of the labor market by shaping demand and preferences for specific categories of workers, which are based on deeply embedded expectations about gender-appropriate work. Salzinger interrogates the assumption that globalization is a gendered process to show how the gendered structure of the labor market is made through the circulation of the trope of "productive femininity." The trope of productive femininity references a feminized assembly-line worker, applying to particular women, usually young women, as well as emasculated men. The preference for women workers plays on the old rationale that tied women to repetitive work in nineteenth-century factories in the US. Her research demonstrates why and how the local (micro-level) becomes important for the study of globalization (macro-level processes) by focusing on the social construction of gendered workers.

Feminist theories of globalization offer various accounts of the linkages between production and social reproduction, between the intimate sphere and abstract economic laws, and between micro-level and macro-level political-economic relationships. More specifically, a dialectics of globalization, to use Chow's terminology, compels theoretical engagement that analyzes gender and class relationships within and across households, communities, and nations. Considering these relationships can "disrupt the gendered mapping of global/masculine space" (Freeman 2001: 1019). Another way to formulate the dialectical relationship is through the narration of women's "lifelines" (Lal 2010) and through the "local in/of the global" (Mohanty 2006: 229).

Conclusion: gender from internationalization to globalization

Theories of economic governance and work transformation contrast internationalization and globalization to highlight what is distinctive in this current phase of capitalism. Globalization theories emphasize interactions and interconnections of people, places, and production processes. Feminist interventions show why it is critical not only to point out that gender is absent from traditional political economic theories, but also to show what difference it makes when gender is missing from these accounts. A new generation of feminist scholarship revitalizes earlier "women and development" approaches.

Feminist criticisms seek to show that processes of globalization do not occur simply "'over there' but also, here, at home" (Fernandez Kelly & Wolf 2001: 1248). It is unavoidable, and in fact necessary, to push the frontier of research on gender, work, and economy beyond a single country or geographical binary. Globalization intensifies linkages both within and between countries through migration flows, commodity chains, and rescaling of political institutions and politics. Using a feminist political economy, and the sensitizing tool of geographies of power, gives us a theory and a set of categories for analyzing these linkages from micro-level to the macro-level in the Global North and South. The language of Global North and South articulates a relational geography of power, "draw[ing] attention to the continuities as well as the discontinuities between the haves and have-nots within the boundaries of nations and between nations and indigenous communities" (Mohanty 2006: 227).

Feminists, observing recent economic transformations, direct our attention to how globalization intensifies interconnections of spheres of activities thereby changing the material conditions facing different groups of women and men. In this sense, globalization opens up new vistas of research, and calls for both reimagining and problematizing fixed categories of analysis. Drawing on earlier theories, "revitalized feminist approaches" not only examine multiple effects of globalization on women's work, both paid and unpaid, but also consider how globalization is itself gendered (Fernandez-Kelly & Wolf 2001). In particular, feminists examine how gender is embedded in the logic and (re)structuring of global capitalism (Acker 2004), and document the unequal distributional consequences for different groups of women and men within and across countries (Walby 2009a). Feminist theories of globalization are better able to assess the reasons behind the uneven integration and valuation of men's and women's labor in different locations of the Global North and South. An extensive review of feminist globalization theories enables us to uncover the factors driving economic changes and work transformations in the intimate sphere of the household in older and emergent global cities.

The three chapters that follow delve more deeply into processes of economic and political globalization through an examination of the mobilities of people, of production processes, and of politics. Using the feminist lens shows how gender shapes, and is shaped by, economic processes. Beginning with broad economic trends, the next chapter outlines the play of economic forces on multiple scales. The next, about global cities, reveals the concrete work practices of male and female workers who manage and serve the global economy. The last chapter in this section explores the global political landscape.

Global cities and global labor markets weaken former political juris-dictions and governance institutions, challenging and creating new political landscapes. To a certain extent, new political assemblages transgress the old international system of nation states. However, the nation state continues to significantly determine conditions of life and work for male and female workers alike.

CHAPTER 10

Gender, Global Labor Markets, Commodity Chains, and Mobilities: Globalizing Production and Reproduction

L‍ABOR markets are becoming more globally integrated, with some women drawn into the circuits of global capital, while others remain outside them (Browne & Misra 2003; Pearson 2007; Floro & Meurs 2009). Women enter into the paid labor force in greater numbers worldwide as economic globalization processes, like off-shoring, outsourcing, subcontracting, informalization, and migration (UNIFEM 2009: 58), restructure local and global labor markets. This chapter analyzes the processes and structures of economic globalization, off-shoring capitalist production and reorganizing reproduction. Different from internationalization of production, economic globalization interconnects work processes and workers through commodity chains and intensifies these linkages across geographic spaces.

This chapter begins with an examination of globalizing trends. Both labor and capital are on the move, but they encounter different constraints that limit, and forces that drive, their respective mobilities. Using a feminist lens focuses attention on how and when capital feminizes jobs, relocating labor-intensive production in global spaces. These labor-intensive economic activities and low-waged work in global production increasingly take place off-shore in special enclaves, in intimate spaces of households, or through relationships of interactive service encounters. New economic zones designate an extra-territorial space to lure capital. In these zones, capital operates in extra-territorial global spaces where national governments suspend labor laws and other regulations. Social and political considerations along with profit maximization motivate hiring and locational decisions contributing to economic globalization.

Economic globalization not only reconfigures the location of work and workers – that is, who performs particular jobs and in what spaces of production and reproduction – but also is associated with feminizing service work and the feminization of work biographies and migration. As this chapter shows, this process differs from the internationalization of migration during earlier phases of capitalist development. Internationalization involved male labor toiling in extractive industries in their home countries or migrating to the North where they worked in the fields, on construction sites, and in factories. In the current era of globalization, gender influences both the structures of meaning at work and the types of labor extracted in transnational service production. One of the newest trends – discussed in this chapter – transnationalization and commodification of feminized services, extracts emotional and affective labor principally from women workers, many of whom migrate from poorer regions to wealthier ones. At the other end of the spectrum, finance capital and the management of global capitalism fuel the globalization of migration among elites who themselves require services for living in global cities, discussed more fully in the next chapter. Globalization of migration, thereby, intensifies the demand for increasing reproductive services, from dual-earner families in developed countries, from wealthy families in developing countries, and from an elite relocating to global cities. As a result, feminization of migration and a global transfer system of gendered care and emotional labor link micro-level interactions with macro-level economic processes.

Another prominent feature of economic globalization increases non-standard employment in nearly every country. The rhetoric of globalization emphasizes economic reasons to explain why firms have shed regular workers and hired employees on non-standard employment contracts in order to save on personnel costs and to evade obligations for job security among their workforce. This reasoning does not adequately situate and identify political sources and social forces giving rise to the variation in vulnerable employment across different groups in different spaces and places. Though women generally are more likely to end up in non-standard employment, an empirical investigation in latter sections underscores the clear trend of increasing informalization for workers, both female and male, everywhere. The final section of this chapter asks whether informalization is an opportunistic by-product of global capitalism, or intrinsic to its logic. In either case, informalization shifts the burden and costs of reproduction onto individuals and intensifies feminized service work, both paid and unpaid.

Globalizing capital, globalizing labor

In the first decade of the twenty-first century, women make up a large share of the workforce in low-waged labor-intensive manufacturing (Collins 2003; Caraway 2007) and increasingly occupy jobs in new tertiary outsourced services (Hochschild 2003; Gottfried 2009b), such as call centers (Poster & Wilson 2008) and care work located both in developed (Holtgrewe 2007) and in developing countries (UNIFEM 2009). Preference for women is evident in hiring practices among firms dedicated to assembling goods in labor-intensive production processes or to computer-enabled operations, such as secretarial work performed off-shore; other services include individuals and small enterprises specializing in care, health, and custodial services. However, gendered employment patterns vary in ways not easily predictable from analyses of economic variables alone.

To understand the process of economic globalization, it is necessary to distinguish between hiring women on the one hand, and feminizing jobs on the other: the former refers to the more commonly used measure of gender composition indicating the *quantity of labor* performed by women workers (Acker 2004: 35), while the latter refers to the gender ideology socially constructing the *quality of labor* based on the "trope of femininity." According to Acker (2004), the "trope of femininity" has survived because it resonates with the new restructuring of globally integrated labor markets and jobs, for both men and women. Salzinger (2004: 45) developed this idea further in terms of the trope of "productive femininity," which plays on the double meaning of "productive." On the one hand, "productive femininity" signifies the way that the structures of meanings construct and produce gendered subjects. On the other hand, "productive femininity" contributes to the engendering of workers. By distinguishing between hiring women (numerical composition of the labor force) and feminizing jobs (quality of labor), it is possible to view the gendering processes and practices that are altering patriarchal social divisions between men and women within countries and transnationally due to economic globalization.

Economic globalization intensifies interactions and interconnections between people, places and production processes. However, not all types of work and production can be transplanted or relocated. Some types of work processes are more mobile than others. Extractive industries, construction and interactive services, such as female-typed care work, sex work, and restaurants, laundries, and cleaning services, involve a product or process that takes shape in site-specific locations. On the other hand, assembly of textiles and electronics, food processing, and digitized tasks that do not require face-to-face contact (Paus 2007: 5), such as IT-enabled services ranging from back-office processes (e.g. data entry), to call centers, to on-line delivery of professional services (accounting, financial services), are all more amenable to transnational relocation. As a result, work and production processes are globalized in different ways. On the one hand, global capital transplanting labor-intensive production processes in search of lower costs may touch down in places where cheap labor abounds. Knowledge-intensive work, especially finance and other high-end business services, may locate where a density of these activities exist, in either old or newer global cities to take advantage of an existing critical mass of networks and skilled workers. On the other hand, site-specific employers, including those offering face-to-face interactive services, may meet demand by hiring low-waged migrant labor. In these cases, employers may draw on a global labor pool. Whether transplantable or site-specific, employers might resort to using informalized employment arrangements, subcontracting with labor market intermediaries, and hiring migrant labor to realize a saving on wage rates and the payment of benefits. Economic globalization, therefore, involves the movement of capital and of labor, but not in the same manner.

Global Capital, Local Labor: Feminization of Global Production

Global capital extends its reach by off-shoring and subcontracting labor-intensive production, hiring local workers, and integrating women into commodity chains in a new spatial division of labor.[1] The concept of commodity chains fosters a research agenda for analyzing the structure of transnational corporations' global reach. The metaphor of chain emphasizes connectivity between production processes, networked firms, and people who are otherwise spatially dispersed. Initial research analyzed the logic of global capital moving abroad in search of cheap local labor on what became a global assembly-line. In this narrative, capital seeks out labor in low-waged regions of the world to locate labor-intensive production facilities at the lower end of value-added commodity chains. The place for (re)location of production varies with the type of work and the labor process. Some countries, especially in regions with underdeveloped industrial infrastructures like Africa, are further left behind in a race to the bottom. Labor-intensive manufacturing of garments and electronics employs a female work force in the more developed countries of the Global South (e.g. Mexico, Philippines, and China). Other globalized production like call centers, providing routine and customized services, employs an educated workforce with English-language proficiency, and is located either on the edge of cities in the Global North or in former British colonies such as India, Jamaica, and other Caribbean countries – as more countries are incorporated into a global system of production.[2] The process remains uneven, in both the kinds of investments made and the nature of labor employed. As a result, the feminization of global production unevenly incorporates women into the global capitalist labor market.

Global Capital and Relocation of Work

Global capital touches down locally not merely in a race to the bottom, as it seeks to maximize profits, but also bases decisions on factors other than the lowest wages. Collins (2003: 151) positions the relationship between social, economic, and political institutions along a continuum by asking the questions: "how different kinds of firms embed themselves differently in local institutions, how their operations are shaped by local culture, and how law and specific forms of economic organization condition different degrees of connection to workers and foster or inhibit the development of strong workplace communities." She analyzes how place matters to the relationship between local labor and global capital, and finds that firms make labor recruitment decisions based not only on the "price" of labor, skill sets, and knowledge available, but also on the social and political arenas in which they operate. This includes the degree of enforcement of the rule of law and regulations, and the existence of favorable laws and terms of engagement (152). Importantly, low wages of workers are underwritten by individual and "community-based livelihood strategies" that enable social reproduction at no or low cost to companies in the Global South (152). For this reason, countries in Sub-Saharan Africa, prone to famine, receive less foreign direct investment, even though wages would be among the lowest in the world. Unpaid reproductive labor, both individual and community-based, is an unacknowledged yet important consideration for global capital looking to (re)locate production.

　　Studies of the apparel industry trace the threads of global production (Bonacich et al. 1994) pieced together from different locations, still prominently in global cities yet increasingly found in newer assembly sites. US-based multinational companies use different strategies for globalizing production. One strategy involves the creation of "the new sweatshops" in US cities with large female immigrant populations (Ross 2004). The US ranks second after China and ahead of Mexico among the top three clothing producers measured by employment – though the clothing industry in the US is small relative to other industries in the overall economy (47) and has shrunk in absolute size in recent decades. Women make up the vast majority of apparel workers – though no reliable statistics are available on their number in the US. Given the existence of "invisible home sewing machine operators," estimating an accurate number of apparel workers, and gauging their employment conditions, require extrapolation from qualitative studies (33). Citing a 1997 Department of Labor (DOL) survey of the New York City garment industry, Ross found only 75,000 workers, a sharp decline from the 340,000 recorded in 1950. Though difficult to calculate, Ross estimates that the "sweatshop" population in New York City ranges from 40% to 63% of total employment in the industry. The once thriving apparel business organized in the heyday of the International Ladies Garment Workers' Union has declined in the US, and has moved to lower-waged countries.[3] It is not so much that overall employment in apparel has taken a nosedive, but rather that US parent companies outsource and subcontract with firms in other countries (Collins 2003).

Social and political considerations are part of a firm's location calculation. Collins analyzes locational and hiring decisions by comparing two apparel firms at either end of the fashion spectrum, one at the low end (Tultex) and the other at the higher end (Liz Claiborne), to determine whether product differences entail low- and high-road industrial pathways. Founded in the 1930s, Tultex began as a family business in the cradle of the textile industry of southern Virginia, later expanding into a vertically integrated firm mass-producing knitwear in eight factories across the US. The company shifted production to plants in Jamaica and Mexico in the 1990s when faced with the intensification of global competition, especially from rapidly industrializing China. From its inception in the 1970s, "[Liz Claiborne] produces clothes without factories, externalizing risk to manufacturers and supplier networks throughout the world" (Videla 2010: 3). Despite different origins and organizational models, both firms subcontracted with apparel firms located in the interior city of Aquascalientes in central Mexico – 312 miles northwest of Mexico City. The subcontractors, whether producing higher-quality fashion for Liz Claiborne or T-shirts and hoodies for Tultex, took the low road of Taylorist production methods by recruiting rural women with little factory experience and paying them low wages. The rationale for locating in central Mexico, rather than either on the border of Texas where Maquila factories produced output for many US multinational corporations or in Mexico City, becomes more apparent if we consider social and political factors. Aquascalientes is in close proximity to Mexico City for transportation purposes, but is sufficiently far away from the site of many labor disputes and political mobilizations – a common occurrence in the main Zocalo Square. At the same time, the rural community, though poor, collectivizes the costs of reproduction through the provision of food from either subsistence agriculture or local farmers. In this setting, corporations can pay lower wages than would be commanded in Mexico City and Juarez, and also employ a relatively docile workforce at the outset. These two firms' location and hiring decisions contribute to feminization of production in these global factories.

Feminization and Industrialization

The process of feminization occurs in places with different histories of industrialization. To understand this process, *Assembling Women* compares an impressive number of countries in South America, East Asia, and South Asia to explore the question: why don't employers always prefer women over men in order to reap large labor savings by hiring cheaper women workers? Caraway (2007) asks: if low wages are the paramount consideration, then why don't women workers dominate in all economic sectors? The answer requires examination of the historical process of feminization occurring in waves of industrialization. Prior to the new orientation toward globalization, internationalization was embodied by a different model of economic activities and investment. During the 1960s, countries of the Global South adopted export-oriented industrialization, often at the behest of international institutions such as the International Monetary Fund and the World Bank, and of governments through policy manipulation.

Export-oriented industrialization stimulated the growth of labor-intensive production, and, in this initial phase, employers hired both male and female workers. With the shift to more capital-intensive industries, employment growth slows down, and masculinization of the labor force often follows (Videla 2010: 2). Hiring strategies, once established, often prevail over new staffing arrangements. In this way, older firms dominated by a male workforce may retain that gender mix. This "stickiness" keeps companies from overhauling their personnel, despite the possible cost savings likely to result if they hired women to replace men (2). Newer plants are more likely to feminize the workforce, taking advantage of lower wages paid to the women now drawn into it. Once a firm or a sector feminizes jobs, then other companies often follow suit. In other words, a "spillover" describes the learning process through which corporations emulate the gendered practices of other neighboring employers. The final phase, called "snowballing," gathers up more women when increasing demand for the product leads employers to hire additional workers. And, "importantly, the growth in already feminized sectors deepens gendered beliefs and practices" (2). Once in place, feminized jobs are constructed through gendered discourses about proper work for both men and women.

The global reach of transnational corporations intensifies interconnections and linkages in global commodity chains in several ways: by transplanting production or subcontracting work in low-waged regions; by collectivizing costs of social reproduction; and by locating plants or doing business in special zones, but not necessarily in the most impoverished countries. While women are drawn into labor-intensive production, the results are uneven across firms and countries. At the lower end of the value chain, global production takes place in, and creates new, socio-political spaces.

Global spaces of production: Export Processing Zones and commodity chains

Companies transplant production clustered together in newly emergent global spaces called Export Processing Zones (EPZs). These EPZs have facilitated off-shoring and subcontracting of manufacturing at the low end of value-added global commodity chains. Some of the work off-shored is either subcontracted to local firms or performed by subsidiaries of multinational firms in these zones. Regardless of ownership, the factories operating in these zones typically produce for export rather than for domestic consumption. What makes these spaces global is that they function as extra-territorial sites of production. EPZs also are global spaces in another sense. They suspend national regulations and impose militarized discipline on the workforce. While labor standards and enforcement may be weak in the country as a whole, exemptions from labor and environmental regulation (with or without minimal occupational safety and health standards) lower the cost of doing business further for those locating to these relatively new global spaces of production.

Many developing countries have designated Export Processing Zones (EPZs) as special socio-spatial enclaves dedicated to export-oriented, labor-intensive production processes often employing a low-waged female workforce living in dormitories or in nearby housing. The appeal of these zones is evident in the dramatic growth of EPZs from their inception: from being barely in existence prior to 1975, to numbering almost 1,000 in nearly 40 countries just twelve years later. By 2006, over 3,000 EPZs had taken root in more than 120 countries. Women are the preferred labor force in these zones, accounting for approximately 90% of all employees in Nicaragua, about 80% in Bangladesh, 75% in Honduras, Philippines, and Sri Lanka, and over 50% in Korea, Mexico, and Kenya, among other countries (UNIFEM

2009: 61). Feminization of the workforce is clearly apparent not only in the number of women working in these zones, but as a result of these feminized jobs reserved for women.

In an exemplary case study, "The global trotting sneaker" (Enloe 2006) traces the global commodity chain of iconic sneaker production, starting with research and design by the parent companies in the US, and moving to stitching of shoe parts by subcontracting firms in Asia, and finally to the purchasing of the fashion item in metropolises around the world. Though the globe-trotting sneaker is based on data reported from the 1980s, the logic can be applied to the process of economic globalization more recently. By subdividing work into small component parts, multinational corporations with household names like Nike subcontract shoe assembly to local companies paying piece rates with no or few benefits for workers. An astonishing 45–50 people may work on a single pair of shoes. South and East Asian women earn a fraction of the hourly wage paid to their counterparts in the US. Only a small proportion of the cost of production, however, pays workers' wages (see table 10.1). The transfer of athletic footwear assembly to South Korea, for example, occurred during the 1980s when the military dictatorship of President Park suppressed workers' organizing and could guarantee a supply of cheap labor in literally militarized economic zones. Also importantly, access to an international airport kept transportation costs relatively low. Global spaces of labor-intensive production settle in countries guaranteeing the conditions for a low-waged feminized workforce.

Table 10.1 The globe-trotting sneaker	
A: Hourly wages in athletic footwear (1980s)	
Country	Wage range ($)
China	0.10–0.14
Indonesia	0.16–0.20
Thailand	0.65–0.74
South Korea	2.02–2.27
United States	7.38–7.94
B: Allocation of costs of a $70.00 pair of Nike Pegasus sneakers (labor-intensive)	
Item	Cost ($)
Materials	9.18
Labor	1.66
Administration and overhead	2.82
Subcontractor's profit	1.19
Nike profit	22.95
Retail mark-up	32.20

Source: derived from Enloe (2006).

The gender pattern emerges in sharp relief in China's development of Special Economic Zones for labor-intensive manufacturing of textiles, shoes, toys and electronics, destined for export to markets in the US and elsewhere. Within these designated zones, the Chinese state began a "controlled" experiment for foreign direct investment in capitalist production. In 1980, women were recruited to work in these labor-intensive industries (Wichterich 2009: 3). During the 1990s the Chinese government initiated a second phase, focusing on more capital- and technology-intensive industrialization. Over the next decade, the government shifted to more knowledge-based industries at the higher end of the global value chain in coastal manufacturing hubs. This shift led to a decrease in the proportion of female workers in manufacturing, dropping from more than 80% to less than 70% of the total manufacturing workforce (5). The existence of global commodity chains, whereby men and women work in different sectors, results in wage disparities. By one account, those recognized as skilled labor (typically men) saw their wages increase in 2003 to 5,000 Yuan per month (approximately $790) while female migrant workers earned only 10% of those wages working in the Special Economic Zones (Dale 2005 cited in Wichterich 2009: 6). In the case of China, the state both directed and dictated the gender composition of the labor force in these zones.

National governments' trade liberalization, transnational agreements, and state-led economic development projects set the background conditions enabling the creation of EPZs as global spaces for the feminization of global production. The political framework eases the movement of capital around the world. Trade and investment liberalization encourages countries to keep women's relative wages low in order to maintain the countries' competitive advantage for foreign investment (Floro & Meurs 2009: 14). Transnational trade agreements, such as the North American Free Trade Agreement (NAFTA) and the General Agreement on Tariffs and Trade (GATT), facilitate the mobility of transnational corporations by lowering tariff barriers. Such agreements, predicated on the principle of "free" trade rather than "fair" trade, either exclude or provide inadequate support for fair labor practices and environmental standards. Thus, companies are "free" to transplant to or subcontract in these spaces where labor regulations are suspended. In addition, subcontracting arrangements with local companies allow parent companies with household names to evade legal and "moral" responsibility for working conditions back home (Enloe 2006: 459). Some companies publicize efforts on behalf of human rights and emphasize the fact that they offer the Third World women making their products a better income than would otherwise be available to them. This is reminiscent of Walmart justifying low wages by arguing that they provide low-cost goods to working families in the US. Yet companies disavow social responsibility for human rights abuses in those same factories. The multiple layers of commodity chains disperse and fragment the labor force, making it hard to hold one employer – particularly the parent company, ultimately – responsible for bad working conditions (Beneria 2001: 39–40).

EPZs represent relatively new socio-political spaces for global production. Companies doing business in these zones often feminize the workforce, taking advantage of lower wages paid to women now drawn into the paid workforce. Once firms or sectors mark jobs as feminized, other companies emulate hiring patterns. Among these firms, labor takes on a gender-specific quality.

Global labor, local employers: gender and migration

The movement of capital across national boundaries is only one side of the process of economic globalization. Labor also joins migratory trails. The lure of Northern prosperity has been called the "globalization of migration" (Castles & Miller, cited in Hochschild 2003: 18). This globalization of migration involves an increasing number of people on the move in search of employment or for the performance of their jobs. Migration tends to be global in that now the distance traveled has increased, no longer just within countries or crossing one border. Economic compulsion is the primary driver of migration from the Global South to the North. However, the mix of choice and compulsion propel different mobilities of men and women from one region to another in the world economy. While low-waged women migrate to the North in search of work, higher-waged men and some women migrate out to manage global production. In particular, transnationalization and commodification of care and other services fuel a feminization of migration. Globalization of migration is not only a story of individual heroism or grit, but also about the changing structures of gender, class, race, and international relationships.

Feminization of Migration: From Global South to North

Economic pressures in home countries and the promise of better pay in places of destination compel more women to migrate to cities, whether in the Global North or South. Many skilled women who leave increasingly poor countries can earn more money as nannies and maids than as nurses, teachers, or clerical workers if they remain in their own country (Hochschild 2003: 18). The changing gender composition of migration (quantitative measure of who migrates) and the changing quality of the labor extracted from migrants (qualitative capacity of labor power) inform the feminization of migration. Feminization of migration is evident in the relative and absolute numbers of women crossing borders to make the journey from their homes to faraway destinations, joining migratory streams in larger absolute numbers than during the past four decades.

More women, both as job-seekers and as family members, embark on migratory sojourns. The female share of migration already hovered at a relatively high level of 47% in 1960, inching upward throughout the 1960s, and then falling a few percentage points from the mid-1970s to the mid-1980s, during the worldwide economic crisis. By the close of the economic downturn in the late-1980s, female migration returned to its former level at 47% of the total, ratcheting upward to 49% in 2005 (UNIFEM 2009: 59). Although the increase remains relatively modest as a percentage change, this growth rate translates into 100 million women migrating from their homes to new destinations (58–9). Variation in the gender composition of migration depends on the country of origin and destination, and these have changed since the end of World War II. Few Algerian and Moroccan women migrated to France immediately following the War; women accounted for less than 3% of total immigrants from these countries in 1946. By 1990, there was a dramatic change, with women accounting for more than 40% of the total (Hochschild 2003: 5). From some countries, the number of women migrating reached parity (as among Filipinos) or exceeded the number of men (women accounted for 84% of Sri Lankan migrants to the Middle East) by the turn of the twenty-first century (6).

Women have always migrated, either by force through enslavement or military conflict, because of economic circumstances, or by choice. What makes the phenomenon new is not only the sheer number of women migrating and the distances they traverse, but also the feminized nature of the labor extracted. Feminization of migration derives from and drives commodification of care and transnationalization of other feminized services. The feminization of migration becomes more visible when studying waged care work and other services in more developed countries, performed by migrants in private households.

Feminized services: gender, race, and migration

Tracking the migration trail of "pioneering" women can highlight the contradictory effects on, and complexity of, gender and class relations in and between both home and host countries (Hondagneu-Sotelo

2001; Parrenas 2008). In other words, theorizing the intersection of gender, class, race, and nation is unavoidable when studying nannies, maids, and home-health-care workers who toil invisibly in the intimate sphere of someone else's household (Hochschild 2003). Like their counterparts among racial minorities, whose experience of domination was documented for an earlier period in the US (Rollins 1985; Glenn 1992; Romero 1992), many women migrating from the Global South perform domestic and care work cast-off by affluent women in the Global North. Women in rich countries, many entering the workforce, are turning over care work to female migrant workers paid low wages with few or no benefits and whose lack of citizenship status deprives them of many social protections and legal rights.

Globalization and the Commodification of Care

The growing demand for a range of paid caring services transforms employment relationships and inequalities on a global terrain. Women's increasing labor market participation in industrial nations and their ability to combine work and family, to some extent, rely on other women's cheap labor. Elite women face different hurdles and opportunities in securing good jobs and can afford different solutions in the face of obstacles such as the time-bind. Some women may pay for services performed by migrant and minority women earning low wages as nannies, maids, and waitresses. Commodification of care involves a global labor transfer system, whereby women migrating from poorer regions of the world replace work once performed largely by mothers and wives in the form of unpaid labor in the home.

The reason that elite women turn to migrant women in part derives from a "care deficit," as more women enter the paid labor force and cannot find adequate care services (Hochschild 2003). Unpaid parental leave and costly privatized childcare accentuate the care deficit in the US. This care deficit is not only the product of public policies, but also the result of men failing to significantly increase their share of domestic labor even when women work full-time: "So, strictly speaking, the presence of immigrant nannies does not enable affluent women to enter the workforce, it enables affluent men to continue avoiding the second shift" (9). In this way, the care deficit helps to drive feminization of migration.

When the care deficit is addressed through the employment of migrant labor, a similar care deficit necessarily is produced in another part of the world through the transfer of commodified sentiments. This global transfer of services associated with and transplanting a wife's traditional role extracts a different kind of labor from that in prior migrations based on agricultural and industrial production

(Hochschild 2003: 20). In the new global era, women's part of the story becomes more prominent than in "male-centered imperialism" in its classic form of openly coercive extraction of natural resources and the production of agricultural output on conquered or colonized lands. Instead, emotional, sexual, nurturance, and physical labor is extracted in this current phase of globalization. In particular, "love is the new gold" (20). The extraction of emotional resources does not typically involve military force, although abusive treatment of care workers has been documented. Among care workers, coercion operates differently, not principally through the barrel of a gun, but rather through economic compulsion (27).

To understand the global transfer of sentiments, Hochschild (2003: 22) argues that love is an "unfairly distributed resource extracted from one place and enjoyed somewhere else." In order to make this argument, she poses the question whether love really can be considered a "resource" which a child has a right to enjoy? And if so, what are the qualities of this immaterial good? According to Hochschild (22), what differentiates love from material commodities is that the former does not constitute a fixed quantity. Instead, love is a renewable resource that creates more of itself. Based on these qualities, love can be seen as a scarce, distributable resource, but cannot be invested as such. Rather, love is displaced in a psychological sense, finding a different object for its expression (23). In this way, love becomes a precious resource not simply extracted from the Global South and implanted in the Global North. Love "owes its very existence to cultural alchemy," occurring in the place that it is imported to (24); loosely analogous to the extraction of raw material, in this case sentiment is "assembled" at the place of work (25). Through cultural alchemy, the nanny extracts love by transferring her affections to the children under her charge, while her own children suffer the loss of her affection. This labor of love produces affection in a display of emotion and care, rather than necessarily expressing genuine affection that is the essence of its commodification.

An analogy to Marx's notion of commodity fetishism allows Hochschild to characterize the experience of a nanny's love as if it obtains a thing-like, unique, and private quality (2003: 26). Hochschild argues that: "We unwittingly separate the love between the nanny and child from the global capitalist order of love to which it very much belongs" (26). Families employing nannies rarely make the connection between the love that their children receive and the love denied to the children left behind. The "magic" of commodity fetishism obscures the exploitative social relationship in which extraction of labor occurs through the global commodity transfer system.[4] The fact that commodity fetishism involves a sentiment, an object of one's affection, does not diminish its exploitative effect. Low wages paid to the nanny and devalued care work are perpetuated through the ideological veil of commodity fetishism that shrouds the fact of the "emotional deprivation of [migrants'] children with the surfeit of affection their First World counterparts enjoy" (22).

Global Labor Transfer System

The concepts of "transnational care chains" and "transnational chains of reproductive labor" created by migrant workers shed light on what propels feminization of migration and its consequences (Hochschild 2003: 18). These chains link families from one region to another region of the world economy in pursuit and performance of reproductive labor. These transnational chains reflect the organization of public and private power relationships between men and women, but also among women divided by class, and often by race, ethnicity, and increasingly by national origins. As Parrenas (2001: 78) describes, "The hierarchy of womanhood – involving race, class, nation, as well as gender – establishes a work transfer system of reproductive labor among women, the international system of caretaking." Both care and remittances are a part of the global labor transfer system.

Who cares for these children left behind depends on local norms and the availability of proximate female relatives. Among the many stories are two about domestic workers from the Philippines. Rowena Bautista hires a local woman to mind her children at her home in the Philippines as she cares for the children of a family in Washington DC (Hochschild 2003). In another case, Jocelyn Santia, a 40-year-old mother, along with her husband who subsequently died, worked as a housekeeper in Milan for 20 years. Jocelyn left grandparents and a brother with the responsibility of raising her four children in Mabini – a city in which 15% of the 42,000 residents live and work abroad (Onishi 2010: A5).

Rhacel Salazar Parrenas (2008) brings together her influential research on Filipina migrants and extends her path-breaking ethnographic analysis to include Filipinas working as domestic workers in Rome and Los Angeles and as entertainers in Tokyo. David Eng[5] incisively captures the importance of Parrenas' analysis when he states, "Extracted from home and homeland only to be reinserted into the domestic spaces of the global north, these servants of globalization exemplify an ever-increasing international gendered division of labor, one compelling us to reexamine the neo-liberal coupling of freedom and opportunity with mobility and migration." The "force of domesticity," as well as economic circumstances, compels transnational movements among migrant women into domestic servitude.

The transnational restructuring of reproduction alters class and gender relations, not only in the host country but also at home, through the "huge transfer of caring and emotional resources globally" (Pyle 2006: 289). A care drain is one of the outcomes of this global transfer system, as women who had cared for their own children and elderly family members in their home countries leave to care for children and elderly clients in their host country. Single mothers or "almost" single mothers migrate from countries with high birth rates, and that are strongly pro-natalist (21). Hochschild (2003) asks: what are the repercussions of a care drain in home countries, and for children left behind in the care of others? Even though women from the Global South may achieve a semblance of liberation, the chance to become independent breadwinners and to improve children's material well-being, still they must sacrifice care for their children to engage in their "commute" across the globe.

Migrant labor may leave behind their families, but many transmit money through remittances to the economies of their home countries. Remittances are financial resources sent by workers to support families back home, and constitute badly needed foreign exchange for poor countries, especially those with large debts as a result of loans taken out from the International Monetary Fund (IMF) and the World Bank (prevalent during the Asian financial crisis of the late 1990s). This transfer of large sums of money to their families serves as an important source of "development aid" to their home countries. According to World Bank estimates, in 2004 developing countries received the equivalent of $126 billion in remittances, double the amount of Official Development Assistance, and approximately 75% of total foreign direct investment. The Philippines brought in remittances totaling $17.3 billion in 2009, up from $7.6 billion in 2003, which accounts for more than 10% of its GDP (Onishi 2010: A5). Much has been made of these remittances from the Global North to the Global South.

Remittances subsidize the costs of social reproduction, not only by paying educational fees for children left behind, but also by supporting public infrastructure projects such as roads and municipal buildings. "Toiling far from home for Philippine dreams" reports on a village where one-quarter of the 1,200 residents work in Italy and contributed 20% of the cost to build the public hall (Onishi 2010: A5). Although no data are systematically disaggregated by gender, some anecdotal evidence suggests that women distribute a significant share of their wages in the form of remittances. For example, female Dominicans working in Spain send as much as 78% of all remittances to the Dominican Republic, even though they account for only 61.4% of all migrants. An overwhelming 97% of all Filipino migrants remit at least some money home, and women send on average about 45% of their income (UNIFEM 2009: 58). Clearly, remittances create a trans-national system of private and informal support of social reproduction in domestic economies. In doing so, this transnational transfer of funds relieves the pressure on government in the home country to socialize costs of reproduction.

Migration affords women a degree of gender liberation from immediate patriarchal constraints because of their "greater contribution to household income and greater participation in public life" (Parrenas 2001: 1140). Through remittances, women may gain greater leverage over domestic decisions regarding budgeting and domestic chores. However, they replace local patriarchy with structural patriarchal relations globally. Migration is often compelled by economic necessity and deprives children of their parents. Cash is not a substitute for emotional closeness and care between parents and children. Dependency does not only characterize power relationships between nations, "but [is] internalized within [and extended across] families," as the local patriarchal relationship between men and women becomes transnationalized (Hochschild 2003: 18).

Finally, less visible is the way that globalization enables the transfer of ideas in both directions. Feminization of migration facilitates not only the circulation of money through remittances, but also the formation of new social imaginaries and empowerment, as liberatory ideologies are transmitted back to the home country when women visit their families. The economic vulnerability compelling globalization of migration also serves as a means for transmission of ideas about organizing and cultural practices of resistance. One can point to how communicative ties between migrants and their families, and others in diasporas, set apart global mobilities today from internationalization of the past.

Global restructuring unevenly impacts on the work of women and creates divisions of labor between women in different regions of the world economy, generating greater disparities in wealth as the gap between the global rich and poor grows (Hochschild 2003: 17). On the one hand, the lure of higher relative wages propels more women workers from poor countries to migrate to wealthier countries in hope of finding better jobs than those that exist in their countries of origin. Many of these women live in poverty, moving from the "Third World to the Third World within" the industrialized world (Chang 2006). On the other hand, globalization has "created more high-paying professional jobs in the United States, stimulating the demand for low-paying jobs that service the needs of professional workers . . . domestic workers are drawn from various parts of the globe to meet these needs, creating an international division of reproductive labor" (Browne & Misra 2003: 503).

With the global economic crisis in 2008–9, some highly paid women are laying-off domestic workers, as a consequence leading to a reverse-migration flow of women back to the Third World. Still, globalization of migration continues to be predicated on gendered assumptions about who is available for what type of work, and is strongly associated with informalized employment and labor relations. The global transfer system of care propels women on sojourns from their homes. In this feminization of migration, many women workers, including those with nursing or teaching backgrounds, end up in care and other personal services, often without benefits and at low wages. Those employed in personal services, particularly prevalent in private households, forgo a standard employment contract and often enter into informalized working conditions. Employers, individuals and families, can evade paying minimum wages and abiding by national labor standards such as maximum hours worked. The process of informalization leaves workers more vulnerable to the vagaries of the market.

Informalization, economic insecurity, and globalization

Worldwide, labor faces increasing informalization and economic insecurity as a result of globalization processes. Informalization defines the casualized nature of labor relations lacking formal access to social protections and regulations and without the expectation of continuous employment and work schedules. Contrary to traditional development paradigms, informalization prevails in countries of both the Global South (Beneria 2001; Pearson 2007: 9; Floro & Meurs 2009) and North (Gottfried 2008a, b; Vosko et al. 2009). Modernization theories have posited that the informal economy would eventually disappear as the formal economy "absorbed the marginal working population" (Beneria 2001: 33). More generally, modernization theories and non-feminist globalization theories have underestimated the trend because of their neglect of the way gender influences both the composition of and the types of work that are informalized. More specifically, informalization is linked to feminization of jobs and work biographies. As Guy Standing (1999b) suggests, non-standard employment extends "feminized qualities of work to men on a global basis." By feminized qualities, Standing refers to the nature of work biographies characterized by discontinuity and insecurity, rather than to the sex of the individual worker. Thus, informalization ensnares men as well as women and unfolds unevenly across groups differing by gender, race, and class as well as by nation (Beneria 2001; Vosko et al. 2009).

Gender, Informalization, and Vulnerable Employment Worldwide

The numbers tell a story of growth, albeit in an uneven pattern, across economic sectors within countries and across countries as a whole. From 1980 to 1999, informal employment grew as a percentage of non-agricultural employment in every region of the world: Asia saw a 10 percentage-point increase from 53.0 to 63.0, and there was a smaller percentage increase in North Africa (38.8 to 43.4), Sub-Saharan Africa (68.1 to 74.8), and Latin America (52.3 to 56.9) (Charmes, cited in Beneria 2001: 35). Women's share of informal employment ranges from 52.3% in Sub-Saharan Africa, to 45.9% in Latin America and 39.9% in Asia (35), and an estimated two-thirds of women work in the informal economy in the Philippines (Floro and Meurs 2009: 28), and around 94% in India (Vosko 2007: 276). In China's coastal urban centers, informal employment already exceeded formal employment in 2003 (Wichterich 2009: 4); and more recent estimates range from 37% to 60% informal employment out of the total workforce in 2008 (Swider 2010). Despite such extraordinary numbers, we do not have good measures of informal employment and informalization.

UNIFEM established the indicator of "vulnerable employment" to approximate the extent of informalization in a regional comparative perspective. Vulnerable employment is a measure adding together own-account workers and contributing family workers. Own-account workers are self-employed producers or service providers with no employees working for them, contributing family workers are own-account workers who work without pay in an establishment operated by a relative living in the same household (UNIFEM 2009: 54). These own-account workers are among the most vulnerable workers because they must rely on their own income generating activity under highly variable and unpredictable economic conditions and without the institutionalized support of a safety-net. The gender composition of vulnerable employment skews toward women in most regions. In 2008, the magnitude of women's vulnerable employment reached more than 80% in some regions, such as Sub-Saharan Africa and South Asia, and nearly two-thirds of women in East Asia and the Pacific (see table 10.2). Vulnerable employment encompasses one-third of the male and female workforce in Latin America and the Caribbean. In the Middle East and North Africa, a larger percentage of women (37.7%) than men (26.9%) work in vulnerable employment. Men share a similar fate in the same countries and regions where a large informal economy exists.

To some extent, vulnerable employment is related to underdevelopment. This is supported by the fact that the highest overall rate of

Table 10.2 Percent in vulnerable employment, by region (2008)[a]

	REGION					
	Developed regions	Sub-Saharan Africa	South Asia	Middle East and North Africa	East Asia and the Pacific	Latin America and the Caribbean
Male	9.0	64.3	73.0	26.9	53.1	33.6
Female	7.0	80.6	82.3	37.7	60.7	31.7

[a] Vulnerable employment is the sum of own-account workers and contributing family workers.

Source: based on figure 4.2, ILO Labor Market database (UNIFEM 2009: 54).

vulnerable employment appears in the least developed agrarian-based economies of Sub-Saharan Africa where two-thirds of both men and women work in agriculture (see table 10.3). Indeed, countries undergoing rapid industrialization in South and East Asia, still characterized by high levels of employment in agriculture, also exhibit large populations caught in vulnerable employment. In South Asia, 59.0% of women cultivate fields and 82.3% toil in vulnerable employment. The measure of vulnerable employment is an aggregate statistic for the region, and is not broken down by sector. Thus, we can only infer the relationship between agricultural employment as an indicator of economic development and vulnerable employment. However, the high rates across regions suggest that vulnerable employment is widespread throughout the world economy. It is not that underdevelopment is irrelevant for understanding the growth of informalization, but rather that the notion of vulnerable employment as a residual of backward economies still in the throes of an early stage of development does not explain why non-standard employment has become pronounced in economies of both the Global South and North.

Informalization and Insecurity

For countries with otherwise strong labor regulations, such as many European countries, informalization becomes more pervasive and invasive in those areas of production and reproduction least regulated and unionized. More specifically, the trend toward informaliza-

Table 10.3 Percent in vulnerable agricultural employment, by region (2008)

	REGION					
	Developed regions	Sub-Saharan Africa	South Asia	Middle East and North Africa	East Asia and the Pacific	Latin America and the Caribbean
Male	3.5	63.1	42.3	19.1	39.0	24.9
Female	2.1	67.3	59.0	35.0	42.2	10.5

Source: based on figure 4.5, ILO Labor Market database (UNIFEM 2009: 57)

tion has implications for ways of working, the construction of the standard work biography, and collective-based standards and rights. Weakening reciprocal rights and obligations makes non-standard employment more precarious than permanent full-time employment. The process of informalization threatens the economic security of ever-larger numbers of male and female workers across countries of both Global North and South. Informalization of employment and labor relations adds to insecurity and poverty, especially among own-account, home-based, female workers in developing countries (UNIFEM 2009).

Global capital, whether locally based or globally operated, informalizes labor to reap the benefits of a cheaper more vulnerable workforce. In this sense, informalization is a consequence of globalization, whereby employers opportunistically employ workers in non-standard employment relationships in new and expanding areas of work untouched by past regulatory norms. In another sense, the growth of informalization is a tendency intrinsic to economic globalization. That is, the threat of, or the actual, mobilities of both labor and capital undermine the solidaristic conditions that enabled workers to bargain for the post-war social contract. Most notably, unions that were formed in the international system forged identities and engaged in collective bargaining within the confines of legal arenas staged in nation states. Nonetheless, informalized workers are joining together in new forms of organization, as indicated in chapter 8 on labor organizing, and as discussed more fully in the next chapter on global cities. To explain its growth and patterns, then, we must link informalization to off-shoring, subcontracting, and globalization of migration, as well as to changing political institutions on national and supra-national levels.

Conclusion: gender and economic globalization

> [I]nternational conventions, [social norms], corporations, state policies, and local labor markets, as well as class and racial and patriarchal ideologies, mediate the ways in which women's lives and work are organized. (Videla 2010: 1)

Feminist theories identify causes and consequences of the increasing involvement of women in the waged labor market more generally, and their preponderance in commodified services more specifically. They reveal changing power relations and inequalities associated with the expansion of production of immaterial goods, ideas and services in global commodity chains. Using a feminist lens magnifies the power relationships instantiated in less visible unpaid labor and, increasingly, paid labor performed by migrant workers in the domestic sphere, which links the local to the global. Few places or people are untouched by the global reach of commodity production. Economic globalization, when seen through a feminist lens, highlights new geographies of power formed by the linkages of commodity chains in new spaces of production and reproduction.

One side of economic globalization occurs within countries via Export Processing Zones, the designated global spaces where subcontracting of production and off-shoring of jobs takes place. Several studies document the preference for women who are paid low wages in some labor-intensive manufacturing. Preference for women workers, older or younger, depends on the histories of industrialization and the nature of local institutions. A strategy of feminizing the workforce enables companies operating in EPZs to reap the benefit of hiring women in low-waged work in the factories; workers in these zones tend to come from poor rural areas where families cannot provide for their own subsistence. Output produced in the EPZ typically gets transported for final assembly and consumption in developed countries. Underdevelopment, already part of the world economy, breeds distorted development in these extra-territorial global spaces. These zones function to localize work while facilitating the extension of global capitalism.

On the other side of economic globalization is labor's mobility. Globalization of migration not only circulates more people to far-flung places around the world – labor moved in early phases of capitalism – but also involves new integrated processes of production and social reproduction. Differentiating globalization of migration from earlier international migration is the quality as well as the quantity of cross-border economic and political interactions and linkages. More women embark on migratory sojourns. Women migrating from poorer to richer areas provide a cheap source of labor that frees global managers and members of the global male and female elite from taking care of their own domestic tasks, such as cleaning, laundry and child-rearing. This feminization of migration is based on the increasing demand for personal services. Poor countries supply low-waged labor at one end of the commodity chain, which fuels demand for cheaper consumption in the metropoles. The growth of market-based services, especially commodification of care, relieves some women of the responsibility of unpaid household tasks, but shifts the burden onto low-waged workers. A transnational chain of reproductive labor increasingly promotes commodification and informalization of employment relations.

Globalizing labor markets are associated with informalization, characterizing new rights and risk profiles for men and women in different parts of the world (Summerfield 2001: 5–6). The conditions of informalization affect ever larger numbers of workers, especially those in low-waged services and in labor-intensive assembly. Informalization is premised on individualization of employment contracts and privatization of social reproduction, leaving workers without the means of securing their own livelihood and that of their families. Many of these workers risk abuse due to the lack of legal regulation, social protection, and collective representation, and their invisibility in the confines of private spaces of households, commercial buildings, or sweatshops. In this respect, informalization challenges rights and conditions among workers in formerly more protected areas of production in the core, as well as undermining efforts to get formal rights while breaking down cultural practices in home societies on the periphery. Significantly, globalization and individualization disrupt older structures of social support, putting workers and their families at risk, as cultural practices, once supporting social relations and the community, are replaced by new, but often insufficient, means of social reproduction. The importance of social reproduction and care work indicates why it is necessary to apply a feminist lens to the examination of the causes and consequences of informalization extending feminized quality of work to men and women on a global scale.

While expansion of feminized services and export-oriented manufacturing draws more women into the waged labor market globally, whether they stay at "home" or migrate to other places, it has contradictory effects on class and gender inequality. Pearson (2007: 11) cogently argues that "women's increasing role in global production" raises an "unsettling contradiction." Specifically, while women's engagement in paid work does afford them more choices and more control over their lives, much of this work is degrading, underpaid, exploitative, and informalized. Indeed, she suggests that we must rethink the assumption that paid work either automatically "translates into empowerment" (12), autonomy (13–14), or economic security, or is necessarily the main route to achieving gender equality. Gender equality is not simply an issue of equity in the workplace or of comparable wages, but involves a broader project for improving the conditions of work and life. More money will not, in and of itself, empower women. It brings us back to the problematic of the male norm that is based on paid employment without responsibility for social reproduction. Interestingly, women's paid labor may enable them to escape local patriarchy in their home countries, but it is replaced with structural patriarchal relations in the globalized labor market.

Place matters when analyzing globalizing labor markets and how these labor market changes are gendered (Perrons 2007): "In particular, the 'place' of any locality within the global economy gives rise to local employment and household structures, which in turn influence gender relations" (Bruegel 1999: 73). As suggested in this chapter, global production and reproduction are also local activities. The next chapter examines global cities as strategic places where the new economy is reshaping social relations of production and reproduction.

On the Global Economic Grid: Tokyo Tales, London Chronicles, Shanghai Stories

> Thy city, which is so full of envy that already the sack runs over, held me within it in the bright life . . . For the damning fault of gluttony, as thou seest, I lie helpless in the rain; and in my misery I am not alone, for all these are under the same penalty for the same fault. (Canto VI, Dante's *Inferno*, 89)

Dante's *Inferno* vividly imagines the city enticing travelers with its "bright life" caught in an eternal downpour. Like this circle of hell, global cities doom many to extreme misery and deprivation alongside luxury and wealth. As "one strategic type of place" between the global and the national, the city "allows us to recover the concrete, localized [work] processes" (Sassen 2001: 7) sustaining globalization, in order to uncover linkages that tie together the economic fate of men and women. Whereas the global spaces of economic processing zones and other places in developing countries host labor-intensive, often feminized jobs along manufacturing commodity chains, the examination of global cities through a feminist lens provides entry into the ways that local worksites exist within locations of global power relations that are gendered (Acker 2004), and how global processes "enact on local ground" (Freeman 2001: 1008–9). Global cities attract services at both low and high ends for the administration and management of the global economy. These jobs put in sharp relief the stark differences between the unmarked global elite and the strong gender and ethnic marking characteristic of devalued service and care occupations (Clark 1996: 44). In this way, male and female workers gain "presence" or visibility where they were once missing from globalization narratives (Sassen 2004). By focusing on global cities, this chapter further unpacks the concrete work in the global economy.

A tale of two types of global cities in the North and South lends a material setting to Dante's literary lament: "in my misery I am not

alone, for all these are under the same penalty for the same fault."
New York, London, and Tokyo, old financial centers of the capitalist
world economy, are juxtaposed in this chapter with regional and
ascendant global cities like Beijing, Shanghai, and Dubai. This tour
points out contrasting features of gendered work and reveals new
geographies of power and resistance within and between old and new
global cities. In global cities, we can see economic transformations
up-close, and assess the toll they take on low-waged service workers
inhabiting these localities. At the same time, the city is a site for new
imaginaries. Two examples of mobilization among women workers
reveal the ways that the global city both constrains, and opens up new
possibilities for, collective action. Just as peering through a microscope can expose common characteristics of organisms, a sociological
perspective on global cities finds the "shared patterns beneath [what
appear like] sharp differences" (Sassen 2004) between far-flung places
around the world.

The origins and characteristics of global cities

Global cities originated as centers of capitalist production, emerging
in conjunction with industrialization. Before globalization, cities
housed global functions associated with internationalization of
industrial production. New technologies enabled multinational corporations to transplant production processes in different parts of the
world. With the shift to post-industrial production, a select number
of city centers – e.g. in New York, London, and Tokyo – became the
administrative hubs of the global economy. Finance and other business services crowded out industrial production in places like New
York City, which saw much of its garment industry move first from
the Lower East Side, to farther south in the US, and finally across the
border to Mexico. As magnets for business services and knowledge-
intensive work, these global cities drew on a growing number of
low-waged workers to provide reproductive services for those in elite
jobs. The social, cultural, and economic features of these original
global cities thus reflect the organic growth of capitalist expansion.
Interestingly, the same technologies and networked processes enable
the global reach of capital to move further into the former periphery
and intensify the linkages of commodity chains. New global cities
– not coincidentally, concentrated in Asia – are modeled on the old
but are stamped by the political-economic systems from which they
have come. Political actors in these newer global cities orchestrate
command and control economies. A resulting hierarchy of first-
and second-tier cities share defining characteristics even as they

diverge significantly in the conditions and spatial arrangements of work.

Defining a Global City

Several characteristics define a global city. A global city serves as an "extra-territorial platform," a denationalized command site for the circulation of money, goods, ideas, symbols, and people; operate as places of interchange and exchange; and involve hyper-mobile people, products, and production processes. Hyper-mobility gives a global city its distinctive denationalized orientation. Another hallmark of a global city, the growth, extent, and centrality of finance and specialized business services – such as accounting, legal services, insurance, real estate, and Information and Computer Technologies – generally replaces the old industrial base in rust-belt urban areas of the developed world (Orum & Chen 2003: 56). Beside the volume of specialized business services, the relationship between cities and their relative position at the center of global circuits of capital further situate a global city. From this perspective, Sassen distinguishes between globalization and internationalization, juxtaposing the rise of the global cities of London, New York, and Tokyo with the decline of industrial urban centers.

Serving as "command sites" of the global economy, global cities operate in denationalized ways, in contrast to Fordist industrial centers bound to the nation state (Sassen 1996: 10). British-owned banks exemplify denationalization; though based in the City of London, their divestment from local manufacturing led to the decline of automobile assembly in the UK during the 1980s. These same banks invested large sums abroad where they could reap the highest profits, hastening the post-industrial economic transformation of London, and the UK more generally. Through these processes, old hubs of Fordist production, evident in the decay and urban ruins among red-brick factories in places like Detroit, lose out to global cities like London, New York City, and Tokyo that house finance and knowledge-intensive work (Dicken et al. 1997).

Global cities concentrate finance and headquarters of multinational corporations. Employment in finance, insurance, and real-estate industries (FIRE) makes up a significant portion of each city's economy, well above that sector's share in the overall national economy. In New York City, banking and finance employment encompassed just over 10% of the total workforce in the 1980s, declining to 8.8% by 1997. London started at a smaller share of 4.5% in 1981, and then nearly doubled to 8.4% in 1999. In-between, Tokyo had almost 6% of employment in finance by 1997. The number of headquarters of top

Table 11.1 Largest cities by population (2010 and 2025)

Rank in 2010	City	Metro population 2010 (millions)	Projected rank 2025	Projected population 2025 (millions)
1	Tokyo, Japan	35.2	1	36.4
2	Mexico City, Mexico	19.2	6	21.0
3	New York City, USA	18.7	7	20.6
4	Sao Paolo, Brazil	18.3	5	21.4
5	Mumbai, India	18.2	2	26.4
6	Delhi, India	15.0	3	22.5
7	Kolkata, India	14.7	7	20.6
8	Shanghai, China	14.5	9	19.4
9	Dhaka, Bangladesh	11.9	4	22.0
10	Karachi, Pakistan	11.6	10	19.1

Data source: "In pictures: the 10 biggest cities of 2025," Forbes.com, www.forbes.com/2008/03/19/cities-population-pollution-innovation08–cx_tvr_0319futurecities_slide_2.html (downloaded February 10, 2012).

500 transnational corporations shows high density, ranging from 59 in New York City, to 37 in London, and 34 in Tokyo by 1984. On the eve of the twenty-first century, the number of headquarters grew to 63 in Tokyo, surpassing 25 in New York and 29 in London, as compared to Chicago with only 2 in 1999, down from 18 in 1984 (Sassen 2001: 109). This absolute and relative density of employment in finance and headquarters shows that "Some [cities] are profoundly articulated with the global and others are not ..." (Sassen 2004: 377).

All cities are increasingly global, and intermingle a plurality of cultures and people dwelling in urban areas (Huyssen 2008: 3). To be designated as a global city, by contrast, means the city occupies a strategic space for the coordination and localization of global economic processes. The sheer size of the urban population alone does not define a global city (see table 11.1). Yet population size and global functions are highly correlated (Gugler 2004: 3). For example, Tokyo is a global city not simply because of its population – although it ranks first worldwide in terms of its total with more than 35 million people residing inside densely packed neighborhoods in the sprawling metropolis – but rather because of the strategic role played by banks located there. Though no city is untouched by the global economy – even if through destruction and decay as in deindustrialized cities such as Detroit (Huyssen 2008: 11) – all global cities are positioned in relationship to each other. New global cities have emerged in the wake of global economic restructuring and the interventions by state-based actors.

Second-tier Global Cities

Rival cities now compete for prominence in the global economy. Recently, Shanghai, Beijing, Mumbai, and Dubai have emerged as regional global cities, or as "second-tier" mega-cities (Gugler 2004: 3). These cities are considered global to the extent that finance and other business services operate on a denationalized, but primarily regional, scale. However, they are considered *second-tier* based on the relative density of transnational headquarters, at levels higher than most cities but still lower than in older global cities. The location of these cities in poorer nations, without the social and physical infrastructures to support the large number of people arriving in search of jobs, differentiates these second-tier global cities from the first tier. Such rapid in-migration produces *mega-cities* with enormous populations, drawing mostly on migrants from their own domestic hinterlands. Older global cities (New York City, London, and Tokyo) have displaced the poor to the periphery, shedding non-financial work that had once sustained the working class. Urban renewal during the 1950s and 1960s cleared poor and old working-class neighborhoods, replaced by cultural institutions such as the Lincoln Center and other developments in New York City. By contrast, the rapid growth of new global cities attracts an increasing number of poor people. Mumbai, with a projected population of 26.4 million, will exceed the number of inhabitants in metropolitan New York City by 2025 (see table 11.1).

What also makes these second-tier cities global, like their counterparts in Europe and the US, is their increasingly important role in administering global capital accumulation. But, situated in developing countries, these newer regional global cities are rife with extreme levels of poverty, forming distinctive socio-spatial patterns of inequality. Older global cities repurpose the built environment to accommodate shifting economic functions; these new global cities rely on state-directed development efforts to create a new built environment almost in the blink of an eye, with accelerated economic modernization projects appearing as if one is watching the new cityscape through time-lapse photography. Global cities in the periphery depend on strong state authorities able to mobilize abundant resources, both human and financial, in constructing new command sites. In these newer global cities, political rights may be suspended and enclaves created by governmental fiat or by state tolerance. Foreign elites live and work in these enclaves often replacing traditional neighborhoods bull-dozed from and pushed out of central city districts.

This brief story of the genesis of global cities suggests that capitalist firms concentrate service activities in a few strategic places. Older and newer global cities share common characteristics constituting their importance in managing the global economy. Their roots at different historical moments in the formation of globalization processes, and their relative positions in the global economy give old and newer global cities their distinctive features. Though not highlighted in this section, global cities, both old and new, accumulate wealth and attract specialized business services, which in turn beget increasing demand for personal and personalized services. In dense urban spaces, valorization of service activities and labor differs widely by gender, class, and citizenship status, resulting in unique patterns of social inequalities. These economic processes have cultural and social consequences, creating possibilities for collective mobilization even among otherwise vulnerable workers.

Valorization of Services and Service Providers in Global Cities

The economic functions of global cities generate new patterns of social inequalities. Global cities accumulate immense concentrations of economic power; "highly educated workers in the corporate sector see their incomes rise to unusually high levels while low- or medium-skilled workers see their incomes sink" (Sassen 1996: 20), leading to "polarization of every sort" (Clark 1996: 44). On the one hand, professionals working in banks may interact with their peers located in other global cities more often than they do with their local counterparts (McDowell 1997b: 122). On the other hand, to sustain those employed in command functions, downtown business districts require appropriate amenities catering to highly paid professionals: up-market restaurants and health clubs intermingle with office high-rises in global cities. These specialized services replace and crowd out neighborhood shops once tailored to the local needs of formerly mixed-class communities (Sassen 1996: 23). Professional amenities not only service the global (male) elite, but also are part of the business of doing business. The clustering of service activities enables members of the elite to engage in face-to-face interactions while they enjoy the perquisites of city-life. The legions of low-waged service workers performing reproductive labor enable professionals to conduct business often far from their own homes of origin.

Service workers ensure that the managerial and professional elite have continued access to the rarified environments they desire. For example, by carefully replicating the familiar culture and infrastructure of residences and amenities, service workers make it possible for a globe-trotting executive (hyper-mobile elite) to believe that he (or she) is a culturally neutral technocrat. Cleaners, personal secretaries, security guards, messengers, delivery people, and personal concierges absorb traces of the actual physical and cultural location. Global service companies market aspirational luxury goods with brand names and recognizable logos that lose nothing in translation. This is regardless of the local context: companies such as Starbucks operating abroad make small concessions to the local culture, but mostly offer the same menu in every outlet whether dispensing grande lattes tucked away in Beijing's Forbidden City or Tokyo's Ark Mori Building. The global also homogenizes culture, serving the same products disconnected from place. By design, Starbucks is recognizably Starbucks no matter where you consume it. In this way, service workers both appear hyper-visible and fade into the background of carefully cultivated interior spaces and cityscapes.

Saskia Sassen (1996) paints a "chilling picture of the global [male] elite of managers and consultants" (Clark 1996: 43) – clustered in a small handful of central business districts – concentrating power and income. As Gracia Clark (1996: 46) suggests, the creation of globalized spaces is not a process of "eviction," as suggested by Sassen, but one of devalorization. Women, minorities, and immigrants are not excluded from the global city, but are differently positioned within it (often in relationship to other women). Devalorization is accomplished both through immigration laws that exclude many immigrants from coverage by regulations over wages, hours, and safety, and through informalized employment arrangements (46). Immigration laws are least successful in "keeping immigrants from arriving bodily in global cities, [but] have been very successful in maintaining their status as illegal aliens " (46). This devalorization of the "serving classes" sustains the overvaluation of the male elite, as can be seen in the cities of London and Tokyo.

A gendered tale of two old global cities: London and Tokyo

This tale of two global cities surveys post-industrial landscapes in London and Tokyo. Studies examining macro-economic trends (Bruegel 1999) and more finely grained analysis of meso-organizational and micro-practices at work (McDowell et al. 2005) present a complicated picture of gains and losses among different groups of men and women working in global cities. Such research demonstrates the significance of differentiating gender by class, race, and national origins. Sassen leaves the impression that "women and immigrants" occupy similar positions of inequality in relationship to men. Global cities, however, create opportunities for educated women to find employment in finance and other business services, although still not equal to those for men. Using a feminist lens, this section differentiates types of service work and how these jobs are gendered in order to assess the positive and negative impact of globalization on the economic position of women and men in London and Tokyo.

Global cities like London tend to offer better employment opportunities to women overall. As a result, some women have made gains relative to men, improving gender equality, while at the same time widening class inequalities based on income disparities between households, especially those with low-paid or unemployed men (Bruegel 1999). However, service employment increases class disparities among women as well as between men and women. We must look at what happens inside otherwise opaque high-rise office buildings in the financial district of the City of London and in Tokyo to understand the devalued activities that support the global elite. The feminist lens shows that, though less visible, low-paid, often off-the-grid workers of the formal economy, service workers provide amenities that entice the elite to reside in global cities. In the City of London, it is possible to see devalorization and overvalorization of service work and workers around the global city.

Men's work biographies also are changing as a result of economic restructuring apparent in global cities. In Tokyo, young Japanese men, because of either lack of entry-level jobs or decisions to freelance, increasingly take up temporary employment. This new development undermines the old reproductive bargain, and its underpinning of masculinity based on the male breadwinner. Interestingly, in both London and Tokyo, some working-class men find fewer prospects as a consequence of gender-specific work preferences among employers, especially in many of the feminized personal services. As McDowell (2008: 21) observes: "growing numbers of men are disqualified from even low-wage, low-status jobs in the service sector by their inappropriate (stereotypical) gender attributes . . . . the characteristics of docility, deference and a neat embodied performance that are valued by employers of labor at the bottom end of the service sector are mostly closely mapped onto the socially constructed attributes of femininity."

On the one hand, the process of deindustrialization and the decline of manufacturing capacity (and with it many traditional men's jobs) has "led to re-evaluation of traditionally female skills particularly those associated with communication, sales, training and personnel management" (Bruegel 1999: 75). On the other hand, deregulation erodes social protections and promotes the increasing use of part-time work among women and, increasingly, among young men (75). Though women with high qualifications have made inroads into male-dominated fields, they remain at a disadvantage in jobs configured around masculinized embodied characteristics.

The City of London: Inside the "Lads" Club

While manufacturing hemorrhaged jobs, declining by 48% during the deregulatory Thatcher era of the 1980s, companies in FIRE continued to hire new personnel throughout the 1990s (Sassen 2001: 133). However, as another complementary study suggests, Sassen underestimates class differences among women. In the City of London, young, single, educated women advanced in professional positions while less-educated women and men remained stuck in low-waged and increasingly insecure service employment (Bruegel 1999: 78, 87). London offered educated women greater opportunities to enter managerial and professional occupations when compared to the UK as a whole, women working full-time in Greater London received larger paychecks on average, and their earnings increased at a higher rate over the decade from 1983 to 1994. Likewise, immigrants, both male and female, experienced better chances of finding managerial jobs in London than in other parts of the UK, although female migrants still predominated in low-waged personal service jobs. Despite the unprecedented number of women in professional positions, "occupational sex stereotyping and the institutional and everyday structures of workplace interactions have maintained and reproduced patterns of inequality at work" (McDowell 1997a: 182).

Hidden behind women's entry into more highly paid professional and managerial jobs is the persistence of masculinized organizational cultures that discriminate against women and valorize hegemonic masculinity. Appearing on the first anniversary of the financial meltdown, "Sexism in the City Still Rules OK" (Verkaik 2009) describes the "laddish culture" still prevalent in British financial institutions revealed in an investigation conducted by the Equality and Human Rights Commission (EHRC). Most notably, financial institutions pay women less than men despite long hours of work, and routinely lay-off women when they become pregnant. More sensationally, male bankers entertain clients in lap-dancing clubs and hostess bars. These degrading male venues, if not excluding women altogether from after-work activities, disadvantage them in the business of fostering relationships with clients. The investigation concludes that: "It is this culture that denigrates certain tasks, which then become associated with women's work, from which men are encouraged to progress so that women become ghettoized, contributing to occupational segregation" (cited in Verkaik 2009). One woman summarizes the hegemonic masculine performance of investment bankers in stark terms: "If you do not attend large drinking sessions, play billiards and speak and act like a man (that is, not crying and never sleeping and never taking any days off for yourself or your children) then you still have a small chance of success provided you dress like a model and express a wish never to have children" (2009).

An in-depth study of merchant bankers in London reveals that the construction of a dominant version of hegemonic masculinity revolves around a variant of an embodied, manly, heterosexualized, class-based masculinity that disempowers a range of "Others," not only women but men from different class, ethnic, and educational backgrounds (McDowell 1997b: 203). Playing on Goffman's stage metaphor, McDowell (1997a: 12) focuses on the notion of gender as performance, and merchant banking as a world in which role-playing and drama – an embodied performance – are key requirements for both men and women. For example, the task of "impressing and bonding with potential collaborators" involves a gendered performance that can take place in the board room or the night club, or on the golf course. Individual women may try emulating the "unmarked white male," yet remarks that someone is "typical" or "atypical" of their marked category serve to underline their membership in it (Clark 1996). For this reason, women often feel "out of place in the embodied social structures of the workplace precisely because they are unable to [easily] acquire the cultural markers associated with the rational and bureaucratic workplace" (McDowell 1997a: 12). It is this relationship between a female body and lack of power that helps to explain why women are forced to act as if they were men in order to achieve success. However, women who attempt to behave like men are often viewed with suspicion and distrust by both their male and female colleagues (154). That is, women do not comfortably fit in jobs predicated on hegemonic masculine embodiment. Along similar lines, those in support positions, such as secretaries and waiters, "not only disproportionately include individuals of marked gender and racial or ethnic categories, but frequently these individuals also [are required to] enact exaggerated gender and ethnic roles in dress, voice, or behavior as part of performing and keeping their jobs" (Clark 1996: 44).

This sexist culture produces a "massive gender pay gap" between male and female professionals working in the City. Women employed there full-time earn 47% less in annual gross salaries than do men, in comparison to an overall 28% pay gap in the UK nation-wide. Similarly, women receive lower bonuses on average than men. Data on first-time bonuses confirm this wide gender-based disparity: in 2009 women were awarded £300 on average, as compared to £800 for men. Similarly, women earn an average of £2,875 in annual performance-related pay, much less than men's £14,554. A large part of the pay gap is due to the disparity in bonuses and other performance-related incentives. These more discretionary components of compensation rely on subjective judgments by male-dominated authority structures that determine what merits an exemplary performance. But unacknowledged is how gender-related criteria affect differences in performance-related pay. One way to interpret these differences sees men rewarded not only for their hard work, but also for their successful hegemonic masculine performance. Even more intractable is the significance of masculine embodiment to success in the sexist culture of finance. As one male executive was reported to have said: "We won't pay her, we will pay him: he's not going to have a baby" (cited in Verkaik 2009).

An extended interview with a female lawyer in the City underscores how hegemonic masculinity operates in high finance:

> Gill Switalski, 52, a City lawyer, is claiming £12 million in compensation from F&C Asset Management for allegedly forcing her out of a job in September 2007 through bullying. She claimed that she was treated unfairly at the company, despite making "significant bonuses." A London tribunal heard that she had been questioned by managers over flexible working hours, holidays and expenses. One of her managers became "fixated" with her working hours, which had been adapted to give her more time with her family, and often checked up on her indirectly through her colleagues, this despite the fact that she was hitting her performance targets, the tribunal was told. Ms Switalsk has four children, including a son with cerebral palsy and another with Asperger's syndrome. The tribunal heard Ms Switalski's deputy was selected instead of her for the task of securing a hedge fund and she was overlooked for management roles. But, her lawyer said, a male colleague who had children with special needs was allowed to work from home to care for them. (cited in Verkaik 2009)

The reality of lower earnings and limited mobility speaks to the difficulties for combining motherhood and employment in banking and finance jobs, configured around masculine embodiment and non-responsibility for care. Bruegel extracts comparative statistics from the 1995 UK Labour Force Survey to show that 42.8% of male employees and 25.8% of female employees in banking, and 40.7% of male employees to 23.4% of female employees in finance management, were parents. A similar ratio of male to female parents exists in the legal professions (46.0% to 20.8%), marketing (43.0% to 20.4%), and personnel management (47.1% to 25.4%), with a smaller difference among engineers (37.4% to 27.0%), doctors (50.7% to 37.0%), and accountants/economists (39.9% to 30.2%) (Bruegel 1999: 84). Parenthood also has different effects on men's and women's earnings potential. Fathers are more likely to earn the highest salaries in FIRE industries, as compared to mothers, who receive the least compensation. So, motherhood is experienced as a disadvantage due to gendered expectations, both real and groundless.

This tale of London takes us inside the "lads" club, referring to a core cultural idiom at men's disposal for expressing hegemonic masculinity in the UK. Further, this focus on laddish culture in finance exhumes how work practices at the micro-organizational level are related to and affect economic processes at the macro-institutional level. Financial institutions value and valorize risk-taking (some would say gambling) as the *raison d'être* of their work. This is a gendered activity in the sense that men are perceived to be better at risk-taking than women. It is at the micro-level where we can observe the concrete gendered practices and assumptions driving these businesses. At the high end of the job hierarchy, patriarchal social closure limits women's mobility chances even when they manage to secure elite jobs. Although not representative of all occupations, women's experience in finance illustrates how the glass-ceiling effect and other disadvantages are produced. Case studies reveal that success is measured by more than output, and rewards and returns are based on more than a bundle of "human" capital (e.g. educational credentials). Notions of success and merit embed perceptions of appropriate gender embodiment and performance in these occupations and industries. Men in elite finance positions perceive women to be undeserving, and even unable, to fully meet employment demands. Actual or potential motherhood turns female embodiment into a disqualification. Hard work does not uproot laddish culture in upper levels of finance. Rather, it is the production of a sexist culture through everyday interactions, and the close alliance of finance and other business services with the laddish version of hegemonic masculinity, that preserves these positions as male-dominated.

Tokyo: Crossroads of East and West

As a late and rapidly industrialized country, Tokyo experienced major growth spurts later than the more mature economies of New York and London (Gottfried 2000). Tokyo's sprawling and dense built environment grew up and out in bits and pieces, fits and starts, out of the ashes of war destruction. Throughout the 1970s, when oil shocks reverberated in this oil-dependent nation, there was a relative decline of manufacturing, while financial capital consolidated its base in Tokyo. The employment share in manufacturing declined by 12%, while the share increased for wholesale and retail trade, communication, and transport during the decade from 1975 to 1985. Employment mushroomed an astonishing 28% in finance, insurance and real estate over the following decade, whereas employment in manufacturing slid further, declining 15% even though a small percentage of new manufacturing jobs became available in other parts of Japan. A construction boom in Tokyo created jobs for working-class men, whose employment rose by 23% from 1985 to 1997, attesting to this industry's importance as a political boondoggle; the ruling party of the Liberal Democrats subsidized the building explosion even after the country's economy took a tailspin during the lost decade of the 1990s. As reported in the *New York Times*, beneath the surface of civil engineering projects is pork barrel that fueled economic growth in the post-war period, sustaining the Liberal Democratic Party in power for most of the past half-century (Tabuchi 2009: 4), until the Democratic Party of Japan won a landslide victory in the 2009 election (a party now under assault due to their fumbling of the recovery efforts after the Tsunami of 2011, see Gottfried 2011). In Tokyo, global administrative functions spread over decentered business districts connected by intersecting private and public rail-lines.

Financial institutions cluster in one main district close to metro-stops, with clearly marked names of buildings at each exit to guide foot-traffic on city streets not easily navigated using the flat rendering of a map. Professionals from home offices in Europe and the United States tend to live and reside in Westernized sections of Tokyo, where familiar franchises such as Starbucks, KFC, and 7–Eleven collide with local noodle shops along major thoroughfares of Roppongi. Up-market stores and amenities dot the streets of Shibuya, the other favored neighborhood. On a typical work day, bankers, primarily men hailing from foreign offices, queue up for their jolt of morning Starbucks' coffee, while young Japanese women, most often "office ladies," stand in line to purchase hot and cold beverages. At the other end of the age spectrum, more than two-thirds of mothers with young children drop out of the labor force of Tokyo, where balancing waged employment and motherhood is particularly difficult due to long commuting times and long hours of full-time work in this sprawling city (Nagase 2006: 44). About 80% of mothers with new-born babies living in urban areas leave the labor force to become full-time house-wives (44). A lower-than-average fertility rate in Tokyo underscores the difficulty for women in reconciling waged work with childcare responsibilities. This profile and its consequences stems from labor market institutions so strongly linked to the male breadwinner reproductive bargain.

The age-graded and gender profile corresponds to a skewed dis-tribution of workers in the local labor market of Tokyo. Increasing educational parity has not led women to the top of occupational hier-archies in numbers commensurate with their qualifications. Young women with educational credentials equal to young men's do not necessarily sustain their initial positions on the fast track in upper-level professional jobs. An advanced degree does not shield women from long-term loss of income and limited job mobility. Increasingly, younger men experience a similar trajectory, beginning with their precarious employment in the context of weak economic growth over the past two decades. Education tends to mediate the negative effects of having young children, although a large employment gap between mothers and non-mothers exists even among the most highly educated women (Fuwa 2010; Ishiguro 2010). Those mothers who continue working full-time have better chances of employment and advancement in some professions than in others. Ishiguro (2010) found that single women, with or without children, had more success than married women in the male-dominated industries of banking and electronics. By contrast, the publishing company in her study supported more married women in management. It is possible that flatter organizational structures in industries such as publishing may accommodate married women more than the bureaucratic hierarchical structure in banking. With fewer organizational layers, the publishing company seems to offer more flexibility that enables mothers to balance work and family life. On the other side of the ledger, finance's hyper-masculinist culture appears less family-friendly. In Tokyo's maelstrom of people streaming from major railway stations, the grey-suited salarymen and adorned office ladies conform largely to old gender and class patterns. A case study of the temporary work sector in Japan challenges us to think about gender and modes of embodiment as place-bound processes, allowing us to observe business practices that contribute to the production of age-graded and gender-based employment patterns in Tokyo.

Temporary help companies have created a niche to satisfy increasing demand for linguistic skills, such as interpreting and translation, by foreign-owned subsidiaries, and so dispatch female employees to perform specialized skills and administrative tasks necessary for the operation of foreign-owned and Japanese-based multinational companies in Tokyo (Gottfried 2003). Multinational and locally based temporary help firms serve as labor market intermediaries to service finance and other global functions. Temporary help companies seek to attract and manage qualified female workers who embody certain sexualized body traits and can easily assimilate organizational norms that usually are inculcated through in-house training by client firms. The temporary employee's self-presentation is a situated, culturally informed, gendered performance. Temporary help companies prescribe dress codes for wrapping female bodies in either official or iconic uniforms (2003). For client firms, the male embodied bureaucracy marginalizes temporary female employees who have no formal place in either general-office or career tracks. In the Japanese model of bureaucracy, personal favors are a part of the work of doing authority relationships. Personalized favors belong to elaborate gift-giving rituals that convey, through symbolic means, deference and position in the social order. Yoko Ogasawara (1998), who worked as a temporary employee in a large financial institution, received gifts because of her physical proximity to the boss even though she had little personal contact with him on the job. On-site supervisors use their discretion whether or not to include temporary employees in the gift-giving circuit.

Tokyo stories relate the institutional disadvantages experienced by women in this global city. Japan as a strong male breadwinner welfare system creates what might be called a non-marriage penalty for women who opt out of marriage. The societal value placed on corporate men supported by stay-at-home wives renders real change slow and marginal at best. Gender is more of a barrier in Tokyo than in London. Japanese women face a built environment less forgiving to those with care responsibilities. Commuting distances and long hours on top of rigid labor market structures and sexist culture disadvantage women working in Tokyo.

Changing Geographies of Power: Faces of Old Global Cities

Economic geographers have noted the paradox of globalization increasing the importance of local places (McDowell 1997b: 128). Mobility makes the global elite more discerning about where they live, selecting a place to work on the basis of the flavor of local cultures. Gender and class come into play around different concerns and options for single men and women as compared to mothers with young children. Many highly educated, single women living and working in central city districts enjoy similar amenities to men. Yet mothers seeking care and caring services face different options in terms of quality, availability, and cost, depending on whether they live in neighborhoods within or in close proximity to global cities. In the City of London, good-quality care is expensive, which puts formal arrangements out of reach for some working-class women. Middle-class women may utilize formal childcare centers or nannies in their homes, when they return to work soon after childbirth. In Tokyo, working women more often rely on relatives, when available, or find reasonable outside services, while other highly educated mothers drop out of the labor force altogether unable to navigate the long-hours work culture of salarymen. In both cities, however, the lack of sufficient, affordable, good-quality, and publicly supported care services makes it difficult for mothers to combine work and family responsibilities. Though some women can afford personal concierge services in their homes, or other types of care arrangements, the density of finance and other business services pushes up the costs of private reproductive services at the same time as neo-liberal attacks on the welfare state (Sassen 1996, 2001) lead the state to retreat from support of social services.

Paradoxically, the extra-territorial or denationalized business practices that give these services their distinctive global orientation simultaneously diminish the importance of local places. The process of financialization bids up real-estate properties, making it expensive to conduct business in London and Tokyo, which in turn undermines the appeal of these older global cities. Certain global functions are transferred from distinctive financial districts in older city centers to nearby cities, or off-shored to countries with cheaper rents and lower wages. For example, back-office activities and other banking functions have moved to Jersey City rather than staying in lower Manhattan. At least one of the multinational temporary-help firms has relocated its headquarters from Tokyo to Yokohama where there are lower rents, yet they are still in close geographic proximity via frequent trains leaving the main Tokyo Station to link the agency to old and new clients and workers. And changes in the labor process enabled by computer technologies extend the global reach of finance and banking. For example, call centers relocate work to lower-waged areas around global cities, and to English-speaking countries in the Caribbean or to India. Transnational corporations faced with high costs of doing business move operations to cities in the cheaper Global South.

The emergence of new second-tier global cities, then, can be seen to a certain extent as impelled by the inner logic of transnational capital operating in global cities. That is, the imperative to seek profits, but also for elite male professionals to inhabit a place with amenities, eventually makes other locations more appealing. Where these new global outposts will stake a claim is rooted in geographies of power. A new hierarchy of global cities is evolving from the regional ascendance of countries in Asia. London, New York, and Tokyo are at the center coordinating the global economy, but increasingly these nodal sites must compete with emergent global cities in developing countries. Within Asia, Shanghai and Dubai challenge Tokyo for centrality both within the region and on the global economic grid.

Emergent global cities in an ascendant Asia

Second-tier global cities in Brazil (Sao Paolo), China (Beijing, Shanghai), India (Delhi), and the United Arab Emirates (Dubai) vie for administrative control in the global economy. Where global cities take root depends on readily available economic infrastructures supporting transportation, communication, and education (for a skilled labor force), along with strong central state authority. State-directed development projects have accelerated modernization, and thereby have helped to make coastal cities particularly attractive to foreign capital. In so doing, the state catapults industrial economies into service and knowledge-intensive activities. As they are situated in developing countries, distinctive socio-spatial dynamics produce extreme disparities between a small, but increasingly homegrown, capitalist class and a large working class composed of a growing number of migrants in "temporary" employment, pouring into these urban areas from their rural homes. The rapid pace of change occurring in our lifetime puts in sharp relief the process of transformation making Beijing, Shanghai, and Dubai into second-tier global cities in economically ascendant Asia.

The role of the "developmental" state represents one distinctive aspect of global cities in Asia. The state directly intervenes in national economic modernization projects, while it externalizes social reproduction to working people. Second-tier global cities in poorer nations lack well-developed welfare state systems or have enacted welfare retrenchment, as in China,[1] exposing workers to the vagaries of market fluctuations without the buffer of public support systems (Gugler 2004: 3). At the same time, direct state intervention "remakes" the city and promotes global economic activity (Orum & Chen 2003). The state has undertaken "massive and highly selective investment for redevelopment" of infrastructure to house and facilitate global functions (Sassen 2004: 372). Inescapable construction cranes, like metal dinosaurs roaming prime real estate, transform the physical infrastructure of newer global cities. Large-scale construction projects rely on and require a large pool of cheap labor, most often drawing on male migrants from poor rural villages, as in China (Swider 2010), or poorer countries, as in Dubai (Gugler 2004: 15). These men reside "temporarily" in compounds near construction sites or on the cities' periphery in makeshift slums and shantytowns. The state literally bulldozes old neighborhoods and creates new business districts in emergent global cities.

Local and national governments undertake different strategies to mobilize and create a temporary workforce in the twin pursuits of modernization and economic development. The Chinese state regulates movement of labor by granting temporary residence to migrants. China's household registration system (*hukou*) dictates residence for every person in a family, and designates migrant workers' home in their predetermined place of origin. The *hukou* system was established in 1958 as a measure to control movement from rural areas to metropolises. Even though the system was relaxed in 1984, it remains intact for the purpose of determining rights (Wichterich 2009: 5). Official recognition of one's "home" is critical, since residence determines where one receives welfare benefits, such as access to free education, subsidized housing, and pensions (Weiping & Yusuf 2004: 54).

Overall there are an estimated 150 to 200 million migrant workers from China's countryside (Wichterich 2009: 5), of which approximately 40% are women (Solinger 1999). Migrants account for 17.4% of the total population and nearly one-third (31 percent) of the working population overall (Swider 2010: 3). Nearly one in three workers (3) or an estimated 3 million "temporary" migrants work without official residency status in Shanghai (Weiping & Yusuf 2004: 54). The migrant population is difficult to enumerate because many enter the city under a tenuous legal status. Swider (2010) differentiates four types of legal statuses with corresponding rights, including: regular migrants with full rights and officially sponsored by the state and/or the employer; special-status migrants purchasing residency permits with partial rights; and registered and unregistered temporary migrants without economic and social rights. Registered migrants apply for temporary legal status, whereas unregistered temporary migrants live and work in the city illegally. She argues that the *hukou* system situates most of the unskilled migrant workers in the shadows, deprived of legal residency status and corresponding economic, political and social rights conferred by the system (4). Despite their temporary employment status, many continue to reside in the city for a long time. According to one survey conducted in 1997, about half a million migrants lived in Shanghai for over five years (Orum & Chen 2003).

In local labor markets in emergent global cities, occupational sex segregation is neither the simple consequence of abstract economic forces nor only the result of employer preferences, recruitment efforts, and gendered organizational culture. In these cases, the state is directly implicated in the matching process. The Chinese state, both local and national, invokes and evokes gender rhetoric to mobilize and train men and women for different kinds of work. In Dubai, segregation of men's and women's work conforms to both religious mandates and social norms of gender-appropriate work.

But migrant workers share a common fate, especially in second-tier global cities; the state treats them as temporary workers whose real homes are in other places. This migration from rural to urban areas, encouraged and facilitated by the state, results in new geographies of "centrality and marginality" (Sassen 1996: 17). For Dubai and Singapore, national political projects promote economic growth through a "migrant labor regime," which structures employment status through differential citizenship rights. These two authoritarian city-states issue temporary visas authorizing companies to hire migrants on fixed-term contracts of a limited duration. All "foreign" workers must be officially sponsored, and denial of citizenship ensures and reinforces migrant workers' temporary status in the countries or cities where they work. Both appear as economic miracles with low unemployment rates – a fiction, as workers without jobs have no right to stay in these city-states, which is parallel to China's internal controls. Different mechanisms produce the lower status of temporary work in new global cities.

Both local and national government actively regulate the movement of labor, varying the degrees of enforcement of, and access to, employment protections between workers with different residence and citizenship statuses. Even more pronounced in developing countries, local and national government mobilizes a temporary workforce of migrants from rural areas, and engages in huge urban renewal projects, bull-dozing whole swaths of the fabric of city-life. For example, Dubai draws on a labor force of men and women from poorer nations in South Asia to perform services and to fashion the modern cityscape like a mirage on the peninsula. Female migrant labor meets the increasing demand for low-cost reproductive services, either replacing state-based welfare in the transition from a planned to a market economy in China (Otis 2012), or in lieu of state provision of welfare and a social safety net to those deemed ineligible, as non-citizens, in Dubai and Singapore. Through "partial" citizenship, or lack of it, migrants become temporary residents with few or no employment protections and social provisions. Migrants, as temporary workers, may try to exercise their rights in urban areas away from their official homes (Solinger 1999). Though migrant labor builds these emergent second-tier global cities, the role and type of state intervention influence the treatment of migrants. In contrast to Dubai and Singapore, China mixes a socialist political apparatus with an increasingly capitalist economy, enacting new labor laws that, at least rhetorically, serve the purpose of protecting workers from the worst excesses of an unfettered capitalism.

Beijing and Shanghai: changing political economies and gendered labor markets

Beijing and the coastal city of Shanghai offer a contrast in their economic functions and their relative positions in regional and global political economies. Beijing is the national political-administrative center of China, symbolically marked by the fixed visage of Chairman Mao's monumental portrait overlooking Tiananmen Square. In

Beijing, as of 2000, an estimated 63.3% of all jobs were in the tertiary sector (Otis 2012: 59).[2] Shanghai, China's most populous city and the 8th-largest in the world, has become a center of finance and other business services, with a significant, but shrinking, industrial sector. The importance of Shanghai dates back to the nineteenth century when European trading companies established outposts principally in coastal cities, rather than trying to colonize the vast expanse of China's interior. At that time, Shanghai already had assumed a strategic position as a transshipment center in worldwide maritime trade (Gugler 2004: 10). In 1978, Shanghai's industrial and agricultural sectors accounted for the largest share of employment with 44.0% and 34.3% respectively. However, the share of employment in services has more than doubled from a low of 11.6% in 1978, jumping to 41.2% in 2001. Within the service sector, in 1978, wholesale, retail, and catering dominate with 45.6%, compared to finance and insurance with 13.8% and real estate at 0.5%. By 2001, finance and insurance increased their share to 24.7% and real estate climbed to 12.6% of overall service employment (Orum & Chen 2003: 106).[3] Beijing and Shanghai became global cities aided by their strategic locations, historical functions in international trade, and targeted government action.

Preferential treatment from central and local governments facilitated the influx of foreign capital into Shanghai's banking and real-estate sectors (Weiping & Yusuf 2004: 33), helping to underwrite an unprecedented construction boom (Orum & Chen 2003: 103). Shanghai's municipal government sought to revitalize what became known as "New Pudong" as the site of finance and other services, situated across the river from the art-deco buildings on the Bund of the historical Old Pudong district (Gugler 2004: 7). Glass-fronted office buildings and new expensive high-rise apartment complexes have transformed riverfront property as the distinctive Shanghai-style dwellings formerly hidden along the arteries of narrow alleyways were demolished (Orum & Chen 2003: 125). "Unlike market-driven high income gentrification in US cities, the municipal government of Shanghai has orchestrated the neighborhood-level redevelopment and renewal," uprooting 1.6 million residents or one-tenth of the city's population (125). Another example involves the central government literally paving the way for cultural globalization in its arrangement, almost 20 years in the making, with the Walt Disney Company. The Disneyland-style Theme Park will sprawl across 1,000 acres in the Pudong district. Calling it a landmark deal, Brooks Barnes (2009: B1), writing in *The New York Times*, notes the estimated cost of $3.5 billion would elevate this foreign investment to one of the largest-ever in China. Orville Schell, quoted in the same article, projects the likely creation of tens of thousands of jobs at the site, both in construction and in resort and theme park operations (B5). Disney already employs more than 600 people in Beijing, Shanghai, and Guangzhou. The deal with Disney is emblematic of the transition to service-based economies and low-waged service workers made possible through state intervention.

The state's restructuring efforts have reshaped labor market institutions and promoted the shift to services in global cities. Most notably, retrenchment of welfare spending and lay-offs from state-owned enterprises privatize production and reproduction (Wichterich 2009: 3). Such policy decisions allow for and contribute to the explosive growth of services. In turn, rapidly increasing services have had a different impact on women's and men's work prospects (Lee 2007a; Otis 2007: 103). On the one hand, those workers displaced by the closure of state enterprises in Shanghai, especially middle-aged men in the textile industry, have found work in low-skill services (such as retail, repair, grounds maintenance, and cleaning services) where job prospects have increased and the need for retraining is minimal (Weiping & Yusuf 2004: 53). On the other hand, the burgeoning service sector prefers employing young women for the highly gendered jobs of domestics (Hairong 2007), child maids (*baomu*) (Wichterich 2009), bar hostesses (Zheng 2007), beauticians (Otis 2003), and interactive services in hotels (Otis 2007, 2012). At the macro-level, political decisions have economic consequences on the gender composition and distribution of jobs.

Ethnographies of feminized service work map a similar conceptual terrain in their studies of women's local work practices in both Beijing (Otis 2012) and Shanghai (Lee 2007a). In particular, female migrants face scrutiny and disadvantages derived from their social and legal status, both from their rural origins and their temporary residence in urban areas. Through training, formal and informal, female migrants learn to shed their rural roots to become "modern" women workers in the fast-paced, changing, and increasingly capitalist economy. However, migrant workers earn about half the average wage of permanent urban residents. Female migrant workers in the service sector earn as little as 150 Yuan per month (approximately $19.00) for live-in nannies, 800 Yuan (approximately $100.00) for skilled beauticians, and in-between these wages for waitresses and hostesses (Otis 2012). Women workers are subject to gender- and age-specific training regimens to fashion female bodies for gender-appropriate work.

In newly competitive consumer markets in Beijing and Shanghai, one way employers distinguish their product is through "the attention offered by female interactive service workers" (Otis 2007: 105) attracting the male gaze of the business elite. For example, newly built 5–star hotels market the interactive service encounter itself, a personal relationship of being pampered through customized services (105). Feminized aesthetic labor, including the use of gender displays in the art of being seen and self-presentation, caters to businessmen. The presentation of self is a kind of social performance concerned with the creation and management of impressions for doing gender at work. Organizational gendering of service work begins with sorting and selecting particular bodies for gender-appropriate work. A luxury hotel in Beijing recruits young, mostly unmarried, women still living at home with their parents (Otis 2007). These women are expected not only to converse fluently in English, but also to project an urbane and particular feminine aesthetic. The company "trains" this frontline workforce in the art of deference, using instructional manuals that choreograph feminized embodiment, ranging from demure gestures and facial expressions (such as learning to smile) to style and comportment. The training regimen transforms working-class women into flexible, deferential workers in relationship to an assumed elite male clientele. In the process of self-transformation workers develop an acutely feminized bodily awareness and a hyperconsciousness of customer preferences (Otis 2007: 102). Service requirements for bodily performances elaborate on and invite gendered modes of interaction and domination.

At the same time, the luxury hotel sells the status brand to workers themselves: workers are invited into the "community of the exceptional" that encourages workers to identify with the brand and to see themselves as part of it. The practice of carrying a small card that reads, "I am the Transluxury" fuses the self with the brand (Otis 2007: 106). Otis coins the term "virtual personalism" to define the labor regime that cultivates "a brand of deferent, class-inflected femininity which fosters deep and invisible customer control" (101). Transluxury creates virtual personalism by requiring service providers to furnish consumer preference information that is stored on computers for future use in order to develop a personal relationship between the guest and the service provider. By encoding workers' tacit knowledge, the company can more easily replace women whose aging bodies turn into a depreciating asset in such a feminized aesthetic work environment. Through a virtual personalistic labor regime, guests become hyper-visible to a relatively invisible legion of frontline workers (111). Continuous turnover of personnel enables the company to manage feminized bodies, maintaining a young, exoticized female labor force, paid relatively low wages.

Other feminized services draw on different types of embodied skills and aesthetic labor. The cosmetics industry and direct insurance sales show how hiring decisions for interactive service workers create age-graded gendered labor markets. The beauty service sector, employing an estimated 16 million people, is among the fastest-expanding employment opportunities for young women. According to one study, companies openly discriminate against older women, hiring younger women who conform to a specific age–beauty profile. Cosmetics companies, many from the West, "reinforce the commodification of beauty and new norms of femaleness in the employment market" (Wichterich 2009: 5). China's trade liberalization policies and their accession to the World Trade Organization opened up formerly closed market to imports from Western cosmetics companies (Wichterich 2009: 4). Many companies recruit women in their forties to work as door-to-door sales agents among the legion of 1 million employees in the rapidly expanding private insurance sector. Older women fit a different gendered image of "housewife"; they are expected to exude credibility and to exercise social competencies for congenial communication (4). Many of these sales agents are "self-employed," and thus work without pensions and medical insurance and earn an income below the average in the urban labor market. Sales performance and success are best for those who "adjust to the new market discipline, work around the clock and have no qualms about aggressively exploiting personal relationships in financial transactions" (4).

In China's global cities, governmental disciplinary practices impart moral lessons on the proper conduct of the new socialist/capitalist worker and instruct women on the use of embodied skills and "self-responsibility" (Wichterich 2009: 4). The state creates a spatial hierarchy of beauty in which the beautiful city is a discursive means for inventing the new China (Otis 2012), all accomplished through state-sponsored organizations. For example, the All China Women's Federation trains and encourages women retrenched from state-owned enterprises to take up jobs as domestic workers in private households – a reversal from the taboo against "servants" in the previous socialist era (Wichterich 2009: 5). More generally, the Chinese state elevates and extols women's waged labor through a socialist rhetoric of "serving the people in the service of the nation" (Otis 2003). From the mid-1980s and throughout the 1990s, Chinese political elites articulated a post-socialist national narrative that inverted Maoism, repositioning the binaries of rural/urban, backward/modern, collective/individual as part of the state's modernization project.[4] This contrasts with the way the Chinese state apparatus formerly constructed the prototypical seemingly non-gendered socialist citizen.

After the revolution in 1949, Maoist China integrated urban women into manufacturing. Gender differences were played down in favor of a model worker image shared by both men and women alike. The uniform of baggy, unisex clothing served to minimize the performance of gender differences. To bolster women's identity as workers, the Communist Party celebrated the "Iron Girls' Brigades," emphasizing technical competence and physically challenging work (Otis 2007: 104). Nonetheless, gender inequality persisted, as working-class identity was anchored in a model of masculinity, even as the trope of performative femininity was stigmatized. This working-class hero model downplayed women's responsibility for unremunerated domestic and care labor in the household. Today, the state actively shapes the making of gendered workers for employment in the service sector, and encourages more consumption in the spirit of capitalist accumulation. Changing gender and class relations are central axes of new social inequalities in post-socialist societies and China's global cities.

Dubai: Shifting Economic Sands in a New Urban Center

An examination of work and employment in the regional global city of Dubai puts in sharp relief how gender and class intersect within racialized categories in another part of Asia. The role of migrant labor, most prominently in this different model of the state-controlled migrant labor market, involves cross-border flows altering divisions of labor within and across regions of the global economy. An estimated 90% of Dubai's population of 1.8 million consists of non-citizen workers (Sereni 2010: 15). This once oil-rich Emirate has fueled a building boom; luxury apartments with aerial views from the world's tallest skyscraper, the Burj Khalifa,[5] and iconic hotels such as the Burj Al-Arab, resembling a graceful sail frozen on the waterfront, herald an urban oasis catering to globe-trotting business elites and wealthy tourists. Rapidly depleting oil reserves and their revenues fuel the economic shift; the Emirate is betting on real estate and leisure, establishing business services and its regional sea and airport hub, to replace revenues from oil production. Already, an astonishing 40 million passengers land at Al Maktoum International Airport, according to estimates available for 2010; and the number is expected to rise four-fold to 160 million by the end of the next decade (15). Consumption of goods vies with consumption of symbols in this new shopping and leisure economy built by the Emirate.

The creation of a regional global city requires that the central state embarks on a massive building project. Like other globalizing cities outside of the West, Dubai relies on new construction, literally sprouting out of the desert. On ubiquitous construction sites operating 24/7, an all-male migrant workforce, often recruited from towns and villages primarily located in South Asia, toils long hours in the desert sun. Hierarchies of men inhabit these work zones from dawn to dusk, and these construction workers congregate nearby, not straying too far when they break for lunch – their dress makes them conspicuous targets for police surveillance. After a long work day, buses speed along newly built expansive highways, transporting one shift back to barracks on the outskirts of the city, returning with the nightshift that begins work under the glare of artificial lights and the soft illumination of the moon.

In this Emirate, migrant women's work keeps them primarily in interior spaces of the household, the hotel, or the mall. Limited foot traffic on city streets contrasts with the bustling commerce in mammoth shopping malls. Female migrants tend to be employed in feminized service jobs on short-term contracts usually lasting three years. On a casual walk around several neighborhoods, I observed one nanny, clearly marked by her Indian sari, hand-in-hand with a young child. Her dress denoted that she was not from the Emirates. But the isolation and seclusion of many migrant women working behind closed doors exposes them to bodily harm and sexual abuse as well as the possibility of intimacy with their young charges, complicating gender and class relationships that might lead to collective action.

Dubai, like the city-state of Singapore, treats migrant workers as temporary residents without pathways to citizenship in a migrant labor regime. Temporary status, both as workers and as non-citizens, unites male and female migrants in this Emirate. Labor contracts are renewable, but the state maintains control by issuing visas required as a condition of employment. All migrants who want to work must be sponsored (*kafala*) either by their employer or by an Emirati citizen (Sereni 2010: 15). The state can repatriate workers even before the contract's official termination date, actively regulating bodies through this migrant labor regime. This precarious employment status has until now minimized individual or collective action by vulnerable workers. Visible cracks in the labor control system, as a result of labor mobilizations and short strikes, "point to a tentative negotiation of globalization from below" (Hewison & Kalleberg 2008: 7). Although not yet widespread, such strikes challenge the sustainability of this migrant labor regime.

Changing Cityscapes of Second-tier Global Cities

The speed of economic transition draws attention to spatial dislocations and displacements in second-tier global cities of developing countries. New socio-spatial inequalities result both from their rapid integration into the global economy and from urban renewal unleashing market forces destroying sometimes ancient built environments. Socio-spatial polarization cloisters the global elite in expensive highrises in central business districts and segregates the working poor either in compounds near worksites, in settlements further afield, or in close quarters of an employer's home. A "distinctive enclave" sets regional global cities apart from other cities in poor countries; professionals who come from other cities or foreign countries often live in areas protected by private security companies – increasing the demand for male security guards (Gugler 2004: 17). On city streets, young men gather to guard wealthy patrons' cars in second-tier cities – these informal workers wait for customers outside Starbucks, not only guarding the car but offering to wash it in the up-market neighborhood of Polanco, Mexico City. Car guarding, like other informal jobs, employs an increasing number of men without prospects for finding formal employment (Eligon 2012: A6). These enclaves within cities are similar to Export Processing Zones within countries: the former are located in central business districts surrounded by working-class neighborhoods, while the latter are sheltered by national governments. In global cities, the changing built environment also shapes rhythms of everyday life and cultures of domestic servitude. Apartment complexes replacing single-family dwellings affect gender and class divisions of labor. Smaller apartment units limit the space available for live-in domestic workers and change the relationships between women workers and employers in the household (Qayum & Ray 2003). Emergent global cities transform the way people work and live in new global cityscapes.

New sites of organizing: lessons from global cities

Global cities represent a new frontier for conflicts taking place in major urban centers of the advanced capitalist world where postcolonial battles between a transnational professional class and the working class play out (Hamel et al. 2000: 7). On the one side is an overvalorized new transnational professional class, enacting its global corporate project. They make up the "new city users" who treat the city as a transterritorial environment. On the other side is a devalued low-paid immigrant working class. These workers provide material conditions for the maintenance of that corporate world of power (7). Into this mix, the concentration of "servants" in global cities strategically positions them for gaining a presence that they could never have achieved in small towns and rural areas. This "presence," as Sassen (2004) suggests, translates into the possibility of laying claims on the city, and allows these subordinate actors to unbundle the conditions of their powerlessness. As a result, workers develop a form of politics that not only gives them visibility, but also challenges global elites' political project (Hamel et al. 2000: 7–8).

Global cities concentrate feminized work and labor among women who care for and serve the transnational professional class. For this reason, feminized work creates possibilities and sites of organizing. Two different dynamics related to the condition of women's work inform logics of collective action in global cities (Sassen 1996: 26). On the one hand, women

> are constituted as an invisible and disempowered class of workers in the service of the strategic sectors constituting the global economy. This invisibility keeps them from emerging as whatever would be the contemporary equivalent of the "labor aristocracy" of earlier economic organizational forms.... On the other hand, the access to wages and salaries (even if low), the growing feminization of the job supply, and the growing feminization of business opportunities brought about with informalization alter the gender hierarchies in which they find themselves.

Among immigrant women, waged work improves their access to other public realms and provides a chance to become incorporated into mainstream society. This greater public participation, Sassen (1996: 28) argues, may enable women to "emerge as more forceful and visible actors and may make their role in the labor market more visible as well."

In this way, global cities occasion new possibilities for mobilization among services workers. Sassen (1996: 40) states that "we are seeing the formation of cross-border solidarities and notions of membership rooted in gender, sexuality, and feminism, as well as in questions of class and country status, i.e., First vs. Third World, which cut across all of these membership notions." Clark (1996: 46) re-emphasizes Sassen's point about the "elite's hidden vulnerability" in their dependency on downtown support workers; many recent social movements are fueled by direct reactions against this devalorization process. Further, Clark (48) purports that "with this analytic centrality of decontextualization and recontextualization, the emergence of multiple and diverse women's movements within other liberation movements becomes an expected and positive development, not a danger to feminist activism." The challenge is to "create clear and convincing alternatives for revalorization, recontextualization and local accountability" (49). How can women from such disparate social, cultural, and economic locations, Clark (49) asks, reinforce each others' efforts to regain control of the global economy? She suggests that, "only as we begin to understand how essential each of our different contributions will be to the dismantling of this global overvaluation process can we begin to build a realistic commitment to working together" (49). Clark concludes that Sassen's insights into how the global process works will help us do it more effectively. Local stories set against global connections reveal new forms of mobilization in global cities.

New Forms of Mobilization: New York Stories, Tokyo Tales

Cross-city organizing in old global cities informs New York stories and Tokyo tales. As potential sites of organizing, New York City and Tokyo offer a dense built environment where workers' lives intersect. Though their work may be relatively invisible, workers gain a visibility where they work and reside. Through everyday interactions, workers can share information about their lives, articulate mutual grievances, and identify common experiences. The wealth of accumulated knowledge inspires new imaginaries and possibilities. The formation of the Domestic Workers' United (DWU) organized in New York City, and the development of community-based unions in Tokyo, show how the dialectics of globalization create new terrains of struggle in changing geographies of power.

Founded in 1998, DWU is a city-wide coalition of domestic worker organizations in New York City. Aijen Poo, called the Norma Rae of our times (Ehrenreich 2010: 49), helped establish the organization after she graduated from Columbia University. DWU brought together existing organizations, including: the Women Workers' Project of the Committee against Anti-Asian Violence, representing domestic workers from Southeast Asia, Malaysia, and the Philippines; and Andolan, an organization made up of South Asian domestic workers, primarily from India, Bangladesh, Sri Lanka, and Pakistan. Though starting out small, by June 2005 membership had risen to 800, with about 250 active participants, governed by a committee of 11 domestic workers (Fine 2007: 221). Rather than try to organize one household at a time, the DWU lobbied for, and ultimately convinced, the New York City Council to adopt the Domestic Bill of Rights in June 2003. Their success in recruiting women to affiliate and join the political cause is in part based on social geography and the political landscape of New York City. In addition, they drew on the transnational transfer of ideas from migrants who shared their activist experiences from other countries. For example, Filipina domestic workers recommended that the coalition demand a standard contract or a Bill of Rights, like the one they had won in their successful organizing campaign spearheaded by the community union Committee of Asian Women. Then DWU broadened their lobbying campaign state-wide. Toward this effort, the DWU organized the first National Domestic Workers Congress. About 100 women, representing domestic workers' groups from 10 cities, attended the conference in Manhattan on one hot day in June 2008 (Buckley & Correal 2008). Subsequent rallies in support of the Domestic Workers' Bill of Rights gathered together children and their parents (Ehrenreich 2010: 52). Just two years later, the DWU and its allies added the passage of a state-wide Domestic

Workers' Bill of Rights to their achievements. This significant legislation contains provisions governing overtime pay, a minimum of three
paid days off per year, and legal protection against sexual harassment
(49).

Like New York, Tokyo serves as the geographic hub for cross-border
organizing activity among working women's groups and a host of
community unions. Women's Union Tokyo (WUT) is an exemplary
organization adopting a community-based organizational model.
Since its founding in 1995, WUT's more than 250 members work in
diverse occupations and industries (see chapter 8 for more details).
Initially, the boundaries of WUT stretched across the sprawling
metropolis. Subsequently, Women's Union Tokyo networked horizontally with similar, albeit smaller, working women's organizations in
other parts of Japan. While individual members – many of whom were
activists in labor, feminist, and migrant workers' causes – already had
established transnational connections, WUT has forged solidaristic
relationships with groups in South Korea and Hong Kong, and hosted
activists from other countries in Asia to speak about their own experiences so that they could learn lessons from and provide support
for each other's campaigns. A two-year project in 2003–5, funded by
the Center for Global Partnership, facilitated this cross-border networking. Anne Zacharias-Walsh, currently writing an account of this
democratic impulse from these women's groups including WUT, and
I worked closely with labor activists in a series of workshops on organizing and communication. Feminist scholars and trade unionists met
with their Japanese counterparts, first in Detroit and then in Tokyo,
for workshops. Though satellite meetings took place during the
course of the project, Tokyo, because of its density of activist organizations with overlapping memberships, both from trade union and
feminist movements, provided the training ground for new hybrid
worker associations and social movement unionism. As a global city,
Tokyo is accessible by intersecting mass transit as well as high-speed
rail, and has Narita international airport in close proximity. A one-day
meeting held in Tokyo can draw activists from other cities as far away
as Nagoya/Osaka and Hokkaido.[6]

The old global cities of New York and Tokyo aggregate communicative and organizational resources rooted in a long history of political
engagement, where activists have established strong associational
ties. Recent organizing may or may not formally build on these social
histories of labor mobilization, but such activity appears at this con-
juncture in light of the past. Workers can overcome barriers of isolation and invisibility by taking advantage of old networks, and forging
new ones, made available in these socio-political spaces. New York
has a rich past of labor organizing, and traditional unions continue

to influence local politics. In contrast to the past, recent mobilization reflects the changing dynamics related to the conditions of feminized service work and labor. The domestic workers highlighted here established networks among individuals and organizations across the city. They gained visibility in the spaces of this global city. Cross-border organizing and networking among networks-as-unions turned Tokyo's brutal modernist maze into an asset. Working women leveraged overlapping networks based in Tokyo to extend network organizing across Japan and pan-Asia. Older global cities are spaces where new forms of association around gender, class, and citizenship play out.

Organizing strategies and repertoires of collective action probably will differ in second-tier global cities because workers there confront different employment relations regimes, political structures, and roles of the state. In many cases, workers residing in second-tier global cities are citizens of the nation where they live, even if they may be denied full citizenship rights in the city where they work. Evidence from global and other cities in China finds the emergence of new repertoires and new foci of collective action (see Lee 2007b; Swider n.d.). In the interior city of Wuhan, workers on the production line of the Taiwan-owned Foxconn Technology, one of the largest electronics manufacturers supplying to Microsoft and Apple, threatened suicide to dramatize their grievances of long working hours (up to 16 hours per day) and low wages.[7] These 200 migrant workers due to their differentiated citizenship rights, resorted to this more spectacular strategy following the lead of their colleagues who committed suicide in another labor dispute at a factory located in Shenzhen (Zhang 2012). The intensive scrutiny from the media led Foxconn to promise increased wages and reduced overtime. Local activists wonder whether the company's announcement is merely for rhetorical effect to divert attention away from the reported harsh working conditions in the assembly of branded gadgets, or whether the fanfare will result in real improvements at the workplace (Barboza & Duhigg 2012: B1–2). Because of its central role, whether at the local or the national level, the Chinese state has become a convenient target of protest by workers seeking redress. Capturing imaginations elsewhere, the local protest in Wukan, another village in the southern Guangdong province, directed its collective action against corrupt local officials. The conflict escalated after local authorities cracked down on the protesters (B1–2). The state can, and in the latter case did, unleash the police force to suppress protest activities. However, second-tier global cities consolidate the work and residence of migrant and temporary workers in confined spaces and compounds. These spaces create the platforms for communication among workers sharing their grievances and serve as the staging ground for their protests.

It is difficult to estimate the aggregate number of members in fledgeling labor organizations in global cities. Many operate on the margins with minimal resources and without registration, or even recognition, by traditional unions and the state. Nonetheless, the evidence culled from case studies suggests that labor organizing among women workers reflects increasing organizational capacities in the service sector and in informalized jobs in both developed countries and rapidly developing countries in the global economy.

Conclusion: economic transformations, gendered services, new cityscapes

Like the city in Dante's *Inferno*, the comparative tale of two types of global cities depicts the allure of "Thy city, which is so full of envy that already the sack runs over, held [sic] me within it in the bright life . . ." Both older and newer global cities concentrate transnational administration and localization of economic activities, utilizing knowledge-intensive labor and services at both high- and low-ends. Global cities are defined by their relationships to other cities within a world-wide network. As such, global cities represent strategic places where we can see how the lives of men and women from different social locations intersect in ways and under circumstances not always readily apparent in traditional accounts. Parallel case studies of financial capital located in London and Tokyo, juxtaposed with the emergent regional global cities of Beijing, Shanghai, and Dubai, identify concrete social practices that produce and reproduce gender, class, and race inequalities on a local and a global scale.

This analysis of global cities highlights the labor process of globalized management and control and the central dynamic of overvaluation and devaluation of labor that sustains it. Such analyses, inspired by the research agenda of Saskia Sassen, go beyond an examination of upper circuits of hyper-mobile finance capital and examine service production and social reproduction as place-bound processes. Global cities are incubators for and centers of high- and low-end service production, where low-waged women workers cater to wealthy individuals, often in their homes. Financial and administrative functions concentrated in global cities offer high-paying jobs for male – and an increasing number of female – professionals relying on the purchase of social reproductive services provided by low-waged workers serving and caring for them. Gender intersects with class most clearly among migrant labor which forms a low-waged labor force performing the least-regulated service jobs of both older global cities of the developed world and newer global cities in rapidly growing Asia.

Levels of development and the leading role of local and national government differentiate older from newer global cities. In all global cities, the state facilitates globalization of production, world trade, and low-cost reproduction. But in Shanghai, Beijing, and Dubai, the heavy hand of the state pushes policies aimed at accelerating the creation of global cities and their integration into the global economy. Indeed, these global cities are located in countries and city-states experiencing fast economic growth and prosperity. However, the experience of many new global cities in Asia cannot be explained simply by reference to state-led development. State intervention is the means by which these countries target economic development. Abundant natural (including strategic geographic locations, natural resources such as oil) and human resources (low wages) are the requisite ingredients for exploiting their comparative advantages, enabling these countries to make these particular places into regional global cities.

The focus on global cities in Asia deconstructs geographical binaries to render complex relationships between race, class, gender, and nation more visible and to reveal the historical construction of the political boundaries constituting the region and the imaginary Asia(n). Categories in common usage imply internal coherence and homogeneity in Asia. Asia should not be seen as a neutral or as a natural geographic designation, but rather as a problematized category of historical significance. Criticism of Orientalism has not eliminated the projection of Asia(n) as an undifferentiated mirror image of the West. The influx of migrants, particularly from other parts of Asia, adds a different point of view from workers deemed outside of but within the domestic space and larger region. These international entanglements and complex histories shape configurations of inequality within and across nations in the region.

This chapter differentiates global cities from globalized work in cities in terms of their relative position in "hierarchies of economic and political power" (Schiller 2010: 59). Put another way, "the scalar positioning of cities reflects their relationship to global, national, and regional circuits of capital" (59). Multi-scalar approaches underline the spatial dynamics of social inequalities and political power (Schiller 2010: 60). Global cities, like Export Processing Zones before them, operate as extra-territorial economic platforms for the administration of finance capital and other international business. However, in global cities, non-citizenship and partial citizenship divide men and women working in the same territorial space. Social rights are divided within places like China (for example by *hukou* status), and embedded in gendered corporate citizenship, as in Japan.[8] By contrast, the EPZ designates a socio-political space in which workers, to a large extent, are citizens, generally without legal protections from the state. In global cities, enclaves of male expatriates live in a kind of political limbo between their home countries and the places where they work, but they enjoy the benefits and amenities provided by the concentration of services in a global city. Though these expatriates are non-citizens, their corporate sponsors secure permission for them to work and reside in these cities. In contrast, migrant labor typically enters under less auspicious terms, facing a stay without either political rights or economic security and without the means of easily securing their own, and often other family members' livelihoods. Global cities in a sense internalize power dynamics of gender, class, and racialized hierarchies, whereby male business elites hailing from the Global North encounter female service workers from the Global South.

In global cities new types of political subjects, as well as new hybrid bases of worker organizations, form. By forging new political subjects, disadvantaged populations can gain a presence in the otherwise anonymity of global cities (Sassen 2004: 381–2). Insofar as the "national as container of social process is cracked . . . it opens up possibilities for a geography of politics that links sub-national spaces across borders" (Sassen 2004: 382). The formation of a new type of transnational labor politics is localized in global cities (382). Changing territorial organization both of economic activities and of political power affects the groups, the sites, the modes, and the scales of mobilization. Economic globalization alters the political landscape and political opportunity structures, influencing who the social actors are, how they are organized, how issues and identities are framed, and what communities are imagined.

Shifting territoriality of workers and of production and reproduction processes complicates national-based governance structures and the ability of workers to exercise rights in the jurisdiction where they find employment. The next chapter looks at the rescaling of politics and political institutions in the face of economic globalization. Political globalization changes how economic and employment policies are formulated and enforced on more than one scale. Policy formation and politics largely function in national-based institutions, as previously discussed in chapter 7, but new tensions arise from these changes. Rescaling of politics opens new opportunities and imposes constraints on the claiming of rights and economic governance. It poses the questions of whether and to what extent policies, politics, and political institutions are transgressing the nation state, and what the consequences of this are.

CHAPTER
12 New Political Landscapes: Gender Equality Projects in Global Arenas and Nation States

Economic globalization transgresses national boundaries and thereby seems to render the nation state obsolete, or at least to severely weaken state capacities to govern domestic economies. Increasing global mobilities of labor and capital complicate economic governance and politics formerly predicated on the nation state. While economic and political globalization cracks open the nation state, both as a unit of analysis and as a unified political structure, national institutions remain resilient for the formulation, enactment, and enforcement of policies affecting complex inequalities. One of the recurring themes in this chapter is the tension created by economic globalization for political institutions once predicated on national politics. Economic globalization puts new pressures on the capacity of the state to ensure social reproduction for its citizens. Paradoxically, the increasing importance of supra-national political institutions in response to, and for the management of, flows of labor, capital, and ideas on a global scale results in the resilience of national political arenas and the resurgence of local spaces for pursuing political agendas. New institutions and actors populate a changing political landscape of the global economy.

This chapter begins with a brief history of political globalization to identify institutional restructuring and the ascendance of neo-liberalism associated with new economic realities and priorities, best understood in light of the non-responsibility for care. New opportunities and challenges for national policy formation surface in response to economic and workplace issues enacted at the supra-national scale. The European Union is an example of the uneasy and uneven development of policies that address women's inferior position in paid labor and women's primary responsibility for unpaid labor in the domestic sphere. In particular, issues about and policies addressing social reproduction remain stubbornly within the purview of domestic politics. At the same time, rescaling of political institutions and arenas expands the field of politics in which women's and feminist movements can make claims and lobby around gender equality projects. Women in feminist movements are repositioning themselves vis-à-vis other women within and across social locations, challenging hegemonic masculinities, and transforming patriarchal gender divisions of labor. New policy initiatives transfer through international organizations, most prominently the UN women's conferences, and through cross-fertilization among women's groups and non-governmental organizations, both on the sub-national and national scales.

Turning to an examination of specific agencies of the United Nations, the chapter documents the role of supra-national institutions in promulgating international legal norms around human rights and women's rights. Still, tension exists between the forces of economic globalization and the role of national institutions, leading to uneven adoption of international conventions, human rights norms, and labor standards to protect workers against risks and abuses that arise out of unequal power relations. The chapter then discusses the implications of "denationalization of economies" (Parrenas 2001) for renationalization of policy and politics. Economic globalization generates challenges to and prospects for new domestic politics. Poor and developing countries cannot easily protect their citizens who may suffer abuses when at work abroad. Due to the lack of protections in the countries where they work and from their countries of origin, migrant workers fashion hybrid forms of politics to improve working conditions by pushing home and host countries to recognize their rights, and going further by leveraging the transnational human rights regime. Within developing countries, economic globalization also fosters domestic politics in the intimate sphere. Case studies of female migrants from the Philippines and in India bring us back to active subjects of globalization. Migration empowers some women to redefine the self in the context of changing gender relations at home.

The chapter ends by revisiting new geographies of power prominent throughout the book. Gendering institutional analysis of work and economy reveals the importance of new geographies of power, shaped from above by supra-national organizations and emergent political governance structures, and from below through transnational organizing and intimate domestic politics. The book thus ends on a political note.

History of political globalization, institutional restructuring and new priorities

While internationalization changed power relationships between countries, globalization shifts international rules governing political and economic relationships. Whether or not globalization incapacitates (transgresses) the nation state remains an open question. Fredric Jameson (2000) suggests that such claims may be another way of actually describing the pre-eminence of American "imperial" power. He divides historical forms of imperialism into two main periods: the pre-First World War characterized by a colonialist order; and the post-Second World War characterized by a Cold War form. In the latter period, United States hegemony imposes itself and defines its interests framed around an ideology of neo-liberalism, an ideological expression of ego-centric carefree male dominance. Institutional restructuring and new priorities occur in and develop through a neo-liberal framework of hegemonic masculinity.

Economic globalization beginning to flourish, and the rejection of a Keynesian government role in economic policy from the 1970s onward, follow an ideology of neo-liberalism. This ideological template uses a market-oriented frame for institutional restructuring around new government priorities and social imaginaries, and is based on the logic of ego-centric individualism and non-responsibility for social reproduction. Less support for welfare and more privatized services transfer the burden of social reproduction from the state onto individual women and families. With institutional restructuring, welfare agencies lose while finance agencies gain in prominence (Sassen 1996: 39). All of these efforts are part of government retrenchment within some sectors of the economy.

A shift occurred in the US under the administration of Bill Clinton; the Welfare Reform Act (officially known as the Personal Responsibility and Work Opportunity Reconciliation Act) cut back funds and tightened eligibility for cash assistance to individuals and families living in poverty. This reform marked a rhetorical and institutional change from welfare to workfare, from public assistance to private market measures. Even before the 1996 legislation was passed, Cabinet agencies such as Housing and Urban Development (HUD) and Health, Education, and Welfare (HEW) retreated into the background of government priorities. At the same time, the Treasury loomed ever larger both in policymaking and in the public eye. This elevation of the Treasury Department and the Federal Reserve corresponds to the heightened importance of finance in global economic activities.

Further, the ascendance of neo-liberalism pushes an agenda of political globalization opening up economies by relaxing regulations and lowering trade barriers in countries in both the Global North and South. As Stallings (2002: 1), among others, suggests (also see Acker 2004), "liberalization, then, is the other side of globalization." Neo-liberal policies emphasize deregulation to help transnational corporations conducting business at home and abroad, weakening social protections, increasing the trend toward informalization of jobs in both formal and informal economies, and tightening immigration restrictions on workers' entry into a country. Under the umbrella of neo-liberalism, transnational corporations' restructuring decisions have devastating effects on the environment and local labor markets. In particular, finance capital can wreak havoc, as the world discovered when banks "too big to fail" threatened to bring down the US and Euro Zone economies, or made bad bets on investments allowed in a climate of lax regulation (as in the cases of Iceland, Greece, and Ireland). The ideology of neo-liberalism frees capital to move production across national boundaries, affecting the capacity of states and families to ensure livelihoods and to provide economic and social security. The tenets of neo-liberalism cannot be fully comprehended as an ideology and a set of practices unless analyzed through a feminist lens. It becomes clearer to see that the processes of externalization and commodification of care and reproduction are inextricably bound to the neo-liberal agenda of freeing markets from the state. Consequently, neo-liberalism references gender sources and has gender consequences for individual workers, families, and nations, creating new geographies of power.

Economic geographers, however, appropriately caution against viewing transnational corporations as footloose and placeless. Instead, there are political as well as economic limits to global restructuring (Amin and Thrift 1996; Dicken et al. 1997: 163). The dynamics of political globalization operate not only through and between nation states, but also through institutions of global and supra-national governance, regional and local states and social movements (Dicken et al. 1997: 165). This short history of political globalization suggests that labor and capital face new opportunities and constraints within and beyond the nation state. The rescaling of political institutions and politics is a response to denationalization of economies. In turn, rescaling facilitates cross-border policy formation and transfer. It opens new spaces and sites for political mobilizations from below. But tensions arise from the lack of coordination between national and supra-national governance structures. Such multi-scalar political institutions and politics complicate who will take responsibility for the costs and delivery of social reproduction and employment conditions. Comparative research reveals both the limits on convergence of policy formation and variation of enforcement of common policy agendas across countries within regional political assemblages.

Rescaling political institutions and politics

A relatively new area of comparative research concerns regionalization and globalization of policy formation in the context of feminist politics. The policymaking process has developed through supra-national institutions and the emergence of feminist transnational networks. Both the European Union (EU) and the United Nations (UN) are determinants of, and venues for, successful feminist coalition building and policymaking. Regionalization and globalization can be positive forces, to the extent that they present new arenas for feminist actors in governments and society in their effort to mobilize effective movements for aligning equal employment regulations to internationally based standards. The European Union, through its directives on part-time employment and equal treatment provisions, changes the balance of power within and between nations. Still, policies formulated at regional and international levels must be enacted by national political actors. Underlying tensions between supra-national institutions and nation state governance prevent easy harmonization of policy initiatives and instruments across countries.

The European Union: New Multi-Scalar Politics

The European Union, among other supra-national institutions, belongs to a new regional political assemblage, multiplying the sites where organized interest groups can influence regulatory reform and expand the scope of regulations on a supra-national basis. The European Union institutionally shifts the mode of regulation from an exclusive national affair to a multi-level arena of governance. Jessop (2002: 254) remarks on this shift from "active economic and social steering . . . to [being] run more through soft regulation and reflexive law . . . a key role is also played by meta-governance, that is, the organization of the institutional framework and rules for individual modes of governance and the rebalancing of different modes of governance." The latter refers to meta-governance operations "orchestrating economic and social policy in and across many different scales of action involving a wide range of official, quasi-official, private economic and civil interests" (254). Meta-governance alters the political terrain, and opens new institutional and discursive spaces for engaging in democratic politics, especially among groups (women, migrants, racial and ethnic minorities) formerly excluded from, or marginalized in, national-based corporatist structures.

Through meta-governance, the EU promulgates rules which simultaneously de-regulate economic arenas in the drive for entrepreneurialism and re-regulate social arenas in the drive for equal opportunities and the reconciliation of work and family-life (Walby 1999) via its legally binding directives on equal treatment of men and women. Walby (2004, 2007) presents evidence suggesting that many of the emerging employment forms which have been associated with this new economy are actually related to regulation or re-regulation of the workplace, and that globalization does not necessarily weaken the role of national governments in bettering workplace policies for women. Thus, this feminist lens enables a clearer understanding of the way in which globalization involves not only de-regulation but also re-regulation, and how the larger forces of economic and societal globalization can affect the nature and quality of workplace policies. More specifically, Walby shows how EU policies have stimulated change and, indeed, improvements in women's access to employment and the conditions of women's work, in part by creating new avenues for organizations to pursue gender equality projects.

The frame of equal treatment not only informs regulations specifically aimed at gender equality, but also influences the language used to represent rights and protections in many labor regulations. For example, the 1997 EU Directive on part-time work (97/81/EC) prohibits less favorable treatment between comparable full-time and part-time workers solely based on their employment status, "unless different treatment is justified on objective grounds." The Directive on part-time work compels member states to adopt regulations providing at least minimum employment protections. Women are beneficiaries of the framework agreement on part-time work because of the gender composition of part-time employment. The equal treatment provision diminishes employers' incentive to use part-timers as a low-waged labor pool, which may help to account for the declining numbers of short-term part-timers and the slowing of the rate of increase in part-time employment among women in the UK (Walby 2004).

New regulations are formulated reaching beyond the nation state, but national political forces still condition receptivity to the adoption of, and the specific language used to frame, labor and gender regulations, and mediate the implementation and enforcement mechanisms in place to ensure effectiveness and efficacy of legislative initiatives enacted by member states. Visser (2000: 449) argues that the European employment approach is not a move toward centralization or harmonization. He cites the 1996 EU Directive on parental leave (96/34/EC) as more of a symbolic achievement than a practical change, because "the conditions under which the right has to be secured are left to national regulation since it involves matters of pay bargaining, minimum wages or social security outside the competence of the Community" (443–4). On the one hand, Visser underestimates the impact that transnational measures, such as the Directives on part-time work and parental leave, have on forcing laggard countries to adopt new measures entitling men and women to paid leave (Haas 2004), and on setting minimum standards across the EU zone (Vosko 2010). On the other hand, he correctly points out the difficulty in harmonizing social policy and labor regulations across countries with different political institutional histories, as suggested in chapter 7 on policy formation in different welfare regimes.

A reversion to the national context occurs, especially for those policy domains previously unregulated or newly regulated – such as non-standard employment and social reproduction, both connected to gender equality more generally. For example, the absence of a directive on childcare relegates the organization of reproductive work to resolution in the mixed national economy of privately and publicly provided care. Similarly, the Directive on part-time work remains silent on workers' right to request part-time work without loss of seniority and security. As a result, member states decide on whether, to whom, and under what conditions to make such a right available. Almost two decades before the EU passed the Directive on part-time work, Sweden established a workers' right to request a 6–hour. working day (at pro-rata pay) work schedule until children turned eight. German law grants the right to work part-time to employees in enterprises with more than 15 employees, while a similar right exists, with a lower threshold of 10 workers, in the Netherlands. At the other extreme, there is no statutory right to request reduction of working hours in Italy (Gornick et al. 2007: 6). As a result, uneven and unequal outcomes continue in a context of gender-based hierarchies, especially as it affects women who have primary responsibility for unpaid care work. These policy differences between nations within the European Union reflect welfare state divisions between the more expansive universal rights and working-time regulation in social democratic Sweden and the less generous and less integrative policies in social conservative Germany and Italy.

Though legally binding, the equal treatment approach at the center of many EU directives is aimed at formal equality in the labor market without addressing inequality of circumstances between men and women (Vosko 2006a, 2010). Again, the Directive on part-time work is instructive. The Directive urges rather than mandates that member states eliminate obstacles to part-time employment and instructs employers to "give consideration" to workers who request transfers between full-time and part-time work to accommodate personal or family needs (Gornick et al. 2007: 6). While improving employment conditions of part-time workers across the Community, the Directive has not significantly altered the gendered character of the employment form and its variation across countries.

New Policy Initiatives: From Supra-National to Sub-National

The case of gender mainstreaming illustrates how a policy tool's promise and efficacy for legislating gender equality in part depends on the strength or weakness of women's policy machineries, and/or women's organized lobbying efforts at sub-national and national levels – two factors emphasized by the state feminist theories. "Mainstreaming involves ensuring that gender perspectives and attention to the goal of gender equality are central to all activities – policy development, research, advocacy/dialogue, legislation, resource allocation, and planning, implementation and monitoring of programmes and projects" (United Nations Office of the Special Adviser on Gender Issues and Advancement of Women 2009). Implementation of gender mainstreaming varies from locale to locale within countries as well as across countries in the EU. One reason for this variation stems from the rhetorical ambiguity of mainstreaming language, evident in the confusion over the meaning of the term and the wide disparity of practices under the same rubric. Another reason goes back to the gender politics in different welfare states.

Gender mainstreaming has both innovative and deceptive potentials depending on the success of feminist politics, and "naming" has important policy implications at both symbolic and practical levels. Woodward (2004) maps the transmission from various international and supra-national institutions and systematically studies gender mainstreaming policies as they have been translated into national and sub-national practices. Mainstreaming policy falters in part because it attempts to use the "language of the state against the state" (2004). Thus, the ambiguity or paradox leads to the same policy tool being viewed as both an innovation and a deception by different actors in different places. The scope and scale of gender mainstreaming seems to be broadest where femocrats exercise the "power of definition" – that is, have the ability to define what gender mainstreaming means in practical terms. Women's policy machineries are also important to the success of gender mainstreaming. While not all women's policy machineries have this mission, many of these agencies and femocrats pursue effective strategies and practices for bringing gender into the mainstream of policymaking. Woodward's cautionary tale suggests that gender mainstreaming as an instrument and a discourse can either promote gender equality or serve as window-dressing. As a consequence, equal opportunity offices should not be abandoned but rather supplemented by this new policy tool-kit. An evaluation of gender mainstreaming, to explain its formation, location, and effectiveness, requires a feminist analysis of the policymaking process and institutional context.

Finally, the European Court of Justice (ECJ) offers another institution for policy changes aimed at gender inequality at work in member states of the EU. The ECJ is empowered to adjudicate claims brought by nationally based actors. The application of gender equity policies in the German military exemplifies how the goal of gender justice is put into practice in a very particular type of workplace setting, translating and implementing equal treatment principles enshrined in EU treaties as changes in member state policies. Liebert (2004) builds a theoretical bridge between the forces of globalization, gender dynamics, and workplace policies in the EU and the quest for policies that increase gender equality in actual workplaces. She describes the role of the EU Court and the German state in applying gender equality opportunities to the German military. The EU Court appeared to be a catalyst for gender equality processes already fomenting within the German state. Rapid and apparently full compliance with the Court ruling within Germany suggests that both the government and social system were ready for such changes.

This extended example of EU policy-processes and politics illustrates how supra-national institutions change the political landscape in which actors reform regulations at multiple scales. Meta-governance operates on, and opens up, new political spaces for organized interests to influence policymaking at the EU level, constituting an emerging polity that significantly promotes modernization of gender relations both at the EU level and within member nations (Walby 2004). This more explicitly comparative focus on countries within the regional context of the European Union not only allows for an assessment of how the global affects the local, but also illustrates clearly that national approaches to gender and workplace regulations form a spectrum of approaches, and, while rooted in the historical and social cultures of individual nation states, are also subject to similar regional forces, albeit with varying policy and economic results (Gottfried & Reese 2004).

International institutions, transnational legal norms, resilient nation states

Like regional approaches to gender mainstreaming and equal employment in the European Union, the circulation of human and women's rights norms transcend national territorial borders for making political claims. The UN and its specialized agencies, such as the International Labor Organization (ILO), diffuse legal norms around gender equality and decent work, yet the nation state retains primary responsibility for giving substance to international conventions. Two examples from the UN, the Convention on Elimination of All Forms of Discrimination against Women (CEDAW) and the ILO Convention on Part-Time Work, illustrate the progress and tension in trying to align international legal norms with national action to advance gender equality in globalizing labor markets, and are both regulated and enforced primarily by sovereign nations.

CEDAW: New Rights, Old Barriers

The United Nations General Assembly adopted CEDAW in 1979 after successful lobbying efforts among women's groups involved in the 1975 UN International Women's Year. In turn, this new convention has given women's organizations a symbolic tool for pursuing national legislation aimed at prohibiting discrimination against women. The convention commits signatory states to ensuring the rights of women. Prior to the adoption of CEDAW, the United Nations Declaration of Human Rights (1948), one of the first conventions promulgated after the establishment of the UN, and subsequent conventions on refugees and cultural and political rights, affirmed the principles of the "dignity and worth" of all humans and "equal rights of men and women," but didn't explicitly identify women as a protected "social group" (Benhabib & Resnick 2009: 5). CEDAW represents a landmark convention setting out "a bill of rights" specifically for women as an explicit category. The convention sought to end discrimination against women, defined as ". . . any distinction, exclusion or restriction made on the basis of sex which has the effect or purpose of impairing or nullifying the recognition, enjoyment or exercise by women, irrespective of their marital status, on a basis of equality of men and women, of human rights and fundamental freedoms in the political, economic, social, cultural, civil or any other field" (UN 2009). In so doing, the UN expanded the discourse of human rights and articulated specific protections for women workers.

Beyond moral authority, the UN has no legal status in the international system of nation states. The Westphalian system that took root in the seventeenth century remains a primary organizing framework for the international system of nation states. Conventions formulated by the UN must be enacted by individual member nation states, creating a tension between different levels of governance. At the heart of this tension is that the transnational legal regime fits uneasily with the theory and practice of national sovereignty framed in the era of internationalization. The UN Charter itself is "built upon deference to the national order," prohibiting UN intervention in those matters deemed to be within the "domestic jurisdictions of the state," while leaving the content of those matters unstated (Benhabib & Resnik 2009: 7). Benhabib and Resnick (10) succinctly summarize the source of tension as follows: "First, transnational conventions undermine an absolutist theory of sovereignty that presumes that a sovereign nation has complete control over what occurs within its borders. By becoming states parties, nations cede authority (a form of sovereignty) – at least in theory – as they commit to complying with these precepts." Countries provide the content of legal principles through national legislation, but uneven compliance, in part, occurs "because of the privileging of the national" (10). Political governance remains ensconced in the old international system and thus is unable to fully respond to economic globalization or to effectively regulate it.

Uneven ratification similarly stems from the privileging of national political institutions. By 2011, 186 countries had ratified the CEDAW. One of the hold-outs, the US (one of only seven countries including Iran and Sudan), resists adopting many international norms and ratifying treaties. An ideological tug-of-war between liberals and conservatives pulls against international influence over issues deemed to erode national sovereignty. Also, national institutional roadblocks deter easy adoption of treaties, especially ones focusing on broad social issues. In the US, a treaty requires two-thirds of the Senate to affirm ratification. Perhaps a more insurmountable obstacle is the procedural rule that allows a single senator to hold up a treaty for any reason, and to do so while remaining anonymous. In this particular case, several attempts to ratify the CEDAW failed to muster the requisite 67 votes in the Senate. As early as 1979, then-President Jimmy Carter sent a bill commending the CEDAW to the Senate for approval. The bill died before reaching the Senate floor for a vote. The issue resurfaced in 2002, garnering support from then-Secretary of State Colin Powell and initially from President George W. Bush, only to lose traction when conservative Republicans objected to the implications of the reproductive rights provision of the convention (Riggin 2011). Political procedures diminish the capacity of the US to adopt an international convention or treaty.

An installation at the Museum of Modern Art devoted to a retrospective of Sanja Iveković's feminist-oriented exhibit *Sweet Violence* (Dec. 2011) invokes the disposable political culture in the US, priding itself on liberalism while refusing to recognize the international convention on the Treaty for the Rights of Women.[1] As I contemplated her videos and photomontages, curiously drawn to and repelled by some staged images of women posed as if pictured in an advertisement for luxury goods, only to discover on closer examination that the print told a story of rape and abuse, I stumbled upon the blood-red crumpled sheets of paper littering the ground of the gallery space. Surely, these pieces of paper were intentionally strewn about the space, but why? Then I noticed near the door a similar flyer-sized, colored print at eye-level on the wall. This red sheet announced the Convention on the Discrimination of All Forms of Discrimination against Women (CEDAW), and explained that as of April 2011, the US still had not ratified CEDAW. At the bottom of the sheet it read: "Hesitancy to ratify this important document stems from the unfounded fears associated with the implementation of CEDAW in the US." A Myth v. Fact sheet filled the back. Alongside the sheet on the wall, a typed statement invited patrons to take one of the wadded pieces of papers, which I did sheepishly, feeling like I had stolen art from the museum. In this simple act of reading the wall art, then depositing the flyer in my purse only later to read the document carefully in my office and to present the document in my women's studies class, the artist had moved me to reflect on the tension between national reluctance and international acceptance of human rights and women's rights norms. Undoubtedly, this participatory art exhibit alone will not result in the immediate ratification of this convention. However, the red sheet visible in a pile of papers on my desk reminds me, as it might others, that change requires recognition of the issue first before embarking on collective action. This artistic intervention reveals how using the feminist lens can sharpen our awareness of gender inequality, and maybe move us to action.

Referencing CEDAW, Lenz (2004) adds to the reconsideration of political globalization by arguing that it does not inherently doom consideration of gender issues by countries. Indeed, she highlights aspects of political globalization that enhance the abilities of women's organizations to gain and develop influence within nations. The proliferation of feminist-oriented non-government organizations and transnational women's networks has succeeded in translating and transforming feminist goals into actual policymaking processes at multiple levels. Without the enactment of CEDAW, it is unclear whether the Japanese state, which became a signatory of the convention in 1985, would have adopted the Equal Employment Opportunity (EEO) Law that same year. Japanese policymakers seem more susceptible than their counterparts in the US to external pressures to align national policy with international standards, at least symbolically (Schoppa 1997). The Japanese EEO law, although strengthened several times since its enactment, uses conditional language that translates into weaker mechanisms for achieving gender equality (Gottfried 2009).

The ILO: When Labor Meets Gender Issues

The International Labor Organization (ILO) similarly faces institutional and discursive barriers to establishing an international human rights legal regime inclusive of gender-related rights. As an agency within the UN, the ILO is charged with the promotion of norms around a relatively new campaign on "decent work" and fair treatment of all workers, through conventions on working conditions and new labor standards. The establishment of this long-standing organization actually preceded the founding of the UN,[2] and it retains its original mandate. It is the only UN agency composed of the tripartite interests representing organized labor, employers, and governments (known as the social partners). As for the UN in general, enactment of ILO conventions encounters major hurdles inherent to the ratification process. Even more than in the case of CEDAW, the ILO must contend with its own history, in which workers' rights discourses reflect the legacy of male-dominated trade unions, and tripartite interests are organized around national unions, employers' associations, and governments. Consequently, labor conventions explicitly framed around gender equality issues have lagged behind those conventions more directly focused on the seemingly gender-neutral issues of wages and working conditions. Nonetheless, the ILO has taken up issues of central concern to women workers, and ones that address gender inequality at work.

The relatively recent promulgation of a convention on part-time work is a case in point. The new convention neither names women as the targets of need nor references the gender-specific convention on the elimination of discrimination against women. Instead, the convention resorts to the more gender-neutral language of equal treatment to promote better working conditions (see Vosko 2010). In 1994, the ILO adopted the Part-Time Work Convention (No. 175), and Articles 4–7 enumerate the measures that "shall be taken to ensure that part-time workers receive the same protection as that accorded to comparable full-time workers," including establishment of the right to organize and protection against termination of employment and entitlements to maternity leave, paid annual leave, sick leave, and paid public holidays (ILO 2004). However, few countries have ratified this convention. Legal norms articulated in the Part-time Work Convention effectively apply in European countries through the EU Directive on part-time work. Even so, neither the UK (under Tony Blair's Labour Party) nor Germany (under Gerhard Schroeder's Social Democratic Party) became a signatory, a notable reluctance given these ostensibly labor-friendly administrations in place during the 1990s. Less surprising, given that their weak and decentralized labor movements deprived workers of a voice in national policy-setting in each country, Japan and the US also stayed in the non-ratification camp.

Political institutions continue to shape how countries approach conventions. In the case of working-time regulations, Japan and the US took different approaches. By reforming the Part-Time Labor law in the late 1990s, Japanese policymakers could be seen as conforming to international labor standards. Having rejected becoming a signatory to the ILO Convention on Part-Time Work, these same policymakers could ignore the core principle of equal treatment, even with its limits, in their own labor law reform (Osawa 2001; Gottfried & O'Reilly 2002). A more insulated US government has refused to sign many international conventions and treaties dealing with labor rights and regulations for gender equality. No law on part-time labor has appeared on the legislative horizon or risen to prominence in public discourse in the US. As a result, US labor law remains silent on pay or benefit parity for part-time workers, and only covers remuneration of part-time workers under the national minimum wage law (Gornick et al. 2007: 6). National institutions (collective bargaining and the state) continue to "address various combinations of pay equity, social security and occupational benefits, training and promotion opportunities and bargaining rights" (6).

Lessons from CEDAW and ILO Convention on Part-time Work

Focusing on CEDAW and the ILO Convention on Part-time Work shows how global and inter-national forces can both have strong effects on policies in some countries (EU countries), and have relatively little impact in others (US and Japan). In contrast to the EU, the UN lacks legal authority and cannot impose sanctions to compel governments either to adopt or to comply with labor conventions, and thus, in some cases, has rhetorical importance more than direct impact on regulatory reform. Such supra-national bodies and agencies influence agenda setting and articulate new regulatory norms, but as Streeck (2001: 7) contends, national institutions have the "capacity to impose enforceable sanctions ... and recourse ... to legitimate coercion, in the form of legally binding rules and decisions ..." Faced with similar international challenges and pressures, countries develop different responses, "often with regionally specific manifestations," and at "different speeds of adjustment" (Jessop 2002: 71), helping to explain national variation of employment trends and conditions.

These new legal norms circulate in an emergent transnational human rights regime. On the one hand, new conventions, as discussed above, call attention to, and allow individuals to make, legitimate claims within the United Nations system. On the other hand, human rights designate either a narrow or a broader set of normative principles and entitlements that vary from place to place, with different gender connotations. Issues, such as domestic violence, relevant to women lag behind other international human rights laws (Sassen 1996: 33). Moreover, human rights in practice often are limited to political and civil rights rather than, more expansively, including a host of economic, social, and cultural rights. Some feminists go further to question whether gender equality can be achieved if constructed solely in a rights-based discourse. An alternative approach applies Amartya Sen's "capabilities framework," shifting the focus away from abstract entitlements to lived realities of people's lives (Yuval-Davis 2006: 291) by distinguishing between rights and individuals' ability to exercise them. Rights discourses may be too narrow to frame and ground claims over the distribution of resources and to rein in the excesses of global capitalism.

The emergence of a transnational human rights regime shifts sites of "normativity" for individuals claiming rights away from the state as the exclusive subject, but national boundaries still limit the realization of those rights (Sassen 1996: 33). Sassen pursues this line of argument further when she eloquently describes the impact of the international human rights regime on "undermining the exclusive authority of the State over its 'citizens.'" If all people are entitled to claim human rights, then membership in nation states no longer is the exclusive ground for realizing rights. In this way, "human rights begin to impinge on the principle of nation-based citizenship and thus the boundaries of the nation" (33). Nevertheless, individuals still face significant hurdles in exercising human rights outside of their "home" country and come up against different interpretations and recognition of human rights in both "home" and "host" countries. An international human rights regime still has few effective institutional mechanisms for enforcing, and forcing states to recognize, "women's rights as human rights." There are few available avenues to mandate that a state recognizes human rights of workers who are citizens or non-citizens. Similarly, there are few institutional mechanisms to enforce and claim jurisdiction over interpretation and implementation of human rights when workers suffer abuse in their home or host country. And there are few sanctions to ensure that states will abide by rulings of the International Court of Justice in The Hague, and of United Nations agencies. Although the state is not the exclusive subject of international law, it remains one of its main objects. Institutions and policies for the recognition of citizenship rights and on immigration re-inscribe national boundaries confining the individual and collective bargaining to their territorial home. The transnational human rights regime has less to do with the institutions supporting collective needs for care and solace (interdependence) and more to do with individual claims for freedom and autonomy (independence).

National governments, global labor: citizenship and immigration

The highly contested policy and politics around immigration and citizenship point to the dilemmas posed by, and the tension between, international human rights norms, national-based governmental action, and gender equality projects. Citizenship and, more accurately, non-citizenship divide women who may occupy the same territorial and even intimate spaces, yet who occupy different social locations. The liberal discourse of universal rights conflicts with the prevailing insular, nationalist notions of citizenship: "Liberal discourses of equality and inclusion are left to citizenship law while immigration law performs the dirty work of inequality and exclusion" (Danvergene, cited in Benhabib & Resnik 2009: 11). Practically and legally, citizenship stands "for an (at least relative) ethic of closure" (Bosniak 2009: 136). Immigration policies similarly define an inside and an outside for the recognition of rights in a bounded political space. An examination of citizenship and immigration policies and practices highlights how tension between inclusionary and exclusionary principles impacts on the capability of differently positioned women workers to make claims and to exercise rights in a political community.

Transnational Gendered Work, National Citizenship

The practical and conceptual basis of citizenship is built on the assumption of an exclusionary bounded political community in contradistinction to universalistic claims of inclusiveness. Such bounded notions mark as "other" or as "foreign" those deemed outside the political community. This "ethic of closure" assumes and reifies boundaries that operate not only at the "territorial-edge of a nation," but also "within the territorial interior" (Bosniak 2009: 136). Citizenship designates "distinct practices and institutions" and describes the "quality of relationships among members of a political community and the rules associated with the constitution and maintenance of community membership" (128–9). A broader notion of citizenship moves from one that distinctly refers to political engagement to one that encompasses economic justice, as realized by a universal right to decent work (130). It frames questions such as: who is a citizen, what rights attach to citizenship, and what are the boundaries of citizenship? Feminists go further to make visible the "linkages between women's citizenship and the demands of social reproduction" (131). But feminists and non-feminists alike tend to uncritically view the national society "as the total universe of analytical focus and normative concern" (140). Importantly, the failure to acknowledge the transnational scale of production and, increasingly, of reproduction, particularly transnational care chains, has implications for citizenship as an "aspirational" concept in feminist theory and practice.

An inside look at increasing commodification and transnationalization of domestic and reproductive work reveals the "divided nature of citizenship" (Bosniak 2009: 127), troubling women workers' experiences and feminist thought. Citizenship performs double duty: it affirms a commitment against subordination and toward inclusion; and it is in the service of subordination and exclusion (127). In the first sense, feminists have called for women's participation in the public sphere of paid labor as a means of achieving "full and equal 'citizenship'" (128). At the same time, feminists' attempts to engender concepts of citizenship and to achieve "full-citizenship" falter when the transnational organization of domestic servitude and reproductive labor is not taken into account. As women enter paid labor outside of the home, they increasingly pay for services performed by migrant women either in their homes or in the larger service economy (restaurants, laundries). Bosniak succinctly poses the problematic issue for feminism: "Achievement of citizenship for some women through the participation in paid work increasingly relies on labor of citizenshipless others" (128). In this way, citizenship – or more accurately non-citizenship – becomes an axis of inequality and exploitation, dividing women from the Global North and South. Yet Bosniak cautions against the rhetorically tempting proposition that "First World" women's full citizenship is gained at the expense of "Third World" women's denial of citizenship (137). Exploitation of migrant women is not based on the appropriation or transfer of citizenship. Citizenship is not an object or "single quantity" transferable from some women to others. By contrast, care, and more specifically love, as Hochschild argues and discussed in previous chapters, represents a nonrenewable "good" or resource expropriated in a commercial exchange (137). This "is an exchange that is contingent upon economic inequality – international and domestic – and histories of gender and racial subordination, as well as upon the operation of national immigration controls" (137–8).

The lack of citizenship status deprives migrant workers of avenues of redress available to other workers. Non-citizenship status accords

different protections to workers present in the same political territory of a nation state. Migrant workers, especially those unauthorized
to work in a country, are less able to exercise options of voice and
even voluntary exit. The inherent vulnerability to deportation makes
unauthorized migrant workers reluctant to invoke their inalienable
human rights for fear of being reported. Similarly, being deprived
of income alternatives compounds fear of losing or leaving a job
(Bosniak 2009: 136), even in the face of abuse, for all migrants, regardless of how they enter a country. The global dimension of care work
highlights the "other" citizenship discourse of exclusion (135).

The concept of "partial citizenship" has been proposed to capture
the "degrees and levels of exclusion" of migrants by receiving nations
to recognize the "other" citizenship discourse (Parrenas 2001: 1130;
also see Bosniak 2009: 138). All countries impose restrictions on rights
and benefits of non-citizens and most do not extend equal protections prior to the attainment of full citizenship (Parrenas 2001: 1135).
However, law on eligibility for full citizenship varies, ranging from
more draconian laws denying any pathway to citizenship in migrant
labor regimes in Singapore and Dubai to more welcoming laws granting the possibility of citizenship after a specified length of time, such
as the two-year waiting period in Spain and Canada. In the US, lawful
permanent residents enjoy some basic political and social rights, such
as the right to some social provisions (Bosniak 2009: 136). However,
voting rights are restricted to a few local jurisdictions, and otherwise prohibited in federal elections.[3] Yet so-called "illegal aliens" are
ineligible for most state-sponsored benefits. As a consequence, their
"irregular immigration status renders them vulnerable to subordination in a variety of arenas" (136–7), depriving workers of basic rights
and social protections.

Immigration and Citizenship: Economic and Social Exclusion

Immigration law regulates who can enter a country, specifying the
length and terms of their stay, and restricting the location and type
of jobs available. In particular, the introduction of guest worker
programs creates a category of worker relegated to the tenuous
legal status of "temporary settler" (Parennas 2001: 1135). Some of
these programs restrict incorporation of migrants and often of their
families, denying women migrants the ability to nurture their own
families even as they are permitted to care for others in privileged
families (1134). This forces individual migrants to bear costs of social
reproduction privately when not available from either the home
or the host country. Parennas (1134) concludes that, "in this way
receiving nations can secure a supply of low-wage workers who can

be repatriated if the economy slows down." Through immigration law, the state relinquishes responsibility for social reproduction of migrant labor.

In Japan, relaxation of restrictive immigration policies and practices in the last decade of the twentieth century – not coincidentally, during one of its worst economic crises and in the face of an ageing population – puts in sharp relief differential treatment of migrant workers and the divided nature of citizenship. Short-term programs for industrial training introduced in 1990, and technical internships permitted in 1993, created a pool of temporary labor (Ito 2005: 66). These policy revisions served to induce migration of a relatively cheap female labor force without provoking too much political opposition from conservative members of the Diet or from the population at large (Ito 2005: 66). Recruitment of Filipinas and Indonesian women on short-term training visas to perform health care as trainees guaranteed that women would fill these limited-term contracts. The status of "trainee" deprived these workers of both explicit and implicit contractual commitments to continuous employment and denied recognition of these workers' actual skills, their previous work experience, and their educational achievements. Moreover, the trainee program is part of a policy orientation in which Japan erects a "high wall" for "foreign labor" to stay in the country. A story in the New York Times featured Ms. Fransiska, a 26-year-old nurse from Indonesia who received a three-year visa to work in a hospital outside of Tokyo. In order to earn the right to continue working at the end of her three-year stint, she was required to pass a standardized nursing exam in Japanese – an almost insurmountable hurdle: only 3 out of 600 passed the test from 2007 to 2010 (Tabuchi 2011: A10). Short-term visas, like guest worker programs, function as revolving doors due to legal requirements that direct workers to return home after a fixed time period.

Unique provisions of the Japanese immigration law base migrants' entry and access to work and citizenship on class and gender, as well as heritage. The revised Immigration Control Law of 1990 accords a special status to those with Japanese heritage, Nikkeijin, principally from Latin America, mostly from Brazil and Peru (Roberts 1999: 399). As overseas descendants of Japanese ancestry, Nikkeijin are allowed to stay in Japan as "spouses or children of Japanese nationals or as 'long-term residents' without limitations on work" (Ito 2005: 56). Similarly, political practices privilege Japanese nationals over others as is evident in the example of public employment and enfranchisement, which has been restricted to Japanese nationals, although some municipalities have abolished the nationality requirement (Kibe 2006: 422). In contrast, Filipinas or women from other poor Asian countries enter Japan at a disadvantage in the labor market. The Immigration

Control Law regulates the mode of entry, restricting the terms and conditions of living, reinforcing social exclusion, and privileging some in line for citizenship over others.

More generally, immigration policies and restrictions on pathways to citizenship permit differential treatment of migrant workers and transnational corporations. Migrant labor and international business face different constraints on their mobilities through different political channels, of immigration policy and neo-liberal trade policies respectively. Immigration law, as discussed above, restricts labor's freedom of movement – that is, where they can settle, the duration of their residence, and the type and conditions of work available to them. Migrant labor often ends up in the lowest tiers of the labor market, and in precarious forms of employment. Because of the "illicit" nature of sex work and the isolation of much domestic work, many female migrants face extreme precariousness. This precariousness not only is produced by the informalized nature of the employment relationship and job characteristics, but also is inherent to the differential rights (partial citizenship) and protections accorded to non-citizens. The legal framework controls labor through immigration laws and restrictions on citizenship, while global capital moves more freely, although not completely unconstrained in their activities and locational decisions.

Thinking beyond the boundaries of the nation state highlights what is at stake for women workers on both sides of the citizenship divide. It raises questions about economic and political rights complicated by globalization: should rights and protections be limited to those formally recognized as citizens or to all "those territorially present workers? [and] What obligations do we owe to people whose opportunities for decent work in their own societies have been thwarted, in part, by a system of international political economy that has served to benefit our own nations [including the transfer of care]?" (Bosniak 2009: 141). Finally, can workers from one country be protected in the countries where they work?

Migrant labor and domestic politics

Increasing migration occurs in the context of inequalities between sending and receiving nations, and is fueled in part by economic policies and practices of governments in poor countries. This "denationalization of economies" has had the contradictory effect of "renationalization of politics" (Parrenas 2001). Domestic politics take new forms and address new issues as more citizens seek, and are encouraged, to work outside their homes. In some developing countries, export-oriented development and "denationalization of economies compels poor nations to provide low-waged labor and extend workers as a commodity for export" (Parrenas 2001: 1136).

Global Migration, Domestic Politics: The Case of the Philippines

Migration is a nation-building strategy most notably in the Philippines (Parrenas 2001). The Philippines promotes migration of its own citizens to work in oil-rich countries of the Middle East and developed countries in Europe and North America. In a sense, by promoting commodification of labor for export, the Philippines anticipates remittances sent home by workers living and working abroad. In the Philippines, remittances are the chief source of foreign currency, followed by electronics (1137). Through an exported-oriented political strategy of labor commodification, the Philippine state has become more integrated into the global market economy (1136). An example that follows draws on Parrenas' research on global migration and domestic politics in the paradigmatic case of the Philippines.

The Philippine state actively encourages men and women to migrate so they can find gainful employment, but cannot protect its citizens from abuse or guarantee that employers will comply with contractual terms and conditions of employment in other countries. Finding itself in a no-win situation, the state turns migration into a nationalist virtue for economic development. To promote this goal, the state rhetorically adopts the language of "heroes" to emphasize the importance of migrants in their nation-building project (Parrenas 2001: 1139). The state deploys an "iconic male migrant" as the prototypical hero, despite the reality of the larger number of female migrants. This gendered image of the male migrant downplays the specific exploitation suffered by many female migrants (1137). It also hides the care deficit resulting as mothers and fathers leave their families to work abroad. In this way, the state sidesteps the issue of not being able to protect its most vulnerable citizens.

Gender affects how male and female workers experience and construct their relationship to the state, both as "home" and as the basis of an "imagined global community" (Parrenas 2001: 1131). Female migrants express a desire and nostalgia for home even though many may not return to their country of origin. This stance emphasizes both nationalist and diasporic identities, which both reinforce and transgress the nation state (1139). Nationalist identity empowers Filipina domestic workers, but also deflects them from claiming membership in the countries where they work (1143). Globalization also enables female migrants to forge an imagined community based on national affiliation with other women who are similarly displaced from their homeland. Filipinas construct a symbolic transnational ethnic identity that emerges from their shared experiences of partial citizenship and family separation (1143). A magazine, *Tinig Filipino*, publishes migrant women's stories about their lives. The magazine links domestic workers typically isolated from each other, whether in the same city or in different countries, and creates the possibility for the formation of new solidarities and subjectivities that engage migrant women (1146). However, there are limits to the imagined global communities based on diasporic identities, since most of the women see the Philippines as home rather than establishing a home in the receiving country. As a result, the diaspora migrant community's orientation toward home diverts them from agitating and organizing against abuses by their employers and extending their citizenship rights in host countries.

Female migrant workers are reimagining domestic citizenship, in terms of their relationship both to the spatial imaginary of the nation as their natal home and to the transnational families of their conjugal homes. In the former, female migrants demand rights vis-à-vis the nation state, redefining and extending domestic politics outside territorial boundaries of that state. In the latter, a new domestic politics emerges out of the reformation of family in women's life stories. Female migrants forge new modes of belonging and affective communities with corresponding rights as they negotiate their physical distance and autonomy from their homes. In this way, we can see how home and domestic citizenship take on a double meaning and ground different organizing strategies for female migrants compared to their male counterparts.

"Domestic" Politics, Domestic Citizenship: The Case of India

Globalization localizes and domesticates politics that often go unnoticed by conventional notions of what constitutes the political. What happens if the field of vision shifts to a different register, considering micro-political practices as well as discourses linking domestic citizenship to work? Have feminists' attempts to engender concepts of citizenship been too focused on the abstract legal "content" of rights conveyed in and by states? Do macro-institutional perspectives and abstract philosophical debates deflect from view how women rework "domestic citizenship," as they traverse and stray from the normative gender order? How are women remaking citizenship by constituting alternative family forms and modes of belonging to families, with correspondingly new rights and obligations within the domestic realm (Lal 2009)?

A fascinating case study reveals the presence of women engaged in local politics through an analysis of female factory workers' counter-narratives of "domestic citizenship" in India (Lal 2009). Lal's case study is significant for a country in transition from a domestic to a more public gender regime. Women employed in TV assembly factories represent a relatively privileged category as an "aristocracy of labor" in India. This type of work takes place in contained spaces considered "respectable" because of the clean interiors, rather than on the crowded, unprotected warren of city streets. This is the case even though factory jobs are considered low-skilled and often entail informalized employment relationships.[4] In such globalized spaces of the factory, groups formally excluded from the public sphere engage in a kind of "domestic" politics and citizenship.

The analysis of "domestic citizenship" marks a departure from the literature that typically emphasizes the category of labor or worker, relating to a disembodied and atomized individual as the bearer of a narrow set of political rights. Jayati Lal (2009: 1) appropriates Veena Das and Renu Addlakha's concept of domestic citizenship to make visible the "privileging of the family and community in the construction of women as subjects of the nation and the constitution of women's rights." Her definition highlights the unacknowledged assumption of masculine embodiment associated with the proto-typical citizen that has failed to comprehend the specificity of women's position vis-à-vis the state. Women have derived rights principally through their relationships in the family, as mothers, as sisters, and as wives. The notion of domestic citizenship shines a light on women's lives, but not as simply determined by a set of institutions or legal statuses. Rather, Lal reworks the concepts of politics and publics in terms of women's counter-narratives to articulate new associational forms and affective relations: "It appears that the complex relation between narratives disseminated in the public sphere and experimentation with norms in the domestic sphere might have pried open the domestic space such that new definitions of domestic citizenship emerged . . . opening new avenues for women" (Veena Das & Renu Addlakha 2001: 519, cited in Lal 2009). Women whose life stories produce novel kinship relationships challenge domestic femininity and create new definitions of domestic citizenship.

In "public spaces" at work, women gain a new presence for themselves and for others in factory spaces, where they forge publics enabling them, sometimes unintentionally, to rewrite gender scripts and reconfigure domestic citizenship through the circulation of counter-narratives of their lives. The circulation of counter-narratives "restories" gender in "domestic spaces" of home, turning what signifies outside in and inside out:

> These [women's] stories are suggestive of the multiple sites where ideological betrayals to normative femininity take place – they occur through the creation of alternative forms of households and the fictive bonds of kinship that are forged by women, through the subjective dis-identification with and in the hegemonic patriarchal household, and their commitment to and desire for alternative affective communities at work. (Lal 2009: 32)

Women assemble affective communities at work through the seemingly mundane banter of gossip. Such talk is deeply political because it produces community through communicative interactions (Sotirin & Gottfried 1999). Gossip produces counter-narratives by calling attention to alternative practices, making them visible and available for emulation. In this way, counter-narratives give meaning to and frame alternative biographies pointing to new gender "lifelines."

These new "lifelines" constitute a "politics of refusal," that is, a refusal to inhabit the category of "Indian woman," straying from the gender scripts that sustain and define the category, and even calling the category into question (Lal 2009: 33). The decisions about living arrangements, however, are not necessarily preceded by political intentions. Instead, the influence of the circulation of "other" women's stories enables a woman to try reordering gender relations in her life. Lal's theoretical and epistemological use of the term "life stories" draws on narrative analysis and the narrative construction of identities.[5] Her presentation of women's life stories in the flux of biographical narratives follows a diachronic rather than merely synchronic logic, as implied by the alternative life-course perspective more typical in US sociology. Construction of new lifelines extends the meaning of domestic politics beyond political institutionalized settings.

Reading women's life stories brings work to home and home to work in an analysis of new domestic politics. In matter-of-fact language, women's stories make extraordinary tales out of ordinary experiences. Their life stories unravel the threads that bind women to normative domestic femininity. Echoing Simone de Beauvoir's oft-cited existential statement that "one is not born, but rather becomes, a woman," Lal coins the term "unbecoming women" to denote "the conscious, oppositional, and productive aspects of women's rewriting of their gendered life-scripts," which articulate new possibilities and new modes of belonging. "Unbecoming women" not only suggests the productive aspects of women rewriting their life stories through fictive bonds and familial reformation, but also conveys the enactment of "gender outlaws" who refuse to conform to, and perform in accordance with, norms of femininity deemed appropriate, attractive, and flattering.

The life stories of factory women are shaped by economic globalization in ways that have gone unnoticed in theories of political
globalization focusing on formal political institutions and abstract
legal norms. Deploying the concept of domestic citizenship enables
Lal to excavate logics of social action in women's counter-narratives
of domestic life. Domestic citizenship and politics occur in new spaces
of globalized production and city life. It may well be that the symbolic
and geographic distance from their natal home, created by migration
to work in globalizing cities opens socio-emotional lacunae in which
women can rewrite their gender scripts. A future study might explore
more fully the specificity of spatial-emotional dynamics for women
who migrate to the city.

New multi-scalar feminist movements and new subjects of globalization

Economic globalization alters the contours of politics and the context
for doing politics. What distinguishes international organizing in an
earlier epoch from globalization at the current time is the "intersection of the global with the local, the expansion of popular, decentralized, and democratic forms of interpreting and responding to the top
down challenges posed by a world economy" (Marx-Ferree 2006: 4).
Globalization increases the level of integration and interconnectivity
both structuring positive opportunities for mobilization and impos-
ing new obstacles to it (Marx-Ferree 2006: 9). Feminist organizations
and movements are adopting new spatial forms of politics.[6] The rise
of multi-scalar feminist movements reflects what Marx-Ferree calls a
"multiplicity of 'centers' of power" (Marx-Ferree et al. 2009: 4), which
draws on transnational opportunity structures in new political contexts. Transnational opportunity structures provide new resources,
both discursive and material, as well as spaces for women's and
feminist mobilization to improve working conditions and economic
outcomes.

Newly formed transnational feminist networks affect the success
of women-friendly policymaking at the national level. These feminist
networks may or may not have multinational membership, but their
impulse may come from interactions at global forums. For example,
gender mainstreaming developed in the context of international conferences, and was diffused through NGOs before national and local
governments took up the issue. This finding has particular relevance
for theories of the state, which have neglected the role of women's
mobilization in the making of policy. Japan is a case in point. Theories
of the Japanese developmental state focus on how bureaucracy-

led policymaking operates with minimal transparency and narrow input. These theories fail to take into account how femocrats in the Diet and in the Ministries, along with women's organizations, initiated gender policies and shaped the direction of reforms (Gelb 2003; Osawa 2007). As Lenz (2004) suggests, transnational feminist networks were a potent force for the adoption and reform of equal opportunity laws and for the passage of the Basic Law for a Gender Equal Society in Japan. The term *kansetsu gaiatsu* describes the influence of external norms and movements on gender policymaking in Japan (Gelb 2003).

Transnational feminist organizing involves "conscious crossing of national borders . . . superseding nationalist orientation" (Moghadam 2006: 60–1), mobilizing women across different social locations as well as contexts. Transnational social movements and NGOs disseminate material resources and discursive modes of representation for framing issues across national borders (Marx-Ferree 2006: 14). But race, class, and citizenship divisions among women complicate feminist politics. Without a single common basis of oppression to ground politics, feminists must consider cross-cutting issues and construct cross-class alliances to advance political projects aimed at gender equality. These projects challenge second-wave feminist engagement in "identity politics," whereby members of the oppressed category are constructed as homogeneous, and all dimensions of social location are reduced to a primary one (Yuval-Davis 2006: 277). Acknowledging differences among women has practical and theoretical significance: it "allows us to explain the connections and border crossings better and more accurately" (Mohanty 2006: 226), and thus to build coalitions rather than to expect a false unity of interests.

A transversal feminism is one way to avoid reductionism in feminist politics (Yuval-Davis 2006: 281). According to Yuval-Davis, feminists must engage in dialogue, both horizontally and vertically, in order to achieve a transversal feminist movement. Further, dialogue involves mutual understanding and common interests and beliefs, rather than necessarily roots, in shared social locations. Feminists can *root* and situate knowledge in their own experiences, but then must *shift* to encompass the views of others. As suggested above, there isn't a single women's standpoint from which to derive feminist theory and practice (Yuval-Davis 2006: 286). In negotiating and recognizing differences among women, feminists articulating a vision for the future face pitfalls and potentials for achieving gender justice.

New feminist approaches must attend "to macro-politics of economic and political globalization but also to micro-politics of context, subjectivity and struggle" (Mohanty 2006: 226). Revisiting her influential article "Under Western eyes," critiquing Western feminism, Mohanty argues for a standpoint rooted in the lives of the most marginalized women in the capitalist world economy. According to Mohanty, their standpoint can provide a more inclusive paradigm and expansive vision through critical reflection on their everyday lives as poor women of color in/of the Third World. This does not mean that a transnational anti-capitalist struggle necessarily must originate in a particular geographic space, but rather is based on "place consciousness as the radical other of global capitalism" (235). She recommends that feminists adopt a strategy of "reading up" that can reveal the "concrete effects of global restructuring on race, class, national and sexual bodies of women" (237). The above example of domestic citizenship instantiates a micro-politics in which women in/of the so-called Third World rewrite new gender lifelines. Globalization creates new political landscapes for engagement and construction of counter-hegemonic gender identities, new social imaginaries, and new multi-scalar feminist mobilization.

Conclusion: from local to global and back again

This chapter charts the impulse behind the shift from an international framework of nation states to new multi-level political assemblages. Political globalization entails rescaling of sites and institutions for the staging of politics and policy formation. In this way, political globalization transgresses the nation state by creating new local sites and transnational spaces for influencing policy and engaging in politics. While transnational agents (multinational corporations, NGOs, international organizations and institutions) diffuse legal norms from one place to another, the national context remains an important arena for regulating labor standards and working-time practices, and organizing care. The nation state serves as "more than a pawn in some totalizing and all determining globalization process" (Dicken et al. 1997: 163). However, ascendance of neo-liberalism pushes states to retreat from support of social reproduction, to facilitate recommodification of labor, and to lower trade barriers, all in support of capital accumulation.

The changing role of the state vis-à-vis global capital and labor presents both challenges and new opportunity structures for engaging in politics. Tensions prove difficult for policy transfers in multi-level governance: policy goals formulated by supra-national institutions must be enacted and enforced by national actions. Further, some policies dealing with immigration and citizenship largely remain the purview of the nation state, though the European Union relaxes its strict borders for members of the community. As a result, migrant labor may work in the shadows, unprotected by employment regulation in the country in which they reside yet out of reach of any protections offered by the country of their origin. Political institutions and the realization of rights still are relentlessly located at the national level. Social protections and citizenship are not as mobile as migrant labor, but rather are realized and enforced by local jurisdictions within nation states. Herein lies the disjuncture between economic globalization and the limits to truly political globalization.

Political globalization recasts international relationships between nation states, supra-national institutions, and international organizations; reorganizes institutional priorities within national states; rescales spaces for engaging in politics; and reworks associational modes, meanings, and identities. Gender may seem irrelevant to such large-scale political and economic changes. However, political globalization alters the distribution of risks, opportunities, benefits, and costs among different groups of women workers, as well as influences the circulation, adoption, and modification of regulations and other legal norms around gender equality and human rights. Feminists argue that a narrow view of the domestic economy as a bounded political unit and as a limited set of economic activities misrepresents changing power relationships in the domestic sphere. The political instance is not confined to either large-scale political institutions or abstract legal norms, but is also inscribed in seemingly mundane talk among women who reform their intimate domestic arrangements.

Political globalization also devolves interests and political claims from the statehouse to the household. A reassertion of the importance of "domestic" politics results from women's increasing participation in the "public" sphere. Women are reconstituting and claiming new identities and rights around domestic citizenship. In this way, multi-scalar governance generates spaces for forging new publics and new civil societal spaces for the contestation of gender relations and economic justice. Civil society organizations and social groups are important intermediaries in the policymaking arena. The number of groups, their associational ties and density of relationships between groups, and their political orientations each influence policy and other political outcomes. Transnational experiences seem to strengthen national or sub-national identities in some cases, and open up more expansive social imaginaries at other times. The multiscalar approach applied throughout the book highlights the interconnections and interactions from the local to the global and back again.

Transnationalization of the conditions of social reproduction leads us to understand why this book insists on using a feminist lens to understand economic trends and outcomes. Feminism, as a theory and as a political project, directs attention to how ego-centric capitalism disregards responsibility for the care of others. Capitalism, by shedding workers and informalizing labor, does violence to the economic security of families and communities left in the wake of this economic destruction. The externalization and privatization of social reproduction, then, is part and parcel of this logic, and thereby more prominent as a result of neo-liberal global capitalism. A feminist political economy, in contrast, puts care and social reproduction at the center of analyses and of the framing of new social imaginaries. Without a feminist lens, care seems outside of the economic realm or appears to be some vestige of pre-capitalist relations. It is precisely in our most intimate settings and relationships that we can see the changing nature of work and life. Service production, whether delivered by the state, the family, the civil society, or the market, is associated with female labor force participation, with maternal employment more specifically, with sex segregation in the economy, and with gender inequality more generally. Even more so, the commodification of care and intimacy interjects the market and exchange values into everything and everywhere. An alternative vision, the ethos of caring for others or an ethic of responsibility, can orient action toward interdependence and mutual recognition, and offers a critique of this momentum toward non-responsibility for social provisioning.

Notes

2 Theory of Work and Economy

1 Some sections in this chapter are taken from "Feminist theories of work" (Gottfried 2006). For a more sustained analysis of Marx and Weber, see the edited volume *Social Theory at Work* (Korczynski et al. 2006).

2 The varieties of capitalism approach originated in the scholarship of researchers at two prestigious German research institutes: David Soskice at the Social Science Research Center Berlin (WissenschaftsZentrum Berlin) and Wolfgang Streeck at the Max-Planck Institute for the Study of Societies in Cologne (Gesellschaftsforschung). Literally from their office windows, they could observe and experience first-hand the success and then reversal of economic fortunes of the German economic model.

3 Although little-known today, the publication of *Woman and Labour* by Olive Schreiner in 1891 first made the connection between capitalism and social reproduction (cited in Wise & Stanley 2003: 3).

4 I am grateful to Sylvia Walby for reminding me of the impact of Charlotte Perkins Gilman on second-wave feminism.

5 On January 10, 1918, the Congress approved the 19th Amendment, which said that the right of citizens of the United States to vote shall not be denied or abridged by the United States or any other state on account of sex. Many states granted suffrage to women before the actual ratification of the amendment, but finally, after a year and a half, the Senate passed the amendment on June 19, 1919. The 19th Amendment became part of the US Constitution on August 26, 1920: www.thenagain.info/webchron/usa/19Amend.html.

6 Dorothy Sue Cobble (2003) retrieves the history of 'The Other Women's Movement' from the 1930s to the 1980s.

7 In a similar vein, Colette Guillaumin (1995, cited in Collins 2007: 594) proposes a materialist analysis of gender and racial oppression based on the physical appropriation of the body that bears the capacity to labor, including the "products of the body such as children and sexual services, and the physical care of children, the elderly . . . as well as healthy men."

8 *Patriarchy at Work* (Walby 1986) addresses collective agency to understand how and why jobs (according to length of training, skill, heavy labor required) became typed as either feminine or masculine. The outcome stems from the multifaceted struggle that involves different access to resources, including state power.

9 This book primarily references Western feminist scholarship. However, feminist theories traveled across regions of the world. In her cleverly titled work *Bye-bye Corporate Warriors*, Mari Osawa (1994) translates the

structural approach to formulate the corporate-centered patriarchal society in Japan.

10 For a systematic discussion of gender, see Lorber (1994); Marx-Ferree et al. (1999); Connell (2002).

3 An Integrative Framework for the Study of Gender, Work, and Economy

1 In Japan, hostessing falls under the rubric of reproductive labor; typically, young women serve older men who visit hostess bars "in order to release their stresses from work" (Parrenas 2008: 12).

2 Feminist attempts to gender varieties of capitalism appear in a special issue of *Social Politics* edited by Leslie McCall & Ann Orloff (2005).

5 Serving People: Gender and Services in the New Economy

1 The Supreme Court ruled against certifying 1.5 million female workers as a "class" to take action against the retail giant (Liptak 2011: 5). The significance of the decision will weigh heavily on the ability of women to exercise their collective rights in the future. Columbia University Law Professor John Coffee argues that the suit "could bring a virtual end to employment discrimination class actions filed under Title VII of the Civil Rights Act of 1964."

2 When the new health care law kicks in by 2014, then McDonald's workers presumably will be able to buy better health insurance at lower prices through exchanges (Leonhardt 2010b).

3 See Shire (2007) for a more thorough discussion of the cross-national differences.

6 Caring for People: Gender and Social Reproduction in Service Economies

1 A promising new approach by Kathleen Lynch conceptualizes love, care, and solidarity as forms of labor activity producing nurturing capital, which becomes the basis of "affective inequality." She defines affective inequality in terms of the structure of advantage and disadvantage with regard to the deprivation "of the capacity to develop supportive affective relations . . . As love, care and solidarity involves work, affective inequality also occurs when the burdens and benefits of these forms of work are unequally distributed, and when this unequal distribution often deprives those who do the love, care and solidarity work of important human goods, including an adequate livelihood and care itself" (2010: 2). From her own memories complemented by stories from both domestic workers and their female employers, Gutierrez-Rodrigues (2010: 5) similarly explores the affective dimension and bodily sensations both "disturbing, but also stretching and reaffirming, power relations."

2 We must be careful about interpreting aggregate fertility rates in relationship to labor force participation because fertility varies by class, ethnicity, and religion within a country.

3 In this study, the sample includes women 25–44 years old, in their prime child-bearing ages and living with their partners, and excludes young new entrants into the labor force.

4 Though not the topic of discussion in this section, educational levels affect gender differences in childcare. A mother's higher education leads to both

parents spending more time on childcare in Denmark, France, Italy, and Spain, and less time in German families (Garcia-Mainar et al. 2011: 137)

5 www.bls.gov/ooh/Building-and-Grounds-Cleaning/janitors-and-building-clean ers.htm;   www.bls.gov/ooh/Building-and-Grounds-Cleaning/maids-and-house keeping-cleaners.htm (downloaded, April 27, 2012).

6 For example, estimates of the proportion of employed women in domestic service range between 16% and 20% in Brazil in the 1990s decade (Beneria 2001: 51).

7 State and Economy: Gender, Policy, and Work

1 Australian feminists coined the term "femocrats" to describe feminist state bureaucrats who work in women's policy offices and who advocate for gender equality policies (Stetson & Mazur 1995: 10; Mazur 2001: 4).

2 No comparable data are available for Japan.

3 Only 2% of children up to the age of 3 attend childcare in Germany (Daguerre 2005: 14).

4 This indicator of business leaders includes directors, chief executives and top managers in small enterprises.

5 Haas arrays countries into five clusters, ranging from traditional (Southern European countries) to egalitarian (Scandinavian countries), that loosely follow the tripartite division of welfare states.

6 http://supreme.justia.com/us/479/272/ (downloaded August 10, 2009).

7 The Act covers about 5% of all US businesses, accounting for over half of the total employees in the private sector (Foote 2000: 158).

8 With Sandra Day O'Connor's retirement from the Supreme Court, and despite the confirmation of Sonja Sotomayer and Elena Kagan, the new conservative majority under Chief Justice Roberts has fashioned a more pro-big-business approach.

9 Daniel Foote's (2000: 148) article on US labor law reform dates the liberal impulse "[f]rom the late nineteenth century through nearly the first four decades of the twentieth century, [whereby] courts at both the federal and state levels repeatedly struck down attempts by the states and the federal government to establish laws regulating working hours, workers' compensation, and even workplace health and safety. The most common ground for these decisions was that the laws interfered with freedom of contracts."

8 Terrains of Struggle: Gender, Work, and Labor Organizing

1 This discussion of sources of collective power, especially potent among service workers, was inspired by Eileen Otis' (2012) comments on associational power.

2 Feminists appropriated Gramsci's notion of hegemony to explore the micro-interactions by which men construct senses of masculinity.

3 She retired from this post after losing the election to succeed Andy Stern as President of the Service Employees International Union (SEIU) in the summer of 2010.

4 These numbers are based on a presentation given by the Director of the Gender Equality Office of RENGO in March 2007. She spoke after my own presentation on gender and unions sponsored by the Transnational Labor Studies group in Tokyo.

5 (www.jtuc-rengo.org/about/index.html, downloaded on November 7, 2009).

6 Non-governmental organizations (NGOs) and "new, citizen-initiated movements" (Schwartz 2003: 8) populate the space in civil society between state
and market.
7 Adler in www.citymayors.com/society /nyc_poverty.html.
8 Parts of this section were co-written with Anne Zacharias-Walsh.
9 Already, two affiliated unions, UNITE HERE and the Laborers' International
Union of North America, have returned to the fold of the AFL-CIO under the
leadership of Richard Trumpka who has infused a more politically active presence on the national stage.
10 See Silke Roth (2003) for a history of CLUW.
11 Even traditional unions undergo a kind of political osmosis, either fragment-
ing into smaller parts or merging into larger units. The United Health Care
Workers West, a local representing 150,000 health care workers in facilities
spread across California, charged the International SEIU with undue influence over on-going contract negotiations in 2008. As no resolution to the
dispute could be found, personal animosities and ideological differences
ultimately split the union. The International put the local into trusteeship,
and the former President, Sal Rosselli, and other local leaders set up the rival
National Union of Healthcare Workers.

10 Gender, Global Labor Markets, Commodity Chains, and Mobilities: Globalizing Production and Reproduction

1 Subcontracting reaches into workers' homes in a contemporary version of
the feudal putting-out system. Women represent the majority of home-based
workers, accounting for nearly 80% of the total in Brazil, Thailand, and the
Philippines during the mid-to-late 1990s (Charmes 2000 cited in Beneria
2001: 40). The extent of home-based work is very difficult to enumerate, given
its isolated and sometimes hidden labor process in homes or hard-to-find
sweatshops.
2 The stagnant wage in the US and rising standards of living in traditional locations of call centers in India have resulted in a recent reversal of this pattern,
with centers now relocating in the US. Time will tell if this is a harbinger of a
shift in economic power.
3 The DOL reports that 63% of firms in all of the boroughs of New York, and 90%
of firms in Chinatown, violated monetary provisions of the Fair Labor and
Standards Act that stipulates minimum wage and overtime compensation.
4 A newer trend turns "Third World" women's physical bodies into literal
incubators for the production of children. In such cases, women's surrogacy
can be seen as a kind of gestating work over a nine-month contractual period
– although actual contracts may never change hands. The global transfer
system is one in which the reproduction process takes place in the Global
South and the product of that labor, the children, are adopted by families
living in the Global North.
5 The subsequent quotation appeared on Parrenas' (2008) book jacket.

11 On the Global Economic Grid: Tokyo Tales, London Chronicles, Shanghai Stories

1 I am indebted to Sarah Swider whose work on China and many conversations
on the topic led to this insight.

2 This estimate is based on the China Labor Statistics Yearbook 2001, cited in Otis (2012: 59).

3 For more recent figures, see Chen (n.d.).

4 Interestingly, Japan's symbolic economy inverts this binary. The hypermodern city of Tokyo gained meaning from its juxtaposition with the imagery of the *fursato* (old village) (Robertson 1997). As "curators of the landscape of nostalgia" (Creighton 1998: 131), the Japanese state's evocation of old village life as the site of authentic "Japaneseness" contrasts with the Chinese state's association of the city with modernity.

5 Originally the Burj Dubai, the tower was renamed Burj Khalifa in honor of the ruler of Abu Dhabi, after that oil-rich Emirate bailed out Dubai (Goldberger 2010: 62).

6 Anne Zacharias-Walsh is writing a history of working women's groups in Japan, and detailing the international project, funded by the Center for Global Partnership, which facilitated these organizations' horizontal and vertical networking activities.

7 Foxconn employs 1.2 million Chinese workers who live in dormitories on campuses, which resemble small cities with as many as 200,000 people (Barboza & Duhigg 2012: B2).

8 I am indebted to Karen Shire who made this distinction in personal correspondence on the issue.

12 New Political Landscapes: Gender Equality Projects in Global Arenas and Nation States

1 As in the exhibit's provocative title, the juxtaposition of "sweet" and "violence," staged and real, evokes the seduction of consumption and the harsh realities women face in the production of desire.

2 The ILO was founded in 1919 "to pursue a vision based on the premise that universal, lasting peace can be established only if it is based upon decent treatment of working people. The ILO became the first specialized agency of the UN in 1946": www.ilo.org/global/About_the_ILO/lang–en/index.htm (downloaded August 3, 2009).

3 A permanent resident's (green-cardholder's) simple act of registering to vote or of casting a ballot in a federal election prompts punitive legal action – he/she is either denied the possibility of naturalization or deported from the United States (Semple 2010).

4 Another chapter shows how public factory spaces are "domesticated." Are there differences between industrial home-workers vis-à-vis factory workers, on the one hand, and street vendors and factory workers on the other? Both street vendors and home-workers work in isolation from others plying their trade. These are questions for future research.

5 Jayati Lal made this important point in personal email correspondence (November 27, 2009).

6 Marx-Ferree (2006: 6) distinguishes feminist from women's movements: the former defines activism that is oriented toward challenging and changing gender-based hierarchies; and the latter defines a constituency, not the targets of social change. That is, women's movements name women and build their strategies around "women's" concerns.

Bibliography

Acker, J. (1989) The problem with patriarchy. *Sociology* **23**, 235–40.

Acker, J. (1990) Hierarchies, jobs, bodies: a theory of gendered organizations. *Gender & Society* **4**, 2, 139–58.

Acker, J. (2004) Gender, capitalism and globalization. *Critical Sociology* **30**, 1, 17–41.

Acker, J. (2006) *Class Questions: Feminist Answers*. Rowman and Littlefield: Lanham, MD.

Acker, J. (2011) Welfare states and inequality regimes. Unpublished paper presented to American Sociological Association, Las Vegas, August 20.

Adkins, L. & Leonard, D. (1996) Reconstructing French feminism: commodification, materialism and sex. In: L. Adkins & D. Leonard (eds.) *Sex In Question: French Materialist Feminism*. London: Taylor & Francis, pp. 1–24.

Adkins, L. & Lury, C. (1999) The labour of identity: performing identities, performing economies. *Economy & Society* **28**, 598–614.

Adler, M. (2010) Attacks on welfare largely to blame for New York city's hidden poverty, www.citymayors.com/society/nyc_poverty.html (downloaded April 29, 2012).

Aglietta, M. (1998) Capitalism at the turn of the century: regulation theory and the challenge of social change. *New Left Review* **232** (Nov./Dec.), 41–90.

Aiba, K. (2004) Transformed bodies and gender: an introduction to the study of professional Japanese women wrestlers. Unpublished paper.

Albelda, R., Duffy, M., Folbre, N., Hammonds, C. & Jooyeoun, S. (2010) Placing a value on care work. *Communities & Banking* **21**, 1, 6–9.

Amin, A. (1997) Placing globalization. *Theory, Culture & Society* **14**, 2, 123–37.

Amin, A. & Thrift, N. (1996) Holding down the global. In: A. Amin & N. Thrift (eds.) *Globalization, Institutions, and Regional Development in Europe*. Oxford: Oxford University Press, pp. 257–60.

Amott, T. & Matthaei, J. (1996) *Race, Gender and Work: A Multicultural Economic History of Women in the United States*, revised edn. Boston: South End Press.

Anker, R. (1998) *Gender and Jobs: Sex Segregation of Occupations in the World*. Geneva: International Labour Office.

Anxo, D., Mencarini, L., Pailhe, A., Solaz, A., Tanturri, M. L. & Flood, L. (2011) Gender differences in time use over the life course in France, Italy, Sweden, and the US. *Feminist Economics* **17**, 3, 159–95.

Araki, T. (2002) *Labor and Employment Law*. Tokyo: Japanese Institute of Labor.

Ascher, C. (2009) Women and pay of housework. In: E. H. Altbach (ed.) *From Feminism to Liberation*, 4th edn. New Brunswick: Rutgers University Press, 263–70.

Baca Zinn, M. & Thornton Dill, B. (2009) Theorizing difference from multiracial feminism. In: V. Taylor, N. Whittier, & L. Rupp (eds.) *Feminist Frontiers*, 8th edn. Boston: McGraw-Hill, pp. 89–95.

Bakker, I. & Gill, S. (2003) Global political economy and social reproduction. In: I. Bakker & S. Gill (eds.) *Power, Production and Social Reproduction*. Palgrave, London, pp. 3–16.

Barboza, D. & Duhigg, C. (2012) Pressure, Chinese and foreign, drives changes at Foxconn. *The New York Times* (Feb. 20): B1–2.

Barnes, B. (2009) China approves Disney theme park in Shanghai. *The New York Times* (Nov. 3), www.nytimes.com/2009/11/04/business/global/04disney.html (downloaded May 3, 2012).

Bartsch, K. (2009) The employment projections for 2008–2018. *Monthly Labor Review* **132** (November), 3–10.

Basu, A., Grewal, I., Kaplan, C. & Malkki, L. (2001) Editorial. *Signs* **26**, 4, 943–8.

Beamish, T. & Woolsey-Biggart, N. (2006) Economic worlds of work: uniting economic sociology with the sociology of work. In: M. Korczynski, R. Hodson, & P. Edwards (eds.) *Social Theory at Work*. Oxford: Oxford University Press, pp. 233–71.

Beechey, V. (1979) On patriarchy. *Feminist Review* **3**, 66–82.

Beechey, V. (1987) *Unequal Work*. London: Verso.

Beneria, L. (2001) Shifting the risk: new employment patterns, informalization and women's work. *International Journal of Politics, Culture and Society* **15**, 1, 27–53.

Benhabib, S. & Resnick, J. (2009) Introduction: citizenship and migration theory engendered. In: S. Benhabib & J. Resnik (eds.) *Migrations and Mobilities: Citizenship, Borders, and Gender*. New York: New York University Press, pp.1–46.

Benner, C. (2002) *Work in the New Economy: Flexible Labor Markets in Silicon Valley*. Oxford: Blackwell Press.

Bennett, T. (1994) Popular culture and the turn to Gramsci. In: J. Storey (ed.) *Cultural Theory and Popular Culture: A Reader*. New York: Harvester Wheatsheaf.

Bergeron, S. (2001) Political economy discourses of globalization and feminist politics. *Signs* **26**, 4, 983–1006.

Bergmann, B. (1986) *The Economic Emergence of Women*. New York: Basic Books.

Bergqvist, C. & Nyberg, A. (2001) Alive and fairly well: welfare state restructuring and child care in Sweden. In: S. Michel & R. Mahon (eds.) *Child Care at Crossroads: Gender and Welfare State Restructuring*. New York: Routledge, pp. 287–308.

Bertrand, M., Goldin, C. & and Katz, L. (2010) Dynamics of the gender gap for young professionals in the financial and corporate sectors. *American Economics Journal* **2**, 228–55.

Beynon, H. & Hudson, R. (1993) Place and space in contemporary Europe: some lessons and reflections. *Antipode* **25**, 3, 177–90.

Bird, K. & Gottschall, K. (2004) Erosion of the male-breadwinner model? Female labor-market participation and family-leave policies in Germany. In: H. Gottfried & L. Reese (eds.) *Equity in the Workplace: Gendering Workplace Policy Analysis*. Lanham, MD: Lexington Press, pp. 281–304.

Blackburn, R., Brooks. B. & Jarman, J. (2001) Occupational stratification: the vertical dimension of occupational segregation. *Work, Employment & Society* **15**, 3, 511–38.

Blackburn, R., Browne, J., Brooks, B. & Jarman, J. (2002) Explaining gender segregation. *British Journal of Sociology* **53**, 513–36.

Blauner, R. (1964) *Alienation and Freedom: The Factory Worker and His Industry.* Chicago: University of Chicago Press.

Blum, L. (1991) *Between Feminism and Labor: The Significance of the Comparable Worth Movement.* Berkeley: University of California Press.

Bolzonaro, F. (2010) Book review essay: the uncertain destiny of an incomplete revolution. *Work, Employment & Society* **24**, 3, 591–6.

Bonacich, E., Cheng, L., Chinchilla, N. & Hamilton, N. (1994) *Global Production: The Apparel Industry in the Pacific Rim.* Philadelphia: Temple University Press.

Bonacich, E., Alimahomed, S. & Wilson, J. (2008) The racialization of global labor. *American Behavioral Scientist* **52**, 342–55.

Boris, E. & Klein, J. (2007) We were the invisible workforce: unionizing home care. In: D. S. Cobble (ed.) *The Sex of Class: Women Transforming American Labor.* Ithaca: Cornell University Press, pp. 159–76.

Bosch, G. (2006) Working time and the standard employment relationship. In: J. Y. Boulin, M. Lallement, J. Messenger, & F. Michon (eds.) *Decent Working Time: New Trends, New Issues.* Geneva: International Labor Organization.

Bose, C. & Bridges-Whaley, R. (2009) Sex segregation in the U.S. labor force. In: L. Rupp, V. Taylor, & N. Whittier (eds.) *Feminist Frontiers*, 8th edn. Boston: McGraw-Hill, pp. 233–41.

Bose, C. & Bridges-Whaley, R. (2011) Sex segregation in the U.S. labor force. In: L. Rupp, V. Taylor, & N. Whittier (eds.) *Feminist Frontiers*, 9th edn. Boston: McGraw-Hill, pp. 197–205.

Boserup, E. (1975) *Integration of Women in Development: Why, When, Who.* New York: United Nations Development Programme.

Bosniak, L. (2009) Citizenship, noncitizenship, and the transnationalization of domestic work. In: S. Benhabib & J. Resnik (eds.) *Migrations and Mobilities: Citizenship, Borders, and Gender.* New York: New York University Press, pp. 127–56.

Bourdieu, P. (1990) *The Logic of Practice.* Cambridge: Polity Press.

Boyer, R. (2004) New growth regimes, but still institutional diversity. *Socio-Economic Review* **2**, 1–32.

Bradiotti, R. (1994) *Nomadic Subjects: Embodiment and Sexual Difference in Contemporary Feminist Theory.* New York: Columbia University Press.

Bradley, H. (1999) *Gender and Power in the Workplace: Analyzing the Impact of Economic Change.* New York: St. Martin's Press.

Briskin, L. (2008) Cross-constituency organizing in Canadian unions. *British Journal of Industrial Relations* **46**, 2, 221–47.

Broadbent, K. (2005) For women, by women: women-only unions in Japan. *Japan Forum* **17**, 2, 213–30.

Brook, K. (2001) Trade union membership: an analysis of data from the autumn 2001 LFS, www.bis.gov.uk/filesd/file12445.pdf (downloaded April 29, 2012).

Browne, I. & Misra, J. (2003) The intersection of gender and race in the labor market. *Annual Review of Sociology* **29**, 487–513.

Bruegel, I. (1996) Whose myths are they anyway? A comment. *British Journal of Sociology* **47**, 175–7.

Bruegel, I. (1999) Globalization, feminization and pay inequalities in London and the UK. In: J. Gregory, A. Hegwisch, & R. Sales (eds.) *Women, Work and Inequality.* New York: St. Martin's Press, pp. 73–93.

Brush, L. (1999) Gender, work, who cares? Production, reproduction, deindustrialization, and business as usual. In: M. Marx-Ferree, J. Lorber, & B. Hess (eds.) *Revisioning Gender.* Thousand Oaks: Sage Publications, pp. 161–89.

Buckley, C. & Correal, A. (2008) Domestic workers organize to end an "atmosphere of violence" on the job. *The New York Times* (June 9), www.nytimes.com/2008/06/09/nyregion/09domestic.html (downloaded May 3, 2012).

Budig, M. (2002) Male advantage and the gender composition of jobs: who rides the glass escalator? *Social Problems* **49**, 2, 258–77.

Budig, M. & England, P. (2001) The wage penalty for motherhood. *American Sociological Review* **66**, 204–25.

Burawoy, M. (1985) *The Politics of Production.* London: Verso.

Burawoy, M., Burton, A., Ferguson, A. A. & Fox, K. J. (eds). (1991) *Ethnography Unbound: Power and Resistance in the Modern Metropolis.* Berkeley: University of California Press.

Butler, J. (1993) *Bodies That Matter: On the Discussion of the Limits of "Sex."* New York: Routledge.

Butler, J. (1999) *Gender Trouble: Feminism and the Subversion of Identity.* New York: Routledge.

Calas, M. & Smircich, L. (1989) Voicing seduction to silence leadership. Paper presented at the Fourth International Conference on Organizational Symbolism and Corporate Culture, Fontainebleau, France.

Calhoun, C. (1991) Culture, history, and the problem of specificity in social theory. In: S. Seidman & D. Wagner (eds.) *Postmodernism and Social Theory: The Debate over General Theory.* Oxford: Blackwell, pp. 244–88.

Calhoun, C. (2002) Introduction. In: C. Calhoun, J. Gerteis, J. Moody, S. Pfaff, K. Schmidt, & I. Virk (eds.) *Classical Sociological Theory.* Oxford: Blackwell, pp. 1–18.

Callard, F. (1998) The body in theory. *Environment and Planning D: Space and Society* **16**, 387–400.

Campbell, I., Baxter, J. & Whitehouse, G. (2009) Australia: casual employment, part-time employment and the resilience of the male breadwinner model. In: L. Vosko, M. MacDonald, & I. Campbell (eds.) *Gender and the Contours of Precarious Employment: Developing Common Understanding across Space, Scale, and Social Location.* London: Routledge, pp. 60–75.

Caraway, T. (2007) *Assembling Women: The Feminization of Global Manufacturing.* Ithaca: Cornell University Press.

Castells, M. (2000) Materials for an exploratory theory of the network society. *British Journal of Sociology* **51**, 1, 5–24.

Chang, G. (2006) "From the third world to the 'third world within'": Asian women workers fighting globalization. In: V. Taylor, N. Whittier, & L. Rupp (eds.) *Feminist Frontiers*, 8th edn. Boston: McGraw-Hill, pp. 585–95.

Charles, M. (2003) Deciphering sex segregation: vertical and horizontal inequalities in ten national labor markets. *Acta Sociologica* **46**, 4, 267–87.

Charles, M. & Bradley, K. (2009) Indulging our gendered selves? Sex segregation by field of study in 44 countries. *American Journal of Sociology* **114**, 4, 924–76.

Chen, X. (n.d.) A globalizing city on the rise: Shanghai's transformation in comparative perspective, www.uic.edu/depts/soci/xmchen/Chap1_Chen_Revised%5B1%5D.pdf (downloaded May 3, 2012).

Chow, E. N. (2003) Gender matters: studying globalization and social change in the 21st century. *International Sociology* **18**, 3, 443–60.

Clark, G. (1996) Implications of global polarization for feminist work. *Indiana Journal of Global Legal Studies* **4**, 1, 43–9.

Clawson, D. (2003) *The Next Upsurge: Labor and the New Social Movements.* Ithaca: Cornell University Press.

Clawson, D. & Clawson, M.A. (1999) What has happened to the US labor move-ment? Union decline and renewal. *Annual Review of Sociology* **25**, 95–119.

Clough, P. T. (2008) The affective turn: political economy, biomedia and bodies. *Theory, Culture and Society* **25**, 1, 1–22.

Cobble, D. S. (2003) *The Other Women's Movement: Workplace Justice and Social Rights in Modern America*. Princeton: Princeton University Press.

Cobble, D. S. (2007) Introduction. In: D. S. Cobble (ed.) *The Sex of Class: Women Transforming American Labor*. Ithaca: Cornell University Press, pp. 1–12.

Cockburn, C. (1983) *Brothers: Male Dominance and Technological Change*. London: Pluto Press.

Cockburn, C. (1991) *In the Way of Women: Men's Resistance to Sex Equality in Organizations*. London: Macmillan.

Cockburn, C. (1993) Men's stake in organizations. Paper presented at the "Organizations, Gender and Power" conference, Warwick University, Dec.

Collins, J. (2003) *Threads: Gender, Labor, and Power in the Global Apparel Industry*. Chicago: University of Chicago Press.

Collins, P. H. (1990) *Black Feminist Thought: Knowledge, Consciousness, and the Politics of Empowerment*. Boston: Unwin Hyman.

Collins, P. H. (2007) Pushing the boundaries or business as usual? Race, class and gender studies and sociological inquiry. In: C. Calhoun (ed.) *Sociology in America: A History*. Chicago: University of Chicago Press, pp. 572–604.

Collins, P. H. (2009) *Black Feminist Thought: Knowledge, Consciousness, and the Politics of Empowerment*, 2nd edn. London: Routledge.

Collinson, D. & Hearn, J. (1994) Naming men as men. *Gender, Work and Organisation* **1**, 2–22.

Connell, R.W. (1987) *Gender and Power: Society, the Person and Sexual Politics*. Cambridge: Polity Press.

Connell, R.W. (1995) *Masculinities*. Berkeley: University of California Press.

Connell, R.W. (2002) *Gender*. Cambridge: Polity Press.

Connell, R.W. (2007) *Southern Theory: The Global Dynamics of Knowledge in Social Science*. Cambridge: Polity Press.

Cooley, N. & Stone, P. (2009) Introduction. *Women's Studies Quarterly* **37**, 3–4, 13–21.

Craig, S. & Dash, E. (2010). Study points to windfall for Goldman partners. *The New York Times* (January 19): A1–A2.

Crain, M. (2007) Sex discrimination as collective harm. In: D. S. Cobble (ed.) *The Sex of Class: Women Transforming American Labor*. Ithaca: Cornell University Press, pp. 99–116.

Creighton, M. (1998) Pre-industrial dreaming in post-industrial Japan: depart-ment stores and the commoditization of community traditions. *Japan Forum* **10**, 2, 127–49.

Crenshaw, K. (1991) Mapping the margins: intersectionality, identity politics, and violence against women of color. *Stanford Law Review* **43**, 6, 1241–99.

Crenshaw, K. (2000) Demarginalizing the intersection of race and sex: a black feminist critique of anti-discrimination doctrine, feminist theory and anti-racist politics. In: J. James & T. D. Sharpley-Whiting (eds.) *The Black Feminist Reader*. Oxford: Blackwell, pp. 208–38.

Crenshaw, K. (2011) Demarginalizing the intersection of race and sex: Black feminist critique of antidiscrimination doctrine, feminist theory, and antira-cist politics. In: H. Lutz, M. T. H. Vivar, & L. Supik (eds.) *Framing Intersectionality: Debates on a Multi-faceted Concept in Gender Studies*. Aldershot: Ashgate, pp. 23–42.

Crompton, R. (2002) Employment, flexible working and the family. *British Journal of Sociology* **53**, 537–8.

Crompton, R. (2003) Class and gender beyond the "cultural turn." *Sociologica, Problemas e Practicas* **42**, 9–24.

Crouch, C. & Streeck, W. (1997) *Political Economy of Modern Capitalism: Mapping Convergence and Diversity.* London: Sage.

Curtin, J. (1999) *Women and Trade Unions: A Comparative Perspective.* Aldershot: Ashgate.

Daguerre, A. (2005) Europe's harassed mothers. *Le Monde Diplomatique* (January), 14.

Daly, M. (2002) Care as a good for social policy. *Journal of Social Policy* **31**, 2, 251–70.

Daly, M. (2011) *Welfare.* Cambridge: Polity Press.

Daly, M. & Lewis, J. (2000) The concept of social care and the analysis of contemporary welfare states. *British Journal of Sociology* **52**, 2, 281–98.

Daly, M. & Standing, G. (2001) *Care Work: The Quest for Security.* Geneva: ILO Press.

Davis, A. (1981) The approaching obsolescence of housework: a working-class perspective. An excerpt from *Women, Race and Class.* MIA. Subject Archive: Women & Marxism, www.marxists.org/subject/women/authors/davis-angela/housework.htm (downloaded Nov. 1, 2011).

Davis, A. (2000) Women and capitalism: dialectics of oppression and liberation. In: J. James & T. D. Sharpley-Whiting (eds.) *The Black Feminist Reader.* Oxford: Blackwell, pp. 146–82.

Davis, K. (2011) Intersectionality as buzzword: a sociology of science perspective on what makes a feminist theory successful. In: H. Lutz, M. T. H. Vivar, & L.Supik (eds.) *Framing Intersectionality: Debates on a Multi- Faceted Concept in Gender Studies.* Aldershot: Ashgate.

Davis, M. (2006) Fear and money in Dubai. *New Left Review* **41**, 1–14.

De Henau, J., Meulders, D. & O'Dorchai, S. (2010) Maybe baby: comparing partnered women's employment and child policies in the EU-15. *Feminist Economics* **16**, 1, 43–771.

De Laat, J. & Sevilla-Sanz, A. (2011) The fertility and women's labor force participation puzzle in OECD countries: the role of men's home production. *Feminist Economics* **17**, 2, 87–119.

Dean, A. & Guevara, P. (2001) New economic challenge to Japan's trade union movement. *WorkingUSA* **4**, 4, 59–83.

Delmar, R. (1986) What is feminism? In: J. Mitchell & A. Oakley (eds.) *What is Feminism?* Oxford: Blackwell.

Delphy, C. (1977) *The Main Enemy.* London: Women's Research and Resource Centre.

Demaziere, D. & Hirata, H. (2005) National configurations of unemployment: empirical results and theoretical implications. In: K. Kautoshi & K. Sugita (eds.) *The Unemployed and Unemployment in an International Perspective: Comparative Studies of Japan, France and Brazil.* Tokyo: Institute of Social Science, University of Tokyo, pp. 148–53.

Demaziere, D. & Sugita, K. (2005) Aims and methods of international comparison. In: K. Kautoshi & K. Sugita (eds.) *The Unemployed and Unemployment in an International Perspective: Comparative Studies of Japan, France and Brazil.* Tokyo: Institute of Social Science, University of Tokyo, pp. 4–14.

Dicken, P., Peck, J. & Tickell, A. (1997) Unpacking the global. In: R. Lee & J. Willis (eds.) *Geographies of Economies.* London: Arnold, pp. 158–66.

Duhigg, C. & Bradsher, K. (2012) How US lost out on i-phone work. *The New York Times* (Jan. 22): A1, 22

Durbin, S. (2007) Who gets to be a knowledge worker? The case of UK call centres. In: S. Walby, H. Gottfried, K. Gottschall, & M. Osawa (eds.) *Gendering the Knowledge Economy: Comparative Perspectives*. Houndsmill: Palgrave, pp. 228–47.

Ebbinghaus, B. (2001) When labour and capital collude: the political economy of early retirement in Europe, Japan and the USA. In: B. Ebbinghaus & P. Manow (eds.) *Comparing Welfare Capitalism: Social Policy and Political Economy in Europe, Japan and the United States*. London: Routledge, pp. 76–101.

Ebbinghaus, B. & Manow, P. (2001a) Introduction: studying varieties of welfare capitalism. In: B. Ebbinghaus & P. Manow (eds.) *Comparing Welfare Capitalism: Social Policy and Political Economy in Europe, Japan and the United States*. London: Routledge, pp. 1–24.

Ebbinghaus, B. & Manow, P. (2001b) Varieties of welfare capitalism: an outlook on future directions of research. In: B. Ebbinghaus & P. Manow (eds.) *Comparing Welfare Capitalism: Social Policy and Political Economy in Europe, Japan and the United States*. London: Routledge, pp. 304–15.

Ehrenreich, B. (2008) *Nickel and Dimed: On (not) Getting by in America*. New York: Holt Paperbacks.

Ehrenreich, B. (2010) The nannies' Norma Rae: Ai-jen Poo fights for domestic workers' rights. *The New York Times Style Magazine* (May 1): 49–52.

Ehrenreich, B. & Hochschild, A. R. (2003) *Global Women: Nannies, Maids and Sex Workers in the New Economy*. New York: Metropolitan Books.

Eisenstein, Z. (1984) *Feminism and Sexual Equality: Crisis in Liberal America*. New York: Monthly Review Press.

Eligon, J. (2012) In an informal economy, part valet, part hustler. *The New York Times* (Jan. 16): A6.

Elson, D. (2002) International financial architecture: a view from the kitchen. *Femina Politica: Zeitschrift für Feministische Politikwissenschaft* **11**, 26–37.

Elson, D. (2010) Gender and the global economic crisis in developing countries: a framework for analysis. *Gender & Development* **18**, 2, 201–12.

Encyclopedia of Marxism (n.d.) Commodification. www.marxists.org/glossary/ (downloaded December 3, 2011).

Engels, F. (1968) The origin of the family, private property and the state. In K. Marx and F. Engels (eds.) *Selected Works*. New York: International Publishers.

England, P, (1992) *Comparable Worth: Theories and Evidence*. New York: Aldine de Gruyter.

England, P. & Folbre, N. (2003) Gender and economic sociology. Unpublished paper presented at the "Prospects for Women's Equality in a Changing and Global Political Economy: Varieties of Capitalism, Labor and Gender" conference, Northwestern University, Chicago, October.

England, P., Budig, M. & Folbre, N. (2002) Wages of virtue: the relative pay of care work. *Social Problems* **49**, 4, 455–73.

Enloe, C. (2006) The global trotting sneaker. In: V. Taylor, N. Whittier, & L. Rupp (eds.) *Feminist Frontiers*, 8th edn. Boston: McGraw-Hill, pp. 512–16.

Erikson, R. & Wharton, A. (1997) Inauthenticity and depression: assessing the consequences of interactive service work. *Work and Occupations* **24**, 188–213.

Esping-Andersen, G. (1990) *The Three Worlds of Welfare Capitalism*. Cambridge: Polity Press.

Esping-Andersen, G. (1999) *Social Foundations of Post-Industrial Economies*. Oxford: Oxford University Press.

Esping-Andersen, G. (2009) *The Incomplete Revolution: Adapting Welfare States to Women's New Roles.* Cambridge: Polity Press.

Estévez-Abe, M. (2005) Gender bias in skills and social policies: the varieties of capitalism perspective on sex segregation. *Social Politics* **12**, 180–215.

Evans, M. (2003) *Gender and Social Theory.* Buckingham: Open University Press.

Evans, P. (2008) Is an alternative globalization possible? *Politics and Society* **36**, 271–305.

Eviatar, D. (2002) Is litigation a blight, or built in? *New York Times* (Nov. 22): 21, 23.

Ezawa, A. & Fujiwara, C. (2003) Lone mothers and welfare-to-work policies in Japan and the United States: towards an alternative perspective. Paper presented at the New Challenges for Welfare State Research conference, International Sociological Association RC-19 Poverty, Social Welfare and Social Policy, University of Toronto, August 21–24.

Fagan, C. & O'Reilly, J. (1998) Conceptualizing part-time work: the value of an integrated comparative perspective. In C. Fagan & J. O'Reilly (eds.) *Part-time Prospects: International Comparisons of Part-Time Work in Europe, North America and the Pacific Rim.* London: Routledge, pp. 1–31.

Falasca-Zamponi, S. (2003) Review of Vichy and the eternal feminine. *American Journal of Sociology* **109**, 240–2.

Fernandez-Kelly, P. & Wolf, D. (2001) A dialogue on globalization. *Signs* **26**, 4, 1243–9.

Fine, J. (2007) Worker centers and immigrant women. In D. S. Cobble (ed.) *The Sex of Class: Women Transforming American Labor.* Ithaca: Cornell University Press, pp. 211–30.

Firestein, N. & Dones, N. (2007) Unions fight for women and family policies – not for women only. In: D. S. Cobble (ed.) *The Sex of Class: Women Transforming American Labor.* Ithaca: Cornell University Press, pp. 140–54.

Flexner, E. (1974) *Century of Struggle: The Woman's Rights Movement in the United States.* New York: Atheneum Books.

Floro, M. & Meurs, M. (2009) Global trends in women's access to decent work. Friedrich Ebert Stiftung Occasional Papers, 43. Dialogue on Globalization, http://library.fes.de/pdf-files/iez/global/06399.pdf (downloaded October 3, 2010).

Folbre, N. (2001) *The Invisible Heart: Economics and Family Values.* New York: The New York Press.

Foote, D. (2000) Deregulation and labour law: the United States. *Bulletin of Comparative Labor Relations* **38**, 147–68.

Frank, A. G. (1978) *Dependent Accumulation and Underdevelopment.* London: Macmillan.

Franzway, S. & Fonow, M. M. (2011) *Making Feminist Politics: Transnational Alliances between Women and Labor.* Urbana: University of Illinois Press.

Fraser, N. (1997) *Justice Interruptus: Critical Reflections on the "Post Socialist" Condition.* London: Routledge.

Fraser, N. & Gordon, L. (1994) A genealogy of dependency: tracing a keyword of the US welfare state. *Signs* **19**, 2, 309–36.

Freeman, C. (2001) Is local:global as feminine:masculine? Rethinking the gender of globalization. *Signs* **26**, 4, 1007–37.

Freeman, J. (1995) The revolution for women in law and public policy. In J. Freeman (ed.) *Women: A Feminist Perspective.* Mountain View, CA: Mayfield Publishing Company. pp. 365–404.

Fujimura, H. (2012) Japan's labor unions: past, present, future. *Japan Labor Review* **9**, 1, 6–24.

Fuller, S. (2008) Job mobility and wage trajectories for men and women in the United States. *American Sociological Review* **73**, 158–83.

Gallu, J. & Son, H. 2010. AIG swaps unit "boys club" punished women, ex-workers claim. Bloomberg.com, www.bloomberg.com/apps/news?pid=20670001&sid=aTLgh (downloaded February 25, 2010).

García Márquez, G. (1998) *One Hundred Years of Solitude*. Perennial, New York.

Garcia-Mainar, I., Molina, J. A. & Montuenga, V. (2011) Gender differences in childcare: time allocation in five European countries. *Feminist Economics* **17**, 1, 119–50.

Gelb, J. (2003) *Gender Policy in Comparative Perspective: Japan and the United States*. New York: Palgrave.

Gereffi, G. & Korzeniewicz, M. (eds.) (1994) *Commodity Chains and Global Capitalism*. Westport, CT: Greenwood Press.

Gereffi, G., Humphrey, J. & Sturgeon, T. (2005) The governance of global value chains. *Review of International Political Economy* **12**, 1, 78–104.

Gilman, C. P. (1898) *Women and Economics: A Study of the Economic Relation Between Men and Women as a Factor in Social Evolution*. Boston: Small, Maynard & Co.

Gilman, C. P. (1899) *The Yellow Wall-Paper*. www.library.csi.cuny.edu/dept/history/lavender/wallpaper.html (downloaded March 5, 2011).

Gilman, C. P. ([1903] 1972) *The Home: Its Work and Its Influence*. Urbana: University of Illinois Press.

Gilpin, T. (1988) *On Strike for Respect: The Clerical and Technical Strike at Yale University, 1984-85*. Urbana: University of Illinois Press.

Ginn, J. & Arber, S. (1996) Feminist fallacies: a reply to Hakim on women's employment. *British Journal of Sociology* **47**, 167–77.

Giuffre, P. & Williams, C. (2002) Boundary lines: labeling sexual harassment in restaurants. In A. Wharton (ed.) *Working in America: Continuity, Conflict, and Change*, 2nd edn. Boston: McGraw Hill, pp. 253–67.

Glenn, E. N. (1985) Racial ethnic women's labor: the intersection of race, gender and class oppression. *Review of Radical Political Economics* **17**, 86–108.

Glenn, E. N. (1992) From servitude to service work: historical continuities in the racial division of paid reproductive labor. *Signs: Journal of Women in Culture and Society* **18**, 1–43.

Glenn, E. N. (1999) The social construction and institutionalization of gender and race: an integrative framework. In: M. Marx-Ferree, J. Lorber, & B. Hess (eds.) *Revisioning Gender*. London: Sage, pp. 3–43.

Glenn, E. N. (2010) *Forced to Care: Coercion and Care-giving in America*. Cambridge, MA: Harvard University Press.

Goldberger, P. (2010) The sky line: castle in the air. *The New Yorker* (Feb.), 62–3.

Gornick, J. & Myers, M.K. (2008) Creating gender egalitarian societies: an agenda for reform. *Politics & Society* **36**, 313–49.

Gornick, J., Myers, M.K. & Ross, K. (1998) Public policies and the employment of mothers: a cross-national study. *Social Science Quarterly* **79**, 1, 35–54.

Gornick, J., Heron, A. & Eisenbrey, R. (2007) *Work–Family Balance: An Analysis of European, Japanese, and U.S. Work-Time Policies*. Briefing Paper 189. Washington, DC: Economic Policy Institute.

Gottfried, H. (1991) Mechanisms of control in the temporary service industry. *Sociological Forum* **6**, 699–713.

Gottfried, H. (1992) The impact of skill on union membership: rethinking gender differences. *Sociological Quarterly* **33**, 1, 99–114.

Gottfried, H. (1994). Learning the score: the duality of control and everyday resistance in the temporary-help service industry. In J. Jermeir, D. Knights, & W. Nord (eds.) *Resistance and Power in Organizations*. London: Routledge, pp. 102–27.

Gottfried, H. (ed.) (1996) *Feminism and Social Change: Bridging Theory and Practice.* Urbana: University of Illinois Press.

Gottfried, H. (1998) Beyond patriarchy? Theorising gender and class. *Sociology: Journal of the British Sociological Association* **32**, 3, 451–68.

Gottfried, H. (2000) Compromising positions: emergent neo-Fordisms and embedded gender contracts. *British Journal of Sociology* **51**, 2, 235–59.

Gottfried, H. (2003) Temp(t)ing bodies: shaping gender at work in Japan. *Sociology: Journal of the British Sociological Association* **37**, 2, 257–76.

Gottfried, H. (2006) Feminist theories of work. In M. Korczynski, R. Hodson, & P. Edwards (eds.) *Social Theory at Work*. Oxford: Oxford University Press, pp. 121–54.

Gottfried, H. (2008a) Pathways to economic security: nonstandard employment and gender in contemporary Japan. *Social Indicators Research* **88**, 1, 179–96.

Gottfried, H. (2008b) Reflections on intersectionality: gender, class, race and nation. *Journal of Gender Studies* **11**, 23–40.

Gottfried, H. (2009a) Japan: the reproductive bargain and the making of precarious employment. In: L. Vosko, M. MacDonald, & I. Campbell (eds.) *Gender and the Contours of Precarious Employment*. London: Routledge, pp. 76–91.

Gottfried, H. (2009b) Gender and employment: a global lens on analyses and theorizing of labor markets. *Sociology Compass* **3**, 1–16.

Gottfried, H. (2011) Precarious work in Japan: old forms, new risks? Unpublished paper presented at University of North Carolina, Chapel Hill, Nov. 9.

Gottfried, H. & Graham, L. (1993) Constructing difference: the making of gendered subcultures in a Japanese automobile transplant. *Sociology: The Journal of the British Sociological Association* **7**, 611–28.

Gottfried, H. & Hayashi, N. K. (1998) Gendering work: deconstructing the narrative of the Japanese economic miracle. *Work, Employment and Society* **12**, 25–46.

Gottfried, H. & O'Reilly, J. (2002) Re-regulating breadwinner models in socially conservative welfare regimes: comparing Germany and Japan. *Social Politics* **9**, 1, 29–59.

Gottfried, H. & Reese, L. (2004) Gendering comparative policy analysis. In H. Gottfried & L. Reese (eds.) *Equity in the Workplace: Gendering Workplace Policy Analysis*. Lanham, MD: Lexington Press, pp. 1–28.

Gottfried, H. & Zacharias-Walsh, A. (2007) Network unions: working women's organizing activities in Japan. Union Renewal Web-blog operated by the Netherlands Trade Union Confederation, Dec. 6. http://unionrenewal.blog spot.com/search/label/women (downloaded April 4, 2010).

Gottschall, K. (2010) Women Friendly Welfare States? Understanding the Role of the State as Employer. Paper presented at the International Sociological Association, Goteberg, Sweden, July.

Gottschall, K. & Kroos, D. (2007) Self-employment in comparative perspective: general trends and the case of new media. In: S. Walby, H. Gottfried, K. Gottschall, & M Osawa (eds.) *Gendering the Knowledge Economy: Comparative Perspectives*. Houndsmill: Palgrave, pp. 163–87.

Gottschall, K. & Shire, K. (2007) *Understanding Employment Systems from a Gender Perspective*. ZeS Working Paper 5. Bremen: University of Bremen.

Gramsci, A. (1971) *Selections from the Prison Notebooks*. Ed. and trans. Q. Hoare & G. Nelson. New York: International Publishers.

Grosz, E. (1994) *Volatile Bodies: Towards a Corporeal Feminism*. Bloomington: Indiana University Press.

Gugler, J. (2004) Introduction: In: J. Gugler (ed.) *World Cities Beyond the West: Globalization, Development and Inequality*. Cambridge: Cambridge University Press, pp. 1–24.

Gutierrez-Rodrigues, E. (2010) *Migration, Domestic Work and Affect: A Decolonial Approach on Value and the Feminization of Labor*. New York: Routledge.

Guy-Sheftall, B. with Hammonds, E. (2008) Whither black women's studies? In: J. W. Scott (ed.) *Women's Studies on the Edge*. Durham: Duke University Press, pp. 155–68.

Haas, L. (2004) Parental leave and gender equality; what can the United States learn from the European Union? In: H. Gottfried & L Reese (eds.) *Equity in the Workplace: Gendering Workplace Policy Analysis*. Lanham, MD: Lexington Press, pp. 183–214.

Hairong, Y. (2007) Rurality and labor process autonomy: the waged labor of domestic service. In C. K. Lee (ed.) *Working in China: Ethnographies of Labor and Workplace Transformation*. New York: Routledge, pp. 145–66.

Hakim, C. (1995) Five feminist myths about women's employment. *British Journal of Sociology* **46**, 429–55.

Halford, S. & Savage, M. (1997) Rethinking restructuring: embodiment, agency and identity. In R. Lee & J. Willis (eds.) *Geographies of Economies*. London: Arnold, pp. 108–17.

Halford, S., Savage, M. & Witz, A. (1997) *Gender, Careers and Organizations*. London: Macmillan.

Hamel, P., Mayer, M. & Lustier-Thaler, H. (2000) Introduction: urban social movements – local thematics, global spaces. In P. Hamel, M. Mayer, & H. Lustier-Thaler (eds.) *Urban Movements in a Globalizing World*. London: Routledge, pp. 1–22.

Hananel, S. (2010) Burger retires from change to win, SEIU. August 14, www.google.com/hostednews/ap/article/ALeqM5j1ySdx1JivQncED8zM_tqs5M-GYEgD9HHFING0 (downloaded August 30, 2010).

Hardt, M. (2008) The capacities of democratic citizenship. Unpublished paper presented at Boundaries of Citizenship conference, Wayne State University, March 27–29.

Hartmann, H. (1979) The unhappy marriage of Marxism and Feminism: towards a more progressive union. *Capital and Class* **8**, 1–34.

Harvey, D. (2008) Is this really the end of neo-liberalism? *Counterpunch* April 7 www.counterpunch.org/harvey03132009.html (downloaded May 1, 2010).

Harvey, D. (2010) *The Enigma of Capital*. Oxford: Oxford University Press.

Hashimoto, S. (2012) Unionization of non-regular workers by enterprise unions. *Japan Labor Review* **9**, 1, 25–43.

Hearn, J. (1993) Men and organisational culture. In J. Wajcman (ed.), *Organisations, Gender and Power: Papers From An IRRU Workshop*. Warwick Papers in Industrial Relations 48. Warwick: University of Warwick.

Hearn, J. & Parkin, W. (1983) *Sex at Work: The Power and Paradox of Organization Sexuality*. New York: St. Martin's Press.

Hearn, J. & Parkin, W. (2001) *Gender, Sexuality and Violence in Organizations.* London: Sage Publications.

Hegewisch, A. (2010) Fair and equal paychecks for women. *The New York Times* (Sept. 25): A18.

Hegewisch, A., Hayes, J., Liepmann, H. & Hartmann, H. (2010) Separate and not equal? Gender segregation in the labor market and the gender wage gap. Institute for Women's Policy Research Briefing Paper C377.

Henninger, A. & Gottschall, K. (2007) Freelancers in Germany's old and new media industry: beyond standard patterns of work and life? *Critical Sociology* **33**, 43–71.

Hernandez, D. (1996) *Trends in the Well-Being of America's Children and Youth.* US Bureau of the Census, Washington DC, http://aspe.hhs.gov/hsp/trends/ change.pdf (downloaded February 16, 2012).

Hewison, K. & Kalleberg, S. (2008) Multiple flexibilities: nation-states, global business and precarious labor. Unpublished paper for Social Science Research Council, Dubai.

Hirakawa, H. (1998) Inverted Orientalism and the discursive construction of sexual harassment: a study of mass media and feminist representations of sexual harassment in Japan. Dissertation, Purdue University.

Hirst, P. & Grahame T. (1996) *Globalization in Question: The International Economy and the Possibilities of Governance.* Oxford: Blackwell Press.

Hochschild, A. R. (2001) *The Time Bind: When Work Becomes Home and Home Becomes Work.* New York: Holt Paperbacks.

Hochschild, A. R. (2003) *The Managed Heart: Commercialization of Human Feeling,* 20th anniversary edn. Berkeley: University of California Press.

Hochschild, A. R. (2004) Love and gold. In B. Ehrenreich & A. R. Hochschild (eds.) *Global Women. Nannies, Maids and Sex Workers in the New Economy.* New York: Metropolitan Books, pp. 15–30.

Hochschild, A. R. (2005) Rent a mom and other services: markets, meanings, and emotions. *International Journal of Work, Organization and Emotion* **1**, 74–86.

Hochschild, A. R. & Machung, A. (2003) *The Second Shift.* New York: Penguin.

Hoerr, J. (1997) *We Can't Eat Prestige: The Women Who Organized Harvard.* Philadelphia: Temple University Press.

Holmes, A. (2011) Technical science will be less lonely for women when girls are spurred early. *The Washington Post* (Sept. 22), www.washingtonpost.com/ lifestyle/style/technically-science-will-be-less-lonely-for-women-when-girls-are-spurred (downloaded, September 27, 2011).

Holtgrewe, U. (2007) Restructuring gendered flexibility in organizations: a comparative analysis of call centres in Germany. In: S. Walby, H. Gottfried, K. Gottschall, & M. Osawa (eds.) *Gendering the Knowledge Economy: Comparative Perspectives.* Houndsmill: Palgrave, pp. 248–70.

Hondagneu-Sotelo, P. (2001) *Doméstica: Immigrant Workers Cleaning and Caring in the Shadows of Affluence.* Berkeley: University of California Press.

Hoskyns, C. (2001) Gender politics in the European Union: the context for job training. In A. Mazur (ed.) *State Feminism, Women's Movements, and Job Training: Making Democracies Work in a Global Economy.* New York: Routledge, pp. 31–48.

Huber, E. & Stephens, J. (2000) Welfare state and production regimes in the era of retrenchment. In: P. Pierson (ed.) *The New Politics of the Welfare State.* Oxford: Oxford University Press, pp. 107–45.

Humphries, J. (1977a) The working class family, women's liberation, and class struggle: the case of nineteenth century British history. *Review of Radical Political Economics* **9** (Oct), 25–41.

Humphries, J. (1977b) Class struggle and the persistence of the working-class family. *Cambridge Journal of Economics* **1**, 241–58.

Hunt, G. and Boris, M. B. (2007) The lesbian, gay, bisexual, and transgender challenge to American labor. In: D. S. Cobble (ed.) *The Sex of Class: Women Transforming American Labor*. Ithaca: Cornell University Press, pp. 81–98.

Huyssen, A. (2008) Introduction: world cities, world cultures. In: A. Huyssen (ed.) *Other Cities, Other Worlds: Urban Imaginaries in a Globalizing Age*. Durham: Duke University Press, pp. 1–23.

Hyman, R. (2006) Marxist thought and the analysis of work. In: M. Korczynski, R. Hodson, & P. Edwards (eds.) *Social Theory at Work*. Oxford: Oxford University Press, pp. 26–55.

Isaksen, L. W., Sambasivan, U. D. & Hochschild, A. R. (2008) Global care crisis: a problem of capital, care chain, or commons? *American Behavioral Scientist* **52**, 405–24.

Ito, R. (2005) Crafting migrant women's citizenship in Japan: taking family as a vantage point. *International Journal of Japanese Sociology* **14**, 1, 52–69.

Jackson, S. (1998a) Theorising gender and sexuality. In S. Jackson & J. Jones (eds.) *Contemporary Feminist Theories*. New York: New York University Press, pp. 131–46.

Jackson, S. (1998b) Feminist social theory. In S. Jackson and J. Jones (eds.) *Contemporary Feminist Theories*. New York: New York University Press, pp. 12–33.

Jameson, F. (2000) Globalization and political strategy. *New Left Review* 4 (July/Aug), 49–68.

Jenson, J. (2001) A comparative perspective on work and gender. In J. Jenson, J. Laufer, & M. Maruani (eds.) *The Gendering of Inequalities: Women, Men and Work*. Aldershot: Ashgate, pp. 3–16.

Jessop, R. D. (2000) Governance and metagovernance: on reflexivity, requisite variety, and requisite irony. Lancaster University, Dept. of Sociology, www.comp.lancs.ac.uk/sociology/papers/Jessop-governance-and-metagovernance.pdf (downloaded May 5, 2012).

Jessop, R. D. (2001) *Regulation Theory and the Crisis of Capitalism*. Cheltenham: Elgar.

Jessop, R. D. (2002) *The Future of the Capitalist State*. Cambridge: Polity Press.

Kahn, P. & Meehan, E. (eds.) (1992) *Equal Value / Comparable Worth in the UK and the USA*. New York: St. Martin's Press.

Kalleberg, A., Hudson, K. & Reskin, B. (2000) Bad jobs in America: standard and nonstandard employment relations and job quality in the United States. *American Sociological Review* **65**, 2, 256–78.

Kanter, R. M. (1977) *Men and Women of the Corporation*. New York: Basic Books.

Katzenstein, P. (1999) Regional states: Japan and Asia, Germany in Europe. Paper prepared for "Germany and Japan: The Future of Nationally Embedded Capitalism in a Global Economy," Max-Planck Institute, Cologne, June.

Katzenstein, P. (2005) *A World of Regions: Asia and Europe in the American Imperium*. Ithaca: Cornell University Press.

Keashley, L. & Gottfried, H. (2003) Fundamental violations. *Psychology of Women Quarterly* **27**, 275–6.

Kessler, S. & McKenna, W. (1978) *Gender: An Ethnomethodological Approach*. Chicago: University of Chicago Press.

Kessler-Harris, A. (1982) *Out to Work: A History of Wage Earning Women in the United States*. Oxford: Oxford University Press.

Kibe, T. (2006) Differentiated citizenship and ethnocultural groups: a Japanese case. *Citizenship Studies* **10**, 4, 413–30.

Kohso, S. (2006) Angelus novus in millennial Japan. In H. Harootunian & T. Yoda (eds.) *Japan After Japan: Social and Cultural Life from the Recessionary 1990s to the Present*. Durham: Duke University Press, pp. 415–38.

Kojima, N. & Keiko F. 2000. Non-standard work arrangements in the U.S. and Japan from a legal perspective. Unpublished paper presented at the Non-Standard Work Arrangements in Japan, Europe, and the United States conference, sponsored by W. E. Upjohn Institute, The Japan Foundation and Japan Women's University. Upjohn Institute, Kalamazoo, MI, August.

Korczynski, M., Hodson, R. & Edwards, P. (eds.) (2006) *Social Theory at Work*. Oxford: Oxford University Press.

Korpi, W. (2000) Faces of inequality: gender, class and patterns of inequalities in different types of welfare states. *Social Politics* 7, 2, 127–91.

Kroos, D. & Gottschall, K. (2012) Dualization and gender in social services: the role of the state in Germany and France. In: P. Emmenegger, S. Hausermann, B. Palier, & M. Kaiser-Seeleib (eds.) *The Age of Dualization: The Changing Face of Inequality in Deindustrializing Societies*. Oxford: Oxford University Press.

Krüger, H. (1999) Gender and skills: distributive ramifications of the German skill system. In: P. Culpepper & D. Finegold (eds) *The German Model of Skill Provision in Comparative Perspective*. New York: Berghan Books, pp. 189–227.

Lal, J. (1998) Of Television and T-Shirts: The Making of a Gendered Working Class and the "Made in India" Label. D.Phil. dissertation, Department of Sociology, Cornell University.

Lal, J. (2010) Unbecoming women: factory women's counter-narratives of domestic citizenship. Unpublished paper.

Lavaque-Manty, M. (2009) Finding theoretical concepts in the real world: the case of the precariat. In B. de Bruin & C. F. Zurn (eds.) *New Waves in Political Philosophy*. Houndsmill: Palgrave, pp. 105–24.

Lee, C. K. (1998) *Gender and the South China Miracle*. Berkeley: University of California Press.

Lee, C. K. (ed.) (2007a) *Working in China: Ethnographies of Labor and Workplace Transformation*. London: Routledge.

Lee, C. K. (2007b) *Against the Law: Labor Protests in China's Rustbelt and Sunbelt*. Berkeley: University of California Press.

Leidner, R. (1993) *Fast Food, Fast Talk: Service Work and the Routinization of Everyday Life*. Berkeley: University of California Press.

Leidner, R. (1999) Emotional labor in service work. *The Annals of the American Academy of Political and Social Science* **561**, 81–95.

Lenz, I. (2004) Globalization, gender and work: perspectives on global regulation. In H. Gottfried & L. Reese (eds.) *Equity in the Workplace: Gendering Workplace Policy Analysis*. Lanham, MD: Lexington Press, pp. 29–52.

Leon-Guerrero, A. (2011) *Social Problems: Community, Policy, and Social Action*, 3rd edn. Los Angeles: Sage.

Leonhardt, D. (2010a) A labor market punishing to mothers. *The New York Times* (August): B1, B6.

Leonhardt, D. (2010b) Health care's uneven road to a new era. *The New York Times* (October 6): B1, B6.

Lepinard, E. (2007) The contentious subject of feminism: defining women in France from the second wave to parity. *Signs: Journal of Women in Culture and Society* **32**, 2, 375–403.

Lewis, J. (1992) Gender and the development of welfare regimes. *Journal of European Social Policy* **2**, 159–73.

Lewis, J. (2001) The decline of the male breadwinner model: implications for work and care. *Social Politics* **8**, 2, 152–69.

Liptak, A. (2011) When a lawsuit is too big. *The New York Times* (April 3): 1, 5.

Locke, R. & Thelen, K. (1995) Apples and oranges revisited: contexualized comparisons and the study of comparative labor politics. *Politics and Society* **23**, 3, 337–67.

Lorber, J. (1999) Introduction. In: M. Marx-Ferree, J. Lorber, & B. B. Hess (eds.) *Revisioning Gender*. Thousand Oaks: Sage, pp. i–xx.

Lorber, J. (2009) "Night to his day": the social construction of gender. In: L. Rupp, V. Taylor, & N. Whittier (eds.) *Feminist Frontiers*, 8th edn. Boston: McGraw Hill, pp. 53–68.

Lorber, J. & Martin, P. Y. (2011) The socially constructed body. In: P. Kvisto (ed.) *Illuminating Social Life: Classical and Contemporary Theory Revisited*, 5th edn. Newberry Park: Pine Forge Press, pp. 279–303.

Lovell, V., Hartmann, H., & Werschkul, M. (2007) More than raising the floor: the persistence of gender inequalities in the low-wage labor market. In D. S. Cobble (ed.) *The Sex of Class: Women Transforming American Labor*. Ithaca: Cornell University Press, pp. 35–57.

Lutz, H., Vivar, M. T. H. & Supik, L. (2011) Framing intersectionality: an introduction. In: L. Helma L., M. T. H. Vivar, & L. Supik (eds) *Framing Intersectionality: Debates on a Multi-Faceted Concept in Gender Studies*. Aldershot: Ashgate, pp. 1–22.

Lynch, C. (2007) *Juki Girls, Good Girls: Gender and Cultural Politics in Sri Lanka's Global Garment Factory*. Ithaca: Cornell University Press.

Lynch, K. (2010, July 29) Affective equality: who cares? www.wide-network.ch/pdf/presentations_JaKo/Lynch.pdf (downloadedAugust 10, 2010).

Macionis, J. (2010) *Social Problems*, 4th edn. Boston: Pearson.

MacFarquhar, N. (2010) African farmers displaced as investors move in. *The New York Times* (December 22): A1, A4.

Mandel, H. (2009) Configurations of gender inequality: the consequences of ideology and public policy. *The British Journal of Sociology* **60**, 4, 693–719.

Marquis, C. (2002) Bush to end rule allowing jobless money for new parents. *The New York Times* (December 4) www.nytimes.com/2002/12/04/us/bush-to-end-rule-allowing-jobless-money-for-new-parents.html?pagewanted=print (downloaded May 5, 2012).

Martin, B. & Wajcman, J. (2003) Fun, excitement and passion: positive emotions amongst men and women managers. Unpublished paper presented at the 98th Annual Meeting of the American Sociological Association, Atlanta, Georgia, August 16–19.

Martin, K. (1998) Becoming a gendered body: practices of preschools. *American Sociological Review* **63**, 494–511.

Martin, P. Y. (2001) Mobilizing masculinities: women's experiences of men at work. *Organization* **8**, 4, 587–618.

Marx, K. ([1859] 1954) *The Eighteenth Brumaire of Louis Bonaparte*. London: Progress.

Marx, K. (1976) *Capital*, Volume I. Trans. B. Fowkes, 2nd edn. London: Penguin Classics.

Marx, K. & Engels, F. ([1948] 1978) *Manifesto of the Communist Party*. In: R. Tucker (ed.) *The Marx-Engels Reader*. New York: Norton & Company, pp. 469–500.

Marx-Ferree, M. (1990) Beyond separate spheres: feminist and family research. *Journal of Marriage and the Family* **52**, 4, 866–84.

Marx-Ferree, M. (1992) Beyond separate spheres: feminist and family research. In L. Richardson & V. Taylor (eds.) *Feminist Frontiers III*. Boston: McGraw-Hill, pp. 237–57.

Marx-Ferree, M. (2006) Globalization and feminism: opportunities and obstacles for activism in the global area. In: M. Marx-Ferree & A. M. Tripp (eds.) *Global Feminism: Transnational Women's Activism, Organizing, and Human Rights*. New York: New York University Press, pp. 3–23.

Marx-Ferree, M., Lorber, J. & Hess, B. (1999) Series editors' introduction. In: M. Marx-Ferree, J. Lorber, & B. Hess (eds.) *Revisioning Gender*, Thousand Oaks: Sage, pp. xi–xxx.

Massey, D. (1994) *Space, Place, and Gender*. Minneapolis: University of Minnesota Press.

Massey, D. (1995) *Spatial Divisions of Labor: Social Structures and the Geography of Production*, 2nd edn. New York: Routledge.

Massey, D. (2005) *For Space*. London: Sage.

Mazur, A. (1995) *Gender Bias and the State: Symbolic Reform at Work in Fifth Republic France*. Pittsburgh: University of Pittsburgh Press.

Mazur, A. (2001) Introduction. In A. Mazur (ed.) *State Feminism, Women's Movements, and Job Training: Making Democracies Work in a Global Economy*. New York: Routledge, pp. 3–30.

Mazur, A. (2002) *Theorizing Feminist Policy*. Oxford: Oxford University Press.

McCall, L. (1992) Does gender fit? Bourdieu, feminism, and conceptions of social order. *Theory and Society* **21**, 837–67.

McCall, L. (2001) *Complex Inequality: Gender, Class and Race in the New Economy*. London and New York: Routledge.

McCall, L. (2005) The complexity of intersectionality. *Signs: Journal of Women in Culture and Society* **30**, 3, 1771–800.

McCall, L. (2007) Increasing class disparities among women and the politics of gender equity. In D. S. Cobble (ed.) *The Sex of Class: Women Transforming American Labor*. Ithaca: Cornell University Press, pp. 15–34.

McCall, L. & Orloff, A. S. (2005) Introduction to special issue of *Social Politics*: gender, class, and capitalism. *Social Politics* **12**, 159–69.

McDowell, L. (1997a) A tale of two cities? embedded organizations and embodied workers in the city of London. In R. Lee & J. Willis (eds.) *Geographies of Economies*. London: Arnold, pp. 118–29.

McDowell, L. (1997b) *Capital Culture: Gender and Work in the City*. Oxford: Blackwell.

McDowell, L. (2008) Thinking through class and gender in the context of working class studies. *Antipode* **4**, 1, 20–4.

McDowell, L., Fagan, C., Perrons, D., Ray, K. & Ward, K. (2005) The contradictions and intersections of class and gender in a global city: placing working women's lives on the research agenda. *Environment and Planning A* **37**, 441–61.

McKay, S. (2006) *Satanic Mills or Silicon Islands? The Politics of High-Tech Production in the Philippines*. Ithaca: Cornell University Press.

Michel, S. & Mahon, R. (2006) Introduction: perspectives on child care, East and West. *Social Politics* **13**, 2, 145–50.

Milkman, R. (2007) Two worlds of unionism: women and the new labor movement. In: D. S. Cobble (ed.) *The Sex of Class: Women Transforming American Labor*. Ithaca: Cornell University Press, pp. 63–80.

Miyamoto, T. (2009) After the male employment-oriented regime: towards a dual social compact. Paper presented to conference on Faces of Social Exclusion from a Gender Perspective, University of Tokyo, February 28.

Moghadam, V. (2006) *Globalizing Women: Transnational Feminist Networks*. Baltimore: Johns Hopkins University Press.

Mohanty, C. T. (2006) *Feminism without Borders: Decolonizing Theory, Practicing Solidarity*. Durham: Duke University Press.

Moi, T. (1991) Appropriating Bourdieu: feminist theory and Pierre Bourdieu's sociology of culture. *New Literary History* **22**, 1017–49.

Moi, T. (1999) *What Is a Woman? And Other Essays*. Oxford: Oxford University Press.

Montanari, I. (2003) Gendered work and gendered citizenship: Japan in a comparative perspective. Paper presented at the New Challenges for Welfare State Research conference, International Sociological Association RC-19 Poverty, Social Welfare and Social Policy, University of Toronto, August 21–24.

Moore, B. (1966) *Social Origins of Dictatorship and Democracy: Lord and Peasant in the Making of the Modern World*. Boston: Beacon Press.

Morgan, D. (1998) Sociological imaginings and imagining sociology: bodies, auto/biographies and other mysteries. *Sociology* **4**, 647–63.

Mutari, E. & Figart, D. (2001) Europe at a crossroads: harmonization, liberalization, and the gender of work time. *Social Politics* **8**, 1, 36–64.

National Archive. 2011. The Civil Rights Act. www.archives.gov/education/lessons/civil-rights-act/ (downloaded May 11, 2011).

Nelson, R. & Bridges, W. (1999) *Legalizing Gender Inequality: Courts, Markets, and Unequal Pay for Women in America*. Cambridge: Cambridge University Press.

Nelson, S. R. (2010) Mad men in the he-cession: masculinity, macaroni, and mayhem in America's financial panics. *The Chronicle Review* (Jan. 17), http://chronicle.com/article/Mad-Men-in-the-He-Cession/63510/ (downloaded September 14, 2011).

New York Times (2006). Few cracks in the glass ceiling. *The New York Times Sunday* (December 26): A18.

New York Times Week in Review Staff (2009) The great "he-cession." *The New York Times*, http://ideas.blogs.nytimes.com/2009/06/29/the-great-he-cession/(downloaded January 27, 2012).

Nishikawa, M. & Tanaka, K. (2007) Are care-workers knowledge workers? In: S. Walby, H. Gottfried, K. Gottschall, & M. Osawa (eds.) *Gendering the Knowledge Economy: Comparative Perspectives*. Houndsmill: Palgrave, pp. 207–27.

Nussbaum, K. (2007) Working women's insurgent consciousness. In: D. S. Cobble (ed.) *The Sex of Class: Women Transforming American Labor*. Ithaca: Cornell University Press, pp. 159–76.

Obinger, J. (2009) Working on the margins: Japan's precariat and working poor. *Electronic Journal of Contemporary Japanese Studies* Discussion Paper 1, www.japanesestudies.org.uk/discussionpapers/2009/Obinger.html (downloaded April 11, 2011).

O'Connor, J., Orloff, A.S. & Shaver, S. (1999) *States, Markets, Families: Gender, Liberalism and Social Policy in Australia, Canada, Great Britain and the United States*. Cambridge: Cambridge University Press.

Offe, C. & Wiesenthal, H. (1980) Two logics of collective action: notes on social class and organizational form. In: M. Zeitlin (ed.) *Political Power and Social Theory*, Volume I. Greenwich, CT: JAI Press, pp. 67–115.

Ogasawara, Y. (1998) *Office Ladies and Salaried Men: Power, Gender, and Work in Japanese Companies*. Berkeley: University of California Press.

Onishi, N. (2010) Toiling far from home for Philippine dreams. *The New York Times* (Sept. 19): A5.

Ontiveros, M. (2007) Female immigrant workers and the law: limits and opportunities. In: D. S. Cobble (ed.) *The Sex of Class: Women Transforming American Labor*. Ithaca: Cornell University Press, pp. 235–52.

Oppenheimer, V. (1977) *The Female Labor Force in the United States: Demographic and Economic Factors Governing its Growth and Changing Composition*. Westport: Greenwood Press.

Orloff, A. S. (1993) Gender and the social rights of citizenship: the comparative analysis of gender relations and welfare states. *American Sociological Review* 58, 3, 303–28.

Orloff, A. S. (2008) The current state of gender studies. Paper presented at the Workshop on Inequalities in Japan, Europe, and the US, Reischauer Institute of Japanese Studies, Harvard University, March 1.

Orloff, A. S. (2009) Gendering the comparative analysis of welfare states: an unfinished agenda. *Sociological Theory* 27, 3, 317–43.

Orum, A. & Chen, X. (2003) *The World of Cities: Places in Comparative and Historical Perspective*. Malden: Blackwell.

Osawa, M. (1994) *Bye-bye Corporate Warriors: The Formation of a Corporate-Centered Society and Gender-Biased Social Policies in Japan*, University of Tokyo Institute of Social Science Occasional Papers in Labor and Social Policy.

Osawa, M. (2001) People in irregular modes of employment: are they really subject to discrimination? *Social Science Japan Journal* 4, 183–99.

Osawa, M. (2007) Comparative livelihood security systems from a gender perspective, with a focus on Japan. In S. Walby, H. Gottfried, K. Gottschall, & M. Osawa (eds.) *Gendering the Knowledge Economy: Comparative Perspectives*. Houndsmill: Palgrave, pp. 81–108.

Ostner, I. & Lewis, J. (1995) Gender and the evolution of European social policies. In S. Leibfried & P. Pierson (eds.) *European Social Policy: Between Fragmentation and Integration*. Washington DC: The Brookings Institution, pp. 159–93.

Otis, E. (2003) Serving the people: gender, class, and ethnicity in China's emergent service sector. Unpublished Ph.D. dissertation, Sociology Department, University of California, Davis.

Otis, E. (2007) Virtual personalism in Beijing: learning deference and femininity at a global luxury hotel. In C. K. Lee (ed.) *Working in China: Ethnographies of Labor and Workplace Transformation*. New York: Routledge, pp. 101–23.

Otis, E. (2008) The dignity of working women: service, sex, and the labor politics of localization in China's city of eternal spring. *American Behavioral Scientist* 52, 356–76.

Otis, E. (2012) *Markets and Bodies: Women, Service Work and the Making of Inequality in China*. Palo Alto: Stanford University Press.

Ozyegin, G. (2001) *Untidy Gender*. Philadelphia: Temple University Press.

Padavic, I. & Reskin, B. (2002) *Women and Men at Work*, 2nd edn. Thousand Oaks: Pine Forge Press.

Pangsapa, P. (2007) *The Emergence of Resistance among Garment Workers in Thailand*. Ithaca: Cornell University Press.

Parkin, F. (1982) *Max Weber*. London: Tavistock Publications.

Parrenas, R. S. (2001) Transgressing the nation-state: the partial citizenship and imagined (global) community of migrant Filipina domestic workers. *Signs: Journal of Women in Culture and Society* **26**, 4, 1129–54.

Parrenas, R. S. (2008) *The Force of Domesticity: Filipina Migrants and Globalization.* New York: New York University Press.

Parrenas, R. S. (2011) *Illicit Flirtations: Labor, Migration and Sex Trafficking in Tokyo.* Palo Alto: Stanford University Press.

Patel, S. (2004) Mumbai: a tale of two cities. In J. Gugler (ed.) *World Cities Beyond the West: Globalization, Development and Inequality.* Cambridge: Cambridge University Press, pp. 328–47.

Paus, E. (2007) Winners and losers from offshore outsourcing: what is to be done? In: E. Paus (ed.) *Global Capitalism Unbound: Winners and Losers from Offshore Outsourcing.* Houndsmill: Palgrave, pp. 3–22.

Pearson, R. (2007) Gender, globalization and development: key issues for the Asian region in the 21st century. Keynote Paper for the International Workshop for Junior Scholars: Beyond the Difference: Repositioning Gender and Development in the Asian and Pacific Context, Ochanomizu University, Tokyo, Jan. 12–14.

Pempel, T. J. (1998) *Regime Shift: Comparative Dynamics of the Japanese Political Economy.* Ithaca: Cornell University Press.

Peng, I. (2002) Gender and generation: Japanese child care and the demographic crisis. In: S. Michel & R. Mahon (eds.) *Child Care at Crossroads: Gender and Welfare State Restructuring.* New York: Routledge, pp. 31–55.

Peng, I. (2002) Social care in crisis: gender, demography, and welfare state restructuring in Japan. *Social Politics* **9**, 3, 411–43.

Perrons, D. (2007) Living and working patterns in the new knowledge economy: new opportunities and old social divisions in the case of new media and care-work. In: S. Walby, H. Gottfried, K. Gotschall, & M. Osawa (eds.) *Gendering the Knowledge Economy: Comparative Perspectives.* Houndsmill: Palgrave, pp. 188–206.

Peterson, S. (2008) Intersectional analytics in global political economy. In: C. Klinger & G. A. Knapp (eds.) *UberKreuzungen: Fremdheit, Ungleichheit, Differenz.* Munster: Westfälisches Dampfboot, pp. 210–29.

Pierce, J. (1995) *Gender Trials: Emotional Lives in Contemporary Law Firms.* Berkeley: University of California Press.

Pierce, J. (1999) Emotional labor among paralegals. *The Annals of the American Academy of Political and Social Science* **561**, 127–42.

Pierson, P. & Leibfried, S. (1995) Multi-tiered institutions and the making of social policy. In S. Leibfried & P. Pierson (eds.) *European Social Policy: Between Fragmentation and Integration.* Washington DC: The Brookings Institution, pp. 1–40.

Polanyi, K. (1944) *The Great Transformation.* New York: Rinehart.

Polivka, A. & Nardone, T. (1989) On the definition of contingent work. *Monthly Labor Review* **112**, 12, 9–14.

Pollert, A. (1996) Gender and class revisited: or, the poverty of patriarchy. *Sociology* **30**, 639–59.

Poster, W. (2007) Who's on the line? Indian call center agents pose as Americans for U.S.-outsourced firms. *Industrial Relations: A Journal of Economy and Society* **46**, 2, 271–304.

Poster, W. & Wilson, G. (2008) Introduction: race, class, and gender in transnational labor inequality. *American Behavioral Scientist* **52**, 295–306.

Pringle, R. (1989) *Secretaries Talk: Sexuality, Power, & Work.* Sydney: Allen and Unwin.

Pyle, J. (2006) Globalizations, transnational migration, and gendered care work. *Globalizations* **3**, 3, 283–95.

Qayum, S. & Ray, R. (2003) Grappling with modernity: India's respectable classes and the culture of domestic servitude. *Ethnography* **4**, 4, 520–55.

Quan, K. (2007) Women crossing borders to organize. In: D. S. Cobble (ed.) *The Sex of Class: Women Transforming American Labor*. Ithaca: Cornell University Press, pp. 253–71.

Ramazanoglu, C. & Holland, J. (2002) *Feminist Methodology: Challenges and Choices*. London: Sage Publications.

Ray, R. (2008) Neither factory nor field: global lessons from organizing domestic workers. Unpublished paper presented at the American Sociological Association Annual Conference, Boston, August.

Reskin, B. (2002) Rethinking employment discrimination and its remedies. In: M. Guillen, R. Collins, P. England, & M. Meyer (eds.) *The New Economic Sociology: Developments in an Emerging Field*. New York: Russell Sage, pp. 218–44.

Reskin, B. & Padavic, I. (1994) *Women and Men at Work*. Thousand Oaks: Pine Forge Press.

Reskin, B. & Roos, P. (2002) *Job Queues, Gender Queues: Explaining Women's Inroads into Male Occupations*. Philadelphia: Temple University Press.

Revkin, A. (2007) The art of mapping on the run. *The New York Times* (Sept. 9): A2.

Riggin, J. (2011) The potential impact of CEDAW ratification on U.S. employment discrimination law: lessons from Canada. *Columbia Human Rights Law Review* **42**, 2, 541–611.

Ritzer, G. (1996) *The McDonaldization of Society: An Investigation into the Changing Character of Contemporary Social Life*. Thousand Oaks: Pine Forge Press.

Roberts, G. (1999) Review of Japan's minorities: the illusion of homogeneity. *Journal of Japanese Studies* **25**, 2, 399–403.

Roberts, G. (2004) Globalization and work/life balance: gendered implications of new initiatives at a U.S. multinational in Japan. In: H. Gottfried & L. Reese (eds.) *Equity in the Workplace: Gendering Workplace Policy Analysis*. Lanham: Lexington Press, pp. 305–21.

Robertson, J. (1997) Empire of nostalgia: rethinking internationalization in Japan today. *Theory, Culture & Society* **14**, 4, 97–122.

Robinson, J. (2010) Cities in a world of cities: the comparative gesture. *International Journal of Urban and Regional Research* **35**, 1, 1–23.

Rollins, J. (1985) *Between Women*. Philadelphia: Temple University Press.

Romero, M. (1992) *Maid in the USA*. London: Routledge.

Rose, S. (2004) *Social Stratification in the United States: The New American Profile Poster*. New York: New Press.

Rose, S. & Hartmann, H. (2004). *Still A Man's Labor Market: The Long-Term Earnings Gap*. Washington DC: Institute for Women's Policy Research.

Rosenau, J. (1977) The complexities and contradictions of globalization. *Current History* **96**, 360–4.

Rosenberg, D. (2012) The Pregnancy Discrimination Act of 1978: how the law protects you from pregnancy discrimination at work, http://careerplanning.about.com/cs/legalissues/a/pregnancy.htm (downloaded April 28, 2012).

Ross, R. (2004) *Slaves to Fashion*. Ann Arbor: University of Michigan Press.

Roth, S (2003) *Building Movement Bridges: The Coalition of Labor Union Women*. Westport: Praeger.

Sainsbury, D. (1999) *Gender Regimes and Welfare States*. Oxford: Oxford University Press.

Salem, R. (2009) The death of macho. *Foreign Policy* (July/August), http://www.foreignpolicy.com/articles/2009/06/18/the_death_of_macho   (downloaded January 27, 2012).

Salzinger, L. (2003) *Genders in Production: Making Workers in Mexico's Global Factories.* Berkeley: University of California Press.

Salzinger, L. (2004) From gender as object to gender as verb: rethinking how gender restructuring happens. *Critical Sociology* **30**, 1, 43–62.

Sargent, L. (ed.) (1981) *Women and Revolution: A Discussion of The Unhappy Marriage of Marxism and Feminism.* Boston: South End Press.

Sassen, S. (1996) Toward a feminist analytics of the global economy. *Indiana Journal of Global Legal Studies* **4**, 1, 7–41.

Sassen, S. (2001) *The Global City: New York, London, Tokyo,* 2nd edn. Princeton: Princeton University Press.

Sassen, S. (2004) Afterword. In J. Gugler (ed.) *World Cities Beyond the West: Globalization, Development and Inequality.* Cambridge: Cambridge University Press, pp. 371–86.

Sassen, S. (2008) Two stops in today's new global geographies: shaping novel labor supplies and employment regimes. *American Behavioral Scientist* **52**, 457–96.

Sassen, S. (2010) The re-assembling of territory, authority, and rights. Paper presented at the International Sociological Association XVII World Congress, July 11–17.

Savage, L. (2007) Changing work, changing people: a conversation with union organizers at Harvard University and the University of Massachusetts Memorial Medical Center. In: D. S. Cobble (ed.) *The Sex of Class: Women Transforming American Labor.* Ithaca: Cornell University Press, pp. 119–39.

Schiller, N. C. (2010) Beyond the nation-state and its units of analysis: towards a new research agenda for migration studies. In Study Group: Cultural Capital during Migration (eds.) *Concepts and Methods in Migration Research: Conference Reader.* www.cultural-capital.net (downloaded July 5, 2010).

Schnabel, C. & Wagner, J. (2003) Trade union membership in eastern and western Germany: convergence or divergence? *Applied Economics Quarterly* 49, 213–32.

Schoppa, L. (1997) *Bargaining with Japan: What American Pressure Can and Cannot Do.* New York: Columbia University Press.

Schwartz, F. (2003) Introduction: recognizing civil society in Japan. In: F. Schwartz & S. Pharr (eds.) *The State of Civil Society in Japan.* Cambridge: Cambridge University Press, pp. 1–19.

Scott, J. W. (1986) Gender: a useful category for historical analysis. *American Historical Review* (Dec.): 1053–75.

Scott, J. W. (1996) *Feminism and History.* New York: Oxford University Press.

Scott, J. W. (1999) Some reflections on gender and politics. In: M. Marx-Ferree, J. Lorber, & B. Hess (eds.) *Revisioning Gender.* Thousand Oaks: Sage, pp. 70–96.

Scott, J. W. (2008) Introduction: feminism's critical edge. In: J. W. Scott (ed.) *Women's Studies on the Edge.* Durham: Duke University Press, pp. 1–13.

Semple, K. (2010) For some immigrants, voting is a criminal act. *The New York Times* (Oct. 15), www.nytimes.com/2010/10/17/nyregion/17voting.hotml?pagewanted=all (downloaded May 4, 2012).

Sereni, J. P. (2010) Dubai's blue sky thinking. *Le Monde Diplomatique* (Dec), http://mondediplo.com/2010/12/20emirates (downloaded May 5, 2012).

Shakespeare, W. (1594) *Romeo and Juliet.*

Shannon, V. (2010) The female factor - equal rights for women? Survey says: yes, but ... *The New York Times* (June 30), http:www.nytimes.com/2010/07/01/world/01iht-poll.html. (downloaded on July 1, 2010).

Sherman, M. (2011) Supreme court to take up sex bias claim against Wal-mart. *Huffington Post*, www.huffingtonpost.com/2011/03/27/supreme-court-wal-mart-sex-bias-case_n_841105.html (downloaded March 27, 2011).

Sherman, R. (2010) Time is our commodity: gender and the struggle for occupational legitimacy among personal concierges. *Work and Occupations* **37**, 1, 81–114.

Shire, K. (2007) Gender and the conceptualization of the knowledge economy in comparative perspective. In: S. Walby, H. Gottfried, K. Gottschall, & M. Osawa (eds.) *Gendering the Knowledge Economy: Comparative Perspectives*. Houndsmill: Palgrave, pp. 51–77.

Silver, B. (2003) *The Forces of Labor: Workers' Movements and Globalization since 1870.* Cambridge: Cambridge University Press.

Silver, B. (2005) Labor upsurges: from Detroit to Ulsan and beyond. *Critical Sociology* **31**, 3, 439–51.

Simpson, M. (2010) Pay your nanny on the books. *The New York Times* (July 2): A21.

Skapinker, M. (2010) Companies need to recruit the older woman. *The Financial Times* (Feb. 2): 11.

Skeggs, B. (1997) *Formations of Class and Gender: Becoming Respectable*. London: Sage.

Skocpol, T. (1979) *States and Social Revolutions: A Comparative Analysis of France, Russia, and China.* Cambridge: Cambridge University Press.

Skocpol, T. (1980) Political response to capitalist crisis: neo-Marxist theories of the state and the case of the new deal. *Politics & Society* **10**, 2, 155–201.

Skocpol, T. (1984) Emerging agendas and recurrent strategies. In: T. Skocpol (ed) *Historical Sociology: Vision and Method in Historical Sociology.* Cambridge: Cambridge University Press.

Smith, V. & Gottfried, H. (1998) Flexibility in work and employment: the impact on women. In: B. Geissler, F. Maier, & B. Pfau-Effinger (eds.) *FrauenArbeitsMarkt: Der Beitrag der Frauenforshung zur sozio-ökonomischen Theorieentwicklung.* Berlin: Sigma, pp. 95–125.

Smith, V. & Neuwirth, E. (2008) *The Good Temp*. Ithaca: Cornell University Press.

Solinger, D. (1999) Citizenship issues in China's internal migration: comparisons with Germany and Japan. *Political Science Quarterly* **114**, 3, 455–78.

Sotirin, P. & Gottfried, H. (1999) The ambivalent dynamics of secretarial "bitching": control, resistance, and the construction of identity. *Organization* **6**, 57–80.

Spelman, E. (1988) *Inessential Woman: Problems of Exclusion in Feminist Thought.* Boston: Beacon Press.

Stallings, B. (2002) Globalization and liberalization: the impact on developing countries. In: A. Kohli, C. Moon, & G. Sorensen (eds.) *States, Markets, and Just Growth: Development in the 21st Century.* Tokyo: United Nations Press, pp. 9–38.

Standing, G. (1999a) *Global Labour Flexibility*. Houndsmill: Palgrave Macmillan.

Standing, G. (1999b.) Global feminization through flexible labor: a theme revisited. *World Development* **27**, 3, 583–602.

Standing, G. (2007) Offshoring and labor recommodification in the global transformation. In: E. Paus (ed.) *Global Capitalism Unbound: Winners and Losers from Offshore Outsourcing.* New York: Palgrave Macmillan, pp. 41–60.

Standing, G. (2011) *The Precariat: The New Dangerous Class*. London: Bloomsbury Academic.

Study Group: Cultural Capital during Migration. 2010. Concepts and methods in migration research: conference reader, www.cultural-capital.net (downloaded July 5, 2010).

Steinberg, R. (1990) The social construction of skill: gender, power and comparable worth. *Work and Occupation* **17**, 449–82.

Steinberg, R. & Figart, D. (1999) Emotional labor since the Managed Heart. *The Annals of the American Academy of Political and Social Science* **561**, 8–26.

Stetson, D. M. & Mazur, A. (1995) Introduction. In: A. Mazur & D. M. Stetson (eds.) *Comparative State Feminism*. Thousand Oaks: Sage, pp. 1–21.

Stolberg, S.G. (2009) Obama signs equal-pay legislation. *The New York Times online* (Jan. 30), www.nytimes.com/2009/01/30/us/politics/30ledbetter-web.html (downloaded May 10, 2011).

Stone, P. (1994) Assessing gender at work: evidence and issues. In: J. Jacobs (ed.) *Gender Inequality at Work*. Thousand Oaks: Sage, pp. 408–23.

Streeck, W. (1992) *Social Institutions and Economic Performance: Studies of Industrial Relations in Advanced Capitalist Economies*. London: Sage.

Streeck, W. (1998) The internationalization of industrial relations in Europe: prospects and problems. *Politics and Society* **26**, 4, 229–459.

Streeck, W. (2001) Introduction: explorations into the origins of non-liberal capitalism in Germany and Japan. In: W. Streeck & K. Yamamura (eds.) *The Origins of Non-Liberal Capitalism: Germany and Japan in Comparison*. Ithaca: Cornell University Press, pp. 1–38.

Styhre, A. (2004) Rethinking knowledge: a Bergsonian critique of the notion of tacit knowledge. *British Journal of Management* **15**, 2, 177–86.

Summerfield, G. (2001) Introduction to the symposium: risks and rights in the 21st century. *International Journal of Politics, Culture, and Society* **15**, 1, 5–6.

Suzuki, A. (2004) Explaining Japanese unions' strategies for organizing. Paper presented at the IIRA 5th Asia Regional Conference, Seoul, Korea, February.

Suzuki, A. (2010) Non-regular employment and social movement unionism in Japan. Paper presented at Conference on New Employment Risks in East Asia, DIJ-German Institue of Japan Studies in Tokyo, Nov. 26–27.

Swider, S. (2010) Gender and migration in China: helpless victims and perpetrators of violence. Unpublished paper.

Swider, S. (2011) Permanent temporaries in the Chinese construction industry. In: S. Kuruvilla, C. K. Lee, & M. Gallagher (eds.) *Industry from Iron Rice Bowl to Informalization: Markets, Workers, and the State in a Changing China*. Ithaca: Cornell Press, pp. 138–55.

Swider, S. (2012) Building China: migrant workers in precarious informal work in China's construction industry. Paper presented at the University of California, Berkeley, January 27, 2012.

Tabuchi, H. (2009) Rising debt a threat to Japanese. *The New York Times* (Oct. 20), www.nytimes.com/2009/10/21/business/global/21ven.html?pagewanted=all (downloaded, May 3 2012).

Tabuchi, H. (2011) Despite shortage, Japan keeps a high wall for foreign labor. *The New York Times* (January 3): A1, A10.

Tait, V. (2007) Expanding labor's vision: the challenges of workfare and welfare organizing. In: D. S. Cobble (ed.) *The Sex of Class: Women Transforming American Labor*. Ithaca: Cornell University Press, pp. 177–93.

Tavernise, S. (2011) Gains made in equality of incomes in downturn. *The New York Times* (October 1): A10.

Taylor, V., Fabrizio, C. & Whittier, P. (2009) The women's movement: persistence through transformation. In L. Rupp, V. Taylor, & N. Whittier (eds.) *Feminist Frontiers*, 8th edn. Boston: McGraw Hill, pp. 556–71.

The World's Largest MegaCities. *The Huffington Post*, September 11, 2010, www.huffingtonpost.com/2010/09/11/the-worlds-largest-megaci_n_713185.html#s137741 (downloaded September 12, 2010).

Thelen, K. (1999) Historical institutionalism in comparative perspective. *Annual Review of Political Science* **2**, 369–404.

Tilly, C. (1975) *The Formation of National States in Western Europe*. Princeton: Princeton University Press.

Tong, R. (2009) *Feminist Thought*, 3rd edn. Philadelphia: Westview Press.

Trzcinski, E. (2004) The employment insurance model: maternity, parental, and sickness benefits in Canada. In: H. Gottfried & L. Reese (eds.) *Equity in the Workplace: Gendering Workplace Policy Analysis*. Lanham: Lexington Press, pp. 243–80.

Tsutsui, K. & Ji Shin, H. (2008) Global norms, local activism, and social movement outcomes: global human rights and resident Koreans in Japan. *Social Problems* **55**, 3, 391–418.

Tyler, M. and Abbott, P. (1998) Chocs away: weight watching in the contemporary airline industry. *Sociology* **3**, 433–50.

UNIFEM (2009). *Who Answers to Women: Gender and Accountability, 2008–09*. New York: United Nations.

Vallas, S., Finlay, W. & Wharton, A. (2009) *The Sociology of Work: Structures and Inequalities*. New York: Oxford University Press.

Verkaik, R. (2009) Sexism in the city still rules ok. *The Independent* (September 7).

Videla, N. P. (2010) Engendering global studies of women and work. *Feminist Studies* **36**, 1, 180–99.

Visser, J. (2000) From Keynesianism to the third way: labour relations and social policy in post-war Western Europe. *Economic & Industrial Democracy* **21**, 4, 421–56.

Visser, J. & Van Ruysseveldt, J. (1996) From pluralism to . . . where? Industrial relations in Great Britain. In: J. van Ruysseveldt & J. Visser (eds.) *Industrial Relations in Europe: Traditions and Transitions*. London: Sage, pp. 42–81.

Von Wahl, A. (2005) Liberal, conservative, social democratic, or European? The European Union as equal employment regime. *Social Politics* **12**, 1, 67–95.

Vosko, L. (2006a) Gender, precarious work, and the international labour code: the ghost in the ILO closet. In: J. Fudge & R. Owens (eds.) *Precarious Work, Women, and the New Economy: The Challenge to Legal Norms*. Oxford: Hart Publishing, pp. 53–76.

Vosko, L. (2006b) Precarious employment: towards an improved understanding of labour market insecurity. In: L. Vosko (ed.) *Precarious Employment: Understanding Labour Market Insecurity in Canada*. Montreal: McGill-Queen's University Press, pp. 3–39.

Vosko, L. (2007) Representing informal economy workers: emerging global strategies and their lessons for North American unions. In: D. S. Cobble (ed.) *The Sex of Class: Women Transforming American Labor*. Ithaca: Cornell University Press, pp. 272–92.

Vosko, L. (2010). *Managing the Margins: Gender, Citizenship, and the International Regulation of Precarious Employment*. Oxford: Oxford University Press.

Vosko, L., Campbell, I. & MacDonald, M. (2009) *Gender and the Contours of Precarious Employment: Developing Common Understanding across Space, Scale, and Social Location.* London: Routledge Press.

Wajcman, J. (1993) *Organisations, Gender and Power: Papers From An IRRU Workshop.* Warwick Papers in Industrial Relations 48. Warwick: University of Warwick.

Wajcman, J. (1998) Personal management: sexualized cultures at work. Paper presented at Work, Employment and Society conference, Warwick University, September.

Walby, S. (1986) *Patriarchy at Work.* Cambridge: Polity Press.

Walby, S. (1990) *Theorizing Patriarchy.* Oxford: Basil Blackwell.

Walby, S. (1997) *Gender Transformations.* London: Routledge.

Walby, S. (1999) The new regulatory state: the social powers of the European Union. *British Journal of Sociology* **50**, 1, 118–40.

Walby, S. (2004) Policy strategies in a global era for gendered workplace equity. In: H. Gottfried & L. Reese (eds.) *Equity in the Workplace: Gendering Workplace Policy Analysis.* Lanham: Lexington Press, pp. 53–76.

Walby, S. (2007) Introduction: theorizing the gendering of the knowledge economy: comparative approaches. In: S. Walby, H. Gottfried, K. Gottschall, & M. Osawa (eds.) *Gendering the Knowledge Economy: Comparative Perspectives.* Houndsmill: Palgrave, pp. 3–50.

Walby, S. (2009a) *Globalization and Inequalities: Complexity and Contested Modernities.* London: Sage.

Walby, S. (2009b) Gender and the Financial Crisis. Paper available for download at www.lancs.ac.uk/fass/doc library/sociology/Gender and financial crisis Sylvia Walby.pdf.

Walby, S. 2011. Varieties of modernity: do varieties of gender regime map onto varieties of capitalism? Unpublished paper presented to American Sociological Association, Las Vegas, 20 August.

Wallerstein, I. M. (1976) *The Modern World-System: Capitalist Agriculture and the Origins of the European World-Economy in the Sixteenth Century.* New York: Academic Press.

Ward, K., Fahmida, R., Saiful, I., Rifat, A. & Nashid, K. (2004) The effects of global economic restructuring on urban women's work and income-generating strategies in Dhaka, Bangladesh. *Critical Sociology* **30**, 1, 62–102.

Warnke, G. (2011) *Debating Sex and Gender.* Oxford: Oxford University Press.

Weber, M. ([1922] 1978) *Economy and Society: An Outline of Interpretive Sociology.* 2 vols. Berkeley: University of California Press.

Weber, M. (2006) Class, status, party. In: D. Grusky & S. Szelenyi (eds.) *Inequality: Classic Readings in Race, Class, and Gender.* Boulder: Westview Press, pp. 44–55.

Weiping, W. & Yusuf, S. (2004) Shanghai: remaking China's future global city. In: J. Gugler (ed.) *World Cities Beyond the West: Globalization, Development and Inequality.* Cambridge: Cambridge University Press, pp. 27–58.

Weitz, R. (2009) A history of women's bodies. In: R. Weitz (ed.) *Politics of Women's Bodies*, 3rd edn. Oxford: Oxford University Press.

West, C. & Fenstermaker, S. (1995) Doing difference. *Gender and Society* **9**, 8–37.

West, C. & Zimmerman, D. (1987) Doing gender. *Gender & Society* **1**, 125–51.

Wichterich, C. (2009) Trade a driving force for jobs and women's empowerment? Focus on China and India. Friedrich-Ebert-Stiftung, Dialogue on Globalization, Briefing paper 7, http://library.fes.de/pdf-files/iez/global/06389. pdf (downloaded October 3, 2010).

Williams, C. & Windeband, J. (1998) *Informal Employment in the Advanced Economies: Implications for Work and Welfare*. London: Routledge.

Wise, S. & Stanley, L. (2003) Review article: looking back and looking forward: some recent feminist sociology review. *Sociological Research* (online), **8** www.socresonline.org.uk.

Wisely, N. & Fine, G. A. (1997). Making faces: portraiture as negotiated worker-client relationship. *Work and Occupation* **24**, 164–87.

Wisensale, S. (2004) Solving a problem or tinkering at the margins? Work, family and care-giving. In: H. Gottfreid & L. Reese (eds.) *Equity in the Workplace: Gendering Workplace Policy Analysis*. Lanham: Lexington Press, pp. 215–42.

Witz, A. (1993) Gender and bureaucracy: feminist concerns. In: J. Wajcman (ed.), *Organisations, Gender and Power: Papers From An IRRU Workshop*. Warwick Papers in Industrial Relations 48. Warwick: University of Warwick.

Witz, A. (1997) Embodying gender: society, feminism and the body. Unpublished paper presented at European Sociological Society conference, University of Essex, August.

Witz, A. (1998) Embodiment, organization, and gender. Paper presented at the International Conference on Rationalization, Organization and Gender, Sozialforschungsstelle Dortmund, October.

Witz, A., Halford, S. & Savage, M. (1996) Organized bodies: gender, sexuality and embodiment in contemporary organizations. In: L. Adkins and V. Merchant (eds.) *Sexualizing the Social: Power and the Organization of Sexuality*. London: Macmillan, pp. 173–91.

Wolf, D. (1996) *Feminist Dilemmas in Fieldwork*. Boulder: Westview Press.

Woodward, A. (2004) European gender mainstreaming: promises and pitfalls of transformative policy. In: H. Gottfried & L. Reese (eds.) *Equity in the Workplace: Gendering Workplace Policy Analysis*. Lanham: Lexington Press, pp. 77–100.

Woodiwiss, A. (1996) Review essay: searching for signs of globalization. *Sociology* **30**, 4, 799–810.

Wright, E. O. (1978) *Class, Crisis and the State*. London: New Left Books.

Wright, E. O. (2000a) The shadow of exploitation in Weber's class analysis. Paper presented at the International Symposium on Economy and Society: Max Weber in 2000, Madison, WI, Sept. 21–24. www.ssc.wisc.edu/~wright/weber.pdf (downloaded December 22, 2011).

Wright, E. O. (2000b) Working-class power, capitalist-class interests and class compromise. *American Journal of Sociology* **105**, 4, 957–1002.

Yoda, T. (2006a) A roadmap to millennial Japan. In: H. Harootunian & T. Yoda (eds.) *Japan after Japan: Social and Cultural Life from the Recessionary 1990s to the Present*. Durham: Duke University Press, pp. 16–53.

Yoda, T. (2006b) The rise and fall of maternal society: gender, labor, and capital in contemporary Japan. In: H. Harootunian & T. Yoda (eds.) *Japan after Japan: Social and Cultural Life from the Recessionary 1990s to the Present*. Durham: Duke University Press, pp. 239–74.

Yoda, T. & Harootunian, H. (2006) Introduction. In: H. Harootunian & T. Yoda (eds.) *Japan after Japan: Social and Cultural Life from the Recessionary 1990s to the Present*. Durham: Duke University Press, pp. 1–15.

Young, B. (1999). *Triumph of the Fatherland*. Ann Arbor: University of Michigan Press.

Young, B. (2008) Gender and the financial crisis. Unpublished paper presented at the Garnet Network, University of Kassel, Germany, December 1–5.

Yuval-Davis, N. (2006) Human/women's rights and feminist transversal politics.

In: M. Marx- Ferree & A. M. Tripp (eds.) *Global Feminism: Transnational Women's Activism, Organizing, and Human Rights*. New York: New York University Press, pp. 275–95.

Zhang, L. (2012) China's Foxconn workers: from suicide threats to a trade union? *The Guardian* on-line, www.guardian.co.uk/commentisfree/2012/jan/16/fox-conn-suicide-china-society?INTCMP=SRCH (downloaded January 23, 2012).

Zheng, T. (2007) From peasant women to bar hostesses: an ethnography of China's karaoke sex industry. In: C. K. Lee (ed.) *Working in China: Ethnographies of Labor and Workplace Transformation*. New York: Routledge, pp. 124–44.

Zippel, K. (2004) Implementing sexual harassment law in the United States and Germany. In: H. Gottfried & L. Reese (eds.) *Equity in the Workplace: Gendering Workplace Policy Analysis*. Lanham: Lexington Press, pp. 241–64.

Zunz, O., Schoppa, L. & Hiwatari, N. (2002) Introduction: social contracts under stress. In: O. Zunz, L. Schoppa, & N. Hiwatari (eds.) *Social Contracts under Stress: The Middle Classes of America, Europe and Japan at the turn of the Century*. New York: The Russell Sage Foundation, pp. 1–17.

Documents Cited

(Unless otherwise stated, the URLs in this section were downloaded January 10, 2012.)

19th Amendment, www.thenagain.info/webchron/usa/19Amend.html.

Amendments to the Civil Rights Act. West Encyclopedia of American Law, www.archives.gov/education/lessons/civil-rights-act/ (downloaded May 11, 2011).

Brook, K. (2002) Trade union membership: an analysis of data from the autumn 2001 LFS. *Labour Market Trends* (July), http://webarchive.nationalarchives.gov.uk/+/http://www.berr.gov.uk/files/file12445.pdf.

Center for Health Statistics, Centers for Disease Control and Prevention, Atlanta, www.cdc.gov/nchs/fastats/marriage.htm.

Demographic Yearbook. New York: United Nations, 2001.

Eurostat Yearbook 2002 - The Statistical Guide to Europe. Brussels: European Commission, http://epp.eurostat.ec.europa.eu/portal/page/portal/product_details/publication?p_product_code=KS-40-010319 (downloaded May 5, 2012).

Federal Statistical Office of Germany (2001) www.destatis.de.

Hoovers (2010) McDonald's Corporation, www.hoovers.com/company/McDonalds_Corporation/rfskci-1.html (downloaded February 2010).

Institute for Women's Policy Research (2011a) Women continue to lose jobs in the public sector dobuzinskis@iwpr.org.

Institute for Women's Policy Research (2011b) Quick figures: women and men in the public sector. Washington: IWPR.

International Labor Organization, http://www.ilo.org/global/About_the_ILO/lang–en/index.htm (downloaded on August 3, 2009).

International Labor Organization (2004) www.ilo.org/public/english/region/asro/newdelhi/ipec/responses/index.htm.

Japan Institute for Labor Policy and Training (2010) Datebook of international labour statistics 2010. Ministry of Health, Labour and Welfare, Tokyo, www.jil.go.jp/english/estatis/databook/2010/03.htm (downloaded, September 6, 2010).

Japan Institute of Labor (2002) Basic survey on labour unions. Tokyo: Statistics and Information Department, Ministry of Health, Labour and Welfare.

Japan Institute of Labor (2003) Trade union density rate. Ministry of Health, Labour and Welfare, Tokyo, www.jil.go.jp/estatis/eshuyo/200301/e0702.htm.

Japan Statistical Yearbook (2007) Tokyo: The Japan Institute of Labour.

Japanese Minister's Secretariat (2002) Summary of vital statistics. Tokyo: Statistics and Information Department, Ministry of Health, Labour and Welfare.

Lilly Ledbetter Fair Pay Act (2009) www.whitehouse.gov/briefing_room/LillyLedbetterFairPayActPublicReview.

Muller v. *Oregon*, Findlaw.com, http://caselaw.lp.findlaw.com/scripts/getcase. pl?court=US&vol=208&invol=412 (downloaded on May 24, 2011).

National Statistics UK On-line, www.statistics.gov.uk.

OECD extracts, http://stats.oecd.org/Index.aspx (downloaded September 12, 2010).

Social Watch Gender Equity Index, www.socialwatch.org/en/avancesyRet rocesos/IEG_2008/tablas/valoresdelIEG2008.htm.

Statistical Office of the European Communities, Demographic Statistics.

United Nations (2009) Convention on Elimination of All Forms of Discrimination against Women. New York: United Nations, www.un.org/womenwatch/daw/ cedaw (downloaded May 4, 2012).

United Nations Development Programme (2007) Human Development Report 2007 (on-line).

United States Bureau of Labor Statistics (2010a) Building cleaning workers. *Occupational Handbook, 2010–2011 Edition*. Washington DC: US Bureau of Labor Statistics, http://data.bls.gov/cgi-bin/pring.pl/oco/ocos174.htm (downloaded September 5, 2010).

United States Bureau of Labor Statistics (2010b) Child care workers. *Occupational Handbook, 2010–2011 Edition*. Washington DC: US Bureau of Labor Statistics, http://data.bls.gov/cgi-bin/pring.pl/oco/ocos170.htm (downloaded September 5, 2010).

United States Bureau of Labor Statistics (2010c) Secretaries and administrative assistants. *Occupational Handbook, 2010–2011 Edition*. Washington DC: US Bureau of Labor Statistics, http://data.bls.gov/cgi-bin/pring.pl/oco/ocos151. htm (downloaded September 5, 2010).

United States Census Bureau (2010) Government employment and payroll 2010, www.census.gov/govs/apes (downloaded April 28, 2010).

United States Census Bureau Internet (September 3, 2003).

United States Department of Commerce, Bureau of the Census, *Statistical Abstract of the United States*. Washington DC: US Bureau of the Census, www. census.gov/prod/www/abs/statab.html (downloaded October 9, 2011).

United States Department of Health and Human Services, National Center for Health Statistics, Monthly vital statistics report.

United States Department of Labor. *Employed Persons by Detailed Occupation and Sex, 1983–1999*. Washington DC: Bureau of Labor Statistics.

United States Department of Labor. *Employment and Earnings*. Washington DC: Bureau of Labor Statistics.

United States Department of Labor. Facts on working women, www.dol.gov/wb/ factsheets/hitech02.htm#.

United States Department of Labor. *Highlights of Women's Earnings in 2010*. Report 1031. Washington DC: Bureau of Labor Statistics, www.bls.gov/cps/ cpswom2010.pdf.

United States Department of Labor. Overview of the 2008–2018 Projections. *Occupational Outlook Handbook, 2010–11 Editions*. Washington DC: Bureau of Labor Statistics, www.bls.gov/oco/oco2003.htm (downloaded 3/8/2010).

United States Department of Labor. Quick facts on nontraditional occupations for women, www.dol.gov/wb/factsheets/nontra2008.htm#.

United States Department of Labor. Quick stats on women workers 2008, www. dol.gov/wb/stats/main.htm#.

United States Department of Labor. Quick stats on women workers. Annual averages, 2010, www.dol.gov/wb/factsheets/QS-womenwork2010.htm.

United States Department of Labor. Twenty leading occupations of employed women 2008: annual averages. www.dol.gov/wb/factsheets/20lead2008.htm.

United States Department of Labor, Wage and Hour Division. Fact Sheet #28: the Family and Medical Leave Act of 1993 (revised February 2010), www.dol.gov/whd/regs/compliance/whdfs28.pdf (downloaded January 19, 2012).

United States Department of Labor (2010) *Women in the Labor Force: A Databook*. Report 1026. Washington DC: Bureau of Labor Statistics. www.bls.gov/cps/wlf-databook-2010.pdf.

Women's Bureau (2010) *Women, Wage and Salary Workers, Who Work Full-time*. Washington DC: US Department of Labor.

Index of Names

Index of Subjects